PRAISE FOR
The Black Ha

T0091357

"Award-winning journalist Chris Blatchford establishes new standards for brutal honesty and mind-blowing courage with his latest book, *The Black Hand*, a true masterpiece of investigative reporting. Through his outstanding original research and wonderful storytelling abilities, the author unlocks the mysteries of the Mexican Mafia via one of its most fearsome former members." —DAN E. MOLDEA, author of *The Hoffa Wars*

"Chris Blatchford has the real goods. He has the insightful eye of a predatory creature. He writes about predators with an ease and fluidity that is rare these days. If you really want to know what the belly of the beast in East Los Angeles looks like, read Blatchford's book. I highly recommend it." —PHILIP CARLO, author of *Gaspipe*

"If you care about organized crime in America, then you need to know about the Mexican Mafia, and *The Black Hand* is a great place to start your education. The story of Rene 'Boxer' Enriquez reads like a novel, but the events in this book are all too real. Mr. Blatchford, an experienced crime reporter, has done society a service by uncovering this sordid and chilling tale." —BRUCE RIORDAN, director of antigang operations, city attorney of Los Angeles

"Must-read for police, prosecutors, and politicians." —STEVE COOLEY, Los Angeles County district attorney

"*The Black Hand* is a must-read for anyone fascinated by the Mexican Mafia and the merciless killers it produces. No other book gives more of a first-hand chilling account of the extreme violence this gang has, for decades, brought to the prison system and the streets it controls. This narrative gives a graphic description of the senseless bloodshed the Mexican Mafia engages in to quench their thirst for power and control and shows the depth with which 'the Black Hand' can reach into our communities." —RUSTY KEEBLE, president, National Alliance of Gang Investigators' Associations and Florida Gang Investigators Association, and founder and executive director, Gang Free World Foundation

"If you want to understand the ruthlessness and power of the Mexican Mafia, California's first prison gang, *The Black Hand* is a must-read. This is a fast-paced ride into the illegal drug market, the connection between street and prison gangs, power and murder, through the eyes of a prison gang leader. A shocking reality will set in as you realize that life is cheap and in this 'dog-eat-dog' world anybody can die, including wives, family, and friends, once the Black Hand reaches out and touches you."

—AL VALDEZ, PH.D., retired California gang investigator

"This is by far the most powerful story I've read on the Mexican Mafia. Enriquez tells compelling personal accounts of Mexican Mafia business from inside the prison walls and its deadly reach to the outside world. *The Black Hand* is a must-read for law enforcement, corrections, probation, prosecutors, and educators who want to learn the real deal regarding the Mexican Mafia."　　　　　—NELSON ARRIAGA, president, International
Latino Gang Investigators Association

Courtesy of KTTV/Fox 11

ABOUT THE AUTHOR

CHRIS BLATCHFORD is an investigative reporter and the coauthor of the *Los Angeles Times* bestseller *Three Dog Nightmare*. Blatchford has won numerous commendations and awards for his reports, including nine Emmy Awards, and a Peabody for his investigation into the Italian Mafia infiltration of MCA/Universal's music and home video divisions. He lives in Los Angeles.

ALSO BY CHRIS BLATCHFORD

Three Dog Nightmare

THE BLACK HAND

THE BLOODY RISE AND REDMEPTION OF
"BOXER" ENRIQUEZ, A MEXICAN MOB KILLER

Chris Blatchford

HARPER

NEW YORK • LONDON • TORONTO • SYDNEY

HARPER

A hardcover edition of this book was published in 2008 by William Morrow, an imprint of HarperCollins Publishers.

THE BLACK HAND. Copyright © 2008 by Chris Blatchford. All rights reserved. Printed in the United States of America. No part of this book may be used or reproduced in any manner whatsoever without written permission except in the case of brief quotations embodied in critical articles and reviews. For information, address HarperCollins Publishers, 195 Broadway, New York, NY 10007.

HarperCollins books may be purchased for educational, business, or sales promotional use. For information, please e-mail the Special Markets Department at SPsales@harper collins.com.

FIRST HARPER PAPERBACK PUBLISHED 2009.

Designed by Daniel Lagin

Insert photographs courtesy of the author.

The Library of Congress has catalogued the hardcover edition as follows:
Blatchford, Chris.
    The black hand : the bloody rise and redemption of "Boxer" Enriquez, a Mexican mob killer / Chris Blatchford. — 1st ed.
        p. cm.
    ISBN 978-0-06-125729-2
    1. Enriquez, Rene, 1962– 2. Criminals—California—Biography. 3. Mexican American criminals—California—Biography. 4. Mexican Mafia (Gang)—Biography. 5. Gangsters—California—Biography. I. Title.
        HV6248.E585B55   2008
        364.1092—dc22
        [B]   2008025916

ISBN 978-0-06-194418-5 (pbk.)

24 25 26 27 28 LBC 29 28 27 26 25

*Dedicated
to Martha from Rene*

For she is more precious than rubies and all the things that you desire cannot compare with her.

—Proverbs 3:15

Contents

Foreword

by Rene "Boxer" Enriquez

ON MARCH 22, 2002, I DEFECTED FROM THE MEXICAN MAFIA. AT THE time, I knew it would be a life-altering decision, but I didn't have a clue as to how much. Now I'm housed at an undisclosed location nearly a thousand miles away from my old haunt at Pelican Bay State Prison, and my life seems so removed from the man I used to be—Boxer from the Mexican Mafia.

Today I'm just Rene Enriquez. I'm no longer a Mafioso or a figurehead for a crew of murderous, drug-dealing gangsters, but just a regular Joe clawing my way out of a dark, evil abyss and back into the grasp of humanity.

The transition has been a difficult challenge for me, as if I were Superman turning back into Clark Kent forever. But each day that passes I feel a little bit closer to becoming a normal person.

I no longer have to wake up with a fear of Mafia politics—plotting someone else's death before they plot mine. There is no longer a need to constantly arm myself with a prison shank in an unceasing state of "war-readiness." Nor do I have to continually question the motivations of supposed brothers in crime—men of poor intellect who can't think beyond their own megalomaniacal sense of entitlement.

Even though I am still living behind bars, life now has a true, unfamiliar sweetness to it that is almost beyond my ability to describe with words. I'll try by saying that simple pleasures mean so much more to me. Things I had given up hope of ever feeling again have enriched me: the touch of my wife's hair, the smell of perfume on her neck, the occasional warmth of an embrace by my mother and father, and kisses from my children. These are all experiences that were lost during years of prison visits where

I was separated from loved ones behind glass partitions. Under my current housing conditions, I even get to taste the gift of home-cooked food with some regularity. And for a man who loves to eat, that is truly heaven.

Most importantly, I've pulled from the ashes of my past life what I believe is a nobler calling. Every time I am given the opportunity I strive to educate law enforcement, academics, behavioral scientists, and the general public about the national threat of urban street terrorism and nontraditional organized crime.

In reality, it's not the threat of Al-Qaeda–improvised explosive devices (IEDs) that imperils the streets of Los Angeles. It's street gangs that pose the greatest single threat to public safety and that contaminate our youth with a bankrupt moral code. Gang proliferation and gang migration—mostly emanating from southern California—has spread across the United States and into a number of foreign countries as if it were a disease.

Clearly, I don't possess a cure for that plague, but what I can do is offer the reader an insider's view into a prison and criminal subculture that should scare the hell out of the public.

The Mexican Mafia's tentacles reach far beyond the walls and razor-wire fences of prisons. And sadly, its influence also continues to ignite racial violence between blacks and Latinos in schools, as well as racially motivated street gang wars. The Mafia-induced subculture destroys our most precious commodity—the minds of our young people.

There is no doubt that some skeptics will say this book is nothing more than a glorification of the Mexican Mafia and gang violence. I believe the opposite is true. Laying out the stark brutality in the pages of this book is an attempt to deglamorize the gang philosophy that many young people embrace as a viable status mobility system.

If the publication of this story dissuades one person from participating in the gang lifestyle, enhances the knowledge of even a few law enforcement officers, or enlightens a handful of educators, then the author and I have accomplished our goal.

Also, it would be remiss of me not to acknowledge the carnage of thousands and thousands of victims of gang violence—much of it due to Mexican Mafia brutality. Recognizing my personal responsibility for twenty years of organized crime violence and the negative impact that it has had on others is only a small step in my long walk toward redemption.

I've told these Mexican Mafia horror stories numerous times, but I have never seen them in print. Reading the material in one sitting actually startled me. I was shocked at my own inhumanity, my capriciousness, and my lack of compassion. Intellectually digesting the animalistic way I lived was difficult. The realization that my life was dedicated solely to crime and violence was painful.

I wanted to teach people about the dangers of the Mafia after I dropped out, but a funny thing happened along the way. I ended up learning about myself. Some will understandably believe this turnaround is a manipulative play to get out of prison.

I'm not attempting to hoodwink anybody here. Readers will formulate their own opinions about Rene Enriquez. In all likelihood, many will see me as a monster, and I understand that.

At one point I recall wanting the author to somehow mitigate my responsibility and "pretty me up" to make me appear less evil. But then it dawned on me early on in this project that "there are no swans in the cesspool." This story had to be told as the author wrote it, warts and all.

Regardless of how I am portrayed in this book, those who know me best see that I have changed for the better. My new wife had much to do with that. During one of her visits, I was depersonalizing some of my past victims and rationalizing that they all fell into the NHI category: No Humans Involved.

"They were only mobsters," I said. "No harm, no foul."

She reacted angrily. "How dare you say such a thing! Those people were loved by someone. They were somebody's son, father, or husband." Then she hit me with an illuminating question: "How would you feel if somebody murdered one of your sons, Rene?" I was at a loss for words, dumbfounded. My wife in a burst of anger taught me a quality that was anathema to a mob guy—empathy.

I know that I am no swan, but believe me when I tell you that I no longer want to live in the cesspool. Others will argue that I am not far removed from the criminals who come alive on the pages of this book. What is now different about me? At least I chose to pull myself out of that cesspool. They continue to wallow in it.

I'll probably spend the rest of my life paying for the wrongs that I've done—either physically locked up in prison or emotionally trapped with the ugly memories of what I've done to myself and others. However, I find some comfort in the fact that I'm a better man than I was yesterday, and I will strive to be an even better one tomorrow. I owe that to my devoted wife; my family, who should have bailed on me years ago; and the law enforcement officers and attorneys who took an interest in me, believed in me, and gave me another opportunity for redemption. And lastly, I owe it to myself.

Today I'm just a regular Joe—a son, a husband, a father, a grandfather—and for once in my life, I'm okay with that.

Introduction

IT WAS NEAR THE END OF A LONG DAY IN OCTOBER 1995 WHEN THE phone rang at my office desk. I had just finished presenting the third segment of a long investigative story that explained how a convicted triple-murderer—acting as his own attorney—was abusing the court system to facilitate Mexican Mafia business. It was a court case that launched "Operation Pelican Drop," an expensive, secret, top-security transport of more than a dozen of California's worst "high-risk" inmates, including Rene "Boxer" Enriquez, whom I described as "a notorious mob hit man."

While chasing different organized crime stories in the past, I'd experienced my share of angry calls and more than a few death threats. I wasn't in the mood for any fresh ones, and I hesitated to pick up the receiver. But I did.

A feisty woman on the other end of the line eviscerated me with a torrent of punishing words. She didn't like what she'd seen on TV, especially my portrayal of Rene Enriquez. It was not the only time I had featured him in a piece about the Mexican Mafia, also known as La Eme. I had first done a sweeping, five-part TV news exposé and documentary in October 1991 about the resurgence of the Mexican Mafia and portrayed Enriquez as a brutal, heroin-addicted Mafia hit man. During research on that piece, I'd interviewed an associate of Enriquez's and a recent Mafia dropout, who had both done a number of hits for the mob. It's interesting to note that those two hardened killers agreed to talk to me about any subject with one exception—they would not answer questions about Boxer Enriquez. He generated that kind of fear.

In May 1994, I had described Boxer Enriquez as "a Mexican Mafia killer" during a four-part, in-depth exposé I did on Eighteenth Street, the largest criminal street gang in Los Angeles. With an estimated twenty thousand members, it was involved in extortion, drug dealing, and murder and had close ties to the ruthless La Eme.

Now the angry woman on the phone identified herself as Lupe Enriquez—Boxer's mother. She insisted he was a good-hearted son, not the murderous mobster I had described. I, on the other hand, was something less than pond scum for running down her beloved boy. I figured the last thing I needed to do was insult some notorious Mafia guy's mother, and I tried to soothe her wrath. After about twenty minutes on the phone, she decided I was a "nice man" after all. Lupe Enriquez suggested that if I wrote to Rene, he would probably do an interview with me—so as to warn young people away from the evils of gang life. So I crafted a letter and mailed it to *the* maximum-security prison in California.

A month later, a two-page response, handwritten on lined, yellow legal paper, arrived from Pelican Bay State Prison. The letter expressed "a bit of a surprise" that I had written to him. He informed me that he was aware of the stories I had broadcast about him and that he "was not desirous of that type of exposure." Yet he understood that I was "a journalist merely reporting on events." There was a polite refusal of my request for a TV interview, with a little barb attached: "I have no interest in being splayed across TV screens and dubbed a 'hit man' as you've seen fit to so affectionately entitle me." But the letter writer made it clear I should feel no threat: "Rest assured that I harbor no animosity for you whatsoever. In closing, I wish to thank you for the cordiality with which you treated my mother. I also appreciate the honesty which you displayed in your letter to me and your willingness to be frank. I place a high degree of emphasis on a man's personal integrity. If you feel the need, please do not hesitate to contact me in the future." It was signed, "Sincerely, Rene Enriquez, 'Boxer.'"

In May 1997, Rene wrote me to ask if I could make some still photographs from the videotapes I had shot of him during court appearances. He was locked down in a Security Housing Unit (SHU) at Pelican Bay State Prison and was not allowed to take photos of himself. Rene wanted to send some relatively recent pictures to his family members. I complied with his request and joked that the courtroom photos looked better than mug shots. He quickly sent me a thank-you note, saying, "You're right, they sure beat mug shots." A happy face was sketched right next to the comment.

In the following years, I received a Christmas card from Pelican Bay every year and always sent one in return. The messages were short holiday greetings wishing each other and our families the best. Usually, this legendary mobster wrote a little happy face for emphasis at the end of a humorous sentence.

Then, in the spring of 2003, I heard through contacts in law enforcement that Boxer Enriquez had dropped out of the Mexican Mafia. Frankly, no one could believe it. Several days later, I got a call at the office from John Enriquez, Boxer's father. He said Rene was interested in working on a book about his life in the Mafia, and he wanted me to write it. Would I be interested? The answer was yes.

Days afterward, I was on the telephone with a man I knew quite a bit about as a robber, an extortionist, and a murderer. Through his violent behavior, he had climbed the criminal ladder into the upper echelon of a group widely recognized as California's leading organized crime threat—La Eme. We had never talked before. The Mexican Mafia is supposed to be a secret organization, and members, who refer to themselves as *carnales,* normally speak to the news media under penalty of death. Given the notes we had exchanged during a decade of limited correspondence, I was not surprised that he was articulate, engaging, and gregarious. I quickly found out that he disliked the nickname Boxer and wanted to be called Rene. I was warned that he was a manipulator, and that was true. He still reveled in his somewhat legendary reputation as a mobster, but it was clear from the outset that he had regrets. There was no doubt that he was bright, and at his best he was charming and interesting. It was impossible to leave an encounter with Rene and not wonder what he could have done in life had he not chosen a path of crime. The alter ego of Boxer had dominated his existence, and it was clear he was trying to rediscover Rene. There was a relapse in his drug addiction after four years of sobriety, and early on he went through a period of second-guessing his decision to leave the mob.

Since 2002, Rene and I have met face to face for a total of about thirty hours at different lockup facilities, and we have spent endless hours on the telephone. During the last year of the book project, we talked with each other on an almost daily basis. Our conversations far outreached material for the book. We talked about life and what it meant to be a good man, a father, a son, a Christian. There were reminiscences about his friends in the Mexican Mafia—not just as mobsters but as people. Our talks delved into the depths of evil, drugs, depravity, and death.

As much as two people can when they communicate on the phone and during prison visits, we grew to know each other. I daresay—as shocking as this may seem to some—that we developed a friendship. There is nothing in Rene's criminal past that I admire. It is sad, discouraging, and frustrating to me that so many young people today are choosing lives that imitate the gangster lifestyle. Boxer Enriquez helped keep alive the myth that the Mafia is a fun, glamorous, prosperous, honorable way to live. In the years to come, I hope that Rene Enriquez will do everything he can to dispel that myth. In the end, it is up to him—and only him—to prove that he is a changed man. He is, in fact, another test case for redemption.

A lot of what you read on these pages comes from firsthand accounts by Rene. However, much more comes from research that includes thousands of pages of legal documents, police reports, courtroom testimony, Mafia debriefing reports, published news accounts, and personal interviews with law enforcement agents, prosecutors, defense attorneys, relatives, and confidential informants. In an effort to establish a consistent narrative flow, the information supplied by all of the above is not always referenced specifically.

The eighteenth-century writer, thinker, and statesman Edmund Burke said, "All that is necessary for the triumph of evil is for good men to do nothing." Rapidly approaching forty years as a working news reporter, I have seen too many good men do nothing, not only in the underworld but in the corporate world as well. It makes me sick.

To those in the Mexican Mafia or gang associates who might be angered by this book, I ask simply, do you want your sons to be in the same life? I would argue that they should strive for more. There is no true fulfillment in a life driven by drugs and fueled by blood and violence, looking over your shoulder all the time, wondering when your best friend will put a knife in your back or a bullet in your head. Also, prison walls can be forever—not just locking inmates in, but locking them out of a productive life they chose not to live. Certainly, some who find themselves on the other side of the law were driven there by mistreatment in their own homes while growing up. Others were drawn to the flame of evil through other perceived or true injustices. To them, I can only say: break the chain of mistreatment. A real man nourishes righteousness, not evil.

Lupe Enriquez urged me to say at the beginning of this book that I am not here to blame anyone. I don't stand in judgment. I am trying to tell a story as honestly as I can about a man, his family, and a criminal organization that shaped his life. I tell it in hopes that others can see the warning signs and learn from their mistakes—and from their broken lives. "It wasn't easy," she told me, "for anyone involved." So there it is, Mrs. Enriquez.

CHAPTER 1

Blood In, Blood Out

HE HAD A LOT OF BLOOD ON HIS HANDS—FROM THE STREETS AND from behind bars.

Now he sat in Los Angeles Superior Court waiting for Judge Florence-Marie Cooper to set a trial date. He faced two first-degree murder charges and two attempted-murder charges. If convicted, the death penalty was a definite possibility—at the very least life in prison—and he didn't seem to care.

In fact, as a nearby television news camera videotaped the proceedings, twenty-nine-year-old Rene Enriquez, better known on the gang-infested streets of southern California as "Boxer," calmly turned toward the camera lens, softly mouthed the word "lies," and broke into shoulder-shaking laughter.

He was strikingly handsome with a personality that demanded attention, a certain presence that commanded respect. Thick, jet-black hair combed back. A full mustache turned down at the edges. A sharp, pointed nose and high cheekbones betraying his Mexican-Aztec roots. His wire-rim glasses surrounded friendly eyes that instantly could turn cold and threatening. He was five-foot-eight but carried himself like a man a half-foot taller, trim and athletic. He actually looked good in short-sleeved jailhouse blues. If not for the tattoos that marked both sides of his neck, dotted his hands, and sleeved his forearms, he could easily have put on an expensive suit and passed for one of the slick courthouse lawyers who make a living representing guys just like him—gangsters.

While on parole a year and a half earlier, he had ordered the death of a young woman for stealing drugs from him, and several days later he put five .357 Magnum bullets into the head of an errant mobster who had shown cowardice. Then, while awaiting trial, he did two other bloody hits inside the Los Angeles County Jail—stabbing the rival mobsters so many times that it was only a stroke of fate that kept them from making an early trip to their graves. In truth, authorities believe he had participated in at least ten murders and had personal knowledge of seven times that many.

Boxer Enriquez was a full-fledged member of the ruthless Mexican Mafia, also known as La Eme, a regular modern-day Murder Incorporated. And he was proud of it. "Eme" (pronounced *EH-meh*) is the Spanish phonetic pronunciation of the letter "M"—for Mafia. He has EME tattooed on his left hand. The word EMERO, also for "M," appears on his left bicep. A butterfly, or Mariposa, also signifying the letter "M," is on his neck. An actual life-size black hand is tattooed over his heart with a small "eMe" emblazoned in the middle of the palm—the *e* on each side lightened in color to give prominence to the letter M. La Eme has a saying that, "when the hand touches you, you go to work." That means murder, maiming, mayhem, extortion, drug dealing, robbing, burglarizing, kidnapping, or anything else the Mexican Mafia brothers want done. And Boxer had done them all.

He moved his chair back and forth on its hind legs and stared at Judge Cooper as she set his murder trial date for January 1, 1993. This was no sweat. He stood up straight, already handcuffed and waist-and-leg-chained, and was escorted out of the courtroom under heavy guard. That was the way he would go anywhere outside his cell for the rest of his life. There was the sound of chains clanging as he walked, and he turned and nonchalantly waved as he neared the prisoners' exit door at the side of the courtroom. There would be no bail. Again, he didn't seem to mind. Already Boxer had spent about one-third of his young life locked up. He was reasonably comfortable in prison. Besides, he was a feared killer—even in a world of killers, he knew he would never hesitate. Others would. He was a killer's killer and proud of it—a warrior.

He also knew that the Mexican Mafia controlled not only County Jail but the largest inmate population in the world and all the prison rackets, including drugs, extortion, and gambling. The California Department of Corrections had 160,000 inmates, and La Eme used murder and fear to keep them in line. Yeah, he would be just fine.

By his own admission, it was a "twisted" existence, but he was smart and confident. He knew he not only looked like a gangster, he was one. And after all, it was a life he had bargained for, and there was only one acceptable way out. He'd taken an oath with his Eme brothers—"blood in, blood out." In other words, the only way out of the Mafia was in a pine box.

That was the cardinal rule in this deadly game he played, and he felt he was a player at the top of his game.

And besides, the Mexican Mafia had a Spanish word to describe the position of its members: *rifamos*. Translation: "we rule, we control, we reign." The line that divided life in prison and life in the outside world seemed blurred.

Boxer's criminal career was indicative of the lifestyle of the Mexican Mafia, which did outrageous crimes with impunity, not caring if the brothers got caught or went to prison. They adapted, becoming creatures of the penal system and the cruel streets of the underworld. They had no regard for human life, and still don't.

Rene Enriquez, aka "Boxer," enjoyed being one of them. And to more completely understand what Boxer had become, it's important to first know the bloody history of the organization that spawned and shaped him.

CHAPTER 2

Mexican Mafia History

IT ALL BEGAN IN 1957 AT THE DEUEL VOCATIONAL INSTITUTION (DVI) in Tracy, California, five years before Rene Enriquez was even born. That lockup was then considered the last stop for the state's most incorrigible and violent juvenile inmates. It was in effect a junior prison. Those who were too difficult to handle in reform school were sent to the California Youth Authority (CYA), and those too violent for CYA ended up at DVI. At the time, it was often referred to as "Gladiator School," a place where already tormented teenagers honed their criminal skills and acted out against rivals from enemy barrios.

As the Mexican population grew in southern California, so did a barrio culture that spawned street gangs with traditional rivalries, neighborhood against neighborhood. Deadlier and deadlier gangs were formed to protect home turf. They called themselves *vatos locos,* crazy dudes. In his book *Mexican Mafia: Altar Boy to Hitman,* former Eme member Ramon "Mundo" Mendoza says, "The more aggressive gang members went about the serious business of establishing violent reputations. Along with the reps came the celebrity status. A completely abnormal social value system was established."*

Some of the gang members, in honor of their ancient Aztec or Toltec roots, or even the more recent Apache and Yaquis tribes, took on Indian warrior names such as Caballo, Chato, Crazy Horse, Crow, Cuchillo, Geronimo, and Indio. Others adopted more modern gangster handles like

---

* Ramon "Mundo" Mendoza, *Mexican Mafia: From Altar Boy to Hitman* (Los Angeles: self-published, 2005), p. 15.

Shotgun, Machine Gun, and Capone. In either case, the names were adopted out of pride to generate fear and respect.

At DVI, sixteen-year-old Luis "Huero Buff" Flores of Hawaiian Gardens, a Los Angeles suburb, is credited with coming up with the idea of uniting all the Mexican-American southern California gangs into one big prison "super gang" or "gang of gangs." Together they would cease Mexican street gang rivalries inside prison, control the heroin trafficking, protect themselves against unruly prison guards, and unite as brothers (*carnales*) against rival black and white inmates. Mundo Mendoza observes: "These guys were raging maniacs whose modus operandi was 'all offense, no defense.' They were extremely aggressive, had no respect for their adversaries, and unabated disdain and contempt for the general population. We felt bulletproof."

Prison lore has it that Huero Buff was fascinated with the power and mystique of the Italian Mafia and dubbed the new group the Mexican Mafia, or La Familia Mexicana. There were about a dozen original members, who quickly doubled their ranks and terrorized other inmates, stealing their possessions, mostly canteen items and drugs. Mundo Mendoza notes, "The goal in the beginning was to terrorize the prison system and enjoy prison comforts while doing time." Those who resisted Eme extortion were beaten or stabbed. Huero Buff later said, "It was a kid's trip then, just a branch of homeboys from East L.A. If I felt like killing somebody, I would, if I didn't, I wouldn't. We were just having fun then. The power was intoxicating."*

The majority of the early members did come from East Los Angeles gangs with violent reputations: Hoyo Soto Maravilla, Varrio Nuevo Estrada, White Fence, Big Hazard, Clover, and the Avenues. Everyone was recruited for their fearlessness, aggressiveness, and ruthlessness. Each candidate had to be sponsored by a "made member" and voted in by the entire group. All were supposedly equal in status, were sworn to secrecy about La Eme's existence, pledged their allegiance for life, vowed to kill for the organization, and promised never to show fear, weakness, hesitation, or doubt. Any infraction would be punishable by death.

Memorable names of Eme pioneers include: Mike "Hatchet" Ison, Eddie "Potato Nose" Loera, Jesus "Liro" Pedroza, Alejandro "Hondo" Lechuga, Gabriel "Little Sluggo" Casteneda, Benjamin "Topo" Peters, Joe "Colorado" Arias, and Richard "Richie" Ruiz. Rodolfo "Cheyenne" Cadena, who at the age of fifteen stabbed a local gang rival to death outside a dance hall in

---

* Quoted in Mendoza, *Mexican Mafia*, p. 16.

Bakersfield, is widely known as a cofounder of the Mexican Mafia. He was only five-foot-four and weighed 120 pounds, but he was a handsome, natural leader with tremendous energy, high intelligence, a hair-trigger temper, and undisputed presence. He suggested that the word "Eme" be used along with the term "Mexican Mafia." It added a Spanish flavor for those who still bickered over the name, believing it was too much like the Italians. Also, Eme could be used as a code word around prison guards and others unfamiliar with the language.

By 1961, administrators at DVI, alarmed by the escalating violence, had transferred a number of the charter Eme members to San Quentin, hoping to discourage their violent behavior by intermingling them with hardened adult convicts. It didn't work.

For example, the story goes that Cheyenne Cadena arrived on the lower yard and was met by a six-foot-five, 300-pound black inmate who planted a kiss on his face and announced that this scrawny teenager would now be his "bitch." Chy returned a short time later, walked up to the unsuspecting predator, and stabbed him to death with a jailhouse knife, or shank. There were more than a thousand inmates on the yard. No witnesses stepped forward, and only one dead man entertained the idea that Cadena was anyone's bitch.*

Other young Eme members at San Quentin continued their reign of terror. A pair of Mafia killers, for no apparent reason, stabbed a stunned Robert "Bobby Loco" Lopez, who staggered across the upper yard, hit the pavement in convulsions, and died. A few days later, the deadly duo stabbed another clueless inmate.

Eme's Alfredo "Cuate" Jimenez killed another convict on the lower yard, and Mike "Hatchet" Ison took out another in the prison gymnasium.

Tony Chacon was from Lopez Maravilla, the largest gang in East L.A. at the time; it also had the largest number of inmates in the state prison system. Chacon made the mistake of badmouthing the Mexican Mafia. So Eme hit men Richie Ruiz and Eddie "Pelon" Moreno took him out in the San Quentin Adjustment Center, a unit that housed the worst of prison bad guys.

Charlie White was a black inmate upset about Eme bullying tactics. He shouted obscenities at Eme stalwarts locked up in their cells, singling out Hondo Lechuga. Those who fought with their mouths from behind closed cell doors were derisively called "cell soldiers." Shortly after cell doors were

---

* Robert Morrill, *The Mexican Mafia: The Story*, p. 56.

racked open to let inmates out to the exercise yard, an Eme soldier greeted White on the tier with a series of shank shots that closed that cell soldier's mouth forever.

Juan Zamilpa was a highly feared and respected inmate who had killed an informer about a year earlier. Not to be messed with, he let it be known that he would take no shit from the Mexican Mafia. Cadena—believing Zamilpa might be of some use to Eme—on the yard tried to reason with him to stop disrespecting the brothers. Zamilpa wouldn't hear it. On his way back to his cell, Zamilpa was stabbed eleven times by four Eme members. It was not possible to disrespect someone from a grave.

It was all killing for the sake of killing, to claim superiority on the yard, to let other cons know Eme should be feared.

Ramon "Mundo" Mendoza, who participated in twenty mob hits before he defected in the late 1970s, says that they dedicated their lives to "making a career out of crime." He calls Eme the "special forces" of the gang underworld. Mendoza says, "We recruited the worst of the worst, people who were willing to kill at the drop of a hat for the organization."

In 1967 President Lyndon Baines Johnson increased U.S. military strength to a half-million troops in Vietnam to defeat the Viet Cong army. During that same year, Mexican Mafia strength grew to more than thirty hard-core members, and they controlled drug trafficking, gambling, extortion, loan sharking, and prostitution not only at San Quentin but elsewhere as their numbers and influence spread throughout the DVI and California penal system.

The Eme quest for complete control alienated many other Mexican-American inmates who were fed up with Mexican Mafia bullies stabbing, killing, and stealing their watches, rings, cigarettes, and anything else of value. Some of them secretly formed a new prison gang called Nuestra Familia (NF), or "Our Family." It was first established in the mid-1960s at the California Training Facility in Soledad. Some of the early members were from the Los Angeles area, but NF drew inmates primarily from rural communities in northern California.

The Mexican Mafia saw NF as lame and inferior, just a bunch of farmers, or *farmeros*. However, in 1968 at San Quentin, a full-scale riot broke out after a Mexican Mafia soldier, or *soldado*, stole a pair of shoes from an NF sympathizer. Nineteen inmates were stabbed, and one Eme associate ended up dead. The battle became known as the "Shoe War," and it established Nuestra Familia as a major Eme rival.

After the Shoe War, a number of Mafia heavy hitters were transferred to Folsom State Prison, considered the end of the line for hard-core convicts. Jailhouse legend Joe Morgan was one of the notorious inmates there. He was a tall, muscular, bald-headed Croatian with a near-genius IQ who grew up in East Los Angeles and San Pedro barrios, beat his thirty-two-year-old girlfriend's husband to death with a rubber hammer when he was only sixteen, and buried the body in a shallow grave. He robbed banks, escaped from jail twice, committed multiple murders, and had Mexican cartel heroin connections and ties to the Italian Mafia. Despite the fact that he was not Mexican and he entered the Mafia at the advanced age of forty, Morgan was dubbed the "Godfather" of La Eme within a few years. He had been shot in the leg during a bank robbery; after gangrene set in, it was amputated below the knee.* That earned him the nickname "Peg Leg," but no one called him that to his face.

About the same time Morgan became the Godfather, Nuestra Familia formed an alliance with a Marxist-oriented black prison gang called the Black Guerilla Family (BGF). And the Mexican Mafia formed a loose alliance with a white supremacist prison gang called the Aryan Brotherhood. During the following year, 1972, there was a bloodbath of thirty-six murders in California prisons, and gang experts believed La Eme was responsible for as many as thirty of them.

Meanwhile, the Mafia terror reached out into the streets for the first time.

On December 6, 1971, the body of Mafia soldier Alfonso "Apache" Alvarez was found lying in a pool of his own blood in a local park in the city of Monterey Park, a bedroom community of fifty-five thousand people that rubbed up against East Los Angeles. Apache, three bullet holes in his head, was executed because he failed to pull off a daring escape plot designed to free several incarcerated Eme brothers while on their way to court in San Bernardino County. Police didn't know that, but they found a hand-size blue address book in his shirt pocket. Some of the names listed had the letters "eMe" written next to them.

Detectives comparing notes then found there had been an earlier torture/execution-style murder in San Bernardino County. Jimmy Lopez had been given some Eme heroin to sell on consignment, but instead he

---

* Robert Morrill reports in *The Mexican Mafia: The Story* that Joe Morgan was shot during the holdup of an armored car that was making pickups in front of a department store in a small shopping center in East Los Angeles. Mundo Mendoza believes it happened during a bank robbery.

used it himself. He was methodically shot in the knee, the shoulder, and other parts of the body. He was found with his pants down around his ankles and a bloody fourteen-inch screwdriver lying on the ground next to him. It had been shoved up his rectum. The coroner estimated that Jimmy was tortured for about three hours before he died in a remote canyon in the San Gabriel Mountains.

A number of Eme brothers were now out on parole, stockpiling weapons and setting up drug connections. Apache's execution illustrated that Eme wouldn't even hesitate to take one of their own. Along with the Jimmy Lopez hit, it showed that the Mexican Mafia could get you anywhere, anytime—not just behind prison walls.

On November 18, 1971, a parolee named James "Chapo" St. Claire was found in the Lincoln Park area of Los Angeles, hands and feet tied, three bullets in the head execution-style. St. Claire had been trying to get federal grant money to set up a drug rehabilitation program. La Eme didn't like competition.

Millions in grant money was being handed out during the 1970s for drug rehab programs. It was Cheyenne Cadena's idea to take them over, and the Mafia did infiltrate at least four of these L.A. area–based projects. Eme parolees were hired as counselors, and "ghost slots" were set up where Eme members were paid and never showed up for work at all. Other moneys were siphoned off to buy drugs, finance other illegal activities, or pay for Mafia entertainment. And ironically, the programs gave La Eme direct access to hundreds, if not thousands, of heroin users who would buy their product. It was an effective scam that generated a steady stream of illegal big bucks.

By the end of 1972, Cheyenne Cadena, after brokering a short truce with Nuestra Familia in 1971, arranged transfer to Palm Hall, a high-security lockup at the California Institution for Men (CIM) in Chino, an NF stronghold at the time. Cadena was a visionary and believed that brown men, La Raza, should unite against a common enemy, the establishment.

Bloodthirsty hard-liners like Joe Morgan disagreed. Mundo Mendoza says, "Many of us considered it unacceptable to engage in dialogue with a group we considered inferior—Nuestra Familia. We considered them pests that need to be exterminated." Besides, an enemy was an enemy, forever. The farmeros should die. In fact, Mundo remembers, "while Chy was engaged in dialogue Eme members in different prisons were killing 'farmers.'" In fact, a couple of Eme soldiers, in a different section of the same Chino prison where Cadena was seeking peace, stabbed two NF members.

On December 17, 1972, NF took its revenge. Cadena came out of his cell to go to the exercise yard and was met by a group of angry Nuestra Familia hit men. He was stabbed again and again and clubbed with a lead pipe. His near-lifeless body was then thrown from a second-tier balcony. When he hit the ground, another NF soldado continued to slash away at his torso. The coroner counted fifty-seven stab wounds.

Cheyenne Cadena was dead at the age of twenty-nine. Any thought of peace between NF and Eme died with him.

The carnage would continue for decades. Mundo Mendoza explains, "The outrage over Chy's killing was deeply rooted in our arrogance. We were more offended by the disrespect shown to our organization than the fact that Cadena was killed. It was a blow to our huge egos that a farmer killed a highly placed Eme member."

In 1977 the state of California eliminated indeterminate prison sentences—except for first-degree murder. All sentences were changed to a determinant number of years behind bars, and everyone was given a parole date. This ruling released a new wave of Mexican Mafia members onto the streets. It became apparent in a 1976 photo at the funeral of La Eme's Jesse "Chuy" Fraijo of Norwalk—who died from a drug overdose—when more than a dozen Mexican Mafia members posed for a picture.[*] They all wore collared jackets or sweaters, not just to protect themselves from the nippy air but to more easily conceal the weapons hidden under their clothing. Morgan's bald head stood higher than the others, who still wore their hair long, most of them down below their ears in the fashion of the 1970s. Half of them sported Fu Manchu mustaches, and more than a few hid their eyes behind dark glasses.

Mundo explained afterward that, he, Morgan, and a few others forced heroin dealers to sell only their heroin. "If they didn't," he added, "we killed them. We sent the message—sell our dope or die. We'd kill someone and then go to a Dodger baseball game. It was strictly business, nothing personal."

Eddie "Lalo" Moreno, made in the 1970s and now dead, claimed the average Eme recruit had three or four murders under his belt. "You start to enjoy it after the first time," he said, "to see a person plead and cry for help,

---

[*] The photo featured Gus Rivera, Luis "Huero Buff" Flores, Manuel "Tati" Torrez, Ruben "Rube" Soto, Ralph "Rafa" Mata, Daniel "Dangerous Dan" DeAvila, Robert "Robot" Salas, Jimmy "Jimmy Joe" Lucero, Raymond "Chavo" Perez, Richard "Richie" Ruiz, Gilbert Roybal, and Daniel "Spider" Arriaga.

literally pray to you like a saint. And you just get hopped-up, the blood and everything, it's just weird. It's a sickness."

It was a sickness that would clearly afflict Rene Enriquez in the years to come as he tried to live up to the bloody, ruthless, treacherous history of those who came before him in La Eme.

CHAPTER 3

Boxer Beginnings

IT WAS A SLIGHTLY CHILLY JANUARY DAY IN 1973 WHEN A FEW Mexican Mafia shot-callers, Luis "Huero Buff" Flores and Richard "Grumpy" Garcia, joined a small group of mourners and family members in a Bakersfield cemetery to pay their respects and bury the first Mafia icon, Rodolfo "Cheyenne" Cadena. Most of the other carnales were still locked up in prison and unable to attend the services. The inscription on the gravestone read, RECUERDO DE TU MADRE Y FAMILIA. In English, "Remembered by your mother and family." The initials EME roughly scratched in the stone beside the commemorative plaque made it clear that family included his Mafia brothers.

One hundred thirty miles to the south, in Cerritos, a new, booming, mostly white, upper-middle-class suburb that borders Orange and Los Angeles counties, Rene Enriquez was enjoying his favorite Christmas present, a brand-new set of slot racing cars. He was ten years old. His mother and brothers often called him "Nene," a family nickname that developed from one of his siblings' inability to pronounce "Rene." He was a bright, gregarious, normal kid who played army with a GI Joe action figure and loved to joke around and be funny. "Batman was my hero," Rene recalled with pleasure, "and every day after school I watched my favorite television shows: *Speed Racer, Little Rascals,* and *The Three Stooges.*" He was the middle son who inherited some of his father's restless ambition, and as a boy he often led his brothers in the games they played.

A year earlier, Rene's father had landed a new job and moved his family into a brand-new four-bedroom tract home in Cerritos, twenty-four miles southeast of Los Angeles. It was the state's fastest-growing city at that time, carved out of a community that just a decade earlier had four hundred dairy farms—it had had more cows than people. In the 1970s, acres of feedlots gave way to more than thirty tract housing projects with parks, recreation centers, a regional shopping center, and one of the largest auto malls in the nation. It was not exactly the hood.

There were still dairy farms within walking distance of the Enriquez family's house. Rene and other kids used to play in the pastures—"kicking over cowpies looking for magnets." In the 1930s and 1940s, farmers used to shoot a magnet down the throat of dairy cows to act as a safety device. Occasionally, cows would swallow pieces of broken baling wire that had fallen into piles of hay. The sharp metal pieces could tear up the intestines and kill the cow. On the other hand, the sharp steel wire would stick to a smooth magnet and prevent the cow from being harmed. Sometimes the magnets would work through a cow's three stomachs and end up in the stool— becoming a prized souvenir for neighborhood kids on the lookout for them. "We'd spend hours looking for those magnets," remembered Rene. "We also looked for pollywogs and baby frogs in Coyote Creek. And there was an urban legend that deadly quicksand lurked beneath the water's surface, so we always stayed on the edges of the creek."

Other times the dairy farmers would pay Rene and his childhood friends with an ice cream Dixie cup or pint of chocolate milk for raking dung into a pile or picking up the trash in front of the drive-through dairy store. "It was a beautiful little area," remembered Rene, "and the entire world was right. My biggest concern was the Fourth of July, Christmas, Halloween, and my birthday. I didn't have a worry in the world. It was great."

The Enriquez family moved to Cerritos from Thousand Oaks, another tract home community forty-two miles northwest of Los Angeles, where they had lived for a few years in a trilevel house with a balcony and built-in deck in the backyard, just minutes from the Sunset Hills Country Club. It was very nice. Thousand Oaks still has a reputation for being California's safest city.

Rene was born July 7, 1962, at Hope Hospital in Los Angeles, and the family lived on Ninetieth Street in South-Central Los Angeles during his preschool years, surrounded by relatives and mostly black neighbors.

His father, John Palacios Enriquez, was an old-school, stoic, macho man who was born in Arizona and raised in Guadalajara, Mexico; he came to the United States when he was twelve years old, not speaking a word of English. He went to work in a furniture factory when he was sixteen, learned the trade, worked hard, became a shop supervisor, foreman, and plant manager, and in 1978 opened his own factory. Called Resin Craft Decorating Industries, John Enriquez's factory made custom furniture that ended up in fancy restaurants and bars at places like the Bonaventure Hotel in Los Angeles and the MGM Grand in Las Vegas. He also owned commercial real estate and a liquor store. It was the American dream come true. He was prosperous and proud—maybe too proud.

He was thirty years old when he married Lupe Olmos on April 18, 1959, a second marriage for each of them. She was a twenty-four-year-old, brown-haired, hazel-eyed young woman from a little old town of *haciendados* called Lanoche Buena, just outside the city of Jerez, Zacatecas. Her family was well off for Mexico. John and Lupe were Catholics. She also secretly practiced a little *brujeria,* a Mexican witchcraft that combined some of the old Indian ways with Spanish Christianity. Rene walked in on his mother and grandmother once while they were working up something mysterious with Tarot cards, and his mom quickly tried to hide them. He looked at them both and said good-naturedly, "All right, *brujas!*" (witches). Rene said, "I loved my mother dearly and affectionately called her 'Shorty' because she wasn't even five feet tall. She was warm, full of Mexican folklore and unconditional love." She also was permissive to a fault.

John and Lupe had two daughters and three sons together: Perla, Marco, Danina, Rene, and John. Lupe could never control her children. John was the strict disciplinarian, always a bit standoffish with the kids and easy to anger. However, Rene remembered, "there were moments of tenderness with him curling up on the couch with us when we were little. One night he came into my room and taught me my first prayer, the Our Father. And he told all of us about St. Jude, the patron saint of lost causes, helper of the hopeless. He made us go to catechism classes and went to church with us on the Holy Days."

John wanted his children to be good people and blamed his wife's liberal, permissive ways for any troubles they encountered. He and his wife argued often, and he would call her by the nickname "Animal." "Animal," he'd scold, "no! Eso no esta bien" (This is not good!).

She called him "Viejo," the old one. "Leave them in peace, Viejo," she'd respond.

Rene said, "The constant arguing embarrassed me, and there were few displays of affection between my parents. Once in a great while I saw them kiss, but I never saw them hug, walk arm-in-arm or hand-in-hand."

The sons would always go around their father's back to their mother when they wanted something, and they would get it. She was always a soft touch. Her husband more and more began to think she was "crazy," and he looked down his nose at her for being from the Mexican hill country.

Years later John Enriquez would write to the parole board for his son Rene: "By the time he was three years old, his mother and I did not get along and couldn't stand each other. We remained together, because we thought it would be best for the kids. She did what she wanted, so did I. Neither one of us realized how much harm we were causing them. We failed to give them the nutrient that all kids need to grow of sound mind and body, and that is love."

John was also a sociable womanizer who, according to his wife, was a heavy drinker for years. The womanizing was often fodder for fights. "My mom once caught him in a compromising position with an employee at his shop," remembered Rene, "and she confronted the woman with a screwdriver. She just didn't want some tramp to steal away her man. During another argument at home, my mother smashed a glass ashtray over my father's head. The children were all crying. I never saw him hit her back. He just took it and told her to stop. On that occasion, my brother Mark actually called the police, who came to the house and broke up the argument."

John Enriquez spent more and more time at work and less and less time at home. Lupe said, "He was never there to be with the kids, talk to them, and bring them up. I did it my own way, and I did it with love. Sometimes love doesn't do that much. I did the best I could."

There weren't many minority kids in Cerritos, and that at first led to a few playground scuffles for Rene until he learned "to take care of himself." He didn't fit in that well, struggled with math, and was an average student. "When I was eleven," he said, "I broke into a neighbor's house and stole some firecrackers." He was ordered by a Juvenile Court judge to pay for what he stole and was put on informal probation for burglary. It was his first brush with the law. In sixth grade, he attended the Aesop School, which was only for Hispanic and minority children. That's when he started to ditch school—a lot.

For the Enriquez family, the American dream began turning into a nightmare. The two daughters, Perla and Danina, "were always good girls," according to Rene. It was the three sons, mostly Rene and Marc, who were drawn to the dark side.

Just a few minutes' drive from the family home in Cerritos were Artesia, Hawaiian Gardens, and Norwalk—the other side of the tracks—all communities with a significant presence of Mexican street gangs. Rene's older brother Marc was the first to join. The gang was called Arta, short for Artesia 13.

Rene immediately thought the gang members were charismatic with their tattoos and sharp cholo outfits: beanies, wool Pendleton shirts with white T-shirts underneath, baggy khaki pants, and shiny black leather shoes. They were "cool"— to a twelve-year-old kid, they seemed powerful and respected, and they seemed to get the girls too. They were "rebels," and Rene figured that "being a rebel was a chick magnet." Besides, his older brother Marc, now in the thick of it, was Rene's hero. He wanted to be just like him and frequently tagged along with Marc and his homeboys.

The Arta gangsters were bad guys. A lot of them lived in a small ghetto in a seedy part of Artesia. It was not far from the Pat Nixon Park and Recreation Center located near South Street and Norwalk Boulevard. The wife of newly elected President Richard Nixon came to the project groundbreaking in September 1969. There was a historic landmark house there on property where Pat Nixon grew up on her family's farm. Members of the Artesia 13 gang actually burned the little house down—for the hell of it.

One day when Marc was at his girlfriend's house, Rene—now twelve years old—was walking along with Bobby "Apache" Guerrero and another homey called Sparky when suddenly they pulled him into an alley behind the liquor store.

Apache said, "We're going to jump you in!"

Rene was just a wide-eyed kid, still a little square and frightened.

"No! No! I don't want to be in the gang."

Apache's fist found the soft part of Rene's stomach, and he doubled over in pain, his wind gone, gasping for air. Then *boom, boom, boom*—from all directions—hard teenage knuckles pounded against Rene's limp body until the two older boys ran out of steam. Tears began to well up in his eyes, and there was a little sniffle from his nose when he heard, "All right. You're all right. Knock it off! You're a homeboy now. Homeboys don't cry."

Rene swallowed his pride and then coughed it up again. He was a gang member now, a tough guy.

A few days later, Marc, Rene, and a homey named Junior began some training at Montebello Youth Boxing on Whittier Boulevard. It was Marc who decided "Boxer" would be a good moniker for his little brother.

"Yeah, that'll be a good nickname for me," Rene agreed.

Everybody said, "Yeah, he's Boxer."

"At first I just loved having a *placa* [moniker]. It made me more like my brother and his friends—a member of the gang. But as I grew older I also grew to dislike the nickname." However, the name stuck.

Unbeknownst to all of them at that point, they had planted the seed that would grow into a monstrous man-eating plant. Although family and close friends continued to call him Rene, as the years passed Rene and his gangster image became Boxer.

John Enriquez didn't like any of it and was constantly preaching to his sons. He told his boys, "Stay away from those hoodlums. You dress like a bum. You look like clowns in those big clothes!" So they hid their cholo outfits in the garage and halfway down the street put their gang garb back on for the day. They blatantly ignored their father's wishes. Rene thought his dad was "an uncool, old-style Mexican." Besides, he and his brother had a new family now, and they *were* cool—the Arta gang.

CHAPTER 4

Drugs, Dealing, Robbing, and Rebellion

RENE STARTED TO DRINK ALCOHOL WHEN HE WAS THIRTEEN, BREAKING into a pantry cupboard where his dad kept the liquor. He and Johnny Mancillas, a school buddy who lived in the next tract over, poured a combination of Johnnie Walker Red, Bacardi rum, and Kahlúa into a tall glass and chugged it down. By then, Rene had already been smoking marijuana for a year.

A neighborhood character, Becky, five years older, was the famous local head who introduced him to weed. Her parents were old hippies who always placed a big peace sign in blue Christmas lights on the roof of their house during the holidays. She was a tall, blue-eyed, blond hippie chick who wore cutoff Levis and a vest, marijuana patches on her shirt, and biker chains looped from her waist to her wallet. He was walking by her house when he heard this feminine voice ask, "Hey, you want to smoke?" She had some cheap grass. Rene decided, "Yeah, that's cool." So they went out to this empty field where there was a big hole in the ground and lit up. He got loaded, hung out for a while with Becky, then threw up. Honestly, he didn't much like that first experience with marijuana, but after that he smoked it on an almost daily basis. So did most of his new homeboys.

Older gang members would insist that they didn't force the younger ones to imbibe or toke up, that it was a twelve- or thirteen-year-old's own choice. But a kid trying to fit in, trying to impress his older, cooler peers— he did it. The Arta homeboys, like so many other gangsters, washed their hands of responsibility for the younger ones. And Rene, just past puberty, had already slipped into a pattern of substance abuse that arguably helped shape who he would become.

His second brush with the law wasn't any more spectacular than his first arrest for stealing fireworks from a neighbor's house. He and two thirteen-year-old friends ditched school and were headed to the house of a girl who had promised them sex. They had already shared some heavy petting, but she was going to go all the way this time. As the three anxious junior high lovers headed down the street, Rene noticed a yard where a new sprinkler system was being installed. He couldn't resist kicking over some of the elevated sprinkler heads just "for the hell of it." A neighbor saw him do it and called the police. Rene didn't make it to the end of the block before he was arrested for malicious mischief, counseled, and released.

The Enriquez house, one of only a relatively small number in Cerritos lived in by a minority family, became a meeting point for the gang members. They all lived in nearby Artesia, but the garage at the Enriquez house became a safe place where they'd go and get high. It became part of Arta's turf. It didn't take rival gangsters from Hawaiian Gardens long to figure that out, and twice they came by shooting up the front of the house. The phrase "drive-by" hadn't been coined yet. They called it "going capping"—just pick an enemy gangster, drive by his house, and shoot. Arta always retaliated.

Marc, three years older than Rene, also got into a problem with a local drug dealer. He owed the dealer quite a bit of money that he didn't have. This guy was no punk, and he was going to make Marc pay one way or the other. Marc took the problem to his father, who reacted angrily, "This is wrong, son." John wanted to call the police, but Marc and Rene, creatures of a street code that said no cops, begged him not to do it. Their father eventually relented, agreed to pay off the drug dealer himself, and admonished his sons to never get involved with the guy again. Thirteen-year-old Rene hid in the bathroom with his dad's hunting rifle when the drug dealer showed up to collect. He was ready to shoot him if something went wrong. Afterward, the brothers ignored their father's pleas to stay away from the drug scene. He whooped them a few times when they came home high, but they fended off the blows and went on with their druggie/gangster lifestyle.

In fact, Rene became a regular user of PCP when he was fourteen. Not only did he use it, he made it and sold it too. He bought mint leaf by the ounce and *cocui* dust at the local Safeway supermarket, mixed it up at home, put it on dry ice, and let it crystallize. He sold it to other school kids and had a lucrative little business for an eighth grader. PCP is a drug that gives you a stuttering, stupid euphoria. It clearly had an effect on Rene. He would often wake up in a drug-induced daze. He had no idea where he'd been or what he'd done. It was another great ingredient for self-destructive behavior, and it improved his chances of ending up behind bars.

Johnny Mancillas was a gang member from the Compton Varrio Largo who moved into a tract housing complex next to where the Enriquez family lived in Cerritos. He was the only other Mexican-American kid in the immediate area who was Rene's age. The two of them met at school, started drinking together, and became partners in crime, breaking into local homes. Whatever they stole they would sell on the street or trade for drugs.

Johnny's next-door neighbors left for vacation, and this high school freshman burglary team broke into their house as soon as they left. It was 1976, right before Thanksgiving. Inside, they found a stash of guns, including a .22-caliber pistol, a .38 special, and a .410/.22 over-and-under shotgun. In the garage was an Oldsmobile 98. They got the keys and stole that too. Two skinny little fourteen-year-olds without a driver's license between them were rocking back and forth down the street in this big old boat of a stolen car with holsters and guns strapped to their bodies. They did donuts on the grass in front of Cerritos High School and drove all over town, making sure all their homeboys and homegirls got a good look at them in their entire cholo splendor. Then Rene decided to get revenge against the Hawaiian Gardens gang members for shooting up his house earlier.

It was broad daylight. Johnny was at the wheel as they drove up to a little corrugated-metal shack that served as a teen post and saw two rival gangsters about their age. Boxer was seated on the window ledge, hanging over the top of the car roof with his .38.

He shouted, "Where you from?"

He locked eyes with one kid who knew what was about to happen, turned, and took off with his homey. Boxer fired away wildly as the two enemies scurried over a nearby fence and escaped, shaken but unharmed. A police report would later confirm that more than a few of the bullets went into the roof of the Oldsmobile. Rene was a kid with a gun, no Dirty Harry.

Next they drove by an enemy household, saw a group standing out front, and repeated the same drill. They later heard that a girl was hit in the wrist, and Rene thought he winged a couple cholos but never knew for sure.

Then they drove into Orange County, robbed twenty dollars from a gas station attendant, dumped the stolen car in an industrial park, and walked home.

Rene kept the guns, a bunch of them, and laid them out on his bed to show his little brother John. That's when his father walked into the room. He called to his wife, "Call the police. He's got guns!"

The cops were there within minutes. Rene never moved. "My father held me there with his stare." Mr. Enriquez thought it would be good for his wayward son to spend a night in jail. Rene remembered his dad telling the police, "Take him overnight and scare him." He was sure it was the right thing to do.

Sheriff's deputies took Rene to Los Padrinos Juvenile Hall, ten miles away in Downey. It was scary. Four hundred juvenile delinquents housed together on a twenty-six-acre site built in 1957 as Los Angeles County's second reform school. There was constant tension and confrontation between different races and gangs. Rene had more than one fistfight with gang members from other neighborhoods. It was an alien place, especially for a kid who had never even been away from home by himself, and it wasn't for just one night. He was there for seven weeks awaiting trial. His parents dutifully visited him every weekend and hired a lawyer to defend him in Juvenile Court. There are no jury trials in the juvenile justice system, just a hearing before a judge, who has the ultimate power to decide what's best for the defendant.

His parents were as shocked as Rene when the judge made him a ward of the state and sent him to Boys Republic in Chino Hills, a sprawling, two-hundred-acre, self-contained farm and school campus twenty miles northeast of Cerritos. The wards lived in twenty-five separate cottages, but it was a reform school that offered "multidisciplinary treatment for teenagers in need of highly structured supervision." He was confined there for seven months but was allowed to spend weekends at home with his parents. He hated it.

Rene couldn't understand why his dad had called the police in the first place. "I thought my father betrayed me." He resented his father because of it. On the other hand, John Enriquez didn't understand why his son felt that way. He came from another world, deep in Mexico, where a father's word was law. His son didn't respect that, or the simple truth that his father had only been trying to do what he thought was right. The bitterness and distance between them grew. Rene explained, "Every argument we ever had after that, I brought up what I perceived as my dad's betrayal. It became a wedge between us and strained our relationship for years." In the end, reform school only furthered Rene's gang education. "I was baptized in jail, my first twist, and I handled it okay."

His rebellious streak shot off the map as he entered ninth grade at

Cerritos High School and again hooked up with his old crime partner, Johnny Mancillas, who had spent only one night in jail for their last caper. After all, Rene was the one caught with all the stolen guns.

Fresh out of Boys Republic and broke, Boxer picked up a sawed-off shotgun from some homeboys and recruited Johnny to help him with a robbery. Rene recalled, "Anytime I needed money badly I did a robbery."

There was a six-foot wall surrounding the tract housing complex where the Mancillas family lived, and a hundred yards away was an Arco gas station. The plan was to rob the Arco under the cover of dark at closing time, run the hundred yards, hop the fence, and escape into Johnny's house with the loot. The fifteen-year-old robbers snuck into the station through an empty mechanics bay and hid in the back office. They could see the heavyset woman clerk up front collecting the day's cash receipts from a small round safe in the floor. It was late at night when she turned off the lights, and there was the sound of doors clicking and locking. The juvenile thieves, shotgun readied, waited to jump the woman as she came to the back office. Ten minutes passed, and she never showed.

Johnny said, "I think we better check."

They crawled across the garage floor on their bellies only to find the clerk and the money gone, all the doors shut tight, and the alarm system activated. The two robbers were locked inside!

Quickly, they took all the cigarettes off the shelf, stuffed them into a bag, and slammed through a door equipped with an emergency escape swing bar. The alarm went off, they ran like hell, scaled the wall, and escaped into Johnny's house. Robberies were always risky.

Drug dealing was the steady, easy money. "That was the money," explained Boxer. "And girls gravitated toward you. Homeboys gravitated toward you because you had things. And I was a hustler in that respect."

This was the 1970s, and Rene was barely a teen as he slipped into a free-spirited stoner phase during which he frequently sold and smoked marijuana but also dropped acid (LSD) and sold it and any other experimental drug he could get his hands on. "With these stoner guys, it was like an all-out twenty-four-hour party," explained Rene. "You just got loaded until you couldn't stand it anymore and you dropped." There were trips to the Colorado River, where he partied with and screwed biker babes, hippie chicks, and surfer girls. "Girls would have sex with you at the drop of a hat." Sometimes he even traded in his cholo outfit for a Hawaiian surfer shirt, sandals, and jeans. He went to rock concerts and listened to ZZ Top, Peter Frampton, Ted Nugent, Santana, Heart, Led Zeppelin, and Pink Floyd.

He stayed out late at night and got up around midmorning. Whoever had a party—cholos or stoners—Rene was usually there getting high and selling dope. His father more than once caught him on a high, sat him down in the house, and watched him so he couldn't go out. Again he'd preach, "Those guys you are hanging out with are no good." A couple of times he hit his son with a belt, hoping to enforce some discipline. He would order him not to leave the house, but Rene would sneak out a bedroom window when no one was looking. He was uncontrollable, and his frustrated father didn't know what to do. His mother was just glad when he was home and off the streets.

Rene ditched school more and more because he thought "it wasn't cool. I thought it was cool to be a goof-off." He only liked two classes, auto body repair and safety. That was it. "It finally got so I attended homeroom in the morning, hooked up with my friends, ditched the rest of the day, and got high in Freedom Park, right across the street from the high school." He eventually dropped out after the ninth grade.

His father gave Rene a job at his newly opened custom furniture factory and tried to teach him the skills of a finish carpenter—good old-fashioned hard work. He moved his son from job to job. There was staining, sealing, lacquering, and working with resins, Formica, and wood. Also, there was sweeping floors with minimum-wage Mexican workers. Rene "hated it." His older brother Marc worked at the factory too, and he felt the same way. Every couple of weeks they'd "get paid, quit, go party, and do drugs," until their father dragged them back to work again.

At the same time, the Enriquez family took in a few of the local runaways, middle-class white kids who got in trouble with their families and had nowhere else to go. "The troublemakers or rabble," explained Rene, "gravitated toward our house. Anglo families seemed to throw their noaccount kids out of the house when they turned eighteen. Mexican families don't do that. Families are sacred to us. My dad at first would give the new houseguests the 'dirty eye,' but the softhearted part of him even gave them jobs at his factory."

Meanwhile, the Enriquez family garage became a serious party spot with all the ingredients for the downfall of a teenager—cases of beer, acid, sensimilla weed, hash oil, a couch, stereo, strobe light, and willing teenage girls. "It was like a love shack," said Rene, "and everyone knew if the door was open there was a party. Homeboys and stoners would come by and jocks and cheerleaders, surfer chicks, and even nerds. It was a mixture of ethnic and social groups, neutral turf for everyone who wanted to party, but especially a magnet for bad boys. Even some of the neighborhood good girls found their way into this teenage den of iniquity, and more than one lost her virtue. It was always packed."

Rene's father would get angry when he found beer cans on the lawn and when the unbridled revelry kept him awake at night. Besides that, the parents basically didn't interfere, because at least their sons were off the streets. The garage scene made Rene "a popular teenager with a wide range of contacts. There were drugs to be had, and my interaction with different groups enhanced my effectiveness as a dealer."

It was during this period that Rene went to score some dope and bought a half-spoon of heroin. He took it home. His brother Marc cooked it up and found a syringe left in their bedroom by an older homeboy; they both shot up. It was Rene's first heroin high: "I remember getting horribly sick, throwing up, vomiting, becoming violently ill. But after that was euphoric warmth. You sit back, and you're in this drug cloud, this euphoria that's just so attractive and alluring." He didn't do it again the next day, or the next week, but that euphoric feeling was trapped deep inside his mind. He started chipping, doing heroin more and more frequently, and became a serious heroin addict at the age of sixteen. Rene would "chase the dragon" for the rest of his life.

Pam Jonas was a pretty, blue-eyed, sandy-haired blonde three years older than Rene. He first met her when she came to his house with some of her girlfriends to buy PCP. She came from a middle-class, dysfunctional family with divorced parents, a high-maintenance mom who liked to drive flashy Cadillacs, and a heavy-drinking father who threw Pam out when she became pregnant. The baby was lost when she miscarried. That was before she met Rene. "Pam didn't drink or do drugs, was actually a bit naive, and for some reason was always infatuated with gangsters and our wild lifestyle," said Rene. In truth, she was his opposite, but she was kind of a wannabe. There was never a strong emotional bond between them, but they became an item, a novelty for Rene, and she moved into the Enriquez home.

Rene gave his pliant mother an ultimatum: "Either I'm moving out or she's moving in!"

Pam moved into Rene's bedroom and within a few months was pregnant again. They got married when he was only seventeen. It was "normal," Rene observed, for them to live at home with his parents. "I loved waking up to the smell of my mother's cooking—coffee, chorizo, and tortillas—and hearing the sizzle of eggs and sausages on the grill." He felt "kinda proud" that he impregnated Pam and wanted "to do the honorable thing," and so he married her. "I thought it was going to make me a man." It didn't. He cheated on her all the time with her friends. The relationship was doomed from the start, and it didn't set well with Rene's father. He wanted his son to be responsible and develop a work ethic. That wasn't happening either.

Rene was quitting his job every other week. That continued to frustrate his father. Also, Rene was coming to the job loaded and selling drugs to other employees. On one occasion, an angry Mr. Enriquez snapped his son's head back with an open hand across the face while at the coffee shop near his office at the furniture plant. Rene remembered that he glared at his father "with death in my eyes."

"You want to hit me?" asked his dad.

There was a large cake knife on the counter where they stood, and John Enriquez slid it toward his boy. "Go ahead and do it, tough guy."

Not even a knife could cut the tension in that room as the father turned and left. Rene called his new wife to come pick him up at work and once again quit his job.

A few weeks later, Rene had been out all night partying and had had only an hour of sleep when his dad came in. "It's time to go to work. Let's go. Wake up!"

Rene resisted. "Hell, no, screw your job!"

His father was seething. "Get that whore out of my house!"

Rene slipped out of bed. "Don't ever say that. That's my wife, Dad!"

The words stung again. "Get that whore out of my house!"

The son, a few inches taller, swung a fist at his father and struck him in the eye. The blow didn't faze the older man. John Enriquez, who had done some boxing in his youth, came back with a quick combination of punches, boom-boom, a busted lip, boom-boom, a black eye, boom-boom, and the rebellious son was on the floor.

Rene shouted with angry tears in his eyes, "Fuck you! I hate you!"

"Don't ever raise your hand to me, kid!" The disappointed father walked away and went to work. His son stayed home and got high. Later that night, Mr. Enriquez called from the shop in a trembling, tearful, apologetic voice and invited Rene to the company Christmas party. The son said, "I don't want shit from you," and slammed down the phone. The anger lived in both of them.

"It drove us even farther apart," said Rene with regret. "But at the time it felt good. Prior to that fight, my father used to grab me by the back of the neck or the short hairs on my scalp. Sometimes he pinched my ear until the cartilage popped. He never laid a hand on me again."

At one point, his father gave Rene a self-help classic he embraced, a book called *As a Man Thinketh,* written in 1904 by James Allen. Basically, it taught that a person's thoughts influence what he achieves. Rene read it and dismissed it as corny. He didn't need books written by some old square to tell him how to live. He was already Boxer from Artesia 13.

There was constant gang friction. For example, he and a half-dozen homeboys were at Grauman's Chinese Theater in Hollywood, where movie stars have their autographs and hand- and footprints embedded in the cement out front. Some gang members called North Side Rebels said, "Where you from?" It was their turf. Everyone ended up in the parking lot swinging belt buckles, trading insults, and circling each other. One pulled a knife, but no one was seriously injured.

Another time, the Enriquez brothers, Marc, Rene, and John, along with a couple of other Arta homeboys, wandered into a carnival in the nearby town of Buena Park. Rival gangsters there "mad-dogged" them and demanded to know, "Where you from?" This question on the streets is normally perceived as a challenge. So Rene flicked a cigarette into a gangster's face and bitch-slapped him. That sparked a fistfight free-for-all that quickly ended when police showed up with attack dogs and dispersed the gang members without making any arrests.

Later that day, the Arta homeboys were talking to some girls at a duplex in Fullerton (another Orange County community) when the same rival Tokers Town gang members spotted them. The words "Where you from?" were hanging in the air for barely a second when steely blades started flashing. Rene, who was knifed in the back, fought furiously with a bumper-jack to save Marc, who somehow ended up down the street on the sidewalk, stabbed repeatedly. A buck knife and a pocketknife were sticking into Marc's blood-covered stomach when Rene and a few others pulled him into a waiting car to escape. Even thirteen-year-old John had a slash wound on his leg as Rene dialed an ambulance from a nearby 7-Eleven convenience store.

Rene and John were stitched up and released that night. Marc almost died and spent weeks in the hospital recovering from his wounds. Their mother and grandmother put eggs and oil on his stomach and prayed to the saints in brujeria. The night of the attack John and Lupe Enriquez rushed to the hospital and spent much of the night crying for their sons. Rene had a vivid recollection that his father "didn't get mad. He hugged me with tears in his eyes knowing we fought to save Marc's life and that I would never abandon my brothers."

The police that night arrested Rene and Marc, but the case was later dropped. The Orange County District Attorney's Office determined that the Enriquez brothers had a good argument for self-defense.

Still, the gang chaos never ended. Once, while driving their mother's car, they spotted a cholo named Bobby from Hawaiian Gardens, stopped on his motorcycle at a red light and headed to work in the opposite direction. He saw them too, flipped some HG gang signs, gave them the finger, and took off.

Marc said, "I know where he's going."

Rene pulled a star-shaped lug wrench out of the trunk and got back in the car. His brother took off on a shortcut through some residential areas to catch up with Bobby at the nearby industrial park where he worked. "We pulled up behind him right as he turned off the main boulevard into his job site," remembered Rene, "and I leaned out the window with the lug wrench." Marc accelerated like a cop car giving chase. Bobby heard the noise, turned, and moved the bike just enough to avoid a full blow. The lug wrench slammed against his motorcycle and glanced into his body, almost knocking him over. Marc stopped the car and rammed back into the faltering bike. Bobby took off, the motorcycle crooked and wobbly, but operational enough to make it to the safety of his workplace a few blocks away.

The Enriquez brothers began carrying guns for protection and four or five more times shot up a house where some rival Hawaiian Gardens gang member lived. They'd sometimes sit in their own front yard or garage—waiting with guns—because they expected retaliation.

Their father hated it. "I couldn't get them to understand," he said, "that that was not the way I was taught to live."

The pattern of violence escalated along with the use of harder drugs—heroin, cocaine, and methamphetamines, called "crystal" at the time—and Rene sank deeper into the gang member abyss. Not even he understood it at the time, but drug addiction and the gang lifestyle—referred to by gang members as la vida loca, or "the crazy life"—were narrowing his choices and shaping his life.

Prevailing cholo logic was simple. Why work to support a habit when you could deal drugs or rob to get money? So that's what Rene did.

In East Los Angeles visiting his grandmother, he and a family friend named Hector decided to pick up a quick few bucks. There was a little mom-and-pop grocery named Steve's Market. Rene walked in and pulled out a knife: "Give me the money!" The seventy-year-old woman behind the counter pulled out a little children's broom and started beating him over the head with it. She chased him out into the street, yelling, "Largate, ladron, ladron!" (Get out, thief, thief!) Little bumps appeared all over his head and hands as the broom struck him, and the beanie he was wearing was askew. Hector pulled up in the getaway car, laughing, and said, "Come on. Let's go!"

Rene jumped in the car angrily. "What are you doing? Why didn't you help me?"

"What am I going to do?" answered Hector. "It's an old lady."

He stepped on the gas. The two robbers looked at each other and burst into hysterical laughter. It was a bungled job, but most of them weren't.

CHAPTER 5

Boxer Graduates to College (Prison)

SUPERMARKETS, GAS STATIONS, AND JEWELRY STORES WERE ALL targets. Over the course of a year, Boxer and Johnny Mancillas paired up to do a robbery about once a week—every time they ran out of money. Their favorite spots were large supermarkets that were next to a freeway for a quick escape and miles away from their Cerritos neighborhood. Each heist was usually good for at least a couple thousand dollars, sometimes twice that much.

They used a similar MO every time. They parked the getaway car nearby, went in together like regular customers, waited in line with a carton of cigarettes, pulled back a shirttail to expose the butt of a handgun in their waistbands, said calmly, "This is a robbery," and cleaned out all the cash registers, the petty cash vault up front, and all the cash that customers had in their wallets. Victims were ordered to put all the money in brown grocery bags.

Boxer was strung out on heroin all the time and usually carried a .45 automatic pistol. Occasionally, he had to point the gun in a reluctant cashier's face and cock it, but he considered himself a polite bandit, not mean. Some witnesses might have argued that point. He ordered a night manager at a Market Basket in Bellflower, "Stop or I'll blow you away!" And Boxer told a cashier at an Alpha Beta store in Lakewood that he "would blow his fucking head off!" Police reports were replete with statements from victims who were "in fear for his life" or "afraid for his life." However, he never stole anyone's wedding ring, and no one was ever pistol-whipped, shot, or beaten.

Afterward, the alarm call always came in to police: two male Hispanics fleeing on foot. But as they drove off, one of them always lay down on the floorboards while the other one drove. They'd also change clothes on the way.

Also, no one ever chased them. The supermarket robberies worked like a charm over and over again. That is, until they met off-duty officer Howard Dallies on February 17, 1981.

He was a young cop's cop. A big, quick-thinking, good-looking ex-military man with blue eyes, blond hair, and excellent instincts, Dallies was always the first one through the door on search warrants. He had just gotten off the night shift at the Placentia Police Department and had driven his motorcycle to an Alpha Beta store in Buena Park, just a few blocks from his apartment, to pick up some cigarettes on his way home. On his way through the automatic doors, he saw two young Mexican-American teenagers walk in right behind him. Inside, next to the cigarette rack, he noticed the same two nervously looking around the store as if they were casing the place. As he grabbed some cigarettes and checked out, he noticed that Mancillas had disappeared and Boxer was standing in another line near the front main entrance with a carton of nonfilter Camels. During every job, Boxer took a carton of Camels for himself and a carton of Salems for his mother.

Outside, Dallies walked back to his bike, but a burning suspicion quickly brought him back to the front entrance, where he stood behind a pillar. He saw Boxer brandishing a six-inch butcher knife in a grocery checker's face and spotted the butt of a handgun tucked into Boxer's waistband. Mancillas was walking quickly up the main aisle in front of the checker counters. Dallies sent his girlfriend—who had ridden with him—to telephone Buena Park police for backup.

As Boxer stepped toward the double-door entrance/exit and the automatic doors flew open, he heard in a loud clear voice, *"FREEZE!"* Officer Dallies—dressed in street clothes—stepped even closer to the front entrance showing a badge in one hand and a .38 revolver in the other. The cop ordered him to a prone position, cuffed him, ripped a brown watch cap off his head, and discovered that the weapon in the crook's belt was only a Crossman repeater BB gun. The stolen cash and cigarettes were spilling out of a paper bag that lay next to him on the pavement. Mancillas ran to the back of the store as backup arrived.

Other policemen swarmed the market, and employees were herded into the manager's office as the voice of a Corporal Kirby came over the intercom asking anyone left inside the store to slowly walk to the front with their hands in plain sight. Two or three customers trickled down the aisles and out. Five minutes later, Johnny Mancillas came walking down an aisle carrying a five-pound bag of Quaker Instant Masa Karina on his shoulder and wearing a big white cowboy hat and a brand-new brown sweater he'd taken off the store shelves. He had stuffed the blue shirt he had on during the robbery inside a towel display on aisle 1, but Officer J. Sells noticed that this approaching cowboy fit the general description of the second robbery suspect. He ordered Mancillas to put the bag of Masa on the counter and his arms above his head, patted him down, and found a six-inch steak knife in his right rear pocket.

A twenty-one-year-old grocery clerk came over, lifted the cowboy hat, and said, "That's him. He's the one." The gig was up. Johnny at first protested to the cops, "I don't know anything, man." Minutes later, he showed them where he stashed the other bag of money inside a walk-in refrigerator at the rear of the market. The total take was $1,128.83 and $15 worth of food coupons.

Boxer and Johnny were locked up in the Orange County Jail, and for several days Enriquez felt a gut-wrenching sickness. "I threw up violently," said Boxer, "and my cellmate asked, 'What's wrong'?" He described his symptoms, the sweats and this constant weird feeling in his belly.

There was no shortage of jailhouse junkies, and this cellie quickly had a diagnosis. "You're kicking, man. You're kicking."

Boxer was going through heroin withdrawal, and he didn't even know it. "I'd never been through that. If I ever felt even edgy, I always had heroin. I never ran out. I was never at a point where I couldn't get heroin."

Five weeks later, Boxer had shaved his mustache, but ten witnesses picked him out of a lineup as the gunman in three different supermarket robberies, including the Alpha Beta holdup. That was only the beginning. Their similar MO made Boxer and Mancillas suspects in more than two dozen robberies, and witnesses had an easy time remembering Boxer because of the butterfly and dragon tattoos prominently displayed on each side of his neck. "Everybody in the world was identifying us, even for robberies we didn't even do."

In April, he ended up pleading guilty to twenty-one counts of robbery in Orange County Superior Court and was sentenced to seven years in state prison. That wasn't the end of it.

Los Angeles County sheriff's detectives tied him to another eight robberies in their jurisdiction. Facing an additional fifteen years behind bars, he made a deal with the District Attorney's Office and pleaded guilty to those eight counts too.

The probation officer's presentencing report read, "The defendant since age 14 has expressed a serious anti-social behavior which remains unabated and unchecked. His stated reason for committing the present offenses was that he was strung out on heroin. The defendant's motivation to better his situation in life and his prognosis are considered non-existent." He recommended twelve years in prison.

An anguished John Enriquez, with "a pain in his heart," addressed the court: "My son has been somewhat unknown to me because of a drug situation. I have never condoned violence, nor have I ever condoned breaking the law; but neither have I condoned the dispensation of drugs or the manufacturing of chemicals that are robbing our children of their mentality. This is the end result of what happens. . . . I speak for millions of families that find themselves in the same situation. My son is not—and I'm sure thousands of parents will say the same thing—my son is a good son."

Then, on August 31, 1981, a judge in Los Angeles County Superior Court added only two years and eight months to Boxer's seven years, for a total sentence of nine years and eight months in state prison. This time Johnny Mancillas got the same.

Rene's mother and wife were weeping, but he was already resigned to the fact that he was headed to prison. "Prison wasn't a bad thing back then. It was kind of like going to college. Once you get there, you're just considered a homeboy who's been to the joint. Homeboys who go to prison are considered *veteranos*. They're well respected in the neighborhood."

It didn't seem to faze him. Maybe his father was right when he told the court that his son's "mind was warped" by the druggie/gangster lifestyle.

Rene "Boxer" Enriquez was only eighteen years old, leg-chained and cuffed, as corrections officers loaded him on a big long bus—inmates called it "the Gray Goose"—headed for Soledad Penitentiary, six hours away in upstate California. He wore a red jumpsuit with the words CALIFORNIA DEPARTMENT OF CORRECTIONS (CDC) stenciled on the back—his new wardrobe.

A year earlier, he and other Arta gang members were having a party at Boxer's, smoking weed, drinking beer, and talking gangster bullshit. Homeboy Victor Ruiz said that, if you're not a member of the Mexican Mafia, "they'll kill you as soon as you get to prison." Boxer remembered thinking at the time, *If I go to prison I better get in the Mexican Mafia*. But it was just a fleeting thought, one that didn't even enter his mind as he sat on the Gray Goose smoking a cigarette and looking out the window at the California countryside.

La Eme is supposed to be a sacred, secret trust in which nobody speaks about being a member or asks to be a member. You don't seek the Mafia—it finds you. As the Gray Goose continued to roll up Interstate 5, Boxer had no idea that the Black Hand would reach out and grab his mind, body, and soul—his entire life.

The exploits of Eme soldados were almost mythical to young gang members in the barrios, jails, and prison yards across the state. Boxer was no exception. When he arrived at Soledad, every tough-looking Mexican with tattoos and a mustache looked to him like a Mafioso.

Every Latino gang member from southern California was known as a *Sureno* (southerner). And in prison all *Nortenos,* Latino gang members from northern California, all of whom were loyal to the Nuestra Familia, were the enemy. Battles between the two groups were constant. Only a punk didn't participate, and Boxer wasn't going to be any punk. He and his cellmate didn't hesitate to pounce unprovoked on a Nuestra Familia associate, rob him, and beat him on the head with a shaving can they found in his cell.

After that incident, guards locked Boxer up in a disciplinary unit called the Management Control Unit (MCU) for "advocating unrest and violence" between Surenos and Nortenos. On the first day in this new cell for troublemakers, he received a gift of cigarettes and a little note greeting him. It came from a man twice his age, locked up across the tier, a quiet, dangerous-looking convict with the sunken dark eyes of a killer. His name was Daniel Barela. Known as "Black Dan," he was a loved, respected, and full-fledged member of the murderous Mexican Mafia. Barela had a slight twitch on his face when he first began to talk, stuttered, and always greeted other carnales by kissing them on both cheeks as if he were some foreign diplomat. He sat in his cell and read from the Bible every day. At the same time, as one veteran detective noted, Black Dan had a "kill-first-talk-about-it-later attitude."

In 1980 Black Dan beat, kicked, and stabbed a San Diego defense attorney because he was dissatisfied with his work in the courtroom. Lawyer George Manning had represented Daniel Salmeron, a friend of Black Dan's, in a federal drug conspiracy case. Salmeron pleaded guilty, believing he would get four years in prison. Instead, he was sentenced to fifteen years when the probation officer recommended a "substantial period of incarceration." Barela accompanied Salmeron to the lawyer's office, administered the beating, and ordered Manning to return his $8,000 legal fee. The frightened lawyer later told police that Barela said: "This was the only warning I would get. The next time someone would be back and I'd be dead. He said if I reported the incident, he didn't care how long it took him, he'd kill me."

Black Dan Barela had roots in a gang called White Fence, which was located in an East Los Angeles neighborhood where Boxer's grandmother and other relatives lived. He and Boxer would become acquainted for a week in the MCU, then Barela was transferred to San Quentin. A year later, that week would make a big difference in Boxer's life.

In 1982 Boxer was transferred to San Quentin too. It was a rough place, partly because of a relatively new California Department of Corrections policy. Two years earlier, the CDC had decided to no longer spread hard-core convicts out among all the different prisons in the system. Murderers, lifers, and other "management control problems"—which included prison gang members—were sent to San Quentin or Folsom. Prison administrators wanted all the rotten eggs in two baskets.

Boxer was a mainline inmate in the general population at the "Big Q," but he was given a prison job as a trustee, or porter, for the fifth tier in North Block. It was a maximum-security unit that housed a bunch of Mexican Mafia and Aryan Brotherhood heavyweights. He met Benjamin "Topo" Peters from the Hoyo Soto street gang, and Topo introduced Boxer to other Eme carnales.* All of them were seasoned gangster/hit men, ranging in age from forty-one down to twenty-four, all but one a decade or more older than Enriquez. Topo introduced Boxer as "the little brother 'Caja,'" which means "box" in Spanish.

A porter's duties included bringing meals, delivering laundry, and mopping and sweeping floors. As a tier tender, Boxer was free to come and go. So he began conducting business errands for the Eme members, as a "runner." He ran messages, called "kites" or *wilas,* and moved drugs between inmates. There were dozens of hits, and he smuggled in shanks so the Mafia guys could do their killing.

In 1982 three prisoners at San Quentin were murdered and another ninety-one were injured in "incidents" ranging from stabbings to brawls. Boxer saw that deadly Mafia politics accounted for a lot of the carnage. For example, Fat George was stabbed for falsely taking credit for a kill someone else actually carried out. Then Serious Steve was shanked because he

---

* The carnales included Steve "Serious Steve" Murillo from El Monte Hicks, Daniel "Cuate" Grajeda of La Rana, Bill "Hoss" Frisbee of Clanton, Richard "Richie" Pinuelas of Brole, Ruben Barela of Orange County, Michael "Oso" Contreras of Florencia, John "Kiko" Torres of Hoyo Maravilla, and George "Fat George" Lopez of Riverside. The Aryan Brotherhood contingent included John Stinson and Ricky Turflinger.

reportedly grabbed Cuate's arm during the hit they did together on Fat George, attempting to stop him and saying it was enough. That was seen as inappropriate behavior. In another incident, Mafioso Jerry "Wino" Dominguez was stabbed for stealing small amounts of drugs sent to the Eme in North Block. And Kiko Torres was cut up because he voiced some dissent about Eme politics.

Prison social status bumped up quickly for the twenty-year-old Boxer Enriquez. He felt, *Wow! This is pretty cool. These guys are powerful.* He could hear other inmates whispering on the yard as he went by: "Don't mess with him." "He's got big homeys" (a term for Eme members). "He's *camarada*" (another term for a Mafia associate). "He's on his way."

Boxer was getting respect, and he liked it: "Even then I didn't aspire to be a Mafioso. I just enjoyed this little position I was in, this little position of fame that I was placed in just by associating with these people. I benefited tremendously by just running for them."

The inmates at San Quentin called North Block "Hotel California." It's the name of an Eagles song that includes this lyric: "You can check out anytime you want, but you can never leave." It could have been written for the mob.

CHAPTER 6

The Wrecking Crew

ON JANUARY 17, 1984, BOXER ENRIQUEZ WAS TRANSFERRED TO DEUEL Vocational Institution in Tracy, California, with a reputation as an up-and-coming camarada.

On his first day on the yard, two carnales, "Kiki" of Primera Flats and "Gator" of Florencia, both in their early forties, walked up to him on the yard, accompanied by a young camarada nicknamed "Roy Boy." Roy Boy said, "Hey, you're Boxer, right? We want you to do this hit right now."

He didn't even blink. "Okay, let's go. Who is it?"

Boxer was only told that the target was a gang member from Santa Monica named "Angel." He didn't know why they wanted it done, and he didn't ask.

"Take Puppet with you," said Gator. Francisco "Puppet" Martinez was another up-and-comer from the Westside Eighteenth Street gang in Los Angeles. He had a spotted birthmark on his face like Soviet premier Mikhail Gorbachev, and around the yard he was also kiddingly called "Gorbie."

The weapon was a shank made from the handle of a paint roller, a long chrome rod broken off and sharpened to an ice-pick point.

Puppet said, "I'm going to grab him and you stab him."

"Okay," said Boxer. "I'll do that."

It was just that simple. They found Angel on the handball courts and walked straight up to him. It all happened in broad daylight right in front of the gun towers and other inmates—what they called a kamikaze hit. Puppet grabbed Angel and Boxer just started stabbing him over and over again until the untaped plastic handle slid up to cover the point of the shank and made it no longer effective. That's the only thing that saved Angel's life. Boxer handed the bloody knife to Puppet, and they both walked away. Puppet passed the weapon to a third conspirator, who buried it in the grass thirty yards away. It was Boxer's first hit: "It was then I knew I was on the path, I was being looked at [by Eme]. I was honored that I was picked for the mission and exhilarated by the immediate recognition I received on the yard as a 'big homeboy.' It felt as if I'd won a schoolyard fight magnified one hundred times. Yeah, it felt good."

The next hit was Ronald "Chainsaw" Hayward, a member of an outlaw motorcycle club called the Vagos. A notoriously violent biker in his own right, and as big as a house, he didn't get the name Chainsaw for nothing. Boxer was still a skinny young guy. "I was scared to death." But he did it anyway—again right out in the open, kamikaze-style, stabbing Chainsaw until his bloody body looked like someone had attacked him with one. "It's kind of like a blood initiation. Somebody has to do a hit, you keep doing hits, and they've [Eme members] got to see you're reliable." Gangsters commonly refer to it as "putting in work," or "making your bones." "And, yes," Boxer explained, "there is always fear before you do a hit, but there is more fear of what might happen to you if you refuse to do it."

Other older hard-core Mafia members were locked down in segregated units and not allowed out on the yard at DVI. They were Manuel "Rocky" Luna of Big Hazard, Frank "Frankie B" Buelna of Primera Flats, and Senon "Cherilo" Grajeda of La Rana. "They were delegating this authority to us," said Boxer, "and we're handling most of the business on the yard." That meant moving drugs, making sure kites got to the right place, organizing little wars against rivals, and doing the hits.

At DVI, Enriquez arranged a couple of dozen hits on Mafia orders. It was as if he was on a campaign. Traditionally, no one was to outwardly seek Eme membership, but "everything you do," said Boxer, "contributes to your résumé." The young camaradas at DVI, doing the Mafia's bidding and secretly hoping to join their ranks someday, became known as the "wrecking crew."

None of their hit victims died. Boxer learned that "it's not as easy as it looks in the movies to kill a man with a knife—where some guy walks up with a slick move, *shhp, shhp!*—and then walks away casually. No, it's brutal. You feel the shank going in, and you hear them. They're grunting. Their life is draining away. You can see it leaking out of them, but they fight, yell, and scream. They attack you! Killing people is not that easy."

It was also clear that prosecutions for prison yard hits were rare. For one thing, there were no video cameras on the yards at the time. There was also a sense among law enforcement of what was referred to as the NHI factor: No Humans Involved. Why take the time to prosecute a killer who is killing a killer? "Stabbings were so common that they didn't even tape off the crime scene, just picked up the knife and resumed play. A killing might get someone forty-five days in isolation," Boxer discovered, "or forty-five days off a parole date. That means nothing to lifers. And it didn't matter to me if I was caught and prosecuted because I was on the fast track to Eme membership. That was more important than getting parole."

Boxer and others in the wrecking crew saw themselves as soldiers in the Mexican Mafia army, putting in work, growing like a new crop of killers.

CHAPTER 7

Boxer and the Black Hand

ON OCTOBER 2, 1984, BOXER ENRIQUEZ GRADUATED TO FOLSOM
Prison. In those days, Folsom was seen as the end of the road for convicts.
Singer Johnny Cash had it right when he wrote, "Far from Folsom Prison,
that's where I want to stay." Legendary for its toughness, it was an environment that was totally unforgiving—no place for the timid or weak and a
rough place even for seasoned cons.

That didn't bother Boxer, who was becoming a hardened, proven camarada, a man to be feared, and an enforcer. He sat back on a chair in the big
yard at the receiving and release area of the prison, waiting to be processed
in, bullshitting with other inmates, taking a big drag off his nonfiltered
Camel, looking real tough.

Suddenly at three o'clock sharp, a huge steam horn, the work whistle,
blasted the air like an atomic canon, *BOOOOOOOOM!!!* Boxer nearly fell off
his chair. It scared the hell out of him and everyone around him, but he was
supposed to be tough. Instead, he was embarrassed. The noise shattered his
cool-as-ice image. It got worse after that.

A few hours later, he was sent to Administrative Segregation, a high-
security unit known by inmates as "Fish Row." Boxer's violent reputation
at DVI/Tracy had not gone unnoticed by those who made CDC housing
arrangements. As he walked into the area, a Norteno gang member just
released from that section lunged at him from behind and plunged a dinner
fork into the back of his neck. They were strangers to each other, but the
Norteno attacked him after noticing Boxer's tattoos, which marked him as
an enemy from southern California.

Being involved in a rival gang skirmish his first day, Boxer was then taken to an even more restricted lockup called Security Housing Unit II, or SHU II. There, from inside his cell, he met the legendary Mexican Mafia "Godfather," Joe Morgan, known as "Peg Leg," who was at the height of his power and influence in the mob. Morgan was reputedly good for at least a dozen murders on his own and had engineered dozens more.

There was also the infamous Alfred "Alfie" Sosa—five-foot-three inches tall and 120 pounds, but arguably one of the most prolific murderers in Eme history. "Alfie was sick. His lust for blood went over and beyond the call of Eme duty and fellow members would jokingly accuse him of achieving multiple orgasms following an execution."*

And there was Raymond "Huero Shy" Shryock, whose loyalty and enthusiasm for carrying out the most heinous of crimes had made him a Morgan favorite. A half-dozen years earlier, Huero Shy and six other Mafiosi were arrested in connection with ten murders. Boxer estimated, however, that "Huero Shy is responsible for as many as one hundred hits." Along with Morgan, Huero Shy was one of the few white guys in La Eme, and many felt that because of that he killed more readily to prove his worth. One law enforcement source describes him as a "murderous fool." Boxer said, "While in jail, several times I saw Shy break into a cold, clammy sweat. Shy called 'Man Down!' so that guards would take him to the infirmary. He thought he was having a heart attack, but I believe he was suffering from post-traumatic stress disorder [PTSD] from all the violence he'd seen." Eleven years older than Boxer, Huero Shy was also a homeboy from Artesia 13.

They all conversed primarily by passing kites to each other—from cell to cell—throwing out fishing lines with notes attached.

Ten days later, when it was determined that he had been a victim in the fork attack, not the aggressor, Boxer was reclassified by prison administrators and shipped to mainline housing. "I was merely an unfortunate victim, the one time I was victimized in prison."

On a fluke, his new cellmate was Sammy Villalba. Known as "Negro," he was six years older than Boxer, intellectually challenged but street-smart, and also from Artesia 13. Sammy used to roll with Boxer's older brother Marc, and he was also a heroin addict who'd been in and out of jail since he was a kid. He was no stranger to the weight pile, and his fully tattooed upper body was pumped from his frequent use of jailhouse barbells. He and Boxer knew each other from the neighborhood, and as they talked freely it

---

* Mendoza, *Mexican Mafia*, p. 147.

turned out that Negro was a camarada too. In fact, he was the Mafia representative in that cell block, and on the fast track to full membership.

It was a time of race riots at Folsom and San Quentin. There were major
conflicts between blacks and browns, sparked by an Eme hit on a BGF (Black
Guerilla Family) soldier at San Quentin. Daniel Vasquez, who started his
ten-year tenure as warden at San Quentin in late 1983, says, "There were six
hundred shots fired by guards because of yard violence during my first six
months on the job. I stopped counting inmate stabbings and assaults at two
hundred fifty about a year after I arrived." Folsom was no different.

As part of that environment, Negro told Boxer, "we're getting ready to
get down. There are some blacks we got to whack on the tier, and I'm glad
you're here because I was going to have to do it myself." Enriquez had nothing against blacks—he had no racist views—but he knew refusal would be
deadly.

"Yeah, I'm game," agreed Boxer. "Let's go. Let's do this."

The next day Negro was transferred back to the SHU, but before he
left he gave Boxer a knife, pointed out the two targets, and ordered him to
do the hit himself. The tier was filled with black inmates, and Boxer would
have to walk past most of them to get to the other end and do the hit. And
then he had to make it back to his cell, again walking past all the black
inmates after attempting to kill two of them. He said to himself, *Oh man!
This is terrible.*

Then he got a wire telling him that Weasel from Venice was next to
him on the tier and he would help. Suddenly, there was an announcement
that all inmates in their section were going to be brought out together for
a controlled shower.

He looked across to Weasel and said, "Listo?" (Ready?)

"Yeah."

"Okay."

Boxer was dressed only in shower shoes and boxer shorts. He had a
brutal-looking shiv made out of aluminum, two inches wide, a quarter-inch
thick, double-edged razor-sharp blade, made in the prison industries shop.
It was wrapped up in his towel, and it was so big that it stuck out the end
of the roll.

The cell door racked open, and as luck would have it, the main target
was walking right past Boxer, but a couple of correctional officers were right
there too. And a guard with a Mini-14 assault rifle was standing on a catwalk
just a stone's throw away. Boxer was nervous, his hands shaking and adrenaline pumping. "Anyone who says they're not scared to do these things is

pretty much lying. You're going to take a human life and might get shot yourself in the process." There was also the pending reality that he would move up the Mafia ladder by killing people. He made the sign of the cross. This was the devil's work, but a side deal with God wasn't a bad idea.

Then Boxer stepped out of his cell, grabbed the handle of the knife tightly, and plunged the hard silver metal deep into soft black skin . . . there was an ooze of red as the victim ran down the tier. Quickly, he swiped the knife at the second black enemy, whom he didn't even know, and only scratched his arm.

WHOOOOOSH! He felt the live round from a guard's rifle go right past his ear, threw his knife to the floor, and squatted down in a small group of white guys, trying to blend in with them. He could see the first victim, lying on his stomach at the end of the tier, get up and stumble to an officer's desk seeking help. He made it to the prison hospital and lived.

Boxer and Weasel were apprehended by descending guards within seconds.

It didn't matter. He was elated. "It's an accomplishment. You feel a raw sense of power, inflicting violence on someone for the organization. You did it and got away with it, and you're pumped with adrenaline, you're just like, *yeah! yeah!*"

He was shipped back to the "hole," where he joined nearly a couple dozen notorious Eme members. There was Peg Leg Morgan and Rocky Luna and Cherilo Grajeda—he'd "put in work for" Grajeda at DVI but had never even met him. There was Jessie "Pelon" Moreno, Angel Valencia, Corwin "Sloppy" Elmore, and Huero Shy and Black Dan, who would become his mentors. All of them embraced him as a soldado, a camarada. They gave him things—dope, cigarettes, food, toiletries, anything he needed. *This,* he thought, *is cool.*

Boxer and his type-A personality fit in nicely at Folsom after all; like his friend Sammy "Negro" Villalba, he was on the fast track. "I was like a *pistolero* with notches on my gun, a doer." Inmates on the yard knew it. That's how prison works. Boxer learned that quickly: "Unfortunately, in the prison world it is violence that's our status mobility system. We move up the ladder by whacking people. And that's how you progress toward membership in La Eme."

Black Dan Barela and Huero Shy Shryock started coming by Boxer's cell, giving him haircuts and talking—sizing him up and grooming him for a life in the Mafia. They had decided that Boxer was their kind of man—someone who would kill for Eme without hesitation. However, there was a hitch to finalizing his membership in the brotherhood. Members were discouraged from recruiting candidates who came from the same gang neighborhood where they grew up. There was always a paranoia in the mob about one carnal surrounding himself with his own homeboys, creating a loyal following that could give him too much power in the organization. Huero Shy, like Boxer, was from Artesia. Black Dan was from White Fence, where Boxer had a slew of relatives. So they came up with a plan to find another sponsor, or *padrino*, for Boxer. They picked Corwin Elmore of Clanton, aka "Sloppy."

Sloppy was glad to do it. He was a Mohawk Indian known for his ability and willingness to kill, but as far as Boxer was concerned, that was his only attribute. Sloppy was an overweight, five-foot-four-inch, brutish caveman type who was a walking billboard for bad hygiene. He was always dirty and unshaven with boogers hanging from his nostrils, a white flaky substance caked up around his mouth, uncombed hair, and breath that could melt the paint off a wall. Other Mafiosi would take the yard in the morning well trimmed and with pressed shorts—assuming a posture of leadership. Corwin Elmore was, well, Sloppy. "He was gross," said Boxer, and he "always repulsed me."

However, Sloppy had one redeeming quality: loyalty. As Joe Morgan would hang up his prosthetic leg and take a shower out on the yard, Sloppy always walked over and stood bodyguard with his arms folded across his chest, letting no one come near the de facto Godfather. It was as if he were the yard dog protecting his owner.

Morgan seemed to get a kick out of it. Boxer frequently played pinochle with Morgan, Black Dan, and a newly made brother named Mariano "Chuy" Martinez of Varrio Estrada Nuevo (VNE), just four years older than Boxer. (Chuy in later years would become a major Mafia figure in his own right and a loyal Enriquez ally.) Boxer noticed that Morgan cheated at cards, but he never mentioned it to anyone. He went on walks with the mob bosses when they got out on the SHU II yard. His name for months was floated around to all the other Eme members at Folsom, and to any other carnales who could be reached elsewhere. One no vote was an automatic veto of any candidate who was courted for La Eme membership.

Then, in the spring of 1985, it happened. Boxer was sitting in his cell babysitting a batch of jailhouse wine he'd made for the brothers to drink. Other inmates were coming in from the yard and locking up in their cells so the guards could take the daily count. Amid the echoing sound of clanging cell doors, he heard Cherilo Grajeda call out to him, "Hey, Rene! Stick your mirror out." At the time, prisoners were allowed to have little handheld mirrors for personal grooming needs. So Boxer held his mirror out through the bars to see Cherilo in his cell down the row. He was sticking his open hand out into the aisle, and he said, "You see this? That's you now." He meant the Black Hand, Mano Negro, La Palma Negra.

The brothers on the yard had just voted him into the Mexican Mafia. "I felt like I'd just won the gold medal at the Olympic Games. I had—in my mind—arrived, reached a pinnacle of my life. I was now a Mafioso." Rene "Boxer" Enriquez was twenty-two years old. Months later, he would have the signature life-size Black Hand tattooed on his chest with a small unpainted "M" for "Mafia" left in the middle of the palm.

There was no formal induction ceremony. The next time everyone was released from SHU II to their yard, which happened three days a week, more than two dozen carnales took turns shaking his hand and embracing him. "Bienvenidos," they said. "Tu eres carnal" (Welcome. You are a brother).

Huero Shy took him aside and laid out the rules:

1. A member may not be a homosexual.
2. A member may not be an informant, or rat.
3. A member may not be a coward.
4. A member must not raise a hand against another member without sanction.
5. A member must not show disrespect for any member's family, including sex with another member's wife or girlfriend.
6. A member must not steal from another member.
7. A member must not interfere with another member's business activities.
8. A member must not politic against another member or cause dissension within the organization.
9. Membership is for life.
10. It's mandatory to assault/kill all defectors (dropouts).
11. The Eme comes first—even before your own family.

Over time, Boxer would realize that the rules were broken all the time and La Eme wasn't quite the brotherhood he thought it would be. Everyone was supposed to be equal, but Boxer was soon to learn that they weren't.

CHAPTER 8

Mafia Politics: Like Swimming with Sharks in a Bloody Pool

THE MAFIA LIFE AND THE POLITICS WERE TREACHEROUS AND DEADLY, and Boxer Enriquez got embroiled in it shortly after he became a "made guy." There was deceit, dissension, and deception all around him. He remembers "feeling fearful and uncomfortable from the beginning," but he kept it all inside.

His sponsor, Sloppy Elmore, defected, and not long after that he died of AIDS.

La Eme was involved in prison administration–approved peace negotiations with black inmates, and that became a source of Mafia tensions too. Godfather Joe Morgan opposed a truce of any kind, but he was transferred to another prison. It was forty-one-year-old Nick "Nico" Velasquez of La Puente who acted as one of Eme's representatives and negotiated a truce that allowed all Mexican Mafia members and their associates to return to the general population mainline—no more Special Housing Unit II. Nico, during this period, was seen talking to the associate warden on a number of occasions, and some of the hard-core brothers didn't like that. He had also found religion and was outwardly preaching to other Eme members. That didn't set well with the hard-liners either. There wasn't supposed to be any God squad in the mob.

Nico was a heroin addict and a killer—like most of the carnales—but he had an outgoing personality that embraced the younger brothers; he always addressed them affectionately as *mijo*, making them feel like family. He had a face that resembled actor-singer Sammy Davis Jr., and as a big prison dope dealer, he was always willing to share his product to get along. Boxer liked Nico.

A half-dozen other carnales secretly plotted to kill Nico for what they saw as his transgressions. Their private meeting was interrupted by Raymond Garduno, aka "Huero Squire," a tall Vietnam vet who looked a lot like actor Jim Nabors, the main character in the 1960s TV sitcom *Gomer Pyle, USMC*. He'd overheard the conspirators. So Huero Squire confronted them about their scheme to hit Nico without a vote from all the other Eme brothers at Folsom. They ignored his concerns and admonished him not to "rat" them out to the other carnales.

Boxer was enthralled by Huero Squire's war stories and appreciated the fact that he was always calm, methodical, and levelheaded. So he was receptive when Squire came to him and voiced his uneasiness about those conspiring to kill Nico. Enriquez agreed that Nico "was a dedicated Mafioso who had done nothing wrong." More than a dozen other mobsters there felt the same way, including Huero Shy, Negro, Sloppy, and Gilbert "Silver-tongued Gil" Santistevan. The next day, a scared but ready Boxer joined a group led by Huero Shy and Huero Squire as they came out to the yard armed with knives, telling the plotters: "You're not going to kill anybody. We all have knives right now. You try it and we will kill you. Nothing better happen to Nico. He hasn't broken any rules." And the conspirators let it go.

Their hit on Nico would have been unsanctioned. Everyone was supposed to vote on the killing of another brother. Those were the rules. The plotters didn't like the dissent and quickly ostracized Boxer and his closest supporters. Enriquez also suspected he was put on their hit list: "I was a new member. I didn't have much voice, much clout." In Mafia parlance, he lacked *palabra,* or influence. But Nico Velasquez lived—for now.

The rival Eme faction was led by two old-school carnales who did have clout and charisma and were Mafia titans compared to the young Enriquez. One was thirty-eight-year-old Reymundo "Bevito" Alvarez of Wilmas, a highly touted veteran of 1970s prison warfare who had killed a Black Guerilla Family shot-caller and a Nuestra Familia general and stabbed at least a half-dozen other farmeros. The other was forty-six-year-old Ernest "Kilroy" Roybal of White Fence, who had a raspy mobster voice, no tattoos, a strange-looking front tooth framed in gold, and a receding hairline with slicked-back salt-and-pepper hair that had an orange tint from an overuse of Grecian Formula. He stood well over six feet tall, enjoyed boxing in his younger days, and was often called "Shug," short for "Sugar," after well-known prizefighters. Kilroy was a well-respected, straight-up Mafioso until he did heroin. Then he turned into a different person, becoming a clown-like figure who went into a Kung Fu routine, slapping his own face and repeatedly yelling, "I'm on the front row!" "Sometimes," says Boxer, "it was embarrassing, and guards told us to take him off the yard." Kilroy was doing time for armed robbery and murder, had spent most of his life behind bars, and had become somewhat of a legend for his ruthless enforcement of La Eme's rigid code of honor.

Bevito was medium in height and weight, had thick black hair shagged down in the back, with eyebrows and a Fu Manchu mustache to match, tattoos scattered on his arms, and wide-set brown eyes with a hazel ring around the perimeter of his iris. Boxer thought Bevito "had a superiority complex and felt he was better than all the other carnales," an oddity considering that his moniker, Bevito, means "baby" in Spanish. Clearly, he had a lot of political savvy, and he didn't care for the young Boxer at all.

According to internal California Department of Corrections intelligence documents, Bevito felt that new Eme recruits weren't properly screened or voted on: "Eme is not what it was . . . the new Eme are nothing but addicts and have no goals." He also blamed Eme for his wife divorcing him and for the lack of support he had in a dispute with another brother.

That brother was Eme pioneer Michael Ison, known as "Ice Man" for his cold-blooded approach to murder and "Hatchet" for his pure love of violence. Once, he stabbed an inmate fifty-one times in the Greystone Chapel at Folsom. He even threw a spoon at singer Johnny Cash, hitting him in the forehead, while he sang "Folsom Prison Blues." Hatchet, "Acha" in Spanish, then screamed, "You son of a bitch! You're not fucking obligated to sing that song every fucking year."[*] Acha Ison was also a close friend of Peg Leg Morgan's.

Bevito Alvarez and Ison did a residential robbery together in 1982 in Santa Maria, California. Afterward, they were caught, and Ison didn't talk to him at all during the arrest. Acha made bail and Bevito did not. Then Bevito claimed that Acha three days later tried to extort $3,000 from his wife, breaking an Eme rule not to mess with another member's family. Eventually Bevito was convicted of the robbery and sent to prison, where he felt that other carnales were "not supportive" of his complaints against Ison. He planned to kill Acha at first, but then came up with another scheme to "inflict much pain." Bevito decided to cause "confusion and deception" in the organization. It was a grab for power. He got Kilroy to go along.

Once back on the mainline, there was some old Mafia business that

---

[*] Mendoza, *Mexican Mafia*, p. 114.

Bevito and Kilroy thought needed immediate attention. And what developed made Boxer worry about the capricious nature of the Mafia rules. A few years earlier, Alfie Sosa had requested protective custody in prison, which is seen as a cowardly act, after a bloody fight he had with Alejandro "Moe" Ferrel. Moe apparently attacked Alfie from behind while he was washing his face in his cell and beat him up badly. Others believe to this day that Alfie was sexually molested as well.

It's a cardinal rule that a brother is not to raise a hand against another brother without sanction. On the other hand, Black Dan and Huero Shy, Boxer's mentors, were planning to hit Alfie—not Moe—because they felt he showed cowardice when he asked for protective custody.

Thirty-six-year-old Moe Ferrel was another strong, charismatic brother with some smarts, known for his exploits at San Quentin in the 1970s, including the executions of two out-of-favor Eme brothers. Clearly, he was a threat to Bevito and Kilroy.

So Bevito and Kilroy decided to give Alfie a pass and make Moe pay with his life.

On December 15, 1985, Moe was butchered in his cell. Boxer told the story:

"Daniel 'Danny Boy' Pina grabbed Ferrel in a headlock and started to stab him. A husky Angel Valencia then ran in with a knife and escalated the attack as Ruben 'Tupi' Hernandez held the cell door closed. Moe never made a squeak as he tried to fight them off, taking blow after blow, dozens of stab wounds, and when it was over, he looked at his assailants and said, 'All right, you killed me. I'm dying. Go ahead and leave before you get caught.' Sammy 'Negro' Villalba was assigned to keep a lookout for guards, but the assailants were caught in the act anyway.

"Later, Moe walked out of his cell, refusing help from prison staff, made it to a waiting gurney, lay down, and went into a coma. Twelve weeks later, he woke up, ripped out the IVs and tubes in his chest, and said, 'If I can't be a carnal, I don't want to live. That's it. I want to die.'"

He did.

Boxer said, "What happened to Moe Ferrel scared the shit out of me because of the way Mafia rules were applied so arbitrarily." It's not the fact Moe was hit as much as it was that Alfie escaped with no punishment at all.

And the hits kept on coming. According to reports by the California Department of Corrections, between 1985 and 1986 there were approximately one hundred hits at Folsom. Boxer remembers, "We did so many hits and got away with them it was ridiculous. That's how loose it was in prison back then."

Prison stabbings became the norm. It was almost entertainment. Mafiosi on a boring day would sit in the yard bleachers and ask, "Who's getting hit today?" The attacks were accompanied by a grotesque, black humor. Faces contorted in pain, stabbing victims stumbled toward death, and the emptying of a dying man's bladder onto his pant leg induced laughter in the hardened Mafia onlookers. "You get a sick charge out of it," explained Boxer. He and his Eme brothers became desensitized to the real horror of murder.

Boxer and his homey Sammy "Negro" Villalba one afternoon were sitting at the domino tables next to the handball courts at Folsom. Negro usually had a life-of-the-party kind of personality, but he had a hidden dark side—as black as the skin that earned him the nickname Negro—that included a sexual episode with a barnyard calf.

Negro said, "AB is going to whack this guy."

"Which one?" asked a curious Boxer.

Negro pointed out an Aryan Brotherhood associate standing in a line waiting to go back into the cell block for a two o'clock recall. He was holding a large Bible in his left hand, his arm hanging down at his side. The hit man walked up beside him and pulled out a huge knife. "Just the sight of it would kill you," recollects Boxer, "that's how massive it was."

Pow! The sound of the knife blow echoed across the yard. Then again: *pow!* The target jumped back from the impact of each strike before the stabber calmly walked away and dumped the weapon in a nearby ice machine.

The stunned victim was still standing, rubbing his side and feeling his body, searching for the signs of blood oozing from a fresh wound or two. There were none. Then he held up his Bible and noticed two slash marks across the cover. In his panic, he had inadvertently used the Lord's Book to shield himself from the devilish knife blows.

Negro looked over at Boxer. "God was truly with him today!"

The two carnales exploded with laughter.

Not every hit was a kill, but it might as well have been. "Once an inmate was stabbed," noted Boxer, "he was marked as a loser. He was fair game for anyone, and might as well be dead, especially if he was a carnal."

Negro Villalba was ordered to do a hit on a Mexican national named Veracruz—a tough guy with no affiliation who went to the yard surrounded by Eme members and associates and still had the gall to disrespect Alfie Sosa by throwing water in his face. There was an unsuccessful hit on him at the weight pile, and still Veracruz refused to go into protective custody. The next day Negro attacked him in a stairwell on the third tier of three blocks with a huge, foot-long, inch-and-a-half-wide steel shank—a real "bone-crusher." Negro stabbed him so many times that he thought for sure he killed the guy, and shortly afterward he went by Veracruz's cell, expecting to see him balled up on the floor and dying. Instead, he saw his victim pulling out *Time* magazines from inside his shirt. During the attack, he'd worn a protective vest made out of the periodicals, and it saved his life. The next day a robust Veracruz was back out on the yard. This time it wasn't so funny.

Bevito started telling everyone that Negro was a halfhearted coward for failing to kill Veracruz. That was dangerous talk because the Mafia executed cowards. Boxer feared even more that he and Negro might then be on the hit list, and it intensified their political turmoil with Bevito. At the same time, he was having second thoughts about his decision to join Eme: "This is not going to last for me. It isn't the brotherhood I thought it was, and I'm going to quit. This is not what I'm about. I was an uncertain, nervous, scared kid really, trying to function with all these notorious Mafia titans. I wasn't comfortable in my skin as a Mafioso yet. I hadn't become completely cold like these guys who would stab you in a hot [second] as soon as look at you. I hadn't become that guy yet." But he was learning.

Bevito and Kilroy were even bold enough to politick against Godfather Joe Morgan, pointing out that he wasn't Mexican. They insisted that no one should be in La Eme who was not Latino; it was becoming an "All Nations Mob," they complained, and they didn't like it.

The inter-Mafia violence extended to San Quentin, based in part on the bad blood between Bevito and Mafioso Mike "Hatchet" Ison, who was housed at the Big-Q.

In January 1987, all Eme members were transferred out of Folsom and San Quentin because of the rash of violence at those institutions. Unfortunately, Boxer and Negro found themselves on the same cell block as rivals Bevito and Kilroy at a brand-new maximum-security prison, California Correctional Institution (CCI) at Tehachapi.

The bloodletting, infighting, confusion, and ever-shifting loyalties continued. Twenty-five-year-old Raymond Frutos, a not-too-bright Eme associate from the Eighteenth Street gang, had his throat slit out on the yard because he didn't share his coffee with a carnal. Three weeks later, twenty-nine-year-old Jose Chavarria, the Mafia member who hit Frutos, was stabbed by his cellmate, a twenty-six-year-old Eme associate named Rudolph Dominguez. A week after that, forty-four-year-old Eme member "Silent George" Ruiz was stabbed.* All of them were caught up in the Mafia politics.

Boxer felt negative vibes that he and his homeboy Negro Villalba might be next. "We know we're going to get whacked. Anything said could be used against you. They should have posted a sign on the door leading to the yard, 'Say nothing or they'll kill you.' That's how dangerous it was out there." It was like swimming in a pool of sharks when someone throws blood in the water. Luckily, Boxer and Villalba were transferred to another Tehachapi cell block away from the Bevito/Kilroy faction.

Nico Velasquez, the same brother they had stood up for at Folsom, was also housed at the new Tehachapi prison. They had helped save his life. Unbelievably, he did a complete 180-degree turn and started to support Bevito and Kilroy—leaders of the faction that had secretly plotted to kill him a few months earlier. It didn't do him any good.

Two weeks after Boxer and Negro Villalba moved out, Nico was sitting in his cell writing a letter. His cellmate was twenty-nine-year-old Gabriel "Sleepy" Huerta of Wilmas, who was short and beasty-looking with a bushy mustache and thick hair combed back. Other brothers also good-naturedly called him "Burt" because he had an extremely hairy chest like actor Burt Reynolds. Sleepy was studious, smart, and articulate, spoke several languages, and was well liked and respected by other members, including Nico. He was also a killer.

Sleepy Huerta called out to his cellie. As Nico turned to answer, Sleepy stuck a metal shank—cut from a locker—into his lower chest and drove it upward toward the heart. Nico Velasquez wouldn't preach his newfound religious beliefs to Eme members anymore. He was dead. The fact that Sleepy killed him with a single blow earned him an additional nickname: "the Professional." Boxer and others believed it was Bevito and Kilroy who ordered the hit.

Boxer Enriquez was now in a cell block with Eme legends Joe Morgan and Mike "Hatchet" Ison as well as stalwarts Huero Shy Shryock and Fernando "Ferni" Bermudez—they were also all heavyweights in the faction opposed to Bevito and Kilroy. In all, there were about ten Eme members

---

* Prison intelligence documents say La Eme member George Ruiz ordered Dominguez to stab Chavarria and supplied the weapon for the assault. Boxer Enriquez says Ruiz was hit because "he was anti–Bevito Alvarez."

and ten loyal associates on that yard. Everything changed again. Boxer was back in the right car. Sick of their politicking, this group wanted Bevito and Kilroy dead. Both were put on the *lista*—the hit list. It was over for them.

Then Boxer Enriquez—after serving nine years and eight months in prison—was paroled.

He went in a crook and came out a killer—more dangerous than ever. Plus, he had now learned the fine art of deadly Mafia politics. "I learned to prevail. I learned that if you keep your feet planted long enough and firm enough, you're going to come out all right. It's throwing everything you can at a guy for so long that some of the mud is going to stick, whether true or not. You can kill a guy with words. Befriend him. Be nice to him. When it comes to a verbal confrontation, call him out, 'Me and you, let's go!' He's already in a shaky position and doesn't want another weight on the scale. Nine times out of ten he'll back down. If not, you kill him." Boxer was now cold—a true Mafioso.

CHAPTER 9

Back Outside:
The Brutality of the Streets

BOXER AND HIS WIFE PAM WERE ALREADY GETTING A DIVORCE IN
August 1988 when he hit the streets. During his stint in San Quentin, he
had conjugal visits with her, and they had a second child, Rene Jr. Pam had
visited him with regularity while he was in County Jail and at San Quentin.
Later, at Folsom, she warned him, "If you get in the Mafia, I'm going to leave
you." Boxer's answer was curt: "You better leave then, because I just got in
last month." Eventually, they agreed that she had custody of Rene Jr. and
Boxer had custody of their older son, Bobby, who was really raised by his
grandparents, John and Lupe Enriquez.

On parole, Boxer moved in with his father, who was now divorced and
had a house in La Puente, and another relative helped him get a job working construction for eight dollars an hour. John Enriquez still quietly hoped
that his son would choose to live a normal, respectable life. It wasn't going
to happen.

Boxer asked his father if he could have a few friends over for a
barbecue.

John Enriquez asked if they were "good guys."

"Yeah," he answered. "They're good guys, Dad."

In his world, they were. "We have our own standards and expectations
that govern our behavior. Brutality is lauded. A brother is considered a good
man because he has committed acts of violence for the Mexican Mafia. He's
not a snitch or a coward. He's a stand-up guy. What the regular world con-
demns, we praise. Your best friend comes along and brothers vote him out,
even though you like the guy, you got to whack him." It was a bizarro world
where right was wrong and wrong was right, a world where coldhearted

killers capable of the most vicious crimes were considered not only normal but good guys.

So Huero Shy Shryock, Rocky Luna of Big Hazard, and Jesse "Pelon" Moreno of Norwalk, all recently paroled "good guys," came to Boxer's barbecue. They were having periodic meetings trying to get organized. They knew they needed to put the Mexican Mafia name back on the streets, where it had been relatively dormant for more than a decade. In the late 1970s, the prominent Mafia killer Mundo Mendoza had become a government informant/witness and helped lock up three dozen influential brothers for long prison terms, including Joe Morgan, Alfie Sosa, and Huero Shy. It definitely crippled Eme influence outside prison walls. Mendoza says, "We were in the initial steps of organizing outside when all the arrests were made."

The organization continued to be a true criminal meritocracy in which a member's influence grew with the volume of blood he extracted from his victims. "But there was nothing lucrative about being a member, other than status," realized Boxer. "There was no effort at generating finances, no collective focus at advancing. There were carnales on the yard who couldn't afford new tennis shoes. They had nothing because they didn't have the intellect or ability to see beyond a prison wall."

On the other hand, Boxer saw lucrative possibilities. "Finances translate into power. We had the base in terms of terror, but we weren't doing anything with it." A number of old-school Mafia guys thought it was sacrilegious to use the Eme name to make money. Several at the top, like Morgan, saw themselves as big drug dealers, but only they did it. The Mexican Mafia was mostly all about running the prison yards. Boxer thought that kind of thinking was a "thing of the past." La Eme might have started as a prison gang, but there was more money to be made outside those walls.

Rocky Luna walked into the barbecue with the front of his shirt open, exposing a large tattoo that spelled out MEXICAN MAFIA across his upper chest, just below his neckline. Luna was an ugly brute of a man with a pockmarked face, helmet-head haircut, wide nose, big bushy mustache that turned down at the edges, and false teeth. Oddly, he always broke one tooth from his dentures to make them look as if they were real teeth. Rocky was a proven killer who was disarmingly charming, a character with a funny story every minute.

Then Huero Shy showed up with the letter "M" unmistakably tattooed on both of his arms. He was a grouchy guy—often referred to as "disagreeable Shy"—with one blue eye and one green eye and a big, deep, booming, throaty voice. He spoke English with a slight Mexican accent even though he was an Anglo whose mother came from Kansas. Shy had a little too much to drink and warmed up to Boxer's father, calling him carnal this and carnal that.

John Enriquez asked his son, "Are these guys from the Mafia?"

"Don't worry about it, Dad."

Boxer was wearing a slingshot—an armless T-shirt that exposed his shoulders and much of his upper body. His father, who already hated prison tattoos because he felt they limited job opportunities, now saw the Black Hand tattooed on his son's chest.

"It's the Mexican Mafia," Boxer said. "Don't worry. It's nothing."

"You're a member of the Mexican Mafia?"

"Yeah," repeated the son. "Don't worry. It's nothing."

Stunned and bewildered by his son's admission that he was a Mafioso, John Enriquez didn't ask any more questions. He just couldn't do it. The words wouldn't come. It wasn't what he wanted for Rene, but there it was. Besides, Rocky and Huero Shy seemed like personable fellows, and they were after all his son's friends. He preferred not to know the details of who they really were or what they did. "He glossed over it," remembered Rene.

The Mafiosi talked business over potato chips, barbecue chicken, potato salad, hot dogs, burgers, and beer. The other guest was forty-nine-year-old Jesse "Pelon" Moreno, an easygoing moneymaker who had missing teeth, wore thick glasses, and knew a lot of people. Although he liked to stay in the background most of the time, Pelon was a go-to guy who served as La Eme's de facto commissioner out on the streets. Huero Shy and Rocky had introduced him to Boxer, and Pelon had agreed to put Boxer in touch with a Mafia heroin supplier so that he could run his own drug sales operation on the streets.

Huero Shy and Rocky also set him up with a two-man crew of camaradas and asked him to supervise the robbery of some drug connections. "To help you get on your feet," said Shy. "Go do this, and give us a little kickback from it." Rocky gave him some firepower, including a .38-caliber revolver, a .357 Magnum pistol, and a shotgun. Boxer sent his nervous ex-wife Pam to buy bullets at Kmart. She feared that he was going to kill someone. But all the while, his Mafia paranoia told him he might be the one walking into a trap, a setup for his own demise. "I was scared to death." He went ahead on blind faith—always covering his fear.

A few days later, he met the crew. There was "Ray-Ray" Sanchez, Boxer's age and the son of an Eme member from an East L.A. gang called Eastside

Clover, and thirty-four-year-old Ray Soto from La Puente. Boxer gave them guns and followed them down the I-10 freeway in his dad's car at seventy-five miles per hour. It was after midnight, and house lights were already dimmed and people in their beds as they drove up into the hilly area of El Sereno, a dangerously gang-infested neighborhood, and not an unfamiliar spot for body dumps. The armed camaradas pulled off the road at a spot where it was pitch-black, with no streetlights. Boxer slid his car in front of them and saw the two gunmen in the rearview mirror as they exited their vehicle and came his way. He knew they were a couple of paranoid cocaine addicts, and he thought, *This is it, man! I'm on the lista for something I don't even know about. They're going to pop me and take off.* Ray-Ray walked up to the driver's side and squatted down as the other Ray stood back, fiddling with his .38. Neither noticed it when Boxer quickly made a little sign of the cross. *Forgive me, God,* he prayed in his mind. *Accept me into heaven if I get whacked right now.*

The same fingers that he had just used to bless himself now itched for a .357 Magnum pistol. He had regretfully left it behind, thinking he was just supervising this job and knowing a chance stop by police would send him back to prison on a parole violation if he was in possession of a firearm.

Ray-Ray said, "We're going to do it right now."

"Okay," replied an uneasy Boxer.

Then they took off into the darkness behind him. He still feared it was a classic setup, and he would soon see the white flash of firing gun barrels emerge from the black night. It was a long five minutes before the Rays appeared with a bag full of cash—about $2,000 worth—and handfuls of jewelry. "Follow us!" one of them said. And the two-car caravan went off to split up the money—the shakedown robbery a success. Boxer got 50 percent of the take and took out a taste for Rocky and Huero Shy. Rip-offs like that one became a lucrative pattern.

He still worked his construction job, but at least once a week he and a crew kicked in doors and robbed drug connections. They took cash, guns, jewelry, and VCRs. They even knocked off a few jewelry stores, a Big Boy restaurant, and a gas station along the way.

A new generation of gang members and dealers on the streets lacked a full knowledge of the Mexican Mafia. Boxer knew they had to reinstill terror and flex muscle. "We were putting the fear of God back in everybody. We were going to make our names known. The Mafia was going to be feared again on the streets." Instinctively, Boxer knew that he and his Mafia brothers also had to fear each other: "Every time I went somewhere with a carnal, it was always a scary ride. I thought I wouldn't come back alive. Every day of my life I was scared for my life." The trick was not to show it and to be ready to kill before being killed. He would never again go on a mission without a gun.

On October 15, 1988—just a few months after his release from prison—Boxer had a fresh reminder of just how brutal one carnal could be to another. Jose "Sluggo" Pineda was a bitter, cantankerous old-school Mafioso who spoke mostly Spanish, and if someone didn't understand him, he would get pissed off. His craggy face with puffed-up eyes, his bald head, and his crooked ears gave him a look of perpetual misery, as if he were sucking on sour lemons all day long every day. In fact, he usually stayed high on heroin, whiskey, or anything else he could get his hands on.

Police found his body near the railroad tracks in Hazard Park, just outside the Ramona Gardens Housing Project in Lincoln Heights. The Big Hazard gang's turf, it was the neighborhood he called home, known simply as "Hazard." His throat had been cut from ear to ear—a trail of deep gashes—and his chest was laced with puncture wounds. An examination by the coroner showed that the fatal neck damage had been done with a jagged metal object, possibly a torn beer can found near the corpse. The puncture wounds looked as if the killers had worked him over with a Phillips head screwdriver. Defensive wounds showed that he didn't go without a fight. Boxer said, "It was the handiwork of Huero Shy Shryock and an accomplice, as a favor to original mobster Topo Peters."

Benjamin "Topo" Peters, according to prison records, was "one of the top members of the Mexican Mafia . . . a very hostile, aggressive, predator type individual with a very short temper . . . involved in numerous violent and assaultive acts at various institutions which were committed with prison made weapons." He didn't like Sluggo.

Sluggo had had nothing when he got out of prison about a year earlier. He had no family, no money, no place to live—nothing. It was customary for mobster parolees who had nowhere to go to stay with Paz Gutierrez, Topo's sixty-six-year-old mother. She would make them do yard work and odd jobs around the house in return. Topo was only five feet, four inches tall, and he stood nearly a head taller than his *madre,* who was a fireplug of a woman with short, permed, dyed strawberry-blond hair, huge owl-eyed glasses, and a little crooked smile. She was totally devoted to Topo, her only child, and he was totally devoted to her. According to probation records, Topo's mother and grandmother were "overprotective," and his father was a "physically abusive" alcoholic who abandoned the family when Topo was seven years old.

FBI agents say Paz was also devoted to the Mexican Mafia. The organization used her and her "clean" mailing address to deliver and reroute messages and to set up three-way telephone calls regarding gang disputes, drugs, and other illegal Eme business. The feds say her house was also used for occasional mob meetings. Naturally, it was a good spot for Sluggo to set up for a while after getting out of the *pinta*. It didn't go well.

It's never been clear why, but Paz quickly grew angry with Sluggo. She sent word to her Mafioso son Topo that Sluggo had tried to rape her. Boxer remembers clearly what happened next: "Benny [Topo] flew off the handle. 'This motherfucker tried to rape my mom after I put him in the house. I'll kill that son of a bitch.'" Topo started sending out *wilas* that ordered Sluggo's death. Not wanting to get on Topo's bad side, others agreed without question that the job had to be done.

Then, as carnales dropped by Paz's house to follow up, her story grew a little softer. She claimed Sluggo had simply come on to her, and later she changed her story again, saying Sluggo had raised his hand back to hit her. There were three different versions of the story. Boxer for one thought "it was lame—it all sounded stupid." Meanwhile, Sluggo had no idea what was going on. He moved out and was sleeping in abandoned cars in Hazard, doing crack, living like a bum, and wondering why younger gangsters in the neighborhood were beating him up and shooting at him. The guy probably didn't know there was a green light on him until Huero Shy came to click off his life.

Boxer Enriquez said that Topo's mom was an "evil" little woman: "She was the worst liar in the organization. Arguably, she caused more murders than all of us. So many people got killed for stupid stuff like this. It's a repetitive theme in the mob: guys get whacked for nothing. It's a cannibalistic organization that will eat its own. That's what it does."

CHAPTER 10

Preserving Hoodlum Honor

DENISE WAS AN OLD CHILDHOOD GIRLFRIEND WHO GREW INTO A GORgeous, big-breasted, slim-waisted woman with freckled, alabaster skin, bleached-blond hair, and bright hazel eyes. Boxer hadn't seen her for a decade when she called him after he ran into her sister in a nightclub. They had a date, and she was so much fun that they soon became a couple who frequented restaurants and clubs.

They were at the Inca Room in La Mirada, a ghetto club for gangsters with a pool hall, bar, and dance floor. Boxer noticed his ex-wife Pam across the room, arguing with a nineteen-year-old girl who turned out to be the niece of a well-known heroin dealer from Artesia known as "Flo." He walked across the room and asked his ex if everything was okay.

Then the niece stuck her finger in his chest and yelled, "Who the fuck are you? Get the fuck outta here!"

Boxer shot her a look that would chill a glass of water. "Don't mess with me. I will hurt you." It was over . . . for now.

Several hours later, Denise and Boxer, along with his younger brother John, went to an after-hours party that happened to be at Flo's house in Norwalk near the intersection of the 405 and 605 freeways. It was the turf of a gang called Neighborhood Varrio Norwalk. Flo's roots were in Arta, but she moved periodically, trying to keep her heroin operation one step ahead of the police. The place was filled with gangsters and their painted women. Not too long after arriving, Boxer saw the same niece, and she yelled, "There that *puto* is!"

She'd probably been telling everyone there about the earlier encounter at the Inca Room. Then Flo's daughter Valerie strutted up to Boxer and said,

"Who the fuck you think you are? You don't run shit here!" Her ashtray breath was overwhelming, and her alcohol spittle hit his face. It didn't make him happy.

Then, as Boxer slowly placed the Corona he was drinking on top of a tall stereo speaker, Valerie struck him with her hand. He turned and popped her with his fist right square in the eye, and then it seemed as if every warm body in the room descended on him. Boxer was soon trapped under a dog pile of swarming cholos and cholas when he felt a sharp ping-ping in his chest. Automatically, he reached for the eight-inch, double-edged killing dagger he kept stashed in his rear pants pocket, and it was missing.

Meanwhile, John was standing over his brother, furiously knocking people off of him. The room was filled with the noise of shrill screams and guttural grunts. An older homeboy known as Big Monk was shouting in disbelief, "That's a carnal! What are you doing?" It was a chaotic ghetto brawl.

Boxer somehow got to his feet and saw the two stab wounds in his chest, blood drenching his white-on-gray-patterned shirt. His eye caught Flo's son-in-law, Eddie, standing nearby, holding a knife and trying to hide it behind his leg. Next to him was "Bosco," Flo's son, pocketing a dagger that was all too familiar to Enriquez—it was his. He threatened them both. "I'm going to kill you. You are dead. You are through!"

Girls from the family taunted him as he walked toward the door, throwing beer cans and screaming obscenities. The short, fat, cockeyed beast of a woman known as Flo stood there blind drunk with a trophy in her hand. "Fuck you! I don't know who the fuck you are!"

"I'm coming back," warned Boxer. "I don't care who your family is."

It turned out that Flo was the sister-in-law of an Eme founder. She pleaded to Topo Peters and Cuate Grajeda, imprisoned Mafiosi who benefited from her heroin supply, claiming that Boxer "disrespected us." It didn't matter. The Mafia rules said that any outsider who raised a hand against a carnal could die for his mistake. Boxer knew he had to make a statement to preserve his hoodlum honor. He sent word of what happened to Flo's brother-in-law at Corcoran State Prison (COR). His common-law wife, Flo's sister, delivered the response to Enriquez. "Do what you have to do."

Eddie, Valerie's fiancé, went into hiding. That left Flo's boy, Bosco, out there to hunt down and kill. However, every time Boxer located him at some nightclub or party, he managed to sneak out the door. About three weeks had gone by when Boxer heard that Bosco would be at the Inca Room. Boxer was outside in the parking lot with a Marlin eighteen-shot, two-magazine automatic rifle. He chambered a round and waited patiently in his car. This time Bosco was going to die.

He'd sent his girlfriend Denise in to make sure Bosco was there. Denise was a dope fiend with ties to Flo's family, and unbeknownst to Boxer, she had been tipping Bosco off every time he got close to the kill. This time she told her sister Tina to leave with Bosco so that Boxer wouldn't shoot. She didn't realize that wouldn't be enough.

Denise followed her sister and Bosco out of the club and jumped into the front passenger seat of Boxer's car. His brother John was driving. Boxer sat in the back with his weapon. Bosco screeched out of the parking lot before them and launched into an exercise of evasive driving, sometimes traveling up the wrong side of the street into traffic. John stayed about five car lengths behind, anticipating the right moment. It was about forty minutes into this stalking game—going fifty miles an hour on a surface street—when John pulled up alongside Bosco. It was then that Boxer leaned out the window with the automatic rifle and unloaded. Ricochets were zinging, and innocent people on the sidewalk nearby were screaming for their lives. Bosco whipped the steering wheel to his right and went into a skid as rifle rounds shattered his windows.

Denise was frantic. "You're killing my sister!"

"Shut up!" said Boxer. He wanted Bosco dead. If Denise's sister was killed in the melee, that was just too damn bad. This was Mafia business.

The rifle magazine empty, Boxer told his brother to head back to the freeway and return to East Los Angeles. He found out later that Bosco had some cuts from flying glass, and Tina was left without a scratch. Both had miraculously survived the attack, but Flo asked for a meeting.

A teary-eyed Flo later agreed to pay one thousand spoons of heroin, worth about $10,000 on the street. She was also forced to pay a couple hundred dollars a week in tribute. She resisted at first but changed her mind when she was reminded that her son Bosco sooner or later would end up in jail for some petty crime and the Mafia would make sure he came home in a coffin. It was Boxer's first successful extortion, and it opened his eyes to the possibilities of extorting other neighborhoods too.

Mike Higgins, also known as "Cowboy," was another gang member from Eastside Clover. He was Boxer's age. They had been on the camarada wrecking crew together at Deuel Vocational Institute in Tracy, California, in 1984. Cowboy was a terror back then. He wanted to stab someone every day. Boxer ran into him at a Lincoln Park festival in East Los Angeles. He assured Boxer that he and his homeys had plenty of guns. They exchanged numbers and decided to do some jobs together—not construction.

But it was while working on his construction job out in the Moreno Valley, sixty-four miles east of Los Angeles, that Enriquez learned about another drug connection in Corona. He called Cowboy.

It was late at night when the two of them kicked in the front door shouting, "Police! Police!" That entry always gave them an edge: a drug dealer expecting a bust always hesitated just long enough when he believed the cops were at his house. The connection was just getting out of bed as Boxer, carrying a Tazer stun gun, and Cowboy, brandishing a .38 Smith & Wesson revolver, crashed through the bedroom door. Boxer hit him with the Tazer right on the neck, and it dropped the guy, who was dressed only in little red underwear that looked like panties. The guy started screaming when the shock wore off, and so did the woman with him.

"Shut up!" ordered Boxer as he and Cowboy duct-taped the mouths, hands, and feet of their victims and made off with a stash of heroin and a reasonable collection of jewelry. It was only later that Boxer learned that the house belonged to another Eme member, Carlos "Carlito" Morales of Lomas, and the woman victim was his mother-in-law. He'd committed a crime that was a killing offense in the mob, but he got away with it because Carlito never made it an issue.

By this time, Boxer Enriquez was using heroin again. He was always a hope-to-die kind of user. So he quit his construction job, and his robbery schedule was coming off the hook.

Denise was a registered nurse but also had a nasty heroin habit. Boxer tried to stay clean when he paroled, but he soon discovered that his girlfriend was shooting up when she told him she was sick. That's a junkie code term for "I need a hit now." He took her to a methadone clinic in Baldwin Park, and they put her on a rehab program. She lied to him about staying with it.

It wasn't long before she came to him again. "I need to get well."

"You are going to ruin me," he lamented.

Then he drove her to Jesse Aragon's apartment to get some dope. Jesse was a thirty-five-year-old paunchy, sloppy, slow-witted Mafia member from Artesia known as "Sleepy." Boxer never thought of him as carnal material, but Sleepy was married to one of Eme founder Huero Buff's daughters, Jenny Burgueno. She was a rail-thin, ferociously unpleasant-looking ghetto chick who chugged a can of beer for breakfast and had a personality to match her face. Junkies and small-time dope dealers went to their place to shoot up and sleep on the floor. Enriquez knew he could score some heroin there. He did. Sleepy gave him a spoon for Denise. Boxer took a taste too and started using again.

When he went back to Sleepy's several nights later, he was asked to attend a meeting with Jesse Moreno, Huero Shy, and Rocky Luna. He walked in the door and the phone rang. It was Mafioso Topo Peters calling from prison, where he'd spent the vast majority of his life.

Even juvenile crime records described Topo "as a clever agitator . . . often stayed in the background while agitating others in aggressive acts." Topo started using heroin when he was fifteen, dropped out of high school in the tenth grade, and, despite coming from a fairly well-heeled family, chose a life of crime. By the time he was forty, there were numerous narcotics arrests, thefts, armed robberies, assaults, and a few escapes on his record. He was currently serving a thirty-year-to-life sentence for first-degree murder. In 1980 an angry Topo—eight days after his release from prison—pulled a .44 Magnum revolver out of his shoulder holster and shot a man in the head at close range outside DeBarry's Bar on North Broadway in Lincoln Heights, just east of downtown Los Angeles. Pablo Rucobo, the twenty-one-year-old victim partying with a friend on a Saturday night, had made the fatal mistake of asking a woman to dance. She was with Topo at the time.

Peters wanted Boxer to take Sleepy along with him and whack another carnal named David Gallegos of Maravilla, aka "Pelon."

"Do it for Mariposa," ordered Topo.

Gallegos, according to Peters, was a coward who had to go. The story was that Gallegos accompanied two other carnales, Ernest "Chuco" Castro of VNE and Armando "Perico" Ochoa of Primera Flats, when they went to shake down a drug dealer in the Maravilla gang neighborhood of East Los Angeles. As the Mafiosi walked up the stoop leading to the front door, the connection came out the front door with a gun in hand. Gallegos ran, leaving Chuco and Perico to fend for themselves.

On another occasion, Gallegos was said to have been run out of his own Maravilla neighborhood at gunpoint by a Mexican Mafia dropout named Robert Marquez, aka "Wito." Those two separate incidents in which his behavior, by Eme standards, had been cowardly marked him for death.

Topo asked, "Can you take care of this for me?"

Boxer didn't hesitate. "Yeah, sure I can."

Enriquez remembered that he had been briefly introduced to Gallegos at Folsom when he was a brand-new brother himself. Gallegos had seemed serious and aloof, like "I was supposed to be blessed by meeting this guy." Yeah, he'd kill Pelon, but he didn't get the chance.

The next day, January 5, 1989, Boxer went to check in with his parole officer for a regularly scheduled visit. Boxer's pupils were pinholes, and he'd lost a dramatic amount of weight. As soon as he walked into the office, the PO picked up his phone and said to someone on the other end, "We're going to have tea." It was some kind of code.

He turned his eyes toward Enriquez. "You're on drugs again."

"No," lied Boxer unconvincingly.

"You're going back to jail. We'll lock you up again before you do something crazy."

The PO handcuffed his new parole violator and drove him straight to the California Institution for Men in Chino, California. It had been only five months since Boxer's release, and now he was back in prison.

The murder of David "Pelon" Gallegos would have to wait.

CHAPTER 11

Boxer Meets Steely—Eyed Chuco

AS OF JANUARY 1989, BOXER ENRIQUEZ HAD HEARD A LOT ABOUT the carnal Ernest "Chuco" Castro, but he'd never met him. Once he had seen Castro being escorted while they were both doing time at Folsom, but they were never housed on the same cell block. They didn't know each other.

Castro was a die-hard junkie and was also back at CIM on a parole violation, housed in the Palm Hall section of the prison where all the Eme brothers were housed along with Aryan Brotherhood, Nuestra Familia, Black Guerilla Family, and assorted troublemaking Crips and Bloods. The yard at Palm Hall was divided into four large squares divided by a two-story-high chain-link fence that kept the rival gangs apart. A guard tower stood in the middle with a couple of sharpshooters constantly surveying the hundred-plus inmates below, each one with his hands gripping the stock and barrel of a Ruger Mini-14 assault rifle. The concrete walls surrounding the yard were pockmarked with holes—testimony to the fact that these correctional officers wouldn't hesitate to pull the trigger. There would be one warning shot, then the next one would find human flesh. They shot to kill.

On any given day, prison gang members, mostly Eme and AB, could be seen in formation going through intensive exercise rituals—push-ups, burpies, jumping jacks, sit-ups, and running-in-place. It was all seriously regimented, someone shouting out the cadence as they went through their series of exercises, as if they were recruits at a U.S. Marine boot camp or a college football team doing calisthenics. "We saw ourselves as warriors," explained Boxer, "preparing to go off to other prisons and fight for the dominance of each institution." There was a smattering of inmates of the flab-a-lanche variety, but for the most part the inmates' heavily tattooed muscles rippled in the sunlight. This was no joke. The Aryan Brotherhood members in particular had lightning-bolt tats that signified they had assaulted a black, and some were adorned with large "war bird" tattoos that signified they'd tasted battle behind bars at some time in their prison life.

Chuco was not tall, but stocky. A handsome, light-skinned Mexican with a well-trimmed mustache, he always combed his hair straight back after a shower, and afterward it would stick straight up. He was a self-taught martial artist who looked like a thug. Boxer remembered that Chuco was an impressive figure: "There was no doubt about it when you looked into his eyes—green come-fuck-me eyes that also said, 'I will fuck you up if you mess with me.'" At the same time, Castro was a thinker who didn't rush to judgment. He had emerged as a strong, charismatic, natural leader from the Varrio Nuevo Estrada gang in East Los Angeles, where he was something of a legend.

In 1975 Chuco and his homeboys from VNE were involved in a shoot-out with L.A. County sheriff's deputies that became known as the "East Mob Massacre."

It all started when a young man went to pick up his date in a neighborhood frequented by the Varrio Nueva Estrada gang. There were more than four dozen cholos and their girls drinking beer and flowing out into the street from a two-story house—party central. The guy picking up his date was confronted for being an outsider. He didn't back down and ended up with dents in his car and bullet-shattered windows. A few blocks away he ran into a cop car and asked for help. It happened to be the gang detail.

The deputies decided to return to the scene with the victim so he could identify the suspects. He drove back followed by an unmarked deputy car and a black-and-white trailing. Other gang deputies and a detective's car planned to drive in from an opposite direction.

As the caravan pulled up, all hell broke loose. A gang member with a shotgun stood in the street, another was firing from a second-story window in the party house, and Chuco Castro and a friend were crouched behind a car on the opposite curb, spraying away with a Ruger 10/22 rifle with a ten-round rotary magazine. It was the deadliest gun on the street in those days. Castro was loading the magazine every time it emptied, and his homey was laying on the trigger. The gangsters had the cops caught in a triangle of fire.

The gunman in the street put a round in the side of the unmarked cop car and took off running, with the black-and-white chasing right behind him. Twenty-five-year-old Richard Valdemar, a Vietnam vet turned gang deputy, pulled his vehicle up on the sidewalk for cover and was taking heavy fire from the second-story window as he fired back with his .38 revolver.

The detective unit pulled up along the curb, and a veteran cop in a suit and tie got out and took aim on Chuco's homeboy, who looked down to check his weapon and took a bullet in the top of his head. As Chuco turned to run, a second shot caught him in the lower back, and he went down in a fog.

In the air, there was the smell of adrenaline mixed with gunpowder as two teenage gang members, a body length apart, were sprawled in the street, each in a pool of his own blood.

Deputy Valdemar holstered his weapon and walked up to the lifeless bodies as paramedics worked furiously to revive the gangster who was shot in the head. He'd seen plenty of soldiers shot up in Nam, and he knew instinctively that the guy was dead. In all truthfulness, he could care less if either one of them lived. They tried to kill cops by ambushing them. Good cops with wives and kids, just trying to do their jobs. However, he could see that Chuco was still alive, covered with blood but breathing, barely. "Hey," he said, "that guy's dead. Forget about him. This one might have a chance."

Chuco was temporarily paralyzed by his injuries. Life was literally draining out of him, and half his hip was blown away. The young cop probably saved his life by alerting paramedics. He'd remember the face and voice of Deputy Richard Valdemar.

More than a decade later at Palm Hall, Chuco Castro had that same steely-eyed charisma. Boxer Enriquez said that Chuco quickly earned his admiration and respect: "There was a young hippie-type gang member, known as Payaso from Long Beach, who somehow got crossed up with the Mafia. A hit was ordered to take him out. Payaso stood alone on the yard with a two-inch gash in his neck, dripping blood, after a camarada opened him up with a box cutter knife. The hit man dropped the blade on the pavement right next to the victim and took off. Then a pale and shaken Payaso in an uneasy voice, asked no one in particular, 'Why did you cut my throat?'

"I was watching all this from ten feet away, standing in a loose huddle of Mafia members—Chuco, Senon Grajeda, Tati Torrez, and Carlos Lomas— and what happened next was unbelievable! A gritty Payaso—blood gushing from the wound in his neck—leaned over, picked up the box cutter, and came right at us."

This all happened in a matter of seconds. The guard in the tower was already posing his rifle.

Then, continued Boxer, "Chuco stepped toward the bleeding victim and gave him a death stare saying, 'Flush the razor right now. Go flush the fucking razor!!' There was an open toilet at the corner of the yard, maybe ten feet away. The victim stumbled over there and flushed the weapon just as a warning bullet from the tower guard's rifle zinged across the top of our heads and cracked against the concrete. The guard screamed, 'Yard down! Yard down!!'"

The alarm buzzer whooped away like the sound of a Gestapo truck heading into the Warsaw ghetto. Convicts dressed in their white underwear and tennis shoes hit the ground in a prone position all over the yard. There were fights and attacks at Palm Hall weekly, sometimes daily, and they usually stopped as quickly as they began. It's one thing to invite a warning round from a Mini-14; it's another thing to actually take one in the head.

Boxer thought, *Chuco showed a lot of mettle.*

During the same time period, there was a crazy-ass white guy on their tier who was drinking water out of puddles when he went out to the yard. Boxer said, "He was always cussing at the Mafia inmates and threatening to sodomize us. He was just nuts." The Eme faction had had enough of his antics and wanted him transferred out.

Boxer told the lieutenant in charge, "This guy doesn't belong with us. He's sick. Save him by getting him out of here." The lieutenant pleaded with his CDC superiors to stop putting mental cases on the yard with Mafiosi, but the brass wouldn't listen.

So Chuco, a prolific jailhouse stabber who ordered even more, joined the Eme brothers in calling a hit on the psycho. He enlisted the young camarada Payaso—who'd had his own throat slit a few weeks earlier—to do the bloody deed. "It was one of those shaky Mafia deals," explained Boxer, "assuring Payaso he'd get a clean slate with the mob if he did the hit." Payaso took the assignment, came up behind the mark while out on the yard, pulled his head back by the hair, and sliced open his neck with a razor-sharp box cutter. "It was," in Boxer's words, "an Italian necktie—blood pouring out in what looked like little red chunks of Jell-O." The target screamed in agony and confusion, *"Ahhhhh!"* Boxer recalled. "The sight of it was horrendous." Unbelievably, the crazy ass lived, but he had a noticeable scar across his throat to remind him not to disrespect the Mafia.

None of the Mafiosi could quite remember why Payaso had been hit in the first place, but the kid had won their grudging respect for moving on the crazy ass. Chuco, along with other carnales, gave him the promised pass.

A couple of days later, the lieutenant came to Boxer and asked him why they did the hit. "We got tired of him cussing at us," answered Enriquez. "I'm the devil. Nobody can talk to us that way. We are Mafia."

Chuco and Boxer became cellmates in the following days. They became good friends. Enriquez found that Chuco "wasn't book-smart. He was politically smart, street-smart, mob-smart, and he always supported me. Loyalty was important to him."

That was why the next incident especially unnerved Boxer. He had a big bushy head of hair because he hadn't had it cut in weeks. Chuco offered to give him a trim. Inmates weren't allowed scissors, so they had to jerry-rig their own haircutting tools. Castro popped the blades out of a safety razor and attached them to combs. It was like a hair-whiz that trimmed your locks. Boxer noticed that "Chuco's hands were shaking" as he broke out the blades. He started thinking, *Oh shit! Why is this guy so nervous? What did I do? Some adrenaline rush must be causing his hands to tremble. Maybe he's not going to cut my hair. He's going to cut my throat!*

Then Enriquez felt his own hands start to shake a little bit.

A correctional officer walked by the cell, slowly taking the afternoon count. A sane man, fearing for his life, would have said something. Chuco was well into the haircut, and his hands seemed to be trembling like those of a seventy-five-year-old cerebral palsy victim.

"Move your head," ordered Chuco.

Here it comes, feared Boxer. All through the haircut, over and over again, he thought, *This might be it.* He refused to be a coward and rationalized, *If it comes it comes.*

But it never did. Chuco finally finished the longest haircut Boxer had ever experienced.

A week later, it became apparent that Chuco's hands shook all the time. It was some kind of nervous disorder. In the mob, little clues about threats to your mortality, real or imagined, popped up all the time. Internal fear is something a Mafioso had to get accustomed to: "Every day in my life," said Enriquez, "I was scared for my life."

But he and Chuco formed a lasting relationship.

CHAPTER 12

Hit the Streets Like a Wild Man

RELEASED FROM PRISON ON MAY 5, 1989, AFTER SERVING FOUR months, Boxer hit the streets like a wild man—muscling in on dope dealers with a renewed fervor. He provided the guns, getaway car, target, and meeting point, and his crews this time did a robbery almost every other day. They kicked in doors, pistol-whipped dealers, tied them up with duct tape, and trashed the place. The dealers were first told to kick back a percentage to the Eme. If they didn't agree, all drugs and cash were stolen at gunpoint. Their firearms were taken too. Boxer's crew was building a small arsenal in the process: .22- and .38-caliber pistols, .357 Magnum and 9 mm handguns, a military-type AR-15 assault rifle, an M-1 carbine, a Universal Mini-14 rifle with a pistol grip, and a couple of .12-gauge sawed-off shotguns. Not exactly peashooters.

Boxer made a habit of always telling his victims, "I'm Boxer Enriquez from the Mexican Mafia. If you come looking for us, I will come back and hunt you down and kill you like a dog!" It was brutal, and he didn't ignore targets in his old Artesia and Hawaiian Gardens haunts.

"Twisting Jenny" was a big drug distributor in that area. She was a forty-five- to fifty-year-old "hottie" with long brown hair and a nice body, and she loved to bed down with young studs just out of prison. Jenny lived in a small house located behind an apartment complex in an alley along the border of Hawaiian Gardens and Lakewood near the intersection of Carson and Norwalk Boulevards. Her entourage was known as "the Alley Girls." Boxer was more interested in her healthy stash of cocaine, heroin, money, and jewelry.

Gilbert "Lil Mo" Ruiz was a five-foot-seven, 135-pound, acne-scarred gang member from White Fence with beady brown eyes, thick black hair, and a pencil-thin mustache shaped like a half-moon, hanging over a pair of thick lips. Enriquez had first met him in Folsom Prison five years earlier. Mo, locked up for a series of robberies, was only sixteen then and wore oversized prison denim pants pulled up to his chest with a large baggy shirt as he walked the yard "mad-dogging" much bigger and more threatening convicts. Boxer thought he had mob potential and told the kid, "I'm going to take over your neighborhood when I get out of prison." Mo agreed to help. Enriquez ran into him on the streets of East L.A. and put him on his crew. "He had the brain of a rock, but he was loyal. We called him 'the Brain Stem.'"

The crew also included two others. Twenty-six-year-old Anthony Aveles, known as "Chino," from White Fence was an "opportunistic little weasel," according to Enriquez. He was Lil Mo's homeboy—four years older, a once-convicted robber who had received plenty of weapons training serving two years in the Eighty-Second Airborne Division of the U.S. Army. Chino had his moniker tattooed on the right side of his neck.

Forty-five-year-old Louis "Rockin' Lou" Lopez of Jardin was a happy-go-lucky, go-along-to-get-along, but absolutely crazy Eme soldado—a tall, wiry, long stringy-haired nut who earned his nickname at San Quentin. There he purposely fought with correctional officers so frequently that other carnales began to shout, "Rock on, Lou!"

The crews almost always struck late at night or in the dark early morning hours. Rockin' Lou and Chino—both armed with handguns—busted through the front door yelling, "Police! *Freeze!* Police!" At the same time, Mo literally crashed through a big bay window at the rear of the house, shattering the glass all over the floor. He killed the dog on the way in and swept through the place with a .12 gauge Mossberg shotgun. In short order, he had Jenny, a naked daughter in her thirties, and a son in his early twenties all rustled out of bed. They were visibly shaken as the intruders laid them all out on the living room carpet.

"Where's the dope," screamed Mo.

Jenny said, "I don't have it."

Meanwhile, her son kept edging across the floor as if he was going for a gun.

"Stay down!" shouted Mo as he motioned with the shotgun.

Then he kicked the son hard in the head and spoke directly to Jenny. "If you don't hand over the dope, I will blow your son's head away!"

Jenny knew she couldn't twist out of this one. Hidden in a sock stashed in a jewelry box on her dresser were a half-pound of cocaine and a baseball-size hunk of tar heroin. The crew also made off with diamond and emerald earrings and a collection of gold rings, necklaces, and bracelets. More important, Twisting Jenny was now ready to kick back a percentage to La Eme on a regular basis.

After the robbery, the crew did "speed balls"—a mixture of coke and heroin—at Sleepy's apartment with their newly acquired dope. During the celebration, Rockin' Lou got paranoid—his face maniacal and shiny with sweat, his teeth grinding—and he put a large bowie knife to the throat of another gangster who came with Boxer, holding him as a human shield while disappearing out the front door with him. He hid outside in some tall bushes for a couple of hours, stripping the guy nearly naked at knifepoint before letting him go. Days later, Lou explained that he imagined the crew was plotting to kill him that night. He was ready to slit the hostage's throat if they moved on him. That's life in the mob.

Big John from Artesia was a humble, obese, teddy bear type who was also a major cocaine connection in the neighborhood. He was an old friend of Boxer's, but one who didn't want to kick down any money. Big worked for Flo, and he mistakenly believed that gave him protection. That mind-set had to change.

It was just past eleven o'clock at night when Boxer came in Big John's kitchen door as if he was making a friendly visit.

"What's up?"

Right behind him came Mo and Chino, who proned Boxer and Big John out on the floor at gunpoint. Enriquez didn't want to beat on John, so he tried to make it look as if he wasn't part of the holdup.

Chino went to sweep the house, holding a shotgun as he went. In a nearby room, he found Big John's girlfriend, a beautiful Mexican homegirl in her twenties with brown eyes and long dark hair, poured into a form-fitting black blouse and skintight jeans. She was hot, Chino thought. And so was the .357 Mark-4 pistol she instinctively began to fire as a startled Chino came through the door. Luckily, she was so scared that the bullets put holes in the wall instead of him.

"Fucking bitch!" Chino blurted as he reached out, socked her in the eye, and wrestled the gun away. His eyes looked like fifty-cent pieces as he came back into the kitchen, pushing the girl ahead of him. "This bitch tried to shoot me!" It was almost comical.

The take was a large bag of cocaine and several hundred dollars in cash.

Big John was suspicious. Two days later, word on the street was that Boxer Enriquez robbed him. Boxer was Mexican Mafia. Boxer had to be paid one way or another—old friend or not.

Still another incident involved Joseph El Fluge, a drug-dealing hustler known on the street as "Big Joe." He lived with a relative of Boxer's in a Boyle Heights apartment building at Whittier and Euclid, right across the street from an elementary school. Enriquez had left some drugs there, and he believed that El Fluge took some of the stash for himself. Stealing from a mobster was not acceptable, so Boxer decided to take the guy's 1990 Cadillac Seville as payment. However, El Fluge was reluctant to sign over the pink slip.

Enriquez started to pistol-whip him with a .32-caliber handgun, a little square automatic that looked like a 9 mm but had a shorter barrel. It cut a two-inch gash in his brow, but Boxer was drugged up and kept striking El Fluge so furiously that he broke his own pinky finger and the gun flew out of his hand. The pistol spun across the room and landed on the floor, wedged in between the wall and a refrigerator. For a second, Enriquez and El Fluge looked at each other dumbfounded, then they both dove for the .32. El Fluge's hand had reached within inches of the firearm when Boxer managed to pull him back. It was a mad scramble as Lil Mo jumped into the battle too. El Fluge was six feet tall and 210 pounds of ferocity, but Boxer and Mo were wailing on him in a murderous frenzy.

"We're going to kill you, you motherfucker," screamed Boxer as his brother John stood nearby frozen in panic, thinking El Fluge was going to die. Even though John hung out with his gangster brothers a lot, he had no tattoos and wasn't a real gang member. He was more of a punk-rocking weed smoker. Later he would do a couple of years in prison for home burglaries and then go straight. Little brother John wasn't into violence. Meanwhile, El Fluge's face was covered with blood and apartment furniture was breaking as the combatants kept fighting for the gun. Finally, John came out of his stupor and picked up the .32. He handed it to his brother.

Mo chimed in, "Okay, let's get the pink slip signed!"

"Why, why?" pleaded El Fluge, apparently confused as to why all this was happening. It didn't matter what he thought at this point.

"Sign it or I'll blow your brains out!" demanded Boxer as he shoved the barrel of the gun into El Fluge's mouth. This time he signed the pink slip. After he handed over the keys to his Cadillac, Enriquez shoved the gun in his eye and delivered the standard message: "If you do anything stupid, I will hunt you down like a dog and kill you." He was persuasive.

Afterward, Boxer, covered with blood, went to Sleepy Aragon's to wash up and slam some cocaine. Rockin' Lou Lopez was there. He put some ice on Boxer's broken pinky finger and said, "Let me do what I'm going to do here." Lopez grabbed on to Boxer's wrist and with his other hand quickly yanked Boxer's finger. The bone popped right back into place with a loud snapping sound—mob medical care.

A few weeks later, Boxer pulled up in front of the same East L.A. apartment complex where he had forcibly acquired his new Cadillac. His mom had been living in the same building since she and Boxer's dad had divorced. She also held some drugs for her gangster son and even struggled with a drug problem of her own. It's something Boxer refuses to talk about, even today: "I feel responsible for it. We exposed my mother to drugs. She never even smoked cigarettes before we started doing it. If I could remove this from her life with the stroke of a brush, I would. I love my mother."

A sleek black undercover car drove up behind Boxer. It was officers from the elite Los Angeles Police Department unit called the Metro Squad—a highly trained special operations team handpicked for their advanced mental and physical abilities. They were part of Operation Hammer Sweep, an LAPD program in which dozens of cops were used in a specific area for a few days to pick up suspicious gang members, parolees, and wanted felons. Boxer fit the bill.

"Don't move!" cautioned one of the cops. It didn't take them long to place him in handcuffs.

They searched inside the car and found shotgun shells and a buck knife. In the trunk there was a baggie of procaine—a cutting agent for heroin that boosted the rush. There was also a baby laxative used to cut cocaine, a triple beam scale to weigh drugs, measuring spoons, funnels, and water pills used to flush out one's system to leave no trace of narcotics. The pills were used to try to beat a drug test. He didn't get a chance to use them.

On June 26, 1989, Boxer Enriquez was sent back to prison for another parole violation. This time he'd been out for only fifty-two days.

CHAPTER 13

Shifting Loyalties and Sweet Revenge

BOXER WAS TRANSPORTED BACK TO THE PALM HALL MAXIMUM—
security unit at California Institute for Men in Chino and once again
landed in the thick of Eme prison politics—now ready to settle a few
scores of his own.

A number of brothers wanted to assassinate Daniel "Cuate" Grajeda of
La Rana, a thirty-eight-year-old, black-hearted, manipulative murderer who
was a self-professed fanatic about his membership in the Mexican Mafia.
"It's as if Eme were his religion," observed Boxer. Cuate actually prayed to
Aztec gods: Mictlantehutli, the lord of death; Huitzilopochtli, the god of
war; and the sun god Tonatiuh. He spoke the ancient language of Nahuatl
and truly believed he was a warrior.

Cuate was six feet tall, muscular, and so dark-skinned that brothers
jokingly referred to him as "Coco," after a gorilla that was the subject of a
Frontline television documentary on the communication of apes. He had the
Mafia Black Hand tattooed inside his left bicep with a circle around it and
an arrow penetrating the perimeter, a nasty scar where someone slashed
him with a steak knife across his left cheek, and a fourteen-inch "X" that he
carved into his own chest. Boxer knew that "Cuate was a violent, aggressive, unpredictable man not to be taken lightly."

Black Dan Barela and Vesi Sagato—both housed at Palm Hall—gave
Boxer a yes vote in regard to whacking Cuate, who was locked up in Los
Angeles County Jail. Cuate had angered other carnales because he liter-
ally tried to take over operations at county, claiming he had Godfather Joe
Morgan's blessing to do so. On top of that, Boxer said, "Cuate formulated a

plan to set up an elite Eme leadership group called 'Los Mejores' (The Best), including Morgan and brothers he designated as worthy. Those carnales deemed nonproductive would be eliminated."

Furthermore, Cuate took it upon himself to order Eme member Henry "Indio" Carlos of El Sereno to hit another carnal in the jail. Cuate threatened him with the words, "Si no lo haces, va a caer el cielo" (If you don't do it, the sky will fall). Boxer said, "Indio felt disrespected and refused. He complained that Cuate was no more than an equal in status and had no right to be giving orders. He figured if Cuate Grajeda wanted someone dead, he should do it himself, or at least be part of the hit team."

Also, a year earlier Cuate had stabbed and killed Eme member Rosario "Chago" Ramirez of Florencia in the visiting room at Men's Central Jail. He stabbed Chago twenty-three times with a sharpened butter knife. Dying in a pool of his blood, as a last act of defiance, Chago lifted his hand and gave a final salute with his middle finger. He was no Boy Scout, but other brothers felt that Cuate had done the hit on his own merely to grab another criminal case that would keep him in the county lockup, where he was making a lot of money selling drugs.

Finally, on September 16, 1989, Cuate was just finishing up a noontime shower down from his B-row cell in the 1700 section of the high-power gang module. He was bald on top and grew his hair six inches long on one side. Always, his last act of grooming was to comb the hanging mane over his bare pate to create a comb-over hairdo that always guaranteed a good-natured ribbing from other carnales.

It was about that same time when Indio Carlos signaled a deputy in the control booth to open the gate on A-row so he could push out some food trays as part of his duties as a trustee. As the gate opened, he ran straight for Cuate in the shower and stabbed him. Cuate was caught naked holding only a towel, which he balled up and threw at his attacker. He slipped on the wet floor and fell, coiled into a defensive fetal position, and tried to fend off the blows as the metal shank repeatedly plunged into his chest, back, and neck. Blood flowed down the drain in a scene reminiscent of Alfred Hitchcock's *Psycho*. Indio was determined to keep stabbing Grajeda until he was dead and planned to attack any deputy who tried to interfere.

Inexplicably, Indio backed off as Deputy Gray Frazier responded to the ruckus, but ignored orders to drop the shank. Only when he got back to A-row did he throw it down and allow himself to be handcuffed.

Later that same day, Senior Deputy Patrick walked into a holding cell where Indio was being temporarily kept, and the Mafioso spontaneously said, "It's one of those things. It's a cruel world."

Deputy Frazier, five days later, was escorting Carlos when the inmate initiated the following conversation.

"Deputy Frazier, the other day, were you going to rush in and break it up?"

"Yes," he answered, "until I saw what was going on. Then I stopped."

"I saw it was you," Carlos continued, "so I backed off. If it had been someone else, I don't know. You been down working (in high power) for a while, and you know me, and I know you. You know what I'm talking about?"

"Yes, I do," replied the deputy.

There is an unspoken code of conduct even among the worst of Eme inmates. Boxer explained: "It's an understanding that there is no reason to mistreat guards who don't mistreat you." It's sort of a go-along, get-along philosophy.

Cuate had been politicking on Indio. So Indio decided to whack him before Grajeda had a chance to close the lid on him. Besides, he knew Cuate was already on the lista. "Carlos didn't do anything wrong," explained Boxer. "He did what he was supposed to do as a carnal. His only mistake was leaving Grajeda alive, which added to his almost mythical ability to survive Mafia politics."

Cuate Grajeda was not an easy man to kill.

The Palm Hall political plots thickened, and it was fairly easy to use the prison system to help the Mafia get it done.

Archenemy Bevito Alvarez—fallen out of the graces of La Eme because of his politicking against other brothers—was still "in the hat." Boxer was housed in Palm Hall with Ruben "Tupi" Hernandez and Ronald "Turtle" Baisa of Ontario Black Angels and Vevesi "Vesi" Sagato of Eighteenth Street—all Mafia members.

La Eme's Freddie "Veneno" Gonzalez of Pomona Twelfth Street, accused of murdering a Nuestra Familia rival at the California Rehabilitation Center (CRC), was on trial for the murder in Riverside, a half-hour drive from the Chino prison site. He had his lawyers subpoena Bevito at prison in Tehachapi to come down to Chino and serve as a character witness in the case. Boxer pointed out, "It was all a ruse to set up the murder of Bevito and force the state to pay for it."

Boxer, Vesi, and Tupi were also subpoenaed as witnesses in the case.

The assassins were equipped with a knife, a garrote, and a handcuff key. The first plan was to murder Bevito in the bus when they were all transported to court.

Alvarez asked Boxer and Vesi—both on the same tier at Palm Hall—if they knew why he was going to court. They played dumb, and Bevito felt there was something wrong. The tier tender, an old prison buddy named "Doc," walked by his cell and said, "Hey, Ray-Ray—wild wild west." Bevito really didn't get what he was trying to tell him, but it added to his suspicions. Then, the night before court, the same friendly face came by his cell again and warned, "Ray, don't you know what's happening here? Ray, they're going to kill you."

The next day there were four different police agencies there for the transport to court and a helicopter flying overhead. Boxer and Vesi were placed together on the bus. Tupi went in a separate car, and so did the target, Bevito. As the convict caravan headed out the prison gates, cops were stationed around with guns at the ready. Officers were blocking traffic at intersections and running red lights. Boxer remembered, "It was like out of the movies."

Headed east for ten minutes down the 60 freeway, suddenly the cars turned down an exit ramp and then headed west on the 60 back to the prison. The conspirators and their prey were locked down again and were told only that court was postponed.

Boxer and Tupi were forced to go to a backup plan—hit Bevito the next day on the yard instead.

Three Mafia associates were assigned to smuggle the weapons out to the yard in their rectums. It's called "keistering." They had big, double-edged, razor-sharp steel knives called "bone-crushers" that were six to eight inches long and an inch and a half wide. The handles were wrapped with strips of bedsheets. Boxer explained how it's done: "First, the knife is wrapped in toilet paper to make it softer or more cushionlike. Then, on top of that, the knife is covered with Saran Wrap taken from prison sandwiches. The whole thing is then covered with a lubricant—some lotion or Vaseline. The inmate then greases his insides with the same lubricant—called 'greasing the tracks' or 'hooping,' as in dunking a basketball in the hoop. The knife is gently inserted in the rectum. The first time that I did it, it felt like I had a broomstick up to my neck. It's excruciating, with enormous pressure on your intestinal tract. Over time it gets easier to do, and I was eventually able to sleep or even exercise with a shank secreted in my bowels. On the yard, you push as if defecating to release the knife, reach back inside your pants, grab the shank, pull off the wrapping, and stab."

The three mob associates designated to bring the bone-crushers out to the yard for the Bevito hit had to insert them while in the shower and pull them out with armed guards watching close by—nerve-wracking for them. It wasn't easy.

Boxer and Tupi decided they would each go for a couple of "kill shots"—deep, penetrating blows—and then lie down. This was a yard for high-risk gangsters, and correctional officers would open fire with their Heckler and Koch 9 mm assault rifles—loaded with Glazer rounds—as soon as they spotted violence. If they stabbed him right, Bevito would bleed out on the pavement before anyone could get to him with medical aid.

There were no security cameras on the yard, so they could probably get away with it. Boxer really preferred not to catch a life term for this hit. It didn't matter much for Tupi; he was already serving three life terms for killing a small-time drug dealer named Mary Lou Davila and two innocent bystanders, Maria Mlourdes, who rented a room at Davila's house, and her fiancé Pancho Ortiz. Tupi tied them all up, hands and feet, and shot them in the head execution-style. Davila died because she had paid $10,000 for the death of a Mexican Mafia associate who was shaking her down for drugs. The young couple—returning home from a night out—was killed so there would be no witnesses. Tupi was amused in court when prosecutors said they would not seek the death penalty. A relative of the young murdered couple, who does not want to be identified, said, "He looked us directly in the face and laughed at us. He thought this was a game. He looked us straight in the eye and laughed."

Now Boxer was ready to roll. He hated Bevito for giving him such a hard time when he was a new Mafia soldado at Folsom and Tehachapi. Revenge was going to be swift and sweet. He was amped up on adrenaline, butterflies in his stomach. He always disliked the waiting and wanted it to be done. He didn't smoke any cigarettes to keep his hands from shaking—the usual ritual for him.

Fifteen minutes went by, and no Bevito.

A half hour went by, and still no Bevito.

Everyone returned to their cells after yard time, and Bevito was gone. What the hell was going on?

What the Mafia didn't count on was Lieutenant Leo Duarte, a gang-savvy officer who had an honest rapport with Palm Hall crooks. Boxer saw him on the tier later that same afternoon.

"Did Bevito lock up?"

"Yeah," answered Duarte. "He's done, Rene. You aren't going to get to him. We know what's going on."

The lieutenant, according to Boxer, was "nobody's fool." Duarte had a certain fascination with prison gangs, made it his business to learn about them, and was always respectful but at the same time wary, perceptive, and tenacious. He found out about the murder plot when he intercepted a kite sent by Tupi. Duarte warned Bevito the day before the planned hit, and the targeted Mafioso chose to go into protective custody. He knew death was waiting for him on the yard, and he could no longer fight it and win. The politicking days in the Mafia for Reymundo "Bevito" Alvarez were over—he dropped out of La Eme and briefed authorities on what he knew. He was in fact done.

Boxer Enriquez still felt a sense of satisfaction. "I wanted to kill him, but seeing him squirm was good enough. Bevito looked nervous when I saw him on the tier. He approached me in a fake brotherly fashion, and I knew it. He looked like I felt at Folsom when he politicked against me and placed me on his hit list. He was scared. I saw it in his eyes. I enjoyed that because I finally saw this guy squirm. He knew we were going to do him, and that was good enough for me. Finally, the shoe was on the other foot. It doesn't feel fun when the rabbit got the gun!" Boxer felt he had won an important Mafia political battle for survival: "It showed me I could prevail in the organization, that I had the political savvy and the knack for survival even against Eme titans."

Ten days later, Enriquez was transferred to the maximum-security SHU unit at Corcoran State Prison to serve out the remainder of his parole violation. There he ran into Senon "Cherilo" Grajeda. Boxer liked Cherilo, a slightly chubby guy who had an outgoing personality, frequently cracking jokes, and they got along well together. He never saw Cherilo angry or bullying camaradas, and Cherilo was loyal to La Eme. Also, he was one of the brothers who helped school Enriquez at Folsom when he was a young recruit.

There were three Grajedas in the Mafia: Cherilo was three years younger than twin brothers Cuate and Thomas, also known as "Big Wino." They all had roots in a Long Beach, California, gang called La Rana. There was a certain magnetism to the family name, and they carried a lot of weight.

Daniel Grajeda, or Cuate, was always caught up in some jam; Boxer had to explain to Cherilo why the carnales agreed to assault his older brother a month earlier at L.A. County Jail. He accepted the explanation but seemed hurt by the fact it was done.

At the same time, Boxer remembered Cherilo once told him, "I'll kill him [Cuate] if I have to. If he done wrong, I'll kill him." It astounded Boxer that someone would actually kill his own brother, or even talk about it, even though that was part of the Mafia code. But in the future he would see that Cherilo was first and foremost a Grajeda: "Grajedas think they are walking gods."

The truth is that everyone in the Mexican Mafia is expendable. During Boxer's last month at Corcoran, word came from the prison grapevine that Ernest "Kilroy" Roybal had been stabbed on the yard at the California Correctional Institution at Tehachapi. This meant Roybal was done in the mob and that Boxer had now prevailed over two powerful Mafia enemies— Kilroy Roybal and Bevito Alvarez.

Ironically, the hit man was Sleepy Huerta, "the Professional," the same Mafioso who killed Nico Velasquez at CCI at the direction of the Bevito/ Kilroy faction. Kilroy—after he was stabbed by Sleepy—began to fight, then backed off and took the hit. He was fifty years old at the time, recovered from his wounds, and spent most of his last four years in the Security Housing Unit at Pelican Bay State Prison (PBSP), where Eme hit men couldn't get to him. "Everyone said he was no good," recalled Boxer.

Kilroy Roybal was released on parole in August 1993 after serving fourteen years for armed robbery and murder, and a month later he became a born-again Christian. In a November 1997 *Dispatch* magazine article about his conversion entitled "Gunning for God?" he said, "I lived and died for Eme."

That is, until the tables had turned. "There are ever-shifting loyalties in the mob," explained Boxer. "It's byzantine. One day I'm friends with a good Mafia member, we do business together in the organization. The next day there is a power shift, and the same brother is my adversary. He won't even say my name. He'll cut me loose, and if there is a vote to kill me, he'll vote yes. That's just how it is."

After nearly six more months in prison, on December 18, 1989, Boxer Enriquez was once again released to the streets on parole. It was time to meet up with his crew and get back to the business of killing.

CHAPTER 14

A Reign of Terror

BOXER HAD BEEN TRANSPORTED FROM CORCORAN STATE PRISON TO Los Angeles County Jail, where he served some additional days for outstanding traffic warrants. Once Boxer's time was completed, Huero Shy and his girlfriend picked him up at the release gate on Bauchet Street near downtown Los Angeles and took him out for breakfast. After eating, they all went to Rocky Luna's and slammed some heroin, saw Lil Mo on Oregon Street and picked him up, and then went to the apartment where Boxer's mother lived nearby on Whittier Boulevard in Boyle Heights, several blocks east of East Los Angeles. Lupe Enriquez knew the neighborhood gossip, and the first thing she told her son was, "Don't hang around Little Mo. He has a lot of heat now. Police are chasing him, and he's going to get you arrested."

Enriquez dumped his jailhouse blues, took a shower, dressed up in a new shirt, pants, and Reeboks, and was ready to go. He, Shy, Mo, and Rocky were headed to the Ramona Gardens housing project, where Luna was known as "the Godfather." There would be plenty of cholas ready to hook up with a carnal for the night.

They piled into Shy's car, and LAPD officers busted them all as they pulled out of the parking lot. Boxer still had parole papers in his pocket as he looked over at Lil Mo and said, "Dirty little dog, you got me arrested."

The officers took them all to a holding tank at the Hollenbeck Division station house but released Boxer five hours later without citing him for any crimes. Everyone was out by the next morning. Enriquez was loaded on dope and couldn't believe he got away—free.

They all gathered again at Luna's and were joined by Jacques "Jacko"

Padilla, a short, buffed-out, heavily tattooed gang member from Azusa. He was two years younger than Boxer and fancied himself a look-alike to heart-throb Spanish actor Antonio Banderas. He wasn't. Enriquez had met him eight years earlier playing cards on 4700 block, a County Jail gang module. A then very young Jacko bragged about stabbing a black inmate with a sharpened toothbrush because the guy stole his food tray.

He and Boxer became reacquainted when Rocky and Shy were using him to sling methamphetamine and heroin in Azusa, a bedroom community with a majority-Latino population located twenty-seven miles northeast of Los Angeles and nestled against the foothills of the San Gabriel Mountains. "Azusa" is most likely derived from the Gabrielino Indian word *asuksagna,* which means "skunk place," but optimistic chamber commerce types for years promoted the lower- to middle-class city's ˌ as an acronym for "everything from A to Z in the USA." That mˌ didn't include gang members, but they had plenty of them noˌ

Boxer, Mo, and Jacko became the nucleus of a new hard-ˌ Rocky and Huero Shy taking a piece of the action, theˌ rorize the street drug trade—hitting dealers all over Fˌ are as many as two hundred different gangs), Arˌ Hawaiian Gardens, and Bassett, all tough gangˌ drug connection not willing to go along witˌ ritual. They stole drugs, cars, jewelry, ˌ anything of value. "Whatever we warˌ reminded the victims he was froˌ stolen property upstate with aˌ Victor "Victorio" Murillo ˌ in return.

In Lincoln Heigˌ had resisted an eˌ Enriquez retuˌ of persuasiˌ stock. Fiˌ

"Somos ˌ have to pay!)

"Nel," came tˌ or English.

There was a pointedˌ Boxer jabbed it in the paisonˌ

"Ustedes tiene que pager!"

"Nel."

The rifle barrel came at him again and again; the sharp flash reducer tore off little chunks of his head until it looked like hamburger meat. Then the crew went to work on him. The take that night was just a small quantity of narcotics, but the message was sent—clearly and painfully.

Jacko had a favorite target in his own neighborhood, a big dealer named Nico. He had a thriving drug trade going out of a house in Azusa. On one occasion, Jacko and Mo went to shake him down, and users kept coming in to buy dope while they were there dealing with Nico. Each customer who came in was greeted by a gun in his face, tied up with duct tape, and robbed. Nico had so much traffic that it was like a fast-food drive-in service for drugs. So in a short period of time, they had about twenty people sitting on the floor in the living room tied up in bundles. It looked like a hostage situation. Jacko and Mo finally felt overwhelmed by the numbers and left with their booty.

Nico drove a sleek, jet-black, fully restored 1978 two-door Dodge BTM. t was a sharp-looking automobile with expensive mag wheels and a black yl top. On another occasion, the crew stuck a gun in Nico's mouth, made sign over the pink slip, and took the car. They called it "the Night Rider." r said it became a symbol of terror: "When we drove the Night Rider, ld see drug dealers down the street take off running. They spotted nd knew it was us. We shot, stabbed, and beat people—sometimes daylight—and we didn't care if we were seen. Now everybody ere out there in force, and their fear made us untouchable." The se who rode in the Night Rider were as black as the car itself.

eady dark outside as they pulled up in front of a little one-story, nish house on Eighth Street in the heart of White Fence. ut of the passenger seat carrying a .30-caliber M-1 carbine. o, was packing a deadly-looking serrated fishing knife in a ped to his belt. Jacko Padilla climbed out of the backseat ved-off shotgun. As was their custom, they walked up ked in the front door.

der homeboys from White Fence, siblings who dealt y had a little buzz on and were too shocked to run. d heard they had a stash of .45-caliber handguns. he weapons, but the gangsters wouldn't sell. So m.

ting on the couch and kept reaching under the at him: "Do not move anymore. Do not put your hand under the cushion!" Enriquez turned around for a second as Mo, he thought, moved to check under the cushion for a weapon. Instead, Mo suddenly pulled out his big, long, razor-sharp, serrated fishing knife with a finger grip plastic handle and shoved it into the victim's stomach—for no apparent reason at all.

As Boxer turned back around, the wounded man was on the floor squirming around in his own blood, stabbed through and through, a small part of intestine protruding through a small hole in his abdomen.

Mo weirdly was trying to hide the knife behind his leg like a nervous little boy, his eyes bugged out, and his hands clearly covered with blood.

"What did you do?" queried Enriquez.

"I didn't do nothing. I didn't do nothing."

Lil Mo had gone haywire—just went off—for some inexplicable reason, and strangely refused to admit it.

"Wow! You stabbed that guy for nothing!"

Again, "No, I didn't. No, I didn't."

As it turned out, these dealers didn't even have the .45s that Boxer and his crew came to take. It seems they spread the rumor hoping word that they had an arsenal would scare Enriquez away. It backfired on them.

Boxer knew intuitively that it wasn't wise to kill the dealers they were shaking down—frightening them was enough. Dead men can't pay. He also knew that "bodies were laying everywhere." The right decision gets easily scrambled in the cerebellum when someone is drugged out of their mind most of the time.

White Fence is an old established neighborhood in East Los Angeles that is set up like a fortress. The gang claims it was started in 1911 by young people who lived in a shantytown just south of the railroad tracks. Electric car commuters from more desirable communities complained that the stinky, squalid, vagrant-filled area was an eyesore as they rode past on their way to work downtown. So the train company built a tall wooden fence to hide the blighted landscape from passing commuters. It was painted white. White Fence was definitely the wrong side of the tracks. According to retired Sergeant Richard Valdemar, "White Fence was the largest and one of the most violent gangs in Los Angeles when I was growing up in the 1950s and 1960s. They claim to be the first to carry out a drive-by shooting and are largely responsible for moving gang warfare from the fair fight to the urban terrorist mentality we see today."

With the blessing of Rocky, Huero Shy, and even Black Dan, Enriquez took over all the drug connections in White Fence. He supervised his own narcotics sales operation out of a house owned by an Eme associate named "Topper," also a White Fence gang member. Topper was a thirty-two-year-old junkie who would do anything to get a shot of heroin. "If I bought him some food," Boxer said, "he would trade it for dope." Drugs had so ravaged his body—he looked so bad—that Enriquez and his crew, also heroin addicts, called Topper "AIDS."

The house was at 714 Camulos Street in East Los Angeles, a white, fairly big two-story located on a corner lot with a high staircase leading to the front door. A gangster with a shotgun or assault rifle, perched above the door, had a good view of what was going on outside. It was a fairly secure location that became Boxer's headquarters, and business was good as he controlled the sales and distribution of dope in the White Fence area.

Cynthia Gavaldon was one of the added reasons that sales were brisk. She was the wife of thirty-two-year-old Roy "Lil Spider" Gavaldon, a gang member from Canta Ranas, and the sister-in-law of Eme member David "Big Spider" Gavaldon. Both of them were in prison, Lil Spider for burglary and his older brother for murder. Cynthia was a nice-looking girl with long brown hair, a good figure, and an outgoing personality—a real party girl who knew everyone. She had a small rap sheet for drug use, theft, and burglary and was at Topper's so frequently that she had a bedroom there, always holding and dealing drugs for Boxer and his crew. Needle marks on both sides of her neck and the inside of her right arm showed she was also a junkie.

Boxer gave her "eight-balls" of heroin to sell, and the money came up short time and time again. Some customers complained she was "stepping on" (removing small amounts) bindles of cocaine. Small amounts of drugs and cash—set down on a table somewhere—disappeared regularly. Boxer suspected Cynthia was taking it, and it made him mad.

"I'm tired of being stolen from," warned Enriquez as he sat in one of the bedrooms getting loaded with Mo and Chino. He and the others had been slamming "speed balls" all day—a mixture of cocaine and heroin that gave an up cocaine rush and a down doper ride.

He'd voiced his displeasure about Cynthia several times throughout the day. Now Boxer called everyone into the living room: Mo, Jacko, Chino, Topper, Cynthia, a homegirl known as Pee Wee, and another White Fence gang member known as "Popeye." They all sold heroin and cocaine for their Mafia boss, and he told them that he "treated them good," that "nobody was sick," and that he didn't like it when someone stole from him. Everyone went stone quiet.

Then he told Jacko, Mo, and Chino to follow him to the bedroom where Cynthia slept. "I know this bitch is taking my shit," he said and ordered them to search the room for dope and money. They found nothing, but Boxer kept repeating, "I know it's her! I know it's her!" His ire reached a drug-induced peak as Jacko reached into his waistband, pulled out a big black revolver, and handed it to Mo. Enriquez gave the order: "Go and do her!"

Lil Mo grabbed the long-barrel .357 Magnum Trooper Mark III with a rubber grip and stuck it in his pants. He found Cynthia in the kitchen and walked up to her, "Let's go!" It was approaching midnight as he drove her up to a place nearby called Russian Hill—an isolated spot where South Concord Street dead-ends at the Pomona Freeway—frequented by lovers, drug users, and occasional transients.

On the way, she knew something was wrong, sensed the evil, and tried to climb out of the car at a stop sign. Mo asked her where she was going, told her not to worry, and lied to her that everything was okay. She sat back in the passenger's seat.

It was a fatal mistake on her part. Minutes later, Cynthia was out of the car in an unlit, vacant dirt lot surrounded by a natural tree-lined bunker on one side and a deserted alley on the other, supposedly helping Mo look for a bag of dope that wasn't even there. She turned and faced him as he lifted the gun and shot her right between the eyes. Her body spun, and he put another slug in her upper back as she hit the ground, dead. Boxer called it "a ride to hell."

Mo returned alone to the hangout at Topper's carrying Cynthia's purse. He, Boxer, and Chino walked into the room where she often slept, and Enriquez said, "Now an example has been set. People will get the message. They will know not to steal from me." Mo gently handed back the murder weapon.

The next morning was cool and dry as one of the residents from a little row of houses across the alley noticed the corpse as he was about to go to work. Police arrived and found Cynthia's body facedown in a bed of leaves, partially hidden inside a growth of green shrubbery. Paramedics turned her over, and her face was caked with blood in the pattern of what looked like a Rorschach ink blot test. Full rigor mortis had already set in, and her right hand was placed on her chest as if to say, "Oh, my God!" She wore a wedding ring, big hoop earrings, a large white beret, a purple long-sleeve pullover shirt, blue jeans, white socks, and a new pair of L.A. Gear tennis shoes.

Detective Jack Forsman remembered thinking: "She was young. Nobody deserved to die that way. It was upsetting." He'd been a cop for five years in his hometown of Rahway, New Jersey, before visiting Los Angeles on vacation. Through a relative who worked as an investigator for the federal public defender's office, Forsman met some retired LAPD detectives. The Jersey cop got hooked, moved to the City of Angels a short time later, and joined the LAPD in 1980. Forsman had been a homicide detective for only a few years when he caught the Cynthia Gavaldon case. "We didn't have a whole lot to go on," he recalled. "Just a body."

The sky was dark again by the time police detectives received a telephone call from the coroner's office informing them that fingerprints confirmed the victim was twenty-eight-year-old Cynthia Gavaldon. It was December 24, 1989—Christmas Eve.

Coroner's investigator David Campbell notified the next of kin, Edward Carlson, that his granddaughter was dead—murdered. Her wedding picture showed a pretty bride in a long white dress. It was easier remembering her that way.

Two days later, LAPD Hollenbeck Division detectives received an anonymous call from a woman who told them Cynthia was murdered by "Boxer from Eme."

The next day Detective Forsman, who had no idea who that was, contacted the Special Services Unit (SSU) of the California Department of Corrections, a group that kept tabs on the "baddest" parolees, especially the career criminals. Boxer was tentatively identified as Rene Olmos Enriquez, a suspected member of the Mexican Mafia.

The day after, a streetwise source—in fear for her own life because of the Gavaldon hit— called investigators, set up a meeting, and told them that Boxer had been "muscling in" on dope dealers in White Fence, was always armed, and was usually accompanied by two or three gang members, one of them Chino from White Fence. She told about the late-night raids on dope houses, the threats, the continual rip-offs of money and cash. She pointed out Boxer's picture.

The informant's boyfriend called next, described the Night Rider car Boxer drove, and identified Mo from White Fence as his "right-hand man." He also told cops that Topper knew everything about the murder but was afraid to talk, and that he was being "bulldogged" by Boxer, who claimed to be Eme.

Detective Forsman now had enough information to put him hard on the killer's trail. He learned that Boxer was "on a reign of terror" and that even other "hard-core killers were terrified of him." What he didn't know was that he had fewer than thirty-six hours to catch him before he murdered again.

Forty-seven-year-old David "Pelon" Gallegos sat in his parents' home in Whittier eating a late lunch of fresh tamales and some gumbo prepared by his mother. It was his last meal.

Pelon had been living with his aging parents since he was paroled from prison twenty months earlier on another in a series of drug-related charges. He was basically "state-raised," first getting locked up in Juvenile Hall for burglary when he was only twelve years old, and then living most of his adult life behind bars. His rap sheet was eight pages long with his repeated drug offenses, break-ins, robberies, extortion, grand theft auto, and murder.

Gallegos had a bald head with ears that stuck out and a full mustache that turned down at the edges and was perched above full lips and tucked under a big wide nose held high enough to give his face a certain appearance of arrogance. It was still a thuggish look, enhanced by an upper body covered by tattoos with ink as faded as his Mafia reputation.

"He was a bum and a no-account who lived by handouts," recalled Boxer, "and we all understood that."

On the street, Pelon used what was left of his Mafioso image to shake down drug dealers for spoons of heroin and cocaine to support his own habit. A friend gave him a ride to East Los Angeles, and it was just bad luck that evening when he walked into the "shooting gallery" operated by Enriquez at Topper's house. He didn't know that, one year earlier, Topo Peters had given Boxer the contract to kill him.

It was Chino Aveles who was watching the door when Pelon Gallegos demanded some free drugs. Aveles was quick to tell him there were no freebies and no credit. Then, after ten to fifteen minutes of haggling, Chino explained that all the dope belonged to Boxer Enriquez, who was in the Mexican Mafia.

"I'm a carnal too," insisted Pelon.

Chino rethought the situation: if this guy really was Eme too, Boxer might get mad if he put him off. If he wasn't, Chino figured he'd just pay for it himself and that way all his bases would be covered. He gave Pelon a ten-dollar bag of heroin, and the anxious Mafioso sat down on a dining room chair, dropped the dope into a spoon, melted it with a lighter, sucked the liquid into a syringe, slammed the needle into a vein, and nodded off into a familiar stupor known only to junkies.

When Boxer walked in the back door an hour later and was told there was a carnal out front named Pelon, he knew this was going to be a hit that just "landed in his lap." This guy was not going to leave alive. Mo, Jacko, Topper, and Chino were all hovering. Boxer kicked them all out of the room for a while and turned his full attention to Gallegos.

"How you doin', brother?"

They started talking politics, Mafia small talk about who was locked up and who was out on the streets. Boxer wanted to "woo him in."

As time passed, Boxer asked, "You want another shot, brother?"

No hard-core junkie could resist free dope. Boxer slid his chair over to Jacko, who had reentered the room: "Fix him up a good one."

He was cooked up a massive dose of oily, black tar heroin. Once it was sucked up into the rig, it was handed to Gallegos, who slowly found another vein and emptied the syringe into his arm. His head slumped down, his lips turned purple, and he passed out cold.

Topper panicked and hurried to the refrigerator for a pack of ice to revive him. *I don't need no murder in my house,* he thought.

On the other hand, Boxer found Chino shooting up in the bathroom and asked for more dope. He came back with nine bags: six heroin and three cocaine. The empty wrappers began piling up on the kitchen counter. Gallegos couldn't even pick his head up.

Later, they lifted him into place for another round. Pelon opened his eyes: "What are you trying to do, kill me?"

"No. Try to relax, man. We're trying to give you some coke to wake you up."

Gallegos looked at the "outfit" filled to the top with familiar, deadly black juice. He had to know they were in fact trying to kill him. But he was in no position to fight—he went easy. Strong hands grabbed his arm and forced the needle into a vein that had many times before welcomed heroin. This time it had had enough.

A few hours after the overdosing began, Pelon's five-foot-eight, 170-pound frame was as limp as a large, well-used bean-bag chair. Chino had gone home. Jacko and Mo helped Boxer lift Gallegos into the Night Rider—parked in the driveway—and they drove to Chuco Castro's apartment, four miles away in Alhambra. Chuco, Boxer's prison pal, was also recently paroled. They stopped off to buy some Yum-Yum donuts and a twelve-pack of ice-cold Corona for Chuco and his wife. It was Chuco who first marked Pelon a coward.

Pelon rode sitting up in the front passenger seat, as if he was passed out from a mean drunk. Boxer planned it that way so that, if they were stopped, they could tell police: "We're just taking him home. The guy is loaded, man. He's messed up. Just look at him, he's still sawing logs."

At Chuco's, they gave the donuts to his wife, gave Chuco some cash and heroin, and all drank a few beers. Boxer said, "Hey, man, guess what I got?"

"What's that?"

"I got a guy in the car. You want to see him?"

"Who is it?"

"That guy, man. I think he's dead."

Chuco walked out to the Night Rider and looked in. "Oh! This fool!"

He told the same story about Pelon acting like a coward when they went to shake down a drug dealer. Then he leaned inside the car and started slapping the limp figure across the head: "You dummy! Look at you. You're dead!"

Still, Boxer wanted to be sure. They all drove back to Chino Aveles's house in East Los Angeles. Enriquez went in and explained only that they had to take care of something.

"Let's go. Get your shit and let's go!" (Chino would later tell police that Boxer slapped him and forced him to go. Enriquez said that was a lie, that Chino went willingly.)

Chino crawled into the backseat of the Night Rider and sat between Boxer and Mo. Pelon—slouched over and unconscious in the front passenger seat—"moaned" as Jacko stepped on the gas and drove off.

Boxer says Chino got the picture immediately and suggested that Spence Street behind the VNE housing projects was "the perfect place for a murder."

Then Boxer barked out some driving directions.

Four turns and a mile away, the car pulled into the mouth of an alley that ran behind a row of small factories on Spence Street in an industrial area about a mile from Topper's. Boxer ordered Mo out of the car. "Watch right here!"

Jacko drove down the alley and stopped in a dark spot—only a shadow of light spilled in from a nearby security lamp. Boxer ordered Chino out of the car to watch the other end of the alley. He hesitated.

"Well! Move! Get the fuck out of the car and watch up the street."

Chino started to walk. Boxer grabbed the back of Pelon's collar and dragged him from the car onto the pavement. He placed a gray sheepskin seat cover over the victim's face to protect himself from blood splatter and put five noisy bullets into Pelon's head with the short-barreled .357 Magnum Trooper Mark III, just in case he wasn't already dead.

Boxer looked up after it was done, and Jacko Padilla was standing there "like a scared little kid with his fingers in his ears. Jacko was a ruthless businessman and a great thug," noted Boxer, "but he never was a killer."

As they left the crime scene, Enriquez couldn't resist telling his crew, "I'm Boxer from Eme. Nobody fucks with me. This is my town." He also explained that he killed Pelon because it was a contract hit. "I take care of contracts," he boasted. They all went off to get loaded again.

David "Pelon" Gallegos was left on his back, legs extended and spread apart, his right arm folded across his nose, laid out on the concrete in a small pool of his own blood. His blue sweatshirt and T-shirt were pulled up over the back of his head, exposing his front and a faded tattoo of Our Lady of Guadalupe that reached from his neck down past his naval. He had 65¢ in his pocket. There appeared to be a little sneer frozen on his lips. It was December 30, 1989—the day before a not very happy New Year's Eve.

Back at Topper's place a few days later, loaded on drugs and shaky with paranoia, Mo was all bug-eyed and sweaty. Jacko didn't look any better. That was enough to make Boxer more than a little paranoid himself. The terrible trio was posing for a photograph when Mo took off running for some unexplained reason. That spun Boxer into a psychotic episode of his own: "I thought, *They are going to do me.*" So he quickly stuck the barrel of a .357 Magnum into the neck of a scared and pleading Jacko, walked him to their car, and ordered him to drive to Olympic and Soto. There, "I was going to shoot him and dump his body in an alley behind a Sears warehouse." "If you're going to shoot me," shouted Jacko, "just shoot me." Boxer couldn't pull the trigger.

After an hour of driving around—Jacko pleading for his life—Boxer finally handed the gun over, and Padilla emptied the cartridges onto the seat. Jacko said, "You're just tripping today." Then he took Enriquez home and dropped him in bed.

Four days after the Gallegos murder, eighteen-year-old Carlos Sanchez and his seventeen-year-old homey Jorge Molina were hanging out on the sidewalk in front of 1115 Rosalind Avenue, several blocks from Topper's in Boyle Heights. It was 5:30 P.M. when the Night Rider pulled up in front of them. Chino and Mo slid out the passenger side of the car.

"Where's your fat friend?" asked Chino as he motioned for Sanchez to come closer.

Mo ordered Molina, "Stay back!"

Chino then pulled a .38 from his waistband and pointed it at Sanchez: "I know you have money, so get on your knees!"

Lil Mo then cleaned out the victim's pockets—thirty-eight dollars in cash. They got back in the car and drove off with Boxer at the wheel.

A woman who watched it happen from the window of her house called the police. She also knew Chino Aveles and identified him as one of the robbers. The victim pointed out Boxer Enriquez's photo as the driver and gave a good description of the getaway vehicle.

More than two hours later, two cops in a black-and-white spotted the Night Rider parked in the driveway of Chino's house. Mo and his girlfriend came out and got into the black Dodge. The officers followed for a few blocks until Mo parked outside Topper's. He got out and was busted, fitting the description of the second robber who was with Chino.

The same day LAPD detectives heard from SSU investigators that Boxer Enriquez knew Pelon Gallegos from Folsom Prison. Detective Forsman had developed a good working relationship with an SSU agent named Brian Parry: "Brian was so knowledgeable about prison life. He and I would get information about different players and fly all over the state trying to beat kites that were coming out of the prison system [about the murder]." At the same time, Los Angeles County sheriff's prison gang experts said there were rumors that Boxer was given the hit by Mafia bosses. Still, there wasn't yet enough evidence to charge him, and they didn't know where he was.

"We searched for him from pillar to post," recalled Detective Forsman. Surveillance vans with LAPD detectives and SSU agents sat outside Topper's place—Boxer's hangout—for days. Agent Parry remembered: "I was in court when I got a page that we had a location [that Boxer frequented], and we spent many nights there on surveillance. We had a couple of unmarked vans, all metal inside, which made it twice as cold. So we started bringing blankets to put on the floor so we wouldn't be constantly kneeling on the cold." Parry knew Boxer was dangerous and would return to his haunt: "They are creatures of habit. We expected to get into a shoot-out with him." Amazingly, there never was a Boxer sighting despite the fact that he was in and out of Topper's dope house every day. Boxer knew from the word on the street that "cops were looking for me, so I always came up a side street and entered and left through the back door."

On January 10, 1990, another anonymous call came into LAPD's Hollenbeck Division with information that Boxer Enriquez could be found at his mother's apartment on Whittier Boulevard. Officer Bill Eagleson and his partner, both in a gang unit known as CRASH (Community Resources

Against Street Hoodlums), arrived to find the front door partially opened. He knocked and it opened farther. Boxer was in a heroin stupor, lying on a bed just three feet away. "We've been looking for you, Rene," said Eagleson as he slapped on the handcuffs and arrested Boxer for his part in the Sanchez robbery.

In a suspect interview room at the LAPD Hollenbeck Division station house, Detective Forsman kept playing with a new Rolex watch on his wrist—a gift from his girlfriend—as he asked Boxer some questions about the murders. Enriquez denied everything. As Forsman left the room, a cocky Boxer told him: "With all due respect, you'll never get this by preliminary"—a reference to a mandatory judicial hearing where a prosecutor is required to show enough evidence to get a case to trial. He couldn't have been more wrong.

Two days later, Chino Aveles was picked up at eight o'clock in the morning a few blocks from his home by a special gang intelligence unit called the Detective Support Division, or DSD. By ten, he was being interviewed by homicide detective Forsman, and at first Chino denied everything too, both the robbery and the murders. An hour into the interrogation, as Forsman talked about the trauma for the victims' families, Aveles changed his mind. Deputy District Attorney Allan Carter of the Organized Crime Division then joined them. The audiotape was rolling as Chino told them all he knew. By seven-thirty that same evening, police had recovered a cache of Boxer's weapons in the trunk of a broken-down 1969 Chevy parked in Chino's driveway and the Gallegos murder gun buried miles away in a trailer park. The next day Chino led them to the five spent casings buried behind a factory several blocks from the crime scene.

Four days after that, Boxer and Mo—already being held in L.A. County Jail for the Sanchez robbery—were booked for the murder of Cynthia Gavaldon.

The next day Topper Aleman told cops everything he knew too, and Boxer and Mo were charged with the murder of David "Pelon" Gallegos as well. Despite the sworn preliminary hearing testimony of Chino Aveles regarding Padilla's role in the murder, Jacko was never charged.

CHAPTER 15

Learning a Sweet Lucrative Scam

WHILE AWAITING TRIAL, BOXER WAS HOUSED IN LOS ANGELES COUNTY Men's Central Jail in module 1700, the maximum-security section known as "high-power," and he found himself on the same tier as Eme's Daniel "Cuate" Grajeda. During his stint at Palm Hall six months earlier, Enriquez had joined others in voting for Grajeda's death. Since then, Cuate had survived a September stabbing attack. Now Boxer got on the phone to Rocky Luna and Huero Shy Shryock and told them, "Just give me the word. I'll take care of it." They told him to stand by.

In high-power, Boxer then met the legendary John Stinson, a top-ranking member of the Aryan Brotherhood prison gang, who was doing life for murder. Thirty-five-year-old Stinson was tall and bald-headed, with Nazi tattoos emblazoned on his skin and "jailhouse lawyer" smarts that had kept him in the County Jail for six years (instead of prison); there he was the architect of a massive drug ring. Prosecutors estimated that he was making at least $5,000 a week while locked up in maximum-security. Stinson was making so much money that he was investing some of it in Disney stock. Boxer liked him immediately.

Also, Stinson was a longtime crime buddy of Cuate's—they had robbed and murdered a dope dealer in Long Beach ten years earlier. He began working on Boxer, telling him that Cuate was a good guy, a good brother, and that people were jealous of him just because he made a lot of money. Grajeda was in the jailhouse drug business with Stinson.

So Boxer made an effort to become better acquainted with Grajeda. It wasn't difficult. Cuate wooed Enriquez with his almost mystical talk about the Mexican Mafia, his devotion to it, the need to be true to its Aztec-like traditions, and the mission to bring Eme back to its old glory. He was a master manipulator. "I succumbed to his spell," said Boxer. "He led me around by the nose for a while."

"Do you want to make some money?" asked Cuate.

"Okay, fine."

Cuate and Stinson cut him in on their drug operation, and from then on Boxer was never without heroin or cash.

It is always difficult for people on the outside to understand that it's quite easy for inmates to get drugs: methamphetamines, heroin, cocaine, and marijuana. Whatever drugs were available on the street were available in County Jail. It was—and still is—big business. Security at county was easier to breach with a large number of inmates coming and going each day. Also, prisoners were allowed at that time to carry cash.

Deputy District Attorney John Monaghan, who eventually prosecuted a number of players in the Stinson drug ring, said at the time: "There are twenty thousand people in the L.A. County Jail system. A good number of them are narcotics abusers, and if you can supply the demand, you can make a lot of money."

Stinson's thirty-nine-year-old wife, Debbie, helped him from the outside, where she lived in a middle-class home in Gardena, California, with two children, including a daughter with Down's syndrome. She had no arrest record but would buy drugs—mostly heroin—and smuggle them into the jail on a weekly, and sometimes daily, basis.

Debbie Stinson knew a woman in South-Central Los Angeles whose boyfriend was a deputy sheriff. The deputy picked up the drugs from his girlfriend and delivered them to an inmate when he went to work. He also smuggled cash payments back out.

Stinson's wife had a private investigator who, during visits to the jail, handed over pens filled with cocaine to inmate drug clients. There were so many people in the visitors' room that it was impossible for deputies to keep an eye on all of them all of the time.

Even prominent defense attorneys were unwittingly used to smuggle in drugs. Paul Leach, a convicted robber and murderer who sold drugs for Stinson on the mainline, testified that the smugglers included Leslie Abramson, who gained national attention representing Lyle and Eric Menendez for killing their rich Beverly Hills parents, and prominent anti-cop defense attorney Gerald Chaleff, an outspoken police reform advocate who was a member of the Los Angeles Police Commission from 1997 to 2001 and who since 2003 has served as an LAPD civilian employee equal in rank to a deputy chief. Leach said, "They were ignorant about it. They didn't know what they were doing." Deborah Stinson would glue a stack of transcripts together and, halfway through the stack, cut up to an inch-thick slot in the paper, which created a little cavity where the drugs were hidden. Then she'd drop the transcripts off at the attorney's office, and the unsuspecting lawyer would deliver them to inmates during private legal visits at the jail. Deputies were not allowed to examine legal documents.

She had other methods as well. At home, Debbie took tar heroin and ironed it out into paper-thin sheets. Then she dismantled a large brown legal folder by tearing back its double-paneled sides, placed the paper-thin heroin flat on one side, and then sealed it back up again with glue. The same trick—sealing heroin between two folds of paper—worked with greeting cards. Also, Debbie would cut the cardboard and insulation out of the covers of calendars and phone books, replace it with sheets of heroin or cocaine, and glue it all back together.

Another Debbie favorite was buying two law books at a time at the local bookstore. Back home, she'd cannibalize one, ripping off the binder and the guts of the cover. She'd then insert the paper-thin heroin and use the undamaged materials from the second new book to rebuild the cannibalized version.

Next, she took the law book back to the store where she bought it, pretended she had just picked it off the shelf, paid for it again, and had it shipped to her husband at the County Jail with the heroin secreted inside.

Visitors were also recruited to bring in golf ball–size bindles of heroin, cocaine, and meth that were wrapped in balloons. They would "keister" the balloons to get past a search, then go to the bathroom, remove the contraband, wash off the balloons, and secretly hand it to the inmate they were visiting. Women visitors used the same method using their vaginas.

Jail trusties, who had work assignments such as janitors or food deliverers, were recruited to deliver dope directly to customers in their cells and collect cash payments. Needles used to inject narcotics were stolen from the jail infirmary.

Inmates could actually place orders through what they called a "mailout": Stinson gave inmate customers a post office box number in Westminster, California. The box belonged to his wife Debbie. Inmates would get a relative or friend on the outside to send a money order to the PO box, and the drugs would be delivered to the jail.

There were special incentives in place to discourage those who refused to pay their bill on time. If the payment for drugs didn't show up in a week, the cost was doubled. If not paid the second week, it doubled again. If not paid the third week, the holder of the delinquent account was killed. It worked well.

Those who sold the drugs, often jail trusties who could freely move around the facility, were compensated for their efforts too. For every six bindles of coke or heroin sold, dealers kept two for themselves. One of more than a dozen dealers working for Stinson testified that he was making between $500 and $800 profit a week—just for himself—selling on the mainline.

Boxer became a major partner with Stinson and Cuate Grajeda. They taught him to go on pro per status, which gave an inmate the right to represent himself in his own criminal case. A maximum-security inmate—such as Boxer, Stinson, and Cuate—is allowed almost no contact with other prisoners. Acting as his own attorney, he was still able to use the system for prison gang business, drug deals, and jailhouse hits.

Deputy District Attorney Frank Johnson, who prosecuted Boxer and is now a Los Angeles Superior Court judge, said at the time about pro per: "It's basically like giving a small child hand grenades to play with. It just causes untold damage."

And that for Boxer was exactly the point. Pro per gave him the right to have a "legal runner" of his choice. The runners were allowed daily, unmonitored, face-to-face visits up to fifty minutes long. There was no glass partition between the inmate and visitor. The runner could hand over as many drug-laced legal documents as humanly possible. Debbie Stinson was her husband's legal runner.

So Boxer married Lil Mo's twenty-year-old sister, Rosie Ruiz, and made her his legal runner. She was five feet, six inches tall, weighed 150 pounds, and had brown eyes and long brown hair. He called it a marriage of convenience. Rosie, who had a drug habit of her own, was then enlisted to slip narcotics into the jail through her legal packages. She brought in heroin, cocaine, and marijuana before she was caught, convicted, and sent to prison for sixteen months.

According to court documents, on one occasion, she even used her legal runner status to call an inmate down to the visiting room, whom the Mafia stabbed on Easter Sunday.

Pro pers were also given free access to the jail law library for two hours a day. A razor blade was used to hollow out the inside of as many law books as a crook might need; messages, drugs, and weapons were kept inside. The law book had a number on it, and it became a "mailbox." Boxer gave an inmate the number, and he could pick up whatever message or contraband that needed to be passed on.

Also in the library was a bank of unmonitored phones. From her two-bedroom apartment in Boyle Heights, Rosie accepted collect calls from Boxer and set up three-way conversations with anyone he wanted to talk to inside or outside prison walls. He could work drug deals and find out who was coming in from the streets, who was going out, and who needed to be hit.

Enriquez also utilized Rosie to implement a PO box mail-out system just like Stinson's. He had a private investigator—paid for by the state—who used to deliver drugs to him during visits.

And there's more. An inmate with pro per status had subpoena power. From the isolation of his cell, Boxer could get a removal order to pull anyone he wanted out of prison and down to the L.A. County Jail, under the ruse of saying he needed the person to be a witness in his case. Rarely was anyone who was pulled down actually a witness. Yet the Mafia could use pro per to call fifteen carnales down from different prisons to have a mob meeting, or call someone down to do a hit, or to get hit. Prosecutor Frank Johnson called it outrageous and one hell of a mess: "It's really laughable. It's like the sheriff and the state prison system are running a Greyhound Bus service for these people at their pleasure, to transport them all over the state, and it's really gotten out of hand."

It was all a sweet, lucrative scam, and Boxer mastered it.

CHAPTER 16

Hungry Piranhas in a Tank

BOXER ENRIQUEZ WAS GRATEFUL TO CUATE GRAJEDA AND LEARNED A great deal from him about the art of Mafia politics. Cuate played it like a chess master, always thinking two moves ahead of the other guy. Interestingly, he was an illiterate dope fiend who taught himself to read and write and used those skills to study war tactics, organizational politics, and philosophy. He once quoted to Enriquez an old Chinese proverb: "If you stand on the bank of a river long enough, you will see the bodies of your enemies and adversaries come floating by."

Yes, Grajeda was a killer's killer, dangerous with a knife and gun. He was also dangerous with his tongue. That's what scared Boxer the most: "The point is he could kill you with his tongue. He'd have everyone wanting to kill you because of his tongue. Cuate has done more killings with his mouth than with his hands, by the way he talked to the brothers and seduced them into murder. He always had this attitude, 'We have to clean house, bring Eme back to its old glory.' And he used those periods of house cleaning to eliminate his adversaries."

It had been eight months since Cuate Grajeda survived the stabbing attack by Indio Carlos in a jail shower room. Now he thought he'd sat on the river bank long enough. It was about time for him to see Indio's body floating by.

Other influential Mafiosi started showing up at County Jail, and Grajeda's future was a topic of discussion. Among them were carnales loyal to Enriquez, including Black Dan Barela, Huero Shy Shryock, and Chuy Martinez. Cuate, who had already won Boxer's favor, got a pass from the others as well. Even Joe Morgan and Topo Peters signed off on it, excused Grajeda for past transgressions, and considered the matter settled.

That didn't sit well with Indio, and he let other brothers know how he felt. He was no competition for the Grajeda poison tongue. Cuate started a campaign, reminding other carnales that Indio had hit him in the shower and that the beef was supposed to be quashed. He lied that Indio was stalking him and posed a constant threat. Grajeda wanted Indio taken out.

"Like a dummy," remembered Enriquez, "I volunteered to do the hit."

Twenty-nine-year-old Indio Carlos, five-foot-five and 140 pounds of rage, was on his way to court at the Criminal Courts Building in downtown Los Angeles. In addition to his Grajeda stabbing, a year earlier he'd stabbed another Mafioso in his cell at Men's Central Jail. At that time, he was already doing life in prison for a fatal drive-by shooting he did when he was only nineteen; he stabbed a correctional officer at San Quentin six years later. He was no stranger to violence.

It was May 21, 1990, shortly after nine o'clock in the morning, as Indio stepped off the elevator on the fourteenth floor, waist- and leg-chained, along with another inmate in K-10 status. That's "keep away from all other inmates" status, a classification for condemned prisoners and those who have been violent to other inmates and/or deputies and need to be separated from the general population. K-10s are escorted by two deputies wherever they go, and they wear red wristbands to distinguish them from other prisoners. Deputies searched a legal folder he was carrying under his arm and patted him down, looking for contraband of any kind.

Indio was now headed for holding cell A. Deputy Shirley Ducre asked if there was any objection to being housed with three other K-10 inmates already inside the holding tank. He asked who they were, and she read their names off, including Rene Enriquez. Indio answered, "That's fine. We get along with everybody." The deputies then freed his right hand from the waist-chain so he could write or use the toilet.

There was a hard-metal door leading to the cell—left open—and a second wire-mesh door barring entry. Deputy Charles Moore hit a switch in the control box on the wall, and the wire mesh rattled open. The first escorted inmate entered, and Indio followed behind him. Boxer was seated directly to the right of the door.

As the deputy pushed the button to close the cell door again, Enriquez, without saying a word, jumped up, grabbed on to Indio's jumpsuit with his left hand, and began stabbing with his right. At first the two deputies thought it was a fistfight and immediately began to yell, "Everybody lie down, get back!" They noticed blood and then continued to let the door close for security reasons. At the same time, they screamed at the floor deputy to put out a call for a disturbance.

By the time they could clearly see the five-and-a-half-inch-long metal shank in Boxer's hand, Indio's jail-blue top was becoming saturated with blood. The assault stopped almost as quickly as it started. Enriquez heard a deputy yell, "Shoot him!" Boxer walked over to the toilet and flushed the knife. It didn't go down.

Indio was still standing in the same spot where he was attacked, one hand still chained to his waist, drenched in his own blood, stabbed twenty-nine times in the stomach, chest, and left arm. There was one scratch on his cheek. He lived. As he was escorted away by the deputies, he muttered to Boxer, "You ain't did shit." Indio knew a true Mafioso doesn't show fear.

The three other K-10 inmates inside the holding cell at the time of the attack told deputies they saw nothing.

Cuate Grajeda was "an evil son of a bitch," according to Enriquez, "willing to do anything or use anyone to conquer his perceived enemies." Not co-incidentally, the jails and prisons were full of young Latino gang members ready "to make their bones" with hopes of someday becoming a Mafioso themselves.

Tony "Santos" Barker, a thirty-one-year-old gang member from Harbor City, was one of them. He'd been in and out of jail most of his life, had a crazy bad-ass attitude with a lot of hate in him, was "looked up to" by his own street gang, and would stab someone in a hot second. Every single day Santos rolled up his thin jail mattress, fixed a couple handles on it with torn sheets, used it like a set of barbells, and did hundreds of repetitions. As a result, he was built like a middleweight collegiate wrestler.

The Mafia "had their eye" on Santos as a recruit with potential, a little brother. Already he had done one hit for them in County Jail—stabbed an Eme associate who had been placed on the lista. Santos knew the target, a homeboy from his own neighborhood, and his family, but that didn't stop him. The Mafia wanted it done. In a "big old fish dorm" with five dozen inmates standing around, he struck the victim once in the heart. The knife he was given bent, and the target ran down the tier. Santos went after him, grabbed him in a headlock, and rode him as he stabbed again and again until the pliable shank collapsed into a useless corkscrew. That probably saved the victim's life.

Still, the brutality of the attack put Santos "in the Mexican Mafia's car." He was looking at fifteen-to-life in prison—if convicted—but he "felt glorified, everybody was glorifying me. I felt like I was somebody."

Eight months later, La Eme turned on him. Santos Barker was sitting up against his cell door getting a haircut. The barber, twenty-five-year-old Albert "Chango" Bribiesca, was standing in the freeway, reaching through the bars with a safety razor. Bribiesca had already done at least three stabbings for the Grajeda brothers—one of the victims died. Suddenly, he pulled out a sharpened butter knife stolen from the kitchen and plunged it into the back of Barker's neck, an inch below his skull. Bribiesca was sure that Barker was dead as his body slumped to the floor. He wasn't.

Santos Barker was no punk. Jelly-like spinal fluid leaked out of the gaping wound in his neck. During a trip to the visiting room a few days after the attack, Boxer noticed that Barker's shirt was shiny and slick with oozing brain matter that looked like egg whites. After that, he began losing equilibrium and coordination. He said that he was showing these guys he had heart and he was ready to die for La Eme. Five days passed before he went to the hospital and had surgery. The knife had pierced his spine.

After Santos Barker fully recovered, Cuate Grajeda admired his nerve and gave him a new assignment to do for La Eme. Los Angeles County deputy district attorney Scott Carbaugh was from the Hard-Core Gang Unit, and he had prosecuted a number of Mexican Mafia defendants, including a short list of Grajedas. Although the case a few years later was overturned on a legal technicality, Carbaugh won a guilty verdict against Cuate's brother Senon and nephew Arthur "Shady" Grajeda for executing a drug dealer who was moving in on their territory. He also successfully prosecuted Cuate's brother Tommy, aka "Wino," on a lesser felony that sent him away for a few years. According to grand jury transcripts, Cuate Grajeda ordered Barker to kill Carbaugh in clear reprisal for carrying out his duties as a deputy DA.

Carbaugh was also prosecuting Santos Barker, who was given instructions to hit the deputy DA during his trial. The plot failed—at the last minute, Santos backed out because he thought he had a chance to win his court case. If he did, he went free. No more jail. Unfortunately for him, he lost the case, and because he didn't attempt the hit, he was marked for death.

On 1750 module, known as high-power, Santos was handcuffed behind his back as he was led from his cell on D-row to go to the visiting room.

Cuate Grajeda was just passing the control booth on his way from C-row to visiting when he noticed Santos coming up the tier on D. He scrambled back to C, was handed a shank by another Mafia associate, and ran back toward Santos, ignoring shouts from unarmed deputies to stop. Santos saw him coming, and just as the knife-wielding Cuate turned the corner onto D-row, he twisted around backward, grabbed the bars with his handcuffed hands, and slammed the gate shut. "You're not getting me!" he screamed at Cuate.

Santos, who eventually testified against Cuate Grajeda in a murder case, described his jailhouse experience with the Mafia: "It's like being in a tank of piranhas with no food, and before you know it, somebody starts moving a certain way, and they are all on them."

Boxer Enriquez, in his next hit, would prove the piranhas wouldn't hesitate to eat anyone.

CHAPTER 17

Die Like a Man, You Punk

SALVADOR BUENROSTRO WAS THE NEXT TO BE THROWN IN WITH THE piranhas, and his time in the tank was especially designed to send out a message that the Mexican Mafia could get anyone, anytime, anywhere. It was set up to happen in the middle of a busy attorney room at the L.A. County Men's Central Jail. The plan was to stab Buenrostro until he was dead. Twice, La Eme had already tried to move on Buenrostro and failed. A cocky and ambitious Boxer Enriquez volunteered to get it done right: "The sheer brutality of the hit, the audacity of what we're doing, that's what we want out there. We are the Mexican Mafia and want everyone to understand that we will even whack our own. We're spreading our terror. It's terrorism. It generates fear, and we'll parlay that into making money."

The forty-five-year-old Buenrostro, known as Mon, was a hard-core, old-school member of the Mexican Mafia. Like most of his brethren, he was a killer; a particularly tough and gritty soldado, he was already doing life for carrying out a $15,000 contract hit on a Pasadena businessman. He later tried to escape from prison. Mon was a stand-up mob guy, but lately he'd been causing some dissension between some older and younger brothers. And there were rumors that he badmouthed Joe "Peg Leg" Morgan. That was viewed as politicking, and politicking was a fatal offense. It was one of those gray-area rules, but this offense did, after all, concern hard-liner and Eme de facto boss Joe Morgan.

Benjamin "Topo" Peters was a close, longtime loyal associate of Morgan's, a right-hand man who had a reputation for deviousness paired with a willingness to carry out Mafia orders without question.

Topo and Mon had come from prison to Men's Central Jail to be witnesses in an unrelated murder trial. The defendant was a Mafia associate on pro per status, and he'd used his subpoena power to transfer the two mobsters down. Of course, neither of them actually had anything to do with the murder case. It was all part of a Mafia ruse to get them to County Jail, where Mon could be killed and Topo could help make him dead.

The hit was set for the evening of July 14, 1991. Boxer Enriquez had made an appointment to see William McKinney, a defense lawyer who was helping him with one of his two homicide cases. They met in one of four glass booths that spanned the wall on one side of the jail attorney room. Twenty-seven-year-old Boxer sat across the table from McKinney, one wrist handcuffed to a chain that was mounted on the floor under his chair. The lawyer recalled that Enriquez seemed "in a good mood." They had talked briefly when he asked McKinney if he would order down two witnesses to get statements about his case. Guess who? He asked for Mon Buenrostro and Topo Peters. It was all part of the setup. Boxer had a handcuff key in his mouth and a six-inch-long, one-and-a-half-inch-wide metal shank stashed in his shoe. His attorney left the booth to speak to another inmate.

Fifteen minutes later, Mon was escorted into the room, followed by Peters. Boxer and Mon immediately locked eyes: "I'm looking at him right through the window, and he knew right then, he's done. He knows it."

Topo had a full head of hair but was a funny-looking, rotund, boisterous, hot-tempered forty-nine-year-old man with a crazy streak. His moniker, or *placa,* came from the fact that he once had a big tooth like a little gopher. *Topito* means "big tooth" in Spanish. Now, after years of heroin addiction, most of his teeth were rotted or missing. He was only five feet, three inches tall, had a confident little waddle when he walked, and, unlike most Mexican Mafia stalwarts, had no tattoos. Peters wore a size 6 shoe, but he had on size 12s to hide a nine-inch knife inside one of them. He was flopping along looking like Bozo the Clown. It was almost comical, but no one was laughing.

As soon as Boxer caught sight of him, he spit out his key and opened up his handcuffs.

Outside the glass attorney booths were three rows of stools where inmates sat across from the visitors, a small partition between them. Mon Buenrostro was seated in the last row, thirty feet away from Boxer, his right hand handcuffed down to a chain between his legs that was anchored to the floor. Topo Peters was seated one stool away. No one was in between them. He too used a smuggled-in handcuff key to free himself.

Boxer waited. Topo took off his shoe, pulled out the shank, suddenly leapt from his seat, and stabbed Buenrostro repeatedly with an over-the-head motion. Deputy Harry Amos, who was seated at the front desk that led into the attorney room, yelled, "Hey! Hey!" That was Boxer's cue. He jumped up and ran across the room, knife in hand, sliding on the slick tile floor with only one shoe on, yelling, "Kill the motherfucker!"

A female probation officer seated nearby screeched, "He has a weapon!" It was too late.

Topo stabbed at Buenrostro's side, one, two, three, four, five, six, seven, eight times. He was screaming, "You're going to die, sucker, and if you die, you die!" Right hand still chained to his stool, Mon fought for his life. He ended up getting Peters in a headlock and grabbed on to the wrist that held his shank.

Deputy Amos came from behind and clutched Topo's shirt as Deputy Clarence Stephenson, who hurried in from the control booth just outside the attorney room, gripped the back of Buenrostro's shirt—both trying to pull the struggling inmates apart.

That was when Boxer slid in. "It's time to pay the devil!" he said scornfully. Mon threw a karate kick that found its mark on Boxer's face, then another quick kick to his chest. So Enriquez plunged his knife into Mon's buttocks. That made him turn and expose his front, and Boxer shoved his jail-made blade into the side of Mon's gut.

Then he took a step toward Deputy Amos. "Stay the fuck out of this!" The deputy backed away and put out a call for assistance. Enriquez swung around and savagely stroked at Buenrostro's stomach ten more times—his shank dripped with blood.

Knowing he couldn't stop the attack alone, Deputy Stephenson suddenly turned his attention to the four dozen attorneys, probation officers, private investigators, and inmates scattered in a panic across the room. "Get out!" he commanded as he directed them toward the release gate at the back of the attorney room. He ran out into the hallway toward the watch sergeant's office and told a few other deputies there was a double shanking in progress.

Boxer was crazed as the karate kicks from Mon caught him again.

Topo's shank "folded up on him," and as he tried to straighten it out he slipped on the slick bloody floor, dropped the knife, and fell with Buenrostro on top of him. Once on the floor, he managed to get Mon in a bear hug from behind, holding his shoulders and neck, screaming, "Die like a man, you punk!" At the same time, Boxer's shank repeatedly ripped through Mon's skin.

All three Mafiosi were on the floor, writhing in the blood and sweat. Enriquez could feel his adrenaline pumping. Buenrostro was facedown, slightly on his side. Boxer just kept stabbing. Every time he struck there was a deep groaning sound as the knife cut through flesh and cartilage. The stench of brutality was thick in the air.

Mon shouted, "Get them off me!"

By now, orders had been given to lock down the entire jail. Deputy Stephenson returned with Deputies Larry Zimmerman and Dan Ordway, who had less than three years on the job between the two of them; none of the three deputies had a weapon. Jailhouse policy was clear. if jailhouse cops carried weapons, there was always the possibility that the heavily out-numbered deputies could be overwhelmed by inmates and their arms taken and used against them. So Ordway and Zimmerman kept barking orders to drop the shank, kicked at Boxer again and again, and backed off a little every time Boxer threatened them with the weapon.

Enriquez wanted to finish the job on Mon. This was Mafia business, and it pissed him off that these deputies—as brave as they were—wanted to be some kind of heroes and save Buenrostro. For a moment, he seemed distracted and looked up at them: "Fuck you! You guys stay out of this. Just back up and let us do what we've got to do!"

Kicks from the deputies snapped at his legs and pummeled his back. A small woman officer pounded on him with a leather-bound notebook, pleading with him to stop: "You're killing him. You're killing him!" He kept sticking the shank in and twisting it as if the cops weren't even there.

Nearly a dozen deputies were now in the room, circling. Boxer, his adrenaline rush wearing off, began to feel the sting of their blows. A kick buckled his knee. The pain was sharp. Another kick knocked him off a stool where he sat delivering a few final strikes with his blade. He was tired and drained emotionally and physically. All three battling mobsters were soaked with blood—their jailhouse blues now tinted a deep red. The smell reminded Boxer of "wet copper pennies." Finally, the handle on his knife bent as if it too had had enough.

Boxer said, "That's it, man."

"Okay, he's dead anyway," replied Topo.

Boxer threw his shank across the room. Deputies descended on him and Topo with a vengeance. The cops were on an adrenaline rush too. Boxer was not abused in any way, but he caught a fist or elbow in the eye, enough to cause a welt. He threatened Deputy Zimmerman, "I'm going to kill you! I'm going to get you if you put your hands on me. Don't you know who I am?"

Boxer still had the chain around his waist, handcuffs attached, the smuggled-in key protruding from one of the cuffs. A deputy had kicked Topo's shank across the room, and his handcuff key sat on the desk above the stool where he was first seated. There was a large pool of blood on the floor. The entire attack had taken no more than two minutes.

Mon Buenrostro was taken by ambulance to a hospital intensive-care unit in critical condition. He had twenty-six stab wounds—one-and-a-half-inch gashes—all over his upper torso and legs, but he lived. Afterward, in true Mafia style, he refused to make any statements.

Boxer and Topo were freshly handcuffed and taken to the medical clinic. Topo had a knife wound on his right hand, either self-inflicted or hit by Enriquez. Boxer complained that he had pain and swelling in his right knee. On his way to the medical facility, Topo told his two-deputy escort: "We were not going to hurt no staff, we respect staff. You guys should have let us finish what we were doing."

Enriquez was more irate. In the medical clinic, he saw Deputy Zimmerman and warned him: "I'm going to get you! I'm going to get you!"

Topo tried to talk him down. "Okay. It's over. Just relax."

A couple of hours later, the two assailants were temporarily locked up in an empty cell block, module 3700. Peters was put in a cell at one end of the tier and Enriquez in his own cell at the other end. They talked as a deputy within earshot was assigned to secretly listen and transcribe their conversation.

"Hey, Boxer, good day, good day, man. I feel so relieved. I've been so stressed."

"Yeah, I feel so good," replied Enriquez.

Topo Peters, also known as Benny, loved to talk, and he went on and on about all the blood, his role in the stabbing, and what he had said during the attack. He had wanted Mon to die, wondered if there'd be a story in the newspaper, and bragged that there was nothing authorities could do to them that hadn't already been done.

"Hey, Boxer," he concluded, "if they try to get us on a murder, just plead guilty so we can go to our cells at Pelican Bay [State Prison] and watch color TV."

Benjamin "Topo" Peters couldn't read or write and was a man of no vision who rarely thought beyond the moment. He was dedicated to La

Eme, but according to Boxer, Peters was basically a hedonist. "All he cared about was getting high on heroin and killing people."

In an interview with deputies five days later, Topo confessed, "I did it. Now all I want to do is plead guilty and get it over." So that's what he did, and he settled into prison for the rest of his life. Prison was home for Benjamin "Topo" Peters.

The attorney room in the largest jail in the country was supposed to be a secure, neutral, safe place for inmates, attorneys, investigators, and parole and probation officers. The Mafia terrorized it, and that's what they wanted to do: let people know the Black Hand had a firm, powerful grip, from the jails and prisons to the streets. The Mexican Mafia was emerging as a powerhouse. And the new, younger generation, noted Boxer Enriquez, understood that terror equaled money.

They had plans—to control not just California but the whole damn country.

Deputy District Attorney John Monaghan knew it was a problem: "There is no threat you can hang over these people who are in prison that continue to commit offenses. There is absolutely, positively, no threat at all. They can pretty much do whatever they want to do . . . secure in the knowledge that nothing else can really be done to them."

After the Buenrostro hit, not only did Topo go back to prison, but so did Cuate Grajeda, Joe Morgan, and John Stinson. County Jail administrators had had enough of all of them.

Boxer was left to face two murder charges and two attempted-murder charges. He was also indicted, along with seven others, for his role in the Men's Central Jail drug-smuggling operation. Grajeda and Stinson weren't even charged in the drug conspiracy. They already had life prison terms, and prosecutors didn't want to give them another case that would again allow them to go pro per, delay trial, stay in L.A., and cause even more trouble.

It turned out that Los Angeles County sheriff's detectives had a jail-house informant working on the inside of the Stinson/Grajeda/Enriquez drug sales scheme.

The Mafia found out who he was and arranged for him to be stabbed when he was transferred to the California Institution for Men in Chino.

Through other informants, cops had now learned that Men's Central Jail was considered the home base for Mexican Mafia and Aryan Brotherhood business activities. It was more comfortable than the harsher prison environment and closer to home, a place where Mafiosi could have meetings, deal drugs, and do hits.

Deputy DA Frank Johnson put it this way: "They really don't care if they get caught or not. They do virtually outrageous crimes with impunity. You really get the impression from dealing with these people, whether they are in prison or out, it's not much consequence to them."

CHAPTER 18

Mafia Gratitude Goes Only So Far

"GIVE IT BACK. GIVE IT BACK! THEY'RE WAITING FOR IT."

Boxer couldn't even move, frozen in a narcotics stupor, looking into the face of Carlos "Carly" Avina from Twenty-fourth Street, a convicted murderer who was now on death row. He was asking for the "rig" back.

Enriquez slowly handed the empty syringe to Carly. It seemed to him as though he was speaking in slow motion.

"Carly?"

"Yeah."

"Call 'man down.'"

Then Boxer blacked out.

He was back in high-power, 1700 module, a few days after the Mon hit. Topo Peters hadn't yet been shipped out to prison. Timmy Tucker, a Crip gang member known as "Funky Beat," had brought in some high-grade heroin for him as a going-away present.

"Make me a good one," said Enriquez a few minutes earlier. "I want to drop a horse." Now he was lying flat on his back in his cell, feet toward the bars, on the edge of death from an overdose.

Funky Beat shouted the news, "Hey, Rene's OD'd."

He pulled Boxer over by the feet and sat him up against the bars.

"What do I do?" he asked.

"Throw water on him."

So people in nearby cells, using little Styrofoam cups, started throwing water toward Enriquez to revive him. One inmate even threw an apple and hit him in the head. At this point, Boxer wasn't even breathing. Outside the bars, there was a hot-water container that inmates used to make coffee.

Funky Beat reached out, grabbed it, and dumped the scalding water in Boxer's lap. It caused third-degree burns on his thighs. He was so numbed by the dope that while he didn't actually feel it, it did wake him up and restore his breathing. The scalding water saved his life.

He fell back into a state of grogginess, and paramedics were throwing water on his legs when he was able to focus again.

Then he heard a deputy's voice. "Hey, Rene!"

"What?"

"Do you hear this?"

"Yeah."

Boxer couldn't see the deputy, but he distinctly heard the click of a shotgun round being chambered.

"You know what time it is then, right?"

It was a warning not to do anything stupid. They were taking him by ambulance to the jail ward at nearby County General Hospital. He was given a shot of something, and his head cleared enough that he could see there was a ring of deputies standing around him, all armed with rifles and shotguns. They weren't taking a chance that this was some kind of Mafia escape plan.

Back at high-power three days later, Funky Beat wasted no time apologizing for scalding a Mafioso. He explained, "You were gone, man!"

"You saved my life, Timmy."

"I was going to pour it on your head at first," Timmy said. Obviously, the scalding water would have badly scarred Boxer's face and chest forever. As it was, some ugly marks were already left on his upper legs.

Boxer looked at Funky Beat and said, "If you would have poured that on my head, I would have killed you."

Mafia gratitude goes only so far.

CHAPTER 19

La Eme Goes to Hollywood

LYLE AND ERIC MENENDEZ WERE BROTHERS WHO SHOTGUNNED THEIR parents to death as they sat in front of the television in the den of their Beverly Hills mansion eating strawberries and ice cream. During two trials, they put on a defense saying their multimillionaire father, president of a media company called Live Entertainment, had molested them for years. The case became fodder for national news coverage and a made-for-TV movie. The sons, who were competitive tennis players, lived a playboy life after murdering their parents. That is, until their psychiatrist told police the Menendez brothers confessed to him during therapy sessions. Ultimately, they were convicted of first-degree murder and sentenced to life in prison without the possibility of parole.

Big drug dealers, celebrities, and people with money in jail or prison are often targeted by the Mafia for extortion payments. The Menendez brothers were no exception. After the Buenrostro hit, Topo Peters and Boxer were working on it in a low-key way. They were now housed in high-power on G-row, a stretch of eight cells enclosed in glass. The food there was terrible. Inmates were given "jute balls," a punishment diet that consisted of ground-up meals containing basic nutrients, all compressed into a single loaf of food. The jute ball isn't pretty to look at, and it tastes even worse.

Eric Menendez was housed within shouting distance on F-row. Boxer and Topo passed him twenty bucks with orders to buy them some candy bars at the jail store. Somehow Eric got caught and couldn't deliver the merchandise to his new Mafioso acquaintances.

Boxer and Topo had no plans to hit the Menendez boys over some canteen items, but apparently the brothers were a little spooked by the predicament. Eric complained to Leslie Abramson, his defense attorney, that he could get killed by La Eme. She in turn went to Cuate Grajeda just before he was shipped off to prison and asked him to intervene—to keep the Mafia off her clients. Boxer later said, "I never understood why they [the Menendez brothers] did that. Actually, I liked those kids."

Boxer noted that when Lyle first entered the jail he was housed just a couple of cells down on A-row in 1700 high-power. All the time, this Beverly Hills playboy was wearing a do-rag on his head like some cholo from South-Central Los Angeles. Enriquez figured the kid—fresh off the tennis court—probably wanted to adjust to the terrain by looking a little tougher in his new jailhouse environment. No problem.

Suddenly one morning a sergeant and two deputies came storming into the cell block and stopped in front of Lyle's cage. Boxer couldn't see them, but it was easy to hear what they were saying. It sounded serious.

"Give it to us!" the cops commanded.

"What?" answered Lyle.

"Give it up now!"

"I don't have anything."

The sergeant's voice was extremely authoritative. "Now hand it over."

Boxer thought, *Wow! This guy is really doing something. He's dealing dope. Maybe his attorney is bringing it in? Or maybe he's caught with a shank—needed it for his own protection.*

"What are you talking about, officer!?"

Then it came. The deputies knew what they were looking for and weren't leaving without it.

"Give us the wig!"

Lyle then handed over this toupee that covered his pate and hung over the top of his upper forehead in little bangs. He walked around with a bald head for the next few months and was thoroughly embarrassed. Apparently, his Princeton playboy image was suffering. Finally, he received a judge's order and was allowed to wear the toupee in court.

"Just shave your head, man. Don't worry about it," Boxer told Lyle. Most of the younger gangsters in jail had full heads of hair and still shaved their skulls. Enriquez didn't understand it. Of course, he'd never hung out at the Beverly Hills Country Club either.

It wasn't all fun and games when it came to celebrity, not when it involved a film about Rene's Eme.

"Paramount Pictures, can I help you?"

"I'd like to talk to this guy Edward Olmos," said Boxer.

During this period following the Indio Carlos hit in the courthouse, the Mon Buenrostro stabbing in the attorney visiting room, the massive jail drug ring bust that even involved his own wife, his court-appointed private investigator smuggling in narcotics and hacksaw blades, and the overdose episode in a high-security gang module, Boxer had been transferred to module 2904. It was an extra-high-security area of the jail where there was one row of only six cells, one man to a cell. Movie actors such as Eddie Murphy and Robert Downey Jr. or other high-publicity inmates, such as the "Night Stalker" serial killer Richard Ramirez, were kept there. All these inmates were deemed unfit to mingle, either for their own protection or for the protection of others. That now included Enriquez. He ate and slept in the small cell and wasn't allowed any visits except from his lawyer. Other than an attorney visit, the only time he was allowed out of his cell was for court appearances. Then he was always escorted by two or three deputies, handcuffed, arms chained to his waist, and his legs in shackles. Even his own lawyer had to give twenty-four hours' notice to see him, and when they did meet, Boxer's hands and ankles were shackled to the table. "He's like Hannibal Lecter," complained his new defense attorney, Joseph Gutierrez.

While Boxer was locked down in module 2904, he had daily access to a telephone. He'd heard that actor Edward James Olmos was producing a movie about the Mexican Mafia titled *American Me,* and he wanted to ask Olmos some questions about it.

The receptionist put him through to Olmos's production office. "American Me."

"I want to talk to Edward James Olmos," said Boxer.

"I can take your message," the reply came.

"No! I want to talk to the guy. I want to talk to *somebody.* This isn't a call from a fan."

Boxer was insistent. Eventually, Danny Haro came to the phone. He played the part of Huero in the movie and was also an assistant to Olmos.

"My name is Rene Enriquez. I'm also known as Boxer."

He never mentioned he was a Mafioso, but Haro instinctively knew he was on the phone with a mob guy, someone who could hurt him. Boxer told him he wanted to see a copy of the script, that he was a "friend of some friends" who'd done some work on the movie. Rocky Luna and Charles "Charlie Brown" Manriquez, both Eme members, had served in some capacity as technical advisers for the film.

"Hey, Rene, you know what?" explained Haro. "We talked to Rocky and CB, and they said it was all cool, man."

That wasn't good enough. Boxer wanted to see a script.

In a 1991 interview with the *Los Angeles Times*, Olmos said: "I want to show there's a cancer in this subculture of the gangs. They'll [Eme] say: 'You've taken away our manhood with this movie.' I say to them: 'Either you treat the cancer or it'll eat you alive.'"

Enriquez told Haro, "I agree with the message [of the film], but not the vehicle [La Eme] that you're utilizing to send the message." He had concerns about how it was being done. The Mafia rumor mill had told him there were some scenes in which Olmos took too much dramatic liberty and did not respect the true heritage of Eme. Enriquez wanted to see for himself. Send him the script. Instead, Haro sent him a production package about the movie. That wasn't enough. Boxer was back on the phone asking for the script again. Haro sent him an address where he could write Olmos, and he did. No response. He telephoned again and was given another address where he could reach the forty-six-year-old actor. Finally, he got a copy of the script, read it, and mailed back his thoughts about it.

What Enriquez didn't know was that Olmos—already petrified that the Mafia was after him—handed the letters over to the FBI. The feds interpreted Boxer's correspondence as a thinly veiled threat.

Boxer had written to Olmos that a lot of people, including him, were upset with the movie. In his opinion, the actor did in fact take dramatic liberties that were offensive. He wrote that he and others were especially displeased with a scene in which the main Mafia character (who was based on Eme icon Cheyenne Cadena) was sodomized in Juvenile Hall. Mafiosi said that was fiction. Furthermore, no man who allowed himself to be raped would be allowed into the Mexican Mafia. The other major objection was that the Cadena character was killed at the end of the movie by other carnales after expressing doubts about their brutal business. In real life, Cadena was murdered by rival Nuestra Familia hit men while trying to forge a truce to unite the interests of La Raza. In truth, he went down as a martyr in the eyes of La Eme.

Those scenes in the film were viewed as an act of disrespect. "If he was going to do a movie," insisted Enriquez, "it should have been a realistic portrayal of what happened."

Boxer concluded his last letter to Olmos by saying that he wished him "health, happiness, and box-office success." The actor felt the message was a warning that the mob was coming after him.

On March 25, 1992—twelve days after the movie's premiere—Charlie Brown Manriquez was gunned down while walking through the Ramona

Gardens housing project in East Los Angeles. It was a Mafia hit. Newly made David "Smilon" Gallardo of Big Hazard later bragged that he shot Manriquez in the face, and when he turned and ran he shot him in the back. He ended up with six bullets from a .380-caliber handgun in his body and a business card in his pocket from *American Me*.

Fifty-three-year-old Charlie Brown had been a hopeless junkie who lived like a bum in an abandoned garage near the projects. "Nobody wanted to waste a bullet on him," remembered Boxer. A year earlier, Manriquez had twice failed to carry out a Mafia-ordered stabbing while at the state prison in Chino. Evidently, he made his contribution to the *American Me* project for a new pair of tennis shoes and Levis. "This was just an affront to the organization," explained Boxer, "and we couldn't tolerate it." CB was a man already marked for death. His participation in the movie sealed it.

On May 13, 1992, Ana Lizarraga stood with her son in the driveway of her home—located just outside the Ramona Gardens housing project—packing the family van to go to her mother's funeral. Ana was known as "the Gang Lady" because of her work with an L.A. County–funded program called Community Youth Gang Services. It was a job that allowed her to cruise the streets, make contact with gang members, and try to cool heated neighborhood gang disputes before they ignited death. A self-described former gang member, Lizarraga told the *Los Angeles Times* in a 1984 interview that she felt a special obligation to work with youths after she lost her husband and two nephews to gang shootings. She said she wanted to be a model for her own children so they would not become gang members.

Two masked gunmen dressed in black came up her driveway firing freely with 9 mm handguns that had fifteen-round clips. As she fell to the ground, the assailants walked up closer and kept on shooting. Lizarraga died with thirteen slugs in her body. Minutes after the hit, police arrested twenty-nine-year-old Jose "Joker" Gonzalez a few blocks away as he tried to flee the scene of the crime. He was a Big Hazard gang member who had been paroled from Folsom Prison just two weeks earlier. Joker was later tried, convicted, and sentenced to life in prison for the murder.

FBI records show that La Eme's Smilon Gallardo more than a year earlier had expressed his desire to kill Lizarraga because he felt she was a police informant who was interfering with his drug trafficking in the Ramona Gardens housing project. Gallardo later sponsored Joker for Eme membership because he killed the Gang Lady.

It was no coincidence that the Lizarraga murder came three months after the release of *American Me*. The forty-nine-year-old gang counselor had worked on the film as a paid consultant with a small acting role. Gallardo saw that as disrespect to Eme.

Boxer recounted that what happened to Lizarraga was "an unfortunate hit, totally uncalled for. In the organization, we believe that violence is the last response, after all else fails. Then you kill. Smilon Gallardo, being the stupid idiot that he was, so hooked on violence, his first response to everything was 'kill 'em, whack 'em.'"

Then, on August 7, 1993, the bullet-riddled body of Rocky Luna, an upper-echelon Mexican Mafia member, was found slumped over in the driver's seat of a compact car parked in a lot at the Ramona Gardens housing project. The car doors had been left open, and the rear window was shattered by gunfire. Rocky had long been known as the Godfather in that area, but that did him little good in the end. He'd made some negative comments about Topo and Black Dan; other Mafiosi claimed that Luna had twice failed to carry out a hit on an alleged informant named Arthur "Mad Dog" Roselli. Twenty-nine-year-old Alex "Pee Wee" Aguirre, an Eme member from the Avenues, was the triggerman who took Rocky out.

Smilon Gallardo, who provided the gun for the hit, also complained that Luna was trying to undercut him in the neighborhood. Boxer Enriquez recalled that it was mob politics for Gallardo, who "wanted to unseat Rocky as the Godfather in Ramona Gardens." Also, Gallardo knew there was another leftover issue that bothered a lot of the carnales: Rocky Luna had served as a consultant for *American Me* and allowed filming to take place in his territory—the Ramona Gardens housing project.

It is no wonder that Edward James Olmos feared that La Eme had a contract on his life. Olmos sought counsel from Eme dropout Ramon "Mundo" Mendoza, who warned him: "Don't underestimate these people. If they're obsessed with getting you, there's nothing you can do to stop it."

Months before Luna was executed, Olmos applied to the Los Angeles Police Commission for a permit to carry a gun for his own protection. "Eddie," said one close friend, "is living with this twenty-four hours a day."* The commission denied his request, concluding that the filmmaker couldn't show proof that he was in "serious and immediate danger." He went everywhere with a bodyguard. L.A. County sheriff's sergeant Richard Valdemar said, "Olmos ran all over the country trying to get away from the Mexican Mafia. Then, on the witness stand before a grand jury, he forgot everything."

---

* "Film Leaves a Legacy of Fear," *Los Angeles Times,* June 13, 1993.

A year after the movie's release, Mafia kingpin Joe Morgan, locked up in Pelican Bay State Prison, actually filed a lawsuit against Olmos, Universal Studios, and several others, seeking a half-million dollars in punitive damages. In the suit, Morgan argued that a character depicting him in the film committed crimes he didn't do and that that hurt his chances for parole. Shirley J. MacDonald, Morgan's attorney at the time, said, "Even if these things occurred, they still don't have the right to appropriate his likeness or his story without permission." The case was eventually dismissed.

Boxer Enriquez maintained that Olmos "was right to be concerned." The prison wing of La Eme discussed hitting Olmos, then finally decided not to take any action—but also not to lift a finger to stop it either. At the same time, he explained, Chuco Castro, Huero Shy Shryock, and Smilon Gallardo—all members out on the street—were plotting to get the actor-director. "Yeah," recollected Boxer Enriquez, "there were people who would have killed him at the drop of a hat. If he would have been at the right place at the right time, they would've killed him."

It's not clear whether Joe Morgan ever got a dime. He died of liver cancer on the Corcoran State Prison hospital ward on November 9, 1993. He was sixty-four years old.

Boxer believes that Olmos did pay extortion money—$50,000 to $100,000—that most likely went to Chuco, Smilon, and Pee Wee Aguirre. Olmos isn't talking.

"I never got anything out of that," said Boxer. "I never participated in that extortion plot. Yet I got blamed for extorting Olmos and having shared in the payoff."

He just wanted a copy of the movie script and a chance to voice his displeasure.

CHAPTER 20

Drive-bys, Drugs, and the Pepsi Generation Mafia

IN THE 1990S, A NEW GENERATION OF EMERGING MEXICAN MAFIA stalwarts saw thousands of loosely organized street gang members in southern California, an unbridled penchant for violence among them, and a booming drug trade. Together, it all spelled opportunity for the mob.

Gang-related murders in Los Angeles County peaked in 1992 with 803. In fact, during the previous five years gang-related murders averaged 570 a year—again, that was just in Los Angeles County.

Grandmothers, teenage girls, and small children were getting killed in the crossfire. "It was looking bad on the Mexican population," said Boxer. "Gang members running indiscriminately in the middle of the street firing and spraying houses." Ironically, it was a senior deputy named Watson in the County Jail gang unit, Operation Safe Streets (OSS), who first suggested to him that La Eme do something about the mindless drive-by problem. Boxer Enriquez began wondering out loud if the Mexican Mafia could stop it from happening. There was a touch of mob morality in the idea, but it was totally bathed in self-interest—control the drive-bys, control the gangs.

Boxer was still the go-to guy at MCJ for the Mafia. From his cell in module 2904, he talked every day on the phone about Eme business with Black Dan Barela, Chuco Castro, and Pelon Moreno—all out on the streets of Los Angeles. Already, they had been discussing how to infiltrate the street gangs more effectively—why not stop the drive-bys? All the Latino gangs constantly shooting at each other created chaos. Together, under Mafia influence, they were a broad force of manpower and muscle.

During the summer of 1992, Eme veteran Peter "Sana" Ojeda gathered five hundred gang members into El Salvador Park in Santa Ana and made them forge a peace treaty. The forty-nine-year-old Sana, a convicted heroin dealer and reputed hit man who controlled narcotics sales for the Mafia in Orange County, stood above the crowd on some bleachers overlooking a baseball diamond. Waving his arms like an evangelical preacher, he ordered the gangsters—many of them longtime rivals—to stop all drive-by shootings against members of their own race, La Raza. Black gangsters were still fair game. Ojeda actually presented a handwritten document warning that anyone who broke the no-drive-by rule would be treated "as a child molester, a rat, a rapist, which all means coward." And that meant dead. Not long after that meeting, Sana was back in federal prison serving seven years for being a felon in possession of a handgun.

Boxer was aware of what Sana was doing but wanted to take it further. During the time he and about thirty others his age were inducted into the Mafia in the late 1980s, there was an advertising campaign by Pepsi-Cola called "the Pepsi Generation." Somehow his generation of Mafiosi got tagged with that identifier. In any event, the Pepsi Generation mob—with Enriquez often leading the way—wanted to grow. Some of the older members were satisfied just being a member of La Eme, with the jailhouse and neighborhood status it gave them. "Why be satisfied with running jails and prisons and shaking down drug dealers in selected neighborhoods?" asked Boxer. La Eme was a murder machine that created terror. It was time to use that terror to expand their reach. "I told them," said Enriquez, "let's run the state, the southwest United States, let's run the world! This is organized crime."

At the time, there were an estimated sixty thousand gang members in Los Angeles County from more than five hundred different gangs. Why couldn't they all be controlled by the Mexican Mafia, with the mob getting a piece of their action? That was a plan.

There was resistance to the idea from certain Eme members. Ruben "Nite Owl" Castro and Francisco "Puppet" Martinez—both from the Eighteenth Street gang—felt that it couldn't be done. They argued that the drive-by mentality was endemic to the gang culture and should be allowed to continue. They felt it fostered a warrior mentality, Aztecas. In the end, however, they went along with Boxer's idea and prospered as a result.

Boxer, with the help of an enthusiastic Lil Mo, started sending *wilas* (messages) to every jail and prison in California. Any gang member who did an unauthorized drive-by shooting got whacked, either on the street or when they ended up behind bars. Either way, they were dead.

At the same time, Mafia-mandated meetings were held in parks all over southern California. Gang members came by the thousands and got the word—no drive-bys. During one meeting at Elysian Park, right next to Dodger Stadium and within walking distance of the Los Angeles Police Academy, one thousand gang members showed up. It looked like the Sermon on the Mount, but with throngs of tattooed, bald-headed, baggy-pantsed gangsters—many of them mortal enemies—tightly packed into a circle on a grassy hillside in the palm tree–lined park. Everyone was searched for weapons. Cholos were asked to raise their shirts to reveal gang tattoos as a check against possible infiltrators. The talk was anything but Christ-like as several Mafiosi laid down the *reglas* (rules): no drive-bys, and violators will die. At one point, Chuco Castro grabbed a teenage face out of the mix, wrenched a gun away from him, cracked him on the head with it, and then slapped him silly, claiming the kid's gang kept doing drive-bys and writing graffiti. That discouraged any questions. Fear and intimidation were still at the guts of the Eme repertoire.

"We get them to stop drive-bys," Boxer told other carnales, "we can then get them to start killing people [for us]." It was all about control.

There were about twenty Eme soldados on the street spreading the word to stop all drive-bys.* Gang members were also told that drive-bys were cowardly. If a rival had to be killed for some reason, the gunman was instructed to walk up to the target face to face and pull the trigger. No more dead grandmas and children would be tolerated. Meetings were held not only in Los Angeles and Orange Counties but in San Bernardino, Riverside, Ventura, and San Diego Counties. That area included a population of twenty million people.

The next step of Boxer's original idea was to require all gangs, or *varrios,* to appoint a representative from their neighborhood. The Mafia could deal directly with that contact, instructing him to get his gang to demand a tax, or *feria,* from every drug dealer in their area. The Eme could get 50 percent of everything collected from every single neighborhood. Dealers not willing to pay the tax—as much as one-third of what they made—were killed.

Black Dan and Chuco tailored the plan a bit differently. They required every gang to pay a monthly quota in guns, dope, or money. The varrio's payment was based on its size. If the neighborhood didn't come up with the

---

* Eme members on the street included Daniel "Black Dan" Barela, Ernest "Chuco" Castro, Jesse "Pelon" Moreno, Victor "Victorio" Murillo, David "Smilon" Gallardo, Alex "Pee Wee" Aguirre, Frankie "Frankie B" Buelna, Antonio "Tonito" Rodriguez, Donald "Lil Man" Ortiz, Juan "China Boy" Arias, Gilberto "Shotgun" Sanchez, Randy "Cowboy" Therrien, Art Romo, and Jesse "Sleepy" Aragon.

agreed-upon amount or refused to comply with the no-drive-by edict, it was put on the "green-light list."

Once a neighborhood was green-lighted, every Latino gang member in southern California (every Sureno)—in or out of jail—was given the go-ahead to kill, or at least assault, any member of that neighborhood on the lista. The lists grew to include more than a dozen different gangs and dozens of individually named gangsters. As time went on, there were two designations on the list: "touch-ups" (beatings) and "hard candy" (stabbings). It was called hard candy because of an unpleasant fact. A shank pulled from an inmate's bowels prior to a hit looked like a brown candy bar. Infections from being stabbed by such a weapon were potentially lethal. In the graveyard humor of the cell block, it was said that the victim "could probably smell the hit before he got it."

The green light worked like a charm. Under this setup, La Eme controlled not only tens of thousands of gang members and drug dealers but anyone else who got in their way.

There was some resistance. The Maravilla neighborhoods in East Los Angeles—which had had a long and bitter battle with La Eme—brought five hundred gang members together for a meeting of their own. Shortly after, the bodies of three of their members were found dead—shot and killed at close range. There were a number of other enforcement executions too.

It is difficult to measure accurately the full impact of La Eme's threat, but it did coincide with a 1993 respite in gang deaths following years of record-setting killing sprees. Los Angeles County Sheriff's Department figures showed about a 15 percent decrease in Latino gang-related homicides. Some LAPD divisions showed numbers down as much as 50 percent compared to the previous year.

A confiscated letter from Sniper, a nineteen-year-old gang member in County Jail writing to his homeboy, illustrated the prevailing attitude fostered by the Eme edict. It was dated November 24, 1993:

> So the homeboy Johnny got the green light by the Eme. Man, that fool is fuckin' stupid. . . . They out there blasting on fools or what? That shit makes the varrio look real bad. They're gonna fuck around and throw the varrio on a green light pretty soon. . . . I say this is what you should do: talk to a couple of the homeboys and see if you vatos can throw a meeting between the varrio. Talk about what's going on with the Eme and about the "Peace Treaty." Those vatos do mean business. Man, you need to get the homeboys on the

right track. It's about making money nowadays, not shootin' your own Raza up. If you guys wanna shoot somebody go shoot up those niggers from Westside 357 or Ghost town. You don't need to blast up your own kind no more. That shit's dead.

At the same time, Mafia shot-callers also fostered racial tension. Black gangs controlled the crack trade on the streets. The Mafia—during the large gang meetings in local parks—constantly preached loyalty to their own race, La Raza, and downgraded blacks, whom they referred to as *terrones*. They placed a green light on all black gangs. The Mexican Mafia wanted to dominate all the drug trade.

Race violence frequently broke out in prisons and jails. The L.A. County jail system averaged one incident a week. Headlines in the *Los Angeles Times* near the end of the year screamed: "Prisoners Are Segregated After Brawl" and "Blacks, Latinos Brawl Again in Court Cell." The *Daily News* followed suit: "11 Inmates Hurt in 2nd Day of Race Fights" and "80 Hurt in Saugus Jail Brawl."

The news media—generally ignorant about the true nature of the disturbances—rarely defined the violence as Mafia-induced trouble. Leo Duarte, a lieutenant who was in charge of monitoring gang activity at the state prison in Chino, knew better. He said at the time, "People don't see it, but there's a war going on right now. It's starting to filter out to the streets."

For example, on the Westside of Los Angeles in the one-square-mile Oakwood section of Venice, twenty people were killed and another thirty were wounded. All were casualties in a battle between two Mexican gangs, V-13 and Culver City Boyz, and a black gang called Shoreline Crips. Historically, there was more violence between the two Latino gangs, but the Eme edict forced them to unite against Shoreline. One Crip, who did not want to be identified, said, "You have to walk to the store with a gun in your pocket." Another worried anonymously, "Give it a couple more months and Venice will be a ghost town."

Both sides were doing the shooting. It was ugly. Nineteen-year-old Chavon Clark, who had no gang affiliation, was shot five times in the back as he walked to his girlfriend's house in the middle of the day. His mother, Sherrie Reed, said he just happened to be the wrong color: "They don't know what they doing. They just shooting somebody for nothing and they shot Chavon for nothing. It's hard."

There were outbreaks at high schools in more than a dozen cities. A special investigation intelligence summary from the L.A. County sheriff's prison gang detail, dated February 3, 1994, warned of black/brown racial unrest at high schools in Compton, Santa Monica, Venice, Pomona, Inglewood, Culver City, and the Inland Empire (Riverside and San Bernardino Counties). The document quoted confidential informants who claimed, "The Eme is supportive or directly linked to the unrest."

It's still going on today.

CHAPTER 21

Dealing with Pure Evil

FRANK JOHNSON WAS A TALL AND TRIM, PALE, SQUARE-JAWED, clean-cut prosecutor from the Organized Crime Section of the Los Angeles County District Attorney's Office. Arguably, he put himself at risk prosecuting a number of Mexican Mafia defendants, but he had courage and commitment. He was a law-and-order Republican, a family man, a successful product of Catholic schools who had a keen sense of what was right and wrong. On balance, he was the antithesis of Rene "Boxer" Enriquez and Gilbert "Lil Mo" Ruiz, who sat across the table from him in Department 110 at the Criminal Courts Building.

Johnson had no love for gangsters who walked through life in a drug-crazed existence of vivacious violence. He had a "moral repugnance" toward men who murdered multiple times, went to prison, and murdered again, all the time snubbing their noses at the system: "Prison is no deterrent for these people. The only way you can prevent them from killing again is to have the death penalty, and apply it. I don't see any other deterrent. I really don't."

At the same time, he was decent; once, outside the courtroom, he referred to Boxer as a "congenial fellow." Enriquez was nonchalantly agreeable in a series of courtroom appearances as lawyers discussed his future. There was no question that included a possible death penalty. In truth, during the three years he spent in County Jail awaiting trial, he'd resigned himself to the fact that he was going to take a trip to death row.

Cynthia Gavaldon's grandparents came to every court hearing carrying two photographs of their murdered granddaughter. Prosecutor Johnson "felt badly for them."

As for Boxer and Lil Mo, the deputy DA knew he was "dealing with pure evil, and I was on the side that was trying to quash it, counter it—it felt important to me." He and his supervisors in the District Attorney's Office were also well aware of the fact that a death penalty case is never a slam-dunk. Guilt has to be proven beyond a reasonable doubt, and all the key witnesses in the murder trials of Cynthia Gavaldon and David "Pelon" Gallegos would be lowly junkies with no more credibility than the accused murderers.

So, on January 7, 1993, after months of legal wrangling, the deputy district attorney finalized a plea bargain that would spare Boxer from the gas chamber. At this juncture, life in prison didn't sound so bad. He agreed to the deal.

Judge Florence-Marie Cooper told Johnson to take the plea.

"How do you plead to the charge in count one: second-degree murder of Cynthia Gavaldon? Guilty or not guilty?" said the prosecutor.

"Guilty."

"To count two: the second-degree murder of David Gallegos?"

"Guilty."

Enriquez also pleaded guilty to assault with a deadly weapon, that being a knife. The agreement consolidated the two murder charges, the two attempted murders on Mon Buenrostro and Indio Carlos, and the drug conspiracy in County Jail.

During an official sentencing proceeding three months later, defense attorney Joseph Gutierrez described Boxer as one of the most courteous and considerate clients he'd ever represented. He argued: "There is some good in Mr. Enriquez, and I think his life is salvageable." Gutierrez, if he believed that, was probably the only person in the courtroom who did. The judge pronounced a total sentence of fifteen years to life in prison.

As part of the same deal, Lil Mo pled out to one count of voluntary manslaughter for the Cynthia Gavaldon murder and one count of manslaughter for the killing of David Gallegos. Ruiz was sentenced to a straight twenty years. Mo was only twenty-five years old and had a definite chance at getting out someday.

Boxer had avoided the death penalty and a harsher sentence of life in prison without the possibility of parole. He made the guilty pleas "rather painlessly." It seemed like the best thing to do. The relatively bright, thirty-year-old Mafioso went back to his County Jail cell anticipating his transfer to prison. He stretched out on his bunk, calmly took a nap, and later woke up suddenly with his mind screaming: *Nooo! What did you do!? You accepted a life sentence!!!* The reality of a life—an entire life—behind bars hit him like a deadly night attack from Freddy Krueger in a scene from the 1984 movie *A Nightmare on Elm Street*. His whole persona was now screaming out against his decision.

It was a recurring dream for the next two years. At least a dozen times he woke up in the middle of the night—disoriented in a pitch-black cell, closed in by stark walls, not understanding where he was—and snapped. "You're in prison, and you're going to be here for the rest of your life, just waiting, and waiting, and waiting"—a profound, desperate feeling that ached with regret.

Rene "Boxer" Enriquez had not been permitted a visitor for more than a year when authorities allowed his father to come and see him before he shipped off to prison forever. He was being housed in the Wayside Super-max, module 900.

The father and son weren't allowed to touch. Rene was in chains. His body was locked up tight, a glass partition between them. They had to talk over a closed-circuit telephone, but the barriers to communication began to dissolve. He had never hated his father, but he'd rebelled against him, rejecting the life of a hardworking finish carpenter that John Enriquez had wanted for his son. They were distant, but "yeah, I always loved my dad," insisted Rene.

An aging John Enriquez was always disappointed that his son was drawn to men he felt were less than himself. He never liked jail visits. They were an ordeal—talking to your boy while surrounded in visiting rooms by tattooed thugs, evil-looking men. The conversations were often stilted and filled with idle chat about different relatives and how they were doing. "I never discussed why he was there. I don't want to know that he's a monster. I still love him very much."

There were so many years they weren't together, so many words that had never been spoken, so many regrets about what could have been, so many tears that were never shed, so much life that was never lived honestly.

Rene now understood that, whatever difficulties there were in the past, his father had always tried to do what he thought was right in his own mind and had provided for his family. He wasn't perfect—nobody is—but he was a good man. John Enriquez told his son, "El respeto al derecho ajeno es la paz" (Respect for the rights of others means peace). It was a quote from Benito Juarez, who is considered one of Mexico's greatest and most beloved leaders.* Rene could feel the clear, salty fluid welling up in the corner of his eyes, but there was no way a Mafioso could cry, especially in front of other inmates or jail deputies. "I think it's okay," he said softly, "for us to be friends, Dad. It's not a bad thing for fathers and sons to be friends."

His father was no Mafioso filled with false bravado. A small tear dripped out of his eye and flowed down his weathered cheek with regret and forgiveness.

Rene wanted to form a new, stronger bond with his father, and this was a good start.

As Boxer opened the door to a more meaningful relationship with his father, he closed the door on another.

Rosie Ruiz, his short-term wife, was released from jail after serving her sixteen-month sentence in prison for smuggling drugs into County Jail. She was only twenty-three years old. Enriquez had married her for expediency and had never even kissed her. He had needed someone to be his legal runner and smuggle drugs into the jail, and she was more than willing to do it. It was never *Romeo and Juliet*. Nor was the marriage ever going to be Ward and June Cleaver from *Leave It to Beaver*.

Boxer divorced Rosie, figuring, "It was for the best." He felt that a divorce was going to happen sooner or later anyway, so he just wanted to get it done. There were no hard feelings on his part. He simply sent a packet of divorce papers to her house.

However, there must have been some bitterness on her end. A week later, she came to visit her brother in jail and asked him "to kill Rene."

"What?" said a disbelieving Enriquez.

"Yeah," said Mo. "My sister wants me to whack you."

They both had a good laugh over it after Boxer reasoned with Mo that "our relationship shouldn't be affected by women. No matter what, we are always carnales first. Eme goes beyond family ties."

According to testimony, Lil Mo Ruiz and Jacko Padilla were both accomplices in the 1989 murder of Cynthia Gavaldon. Only Mo pulled the trigger, and Jacko was never charged, but he reputedly gave him the gun and was there when the killing was planned and executed.

---

* Benito Juarez became president of Mexico in 1861 and instituted a series of liberal reforms that championed the poor. During the French occupation, he refused to accept the rule of the monarchy.

The cold, hard fact remained that she had been the sister-in-law of a Mexican Mafia member, David "Big Spider" Gavaldon. Cynthia was the wife of his younger brother, gang member Roy "Lil Spider" Gavaldon, who was understandably angry that the woman he married was needlessly shot down in cold blood. At one point, Lil Spider went on a verbal rampage against Boxer and the others involved in the hit. He claimed they were on the lista—marked for death under the authority of his Eme big brother.

It was a serious enough threat at the time that Boxer had discussions with his crew about knocking off Lil Spider too. In the end, he decided to give him a pass.

Big Spider had never mentioned Cynthia's murder to Boxer. In fact, the elder Gavaldon once told a gang investigator at Chino State Prison that he knew the hit was "strictly business." Still, Enriquez knew there was animosity toward him. Why wouldn't there be? In reality, he'd had a member of the man's family killed for nothing.

Boxer knew his own status as a carnal gave him some leverage with Gavaldon. On the other hand, Mo and Jacko were more vulnerable—mere camarada pawns on a prison yard chessboard where all the kings were Mafiosi. He felt they needed more clout to survive—some insulation from political payback.

Jacko and Boxer had become great friends. They did a slew of robbery/extortions together and enjoyed each other's company. Padilla had no unbridled lust for blood, but he loved dope and making money. A keen street business sense was his strength.

Mo was low on intelligence but high on the violence scale. Boxer always thought he was a good guy: "He didn't hesitate to kill when you asked him."

So Boxer sponsored Mo for membership in La Eme before he went off to prison. And Mo became a made guy. At the same time, he arranged for Chuco Castro to sponsor Padilla, and Jacko was made too. Their years behind bars would at least be spent with the added potency of being a carnal.

Boxer, who felt he'd taken care of his loyal camarada friends, left the Los Angeles County jail system with a huge Mexican Mafia reputation. He was a dedicated doer, an astute organizer, a prolific drug dealer, and, most important to those in the mob and to those who feared them, a brutal, ruthless killer.

Within days of his sentencing, Enriquez was transferred to California Correctional Institution at Tehachapi for an uneventful six-month stay. Then he was moved to his new home at Pelican Bay State Prison in Crescent City, *the* maximum-security lockup in the entire state of California.

Boxer knew "he would have to dance with the devil" at Pelican Bay. There were enemies there. Among them were Indio Carlos and Mon Buenrostro, who still bore multiple scars inflicted by Enriquez's shanks. There was Spider Gavaldon, who knew Enriquez ordered the execution of his harmless sister-in-law. Hell, even the murdered Pelon Gallegos probably had some old Mafioso friends who might want to settle a score. Mafia politics were always tricky. He knew in the back of his mind that "there were going to be problems. I knew the end was coming, and that I'd be killed or forced out of the organization. No one lasts. I just didn't know when or how the exit would be."

Pelican Bay State Prison opened for business in 1989. It was made for criminals like Boxer and other die-hard prison gang members who have no respect for the law or the system that houses them—inmates who kill in and outside prison with no regard for the consequences of their actions.

Before he even got off the bus at PBSP, a portly Sergeant Aldo Capucci announced, with a thick Italian accent, "You inna the big house now! Start any-a shit and we'll fuck-a you up."

A maximum-security prisoner is held twenty-two and a half hours a day in a windowless solitary confinement cell called a Special Housing Unit (SHU). The purpose of the SHU, according to CDC literature, is "to protect staff and male inmates throughout the system from the few most violent, predatory offenders." Inmates sleep on a poured-concrete slab, molded into the wall, and have an immobile concrete stool to sit on and a small concrete writing platform—no metal parts to make jailhouse shanks. A thick, honeycombed, steel-plated door—no bars—limits an inmate's ability to assault others. Toilets have no removable parts that could be made into weapons. The inmate never sees the outdoors. He can normally exercise ninety minutes a day in a bleak "doggy walk" the size of a two-car garage, caged in on all sides by eighteen-foot-high concrete walls and an open-air ceiling covered by a heavy wire-mesh screen. Anytime he leaves the cell, he is first handcuffed through a small slot in the door. He is waist- and leg-chained, escorted at all times by two or more correctional officers, and video-monitored from a raised control booth where an officer is always ready with a Mini-14 rifle.

No social interaction between inmates is allowed. Most prisoners are housed in single cells. Folsom used to be the end of the road. Now it's Pelican Bay. Boxer insisted that the SHU "didn't bother" him, but prisoners call it "Skeleton Bay" because "you go there to die really . . . snitch, debrief, or die."

New inmates are walked through a sally port and metal detector adjacent to the docks where the prison bus unloads. Inside Pelican Bay is a maze of bland, concrete tunnels that make a fresh prisoner feel lost. A gray, shadowy path is worn into the cement floor where thousands of prisoners have been led to their cells. A half-dozen correctional officers surround the latest arrivals, and there is a gun walk above with an armed guard. The fat sergeant makes it clear that if you move, he will "blow your head off." Welcome to Pelican Bay State Prison.

Ironically, PBSP is a bit of a safe haven because there is no central yard there for inmates housed in the SHU. Arguably, the only man who can kill you is your cellmate—if you are lucky or unlucky enough to have one.

Boxer's first cellie was crime partner Lil Mo Ruiz. There was no scientific selection process. A correctional officer simply announced, "Pick a cellmate or we'll give you one." Each cell block was divided into four to six pods. The pods were like spokes on a wheel emanating from a raised control booth hub. In each pod, there were two tiers, four cells on the top and four on the bottom. Boxer and Mo were stripped naked and escorted into one of the pods. A facade of bravado showed on their faces, but it wasn't easy to maintain a convincing swagger with nothing but your epidermis and private parts showing. On the stairs leading up to the second tier, little metal teeth designed to prevent slippage bit into their bare feet. It was uncomfortable, and the guards wanted it that way. Correctional officers were badly outnumbered—three officers for fifty inmates in each SHU. Some subtle intimidation wasn't a bad idea.

Their nude butts stuck to the plastic mattress when Boxer and Mo sat on the lower bunk. They looked at each other and talked. "Keeping our eyes on the road," recalled Boxer, "and trying to act as if we were clothed." Hours later, COs brought them each a pair of boxer shorts that were a few sizes too small. "Tight-ass, come-fuck-me boxer shorts," complained Enriquez. It was a way for the guards to remind inmates who was in charge at Pelican Bay.

Mo had pea-size acne all over his head, face, shoulders, and buttocks. Boxer was used to seeing it, but not what happened next. Mo sat on his bunk, popped the huge pimples, rubbed the puss and blood between his thumb and forefinger, and wiped it on his underwear. Then he got up and helped himself to cookies or potato chips stocked in their cell, sticking his unwashed hands into the bags. It was disgusting, and Enriquez finally told him, "Do not touch my shit! I will not eat your puss!!" Lil Mo was offended and got angry. He also still harbored some resentment over the fact that Boxer divorced his sister. Mo never tried to kill him, but six months of pimple popping was enough. Boxer Enriquez suffered a bad case of "cellie fatigue" and asked the guards for a switch. It was done.

CHAPTER 22

The Eme Plot to Kill
the Governor of California

THERE IS EVIDENCE THAT, BY THE MID—1990S, MEXICAN MAFIA MEM—bers had plotted to kill the governor of California.

"To date, the SIU has received several reports indicating that the Mexican Mafia prison gang, 'EME,' *may* be involved in a plot to assassinate Governor [Pete] Wilson."

That is an intelligence bulletin from the California Highway Patrol, Special Investigations Unit (which handles security for the governor) that was issued September 7, 1995, to numerous law enforcement agencies.

During 1994, Boxer Enriquez was just settling into his new routine at Pelican Bay—changing cellmates—while Republican governor Pete Wilson was fighting to save his reelection bid by promoting Proposition 187. It was a ballot measure designed to ban undocumented immigrants from receiving public education and other social services. Many Californians, especially those of Latino descent, thought the governor's campaign was race-baiting. Proposition 187 seriously angered a number of Mafia members, led by the murderous, obstinate promoter of all things Mexican and evil—Daniel "Cuate" Grajeda. Boxer didn't need a police intelligence bulletin to tell him what was going on: "I don't know how realistic it was as far as its imple-mentation, but I know there was a Cuate faction in the organization that was talking about killing Pete Wilson. When I heard about it, I said, 'I don't want anything to do with that. You're talking about the governor. That's ridiculous!'"

Boxer also understood clearly, however, why the Eme members were so upset. As unbelievable as it may sound, they felt that they had an investment in Wilson and he had betrayed them. "He did us terrible," said Boxer. "He did the people terrible."

Sixty-six-year-old Rachel Ortiz is a well-known, longtime Latina community activist in San Diego who claims to have recovered from drug addiction in her twenties. She was executive director of Barrio Station, a community center located in the heavily gang-infested Logan Heights area of the city. Ortiz held the job for thirty-five years before retiring in March 2006. Her organization for years has pulled in millions of dollars in government funds to provide counseling, recreation, and job search services for gang members and ex-convicts.

Ortiz, along the way, campaigned to deliver Latino community votes to Pete Wilson, serving as a key adviser as he rose through the ranks as a city councilman, mayor, U.S. senator, and governor. She had pictures taken with him. He even presented her with a distinguished service award.

At the same time, CDC investigators say, Ortiz was making many phone calls and redirecting letters to dozens of Eme members, including Boxer Enriquez, Huero Shy Shryock, and Topo Peters. She had frequent communications with Mexican Mafia heavyweight and murderer Raoul "Huero Sherm" Leon, who was serving a twenty-five-to-life sentence at Pelican Bay. She even bought him a television set. The prison Investigative Services Unit, during a 1996 probe into Huero Sherm's correspondence, "uncovered an organized, criminal gang network wherein Leon corresponded with over one-hundred inmates [including Boxer] in twelve institutions through the use of outside participants who redirected the letters." According to a 225-page ISU report, Leon himself identified Rachel Ortiz as one of those "assisting the Eme," though she has never been charged with any wrongdoing. The investigation concluded that "over one-hundred-fifty crimes were reported or conducted through the use of the United States Postal Service." Those crimes included attempted murder, assaults on other inmates, extortion, drug trafficking, directing gang/racial disturbances (resulting in at least one death), utilizing legal privileges to conduct criminal activity, and organizing Eme-controlled gang leadership. Boxer said, "Huero Sherm seeks his validation through killing people."

Subsequently, Ortiz was banned by the CDC from every prison in the state. She asked the governor for a pardon, but investigators told Wilson she had connections to members of La Eme and warned him to stay away from her.

Huero Sherm was indicted in June 2006 as the leading conspirator in a federal racketeering case in San Diego. Prosecutors accused him of approving murder in a widespread scheme to tax gang members and drug dealers throughout southern California. The feds at first wanted to seek the death penalty, but someone in the Justice Department overruled the idea. He pleaded guilty in 2007 and agreed to a sentence of life in prison without the possibility of parole. Huero Sherm, who has the word MAFIA tattooed on his large belly, told Reuters News Service that his influence spreads far and wide. Three times during a taped interview with a CDC intelligence officer in June 2006 he bragged, "I snap my fingers, and people die." The murder that first sent Huero Sherm Leon to Pelican Bay for twenty-five-to-life may best define the man. The trial judge described it as "a vengeful assassination." On March 19, 1981, Huero Sherm, then a member of a San Diego gang called Gamma Street, and a co-conspirator stole a car from eighteen-year-old George Garcia. Leon made the victim, an athletic, hardworking teenager with two jobs and plans to enter the U.S. Air Force, kneel in the street. Then Huero Sherm blasted him in the back of the head with a shotgun. As if that weren't enough, Leon drove the stolen 1979 silver Camaro once around the block and then ran over Garcia as he lay dying on the pavement.

In 1992 headlines in the *San Diego Union-Tribune* screamed, "Activist Acknowledges Boyfriend's Arrest." It was an article about the apprehension of Rachel Ortiz's live-in boyfriend and his involvement in the sale of twenty-five pounds of methamphetamine to undercover cops and his promise to do future transactions for heroin and cocaine. Her forty-eight-year-old paramour was Ricardo Martinez, a validated Mexican Mafia member known as "Gato."

"And it is well known in Eme circles," according to Boxer Enriquez, "that Gato stole Ortiz from her previous boyfriend—Mexican Mafia member 'Silent George' Ruiz of Logan Heights."

In the wake of boyfriend Gato Martinez's arrest, Ortiz offered her resignation as one of Mayor Maureen O'Connor's nominees to the city's Civil Service Commission.

Boxer insisted that Ortiz has sent him and other Eme members money. She once visited him at L.A. County Jail. And back when his second wife, Rosie Ruiz, was busted for smuggling drugs into L.A. County Jail, it was Rachel Ortiz who came up with the money to bail her out. Topo asked her to do it, and she complied.

"If she doesn't know that we are Mexican Mafia, there is something wrong with her," insisted Boxer. "She knows who she's dealing with."

Most likely, the governor early on didn't know about her Eme affiliation, but the mob did. So when Wilson backed what was perceived as an anti-Latino law in Prop 187, there was in fact serious Mafia talk about assassinating him.

The California Highway Patrol intelligence bulletin stated: "We have heard that the money for the contract hit is coming from 'very important people' in Mexico, the Mexican Mafia, Mexican drug cartels, and the Mexican political party 'PAN.'" The confidential document noted that from February 1994 through September 1995, there were eight reports indicating a threat to the governor.

- The San Diego Police Department reported that an informant described as a "whacko" told them the governor "pissed off some very powerful people" and that a drug dealer offered him a $1 million contract to do the hit.
- An anonymous Hispanic male called LAPD 911 saying that he represented PAN and "the same as Colosio got assassinated in Mexico, Pete Wilson will be assassinated."
- An anonymous caller to a Ventura TV station, possibly a Hispanic male, said, "We're going to assassinate Pete Wilson. By the Eme."
- A letter was sent to the governor from a former mental patient claiming he was kidnapped by two men from the Mexican Mafia because he helped police set up an Eme-related drug dealer. He overheard them talking about a $1 million contract to hit the governor.
- An L.A. County human relations commissioner reported to police that a friend of her son's who spent five days in County Jail overheard inmates say that "the Eme was going to hit Wilson."
- A Vacaville inmate told an ATF (Bureau of Alcohol, Tobacco, and Firearms) agent that he overheard an Aryan Brotherhood member, and later a Black Guerilla Family member, talk about a hit on the governor. The AB brother said, "You're not going to believe this crazy shit!" The informant also felt that "the Eme has heard it."
- An unknown Hispanic gang member, acting as "a concerned citizen," approached an LAPD officer and told him, "The Eme has or will put out a contract hit on Governor Wilson's life, and the money will be coming from Mexico."
- An L.A. cabdriver phoned the FBI and informed them that he had picked up a fare who "talked about a plot to kill Pete Wilson. . . . The assassin was connected to the Mexican Mafia."

"To date," the memo stressed, "there is no confirmed information related to this assassination plot. However, there is enough information to warrant further investigation."

Pete Wilson, now retired from active politics and working for a Los Angeles consulting firm, said that he was "not aware that was the case with the Eme." He'd never heard about the capricious scheme to kill him, but "never had any feelings I was not well protected."

The plan never came off. But according to Boxer Enriquez, had the governor strolled into the wrong neighborhood at the time, there would have been no need to reelect him. He would have been dead.

A final comment on the subject from Boxer Enriquez is chilling: "The real hidden secret was that Governor Wilson was so close to the Mexican Mafia. Rachel Ortiz listens to us [Eme], and those people who work with her listen to her. We may never be able to get next to [in a political sense] a governor or a mayor, but people we know do."

CHAPTER 23

Operation Pelican Drop

IT WAS CALLED "OPERATION PELICAN DROP." NO LAW ENFORCEMENT personnel are on the record describing it quite this way, but it's fair to say that inmates—especially Mexican Mafia inmates—had fucked with the system so much that this time the system was going to fuck them back. One insider who worked on the project called it an "extraordinary security mission."

Bad memories of the entire episode are permanently locked in the mind of Boxer Enriquez: "It was the most treacherous trip I've ever taken. We were all apprehensive and disorientated. They hurt us bad."

It all began with thirty-three-year-old Vincent Bruce, a Venice Shoreline Crip gang member, known as "Honey Bear," who was convicted of a 1987 triple murder. Honey Bear and two accomplices robbed and strangled two reputed drug dealers at an Inglewood apartment and on the same day stabbed one of their girlfriends to death at a home in the Palms area of West Los Angeles. Then Vincent and his girlfriend—referring to themselves as a modern-day "Bonnie and Clyde"—went on a crime spree through five different states, committing a dozen robberies along the way. Caught and jailed in Chicago, Honey Bear sweet-talked his way into a trip to the hospital, pulled out a look-alike .25-caliber pistol he carved out of a blackened bar of soap, and escaped wearing a guard's uniform. Ten days later, he was recaptured as he slept in a stolen car parked in a rest area along Interstate 70 in central Ohio and was extradited to California.

In 1992 he was convicted for the triple murder, but during the penalty phase of the trial the jury deadlocked 11–1 in favor of life in prison without the possibility of parole instead of the death penalty. The judge declared a mistrial. And despite the lopsided vote for life, the district attorney decided to retry the penalty phase of Vincent Bruce's murder trial.

While locked up in L.A. County Jail for seven years during his legal battles, Honey Bear earned a high-risk K-10 (keep away from all other inmates) status. Deputies identified him as *the* head Crip gangster in their 20,000-population facility.

Jailers said that Honey Bear operated a gambling pool, trafficked drugs, was caught with weapons, and tried to kill at least two other inmates. An attorney close to the case said that Bruce was such a risk to jail staff and other inmates that the DA's office believed that the best place for him was the gas chamber.

Honey Bear, wearing a pressed gray suit and tie and looking very much the part, acted as his own attorney (pro per) during the penalty phase retrial. But it was not his articulate manner and seemingly professional demeanor in court that shocked authorities as much as his witness list. He was granted removal orders for twenty-two inmates to testify on his behalf. It was a collection of murderers, escape artists, drug dealers, and ruthless prison gang members.

James Owens, an unassuming but battle-ready county counsel who had spent nearly a decade working with pro per inmates, saw a red flag: "When you see that number of people come down, you get real suspicious." He knew that prison gang members such as John Stinson and Rene Enriquez had for years abused their pro per status by calling down other nefarious inmates to kill or be killed or to participate in prison gang powwows. "They are living a life that is a big game, and they play it day to day," stressed Owens. "And they see how far they can push the game. And how far they can bend the rules."

On the other hand, Honey Bear called any suggestion that he was abusing the pro per system as "totally BS and propaganda." He simply wanted jurors to understand that, in the violent prison environment, "there is a different set of rules that he has to live under." The crooks on his witness list could help show that.

Prominent on that list were nine inmates housed in maximum-security at Pelican Bay State Prison. Aside from Boxer, Cuate Grajeda, Indio Carlos, and John Stinson, they included:

- Eulalio "Lalo" Martinez—a validated Mexican Mafia member doing forty-three years for robbery and assault and well known "for possession of shanks."

- Gilbert "Lil Mo" Ruiz—a validated Mexican Mafia member doing twenty years for manslaughter.
- Jimmy "Smokey" Sanchez—a validated Mexican Mafia member doing thirty-seven-to-life for murder.
- Maurice "Lil Man" or "Vamp" Jones—a member of Eight-Tray Gangster Crips and an associate of the Black Guerilla Family doing life plus twenty-five years for multiple murders, and a well-known "problem child" when he was incarcerated at Men's Central Jail.
- Floyd "Askari" Nelson—a validated associate of the Rolling 60s Crips and Black Guerilla Family doing sixteen months for being a felon in possession of a firearm and known for inciting and leading riots while in jail.

These nine convicts, noted county counsel, were also responsible for a combined seven attacks on deputies and twenty-five assaults on other inmates, including two murders, during previous stays at Men's Central Jail.

The county counsel filed a motion with the court asking for "security measures as may be appropriate" and further stated:

1. Each individual is a demonstrated threat to court room security.
2. The inmates housed in the Security Housing Unit at Pelican Bay State Prison are significant risk for escape, as well as violence on staff and other inmates, and are significantly more dangerous than state prison witnesses housed in other facilities. Expediting the testimony of these inmates and directing their immediate return to state prison would greatly enhance the security measures in both courtroom and jail.

Los Angeles County sheriff's deputy Rodney Elliott was a jail intelligence officer who prepared an affidavit describing the nine Pelican Bay inmate-witnesses for the judge: "Obviously, they are the worst of the worst we have in society, and the worst we have in custody."

The motion was granted by L.A. Superior Court judge John Ouderkirk, and the groundwork was laid for Operation Pelican Drop.

"Vincent Bruce had respect across the board," said Boxer. "He would allow us to stab certain black troublemakers without retaliation because he respected us [Eme]." So Boxer was fine with traveling to Los Angeles to testify for him and try to keep Honey Bear out of the gas chamber. It wasn't all that unusual for crooks to testify for other crooks—even to lie on the stand if necessary. However, Boxer swore that he never lied under oath. There was another reason to make the trip. He felt that he could meet with some other Mafiosi during the trip and discuss Black Hand business.

At six o'clock in the morning of August 28, 1995, he stood in the reception center at Wasco State Prison near Bakersfield. Everyone was given a sack lunch and some coffee. A long bus ride on the Gray Goose had transported him and the others from Pelican Bay to Folsom the day before, and then on down to Wasco. He was talking to the prison institutional gang investigator (IGI), Jerry Negrette, about maybe celling up with Cuate Grajeda. He and Cuate were "smiling enemies," and he knew why Grajeda had volunteered to be his cellmate.

"All right, I'll cell up with you," he told Cuate. "Come on, if you want to talk, we'll talk."

Boxer knew the ritual. If he said no to Cuate, he'd be branded a coward. He also knew what he'd do if he and Grajeda did end up in the same cell. He'd done it before with other cellmates. When he settled in, he'd take his shank out of "the safe," wash it off in the sink, and set it down somewhere within Cuate's reach. Then he'd turn his back as if everything was normal, knowing Grajeda might grab it and stick him with it. "I'm always scared to do it. I don't like it," explained Boxer. "But I do it, just to test myself, and see what a potential adversary would do. It's a scary feeling. I call that testing your mettle." He was sure Cuate wanted to test his mettle, and he wasn't going to disappoint him.

Suddenly, Officer Negrette said, "No." It wasn't necessary to cell up with anyone at Wasco. "You're not going to be here that long. A special transportation unit is on its way."

Meanwhile, the gang investigators had asked the Mafia guys to drop their shirts so they could take pictures of tattoos. It was always the same routine at every prison. "The gang officers want to rub elbows with you."

"Go ahead," said Boxer.

Still, something didn't seem quite right as midmorning approached. Then he saw them pound into the room. They were all wearing badges, protective vests, and riot gear, filing in six deep in British green jumpsuits, big cops, buffed out and physically fit, buzz haircuts with sideburns, and dark glasses hiding their eyes. "You could just tell by their look," said Boxer, "these were the alpha male killer types, the pistoleers. They looked at us, and I knew they were trouble."

There were two teams, three men on each team, from the L.A. County Sheriff's Department Special Enforcement Bureau. Others were there from the Sheriff's Department Transportation Bureau to prepare the necessary paperwork and place the red K-10 (high-risk) wristbands on the nine inmates awaiting transport.

The cops surrounded the crooks in their holding cells, took them aside one by one, stripped them naked, did a visual body cavity search, and redressed them in prison garb and chains. First there was a waist chain, then a bandoleer-type chain across the chest, and finally handcuffs and leg chains. As if that weren't enough, their forearms were attached to the waist chains with plastic flex cuffs.

Boxer made a slight protest, telling them it was "kind of uncomfortable." In reality, it hurt.

He was assured in an evasive manner, "Don't worry. It's just a short drive."

At the same time, Boxer was trying to figure out exactly what was going on. *Where are they going to put us?* he wondered to himself. *Maybe they're going to chain-gang us one in front of the other on the bus.*

Then a CDC officer explained, "They have a helicopter waiting for you guys."

At that point, the inmates became rather excited. Cool! A helicopter ride—that was new. It might be kind of fun. It wasn't.

One by one they were hustled into one of two big white vans staged just outside the door. Waiting in an open field two hundred yards away were two green-and-white Sikorski helicopters emblazoned with the Sheriff's Department name and logo, fired up and ready to fly. Already up in the air were two smaller choppers to be used as chase aircraft for added security.

CDC officers escorted each convict—again one by one—into one of the waiting helicopters. Two SEB deputies stood outside the chopper doors, armed with assault rifles. There were CDC marksmen hidden in the bushes and on rooftops in tactical positions with rifles ready to fire. Others nearby had stun guns and looks on their faces that assured the inmates the weapons weren't just for show.

Boxer's body continued to ache from the pain of the restraints. From the van he could only see each inmate disappear inside the helicopter door. Then there was a tug on his arm. His turn was next. At the door of the helicopter, a deputy turned him and slowly backed him into a row of seats inside. Once seated, the deputies put pads over each eye and used tape to hold them in place. A blindfold was placed over that so that the inmate couldn't see enough to launch an attack on anyone. Additional plastic flex cuffs were tied around the knees and ankles. A strap was added that reached from the chest chain to an anchor on the floor, forcing the inmate into a slightly forward-bending position.

Four inmates were in one helicopter and five in the other. They were seated across from each other and were unable to communicate because the engine noise drowned out any attempt to talk.

Boxer could still see slightly enough out of the corner of one eye to make out a deputy standing in the cockpit with a submachine gun. "These guys," he was convinced, "wanted us to understand who was in charge." In fact, there were three heavily armed Special Enforcement Bureau deputies on each flight.

Why not just drive us to L.A.? wondered Boxer. *Maybe they're just hovering a few feet off the ground to disorient the cons?* He was in fact confused. Then the helicopter banked a bit, and again out of the corner of his eye he could see mountains and little lakes in the distance. They were on their way to Los Angeles.

To say the hourlong flight was uncomfortable is like saying a trip to the dentist to get a root canal really isn't so bad. After they arrived at the heliport atop the new Century Regional Detention Facility, deputies cut off the flex cuffs, and then everyone was deplaned one by one. Boxer could barely walk when he got off the chopper. A few of the inmates had to be gently assisted in order to climb out of the aircraft.

Still blindfolded and chained, the inmates were each given an armed escort into the jail. Deputies from the security team, with big guns and bulletproof vests, were on the rooftop and all over the place. "Every time we moved we saw sharpshooters," Boxer noted, and there was no doubt in his mind "that they would shoot us."

Inside, the nine inmates were rolled down a long corridor in wheelchairs to speed up the operation—the ankle irons slowed everyone down when they were on foot. Each prisoner was placed in a single cell on module 1600, separated from all the other inmates during their entire thirteen-day stay. It seemed like hours before their cuffs were removed. Their arms, hands, and ankles were swollen from lack of circulation. Eventually, everyone was again photographed and fingerprinted. Additionally, there were cameras on tripods recording every move they made. A clear Plexiglas wall cordoned off the end of their unit, not wire mesh. Then a nylon hospital screen was pulled across the entry so inmates couldn't see out.

There was a stationary bicycle they could take turns on for exercise.

Deputies didn't enter the area without a protective vest and without one of them carrying a .40-millimeter block gun that fired less than lethal wooden or plastic bullets.

When it came time to go to court, or anytime they were allowed out of their cell, the inmate-witnesses were required to wear a "react belt"—a security device that gave an inmate ten seconds to comply with an order before an electrical charge shot through his body like a streak of lightning. On the day he was to testify, the prisoner was transported alone in a sheriff's bus. At least three security escort cars were on constant lookout for trouble. Inside the Criminal Courts Building, three deputies escorted each prisoner to and from court. As many as eleven deputies were in the courtroom at any given time during the penalty phase retrial. The judge banned all cameras as inmates were chained inside the witness box during their testimony.

Despite these massive security procedures, cops found a ten-inch jail-made shank in Cuate Grajeda's cell. It was crafted from a toilet fixture and found under his mattress. Also, investigators uncovered a map that described the location of actor-director Edward James Olmos's house, confirming suspicions at that time that the Hollywood figure was on the Eme hit list for his indiscretions in making the movie *American Me*.

Boxer Enriquez actually took the witness stand and refuted a jail deputy's testimony by saying that Honey Bear "didn't make any spontaneous confession" to another inmate about a jailhouse stabbing. Thirteen days after it all began—as planned—sheriff's deputies expedited the trip back to Pelican Bay. This time the inmate-witnesses went on a special bus. It looked like a tractor-trailer cattle truck with three levels of seating, armed guards stationed up front, surveillance cameras stationed around the vehicle, and dark paper taped over the windows so no one could see out. The inmates stopped over for one night at Corcoran State Prison near Bakersfield. The same restraints were used again, only this time the nine prisoners had their bodies firmly pressed against the chair because they were chained to the back of their seat belts, with their feet chained to the post underneath the seat. "So we were bolted back—it was worse," complained Boxer. "By the time I got off that bus I had to be assisted. It was bad. I was praying to God to let the ride be over soon. Someone on the bus actually had tears in his eyes.

"It was announced, 'Twenty more minutes.'

"Then someone would ask again, 'How much longer?' The answer came, 'Fifteen more minutes.' It seemed endless. Every minute was killing me. It hurt so badly. John Stinson had to be carried off that bus. When they cut the plastic cuts off, there were welts on our skin. The marks were so deep it was close to cutting through the flesh. I swore up and down that I would never do another transfer to court."

So perhaps the gambit by the CDC and the L.A. County judicial system paid off. One law enforcement source involved in Operation Pelican Drop said, "Mission accomplished." Nearly a dozen deadly, hard-core prisoners—housed and transported under a heavy security blanket—came and went with no assaults on innocent civilians, deputies, or other inmates. And maybe hard-core prison gang members in the future would think twice before abusing the pro per system by subpoenaing large numbers of inmates across the state—while planning secret skullduggery. Maybe.

Sheriff's coordinators said it cost $12,000 to bus the inmates from Pelican Bay and back, another $16,000 for the helicopter transport, and an estimated $15,000 in security manpower just for the three days the Pelican Bay contingent was in court. Total costs—adding in other expenses for the entire thirteen-day stay—were estimated at more than $100,000.

"It was persuasive," according to Boxer Enriquez more than a decade later.

On the morning of November 7, 1995, Vincent "Honey Bear" Bruce was sitting in the same courtroom with a folder of legal briefs in his lap as a deputy removed his handcuffs. Weeks earlier, he had prevailed, convincing a jury to vote 12–0 for life in prison instead of the death penalty. It will never be clear if testimony from any of the Pelican Bay witnesses actually helped his case. In the end, the court in rare cases can overturn a jury recommendation for death, but has no choice but to accept a jury's recommendation of life in prison.

Judge John Ouderkirk didn't waste any time: "This court recommends that Mr. Bruce never be released from prison." That statement was made shortly after the judge sentenced Honey Bear to three consecutive terms of life in prison without the possibility of parole. The judge went on: "Mr. Bruce is an accomplished confidence man who is capable of regulating his mood, attitude, and emotions to attain his goals. Mr. Bruce used tears to great effect before the jury, and on more than one occasion the court watched him work himself into an apparent emotional state." Ouderkirk wasn't finished yet: "Mr. Bruce is an intelligent and thoroughly evil person who has a capacity to hide behind many masks to achieve his selfish goals. He should never get loose on the world of decent people again."

On this occasion, there was not a drip of moisture emanating from Honey Bear's tear ducts. He showed no emotion as he stood, grabbed his legal folder, and walked out the door as if he had a case in another court-room. The rattle of his ankle chains told the truth. This thirty-three-year-old Crip gangster was headed back to prison forever.

Rene "Boxer" Enriquez, the same age and sitting in his cell back at PBSP after Operation Pelican Drop, was convinced that he would "never go to court again. It was so disconcerting and uncomfortable."

CHAPTER 24

Calling the Shots from Prison

BOXER LANGUISHED AT PBSP FOR NINE LONG YEARS BUT ALWAYS fought to keep up a tough, enduring Mafioso image. There was simply no place for the weak or timid at the Bay, and no way to keep lucrative Eme operations alive in the street without constant communications. It was only through visits and mail that he was still able to call shots on the streets of southern California—eight hundred miles away. Here's how it worked.

A key to good communications was a regular schedule of prison visitors. Boxer had one "trusted confidante" who visited him three hundred times at Pelican Bay between December 1993 and April 2002. That averages out to one visit every eleven days. All visits for SHU inmates are noncontact visits. The prisoner sits in a small secure cell and speaks to the visitor, on the other side of a Plexiglas divider, via telephone. During those visits, Boxer discussed all kinds of mob business, and he could use the visits to send messages to any other gangster back on the street.

Code words are often used to circumvent staff monitoring of the conversation. Mafiosi call it "carnival talk." For example, explained Boxer, "I need to talk about a crew member paying a specific amount of money. I'd say, 'How is everything at home?' The visitor would say, 'Fine, Jorge came by last month and helped me in the garden. He planted four rosebushes and says he will come back every month to help me maintain the yard.' To a person monitoring this conversation, it might sound as if it's a talk about gardening. To me, it means Jorge came by and paid four hundred dollars last month and will do the same each month." There were all kinds of code phrases. "The girls" were crew members. "Go to dinner" was a meeting. "Personal favor" meant a hit or an assault. "Needs help" stood for providing drugs or money. Also, each crew member had a code name to protect his identity.

Various forms of improvised sign language are also used. "We all study American Sign Language in Eme," explained Boxer. "Most understand some form of sign language. There are signs for money, drugs, dead, hit, and so forth." Sign language is used to avoid being recorded by correctional officers monitoring visits.

Notes are another frequently used method of passing secret information to a visitor. The message is secreted in a body cavity to avoid detection, removed during the visit, and held up against the Plexiglas window for the visitor to read.

"It's impossible to stop," claimed Enriquez. "In that visiting room every weekend there are crew instructions going out, hits are being ordered, money laundering is discussed, racketeering. Any crime you can imagine is being planned in that visiting room on a regular basis."

U.S. mail is essential to communication for those locked up at Pelican Bay. "We are able to correspond with anyone," insisted Boxer, "and conduct mob business. One method is jokingly referred to as 'Project X.' We understand mail to Eme members is often flagged for special inspection by an institutional gang investigator. To avoid this, we write out a letter and hand it off to another inmate in our pod, let's say a Mafia associate named Flaco Ramirez. He copies the exact letter in his own hand, signs his name, and sends it to the person I'm trying to reach out on the street. The recipient by prearrangement knows that the letter is really coming from Boxer Enriquez. The recipient answers the letter, sends it back to Flaco, and Flaco hands it back to me at Pelican Bay. The prison staff never sees it, not knowing the communication is really between me and some other mobster. The mail system is one of the best things in the world for the Mexican Mafia."

Prison regulations also prohibit inmates from one institution from writing to an inmate at another penitentiary. A "third-party mail drop" is frequently used to breach this security rule. "It's not all that sophisticated," explained Enriquez, "but it works. For instance, I want to write to a Mafia member at San Quentin State Prison. I'm not allowed to do that. So instead, I write the letter to a third person at their home in Los Angeles. That person opens the letter, places it in another envelope, addresses it to the carnal at San Quentin, and drops it in the mail. So it goes from a Mafioso in one prison to a Mafioso in another prison, again circumventing Corrections Department security regulations." Every Mafia member has multiple third-party addresses at his disposal—people the Mafia can use to communicate with each other. Boxer had third-party addresses not only in California but in Kansas, New Mexico, and Arizona.

It is "legal mail" that is a tremendous bane to CDC efforts to stop mob communications. Under Title 15 of California Department of Corrections regulations, prison staff are prohibited from reading all correspondence or legal documents sent by an attorney. Guards are only allowed to check the envelope, folder, or package for contraband—eyeball it and shake it out. After that cursory procedure, they are required to hand it over to the inmate. Boxer said, "The Mafia actually pays some attorneys to act as fronts, sending blatant messages ordering murder and mayhem. Some lawyers do it because they get caught up in the mystique of La Eme, its influence or power. Others are just unwitting dupes. In any event, we [Eme] have no worries at all about authorities intercepting this kind of communication [legal mail] because we understand it is protected by law."

Highly sensitive Mafia information is also often sent from prison to the streets in yet another manner—by parolee. An inmate who is being released on parole is given a handwritten message to deliver. He wraps it in water-sealed plastic and either swallows it or secretes it in his rectum. The latter option is often called putting it "in the safe." At times, the parolee is trusted to give the message by word of mouth. "But most of the time," according to Enriquez, "you write it in your own hand because then the person who receives it understands, without a doubt, I am the person who wrote it. It came out of Pelican Bay from Eme's Boxer Enriquez."

An actual letter from a carnal is often an endorsement for a certain drug dealer, akin to a letter of safe passage, to sell narcotics in a certain territory. The dealer uses it to ward off other crooks attempting to extort him.

Boxer found that his Mexican Mafia reputation was like a franchise. He said, "Gang-related drug dealers used my name on the streets to deal and protect their interests under the specter of La Eme. And those dealers in turn always kicked back some of the profits to me."

The main one was "Huck," who was originally from a little hangout gang called Street Boyz. He was a short, stocky guy with thick black eyebrows, a bushy mustache to match, and a full head of hair. Huck began by cooking up methamphetamine and selling it wholesale to drug dealers. Eventually, he was selling not only meth but substantial quantities of cocaine, ecstasy, and marijuana—damn near everything. It was hard to guess that he and his friends were criminals. Dressed in hip-hop clothes and driving around in small Euro automobiles, they didn't look the part. Huck drove an expensive BMW and a Cadillac Escalade, not exactly cholo cars. His operation made hundreds of thousands of dollars and expanded into stolen cars and guns and even counterfeit money. The profits allowed him to live in a nice home in suburban Whittier and open a custom rim business and a diesel truck repair shop with his brother. There was even a warehouse with big block letters on the pull-down, metal-corrugated door that read, BEWARE OF HUCK, and he wasn't kidding.

Enriquez met Huck when he got out on parole in 1989 and was staying in Boyle Heights. His mother Lupe—years after her divorce—had a relationship with Huck's dad, and so his son was always hanging around her place. Boxer decided to take him along to rip off a drug dealer for some pocket change. Huck wasn't quite sixteen and always carried a gun. He drove the Mafioso's big, silver, four-door 1980 Cadillac Seville as Boxer sat in the passenger seat with a sawed-off, 12-gauge Mossberg shotgun with a pistol grip. Pulling up in front of the house, Boxer ran inside, and forced the mark at gunpoint to lie down on the floor. Then Boxer, with his finger on the trigger and a round in the chamber, leaned over with the shotgun to clean out the dealer's pockets, and the weapon went off accidentally—*boom!* The round ripped a hole in the floor about the size of a baseball. The sound of the blast scared Enriquez more than it did the victim. Still, he grabbed the guy's dope supply and a small amount of cash and headed for the getaway car. He threw the shotgun into the backseat, hopped in, and told Huck, "Drive!"

Little Huck stepped on the gas and squirmed all over the road as he strained to see over the steering wheel and make a not so elegant escape. He looked scared to death.

"Pull the damn car over!" ordered Boxer.

Huck looked up with eyes as big as the open end of the shotgun barrel. "Did you kill him?"

"No! I didn't kill him. The gun went off by accident."

Nearly five years later, it was no accident that Huck, not quite twenty-one years old, ended up an accomplished crook. There was one problem. Black Dan Barela and a few other carnales were trying to shake him down for some of his profits, and they weren't being congenial about it.

Huck reached out to his old mentor Boxer Enriquez for help, and it worked for both of them. Enriquez convinced Black Dan and others that Lopez was his nephew and told them to leave him and his operation alone. So Huck started calling him "Tio," Spanish for "uncle," and that soon became a street code word for Mexican Mafia members along with the terms "big homeys" and *pilli*. Eme-affiliated contacts such as Huck were then often referred to as *sobrinos,* or nephews.

Huck started paying Boxer about $750 a month to basically use his name. Lopez went around town saying, "I'm here for Boxer Enriquez," or, "This is for Boxer." And if he was ever questioned by another big homey or someone else with more clout than he had, Huck would say, "I'm going up to the Bay to see him this weekend. Do you want me to discuss it with him?" Generally, no one messed with Huck—not even other carnales. "I was his insured safety," explained Boxer, "his protector."

It was the same for "Toker," from the Chivas neighborhood in Artesia. He too was a young gangster Boxer met once, years earlier, while visiting an old homeboy. Toker wrote to him that he was running into "the Wall." "The Wall" was a derogatory nickname for a woman who ran a crew for Eme member Juan "China Boy" Arias of Artesia. China Boy was six years younger than Boxer and in federal prison. The Wall, only in her twenties, invoked China Boy's name and thought she was running the streets. She had a menacing crew of armed gang members and insisted that no one could deal drugs in the Artesia area without paying her an unreasonable sum. The Arias family also owned a bar called the Galleon, which was a hangout for Artesia gang members. The Wall was also referred to as "the Queen Bee" because of her imperious attitude. Enriquez, you might say, upset her beehive.

First, he asked for a "sit-down"—a meeting between a few of his crew members and the Queen Bee and her homeboys. Everyone was heavily armed. Boxer's crew carried the message that he expected "professional courtesy in his endeavors." In other words, stay out of his way. The Queen Bee stood her ground—Chivas, Artesia, Norwalk, and Hawaiian Gardens were her territory. She said she owed Enriquez nothing. That was a mistake.

A messenger came to Pelican Bay to relay what happened at the meeting. Boxer had killed for the mob, taken a life sentence, earned his rank, and was not going to let some woman—even if she was close to a Mafioso—make the rules, especially in the neighborhood where he had his gangster roots. Enriquez felt that China Boy was a made guy mainly because of his drug-dealing talents. He was no killer, no real mob guy by old-school standards, and Boxer was ready to have the Queen Bee exterminated.

It wouldn't be necessary. Enriquez didn't want to start a war that might alienate other Eme members he might need as political allies down the road. Kites went out to Mafia heavyweights on the streets and in prison.

"Look," demanded Boxer, "this is wrong." A woman should not be running Mafia business. Word finally came from Topo Peters: Boxer could do what he wanted. The Queen Bee was left alive, but Enriquez prevailed.

In the end, Toker joined Boxer's crew and ran the Artesia-Norwalk area for him. He sent $1,000 a month up to Pelican Bay.

Rooster, Fat Pete, and Richie Rincon of Artesia-Chivas—prolific cocaine-dealing brothers who had profits invested in their own auto body and repair shops—also tried to restrict Toker's drug selling in that area. Enriquez had Rooster beaten with a golf club, and he wasn't cock-a-doodle-doing much after that: he lost the sight in one of his battered eyes. He and his brothers ended up paying tribute to Boxer and became part of his network of crews.

Enriquez never demanded a set percentage. He told his expanding crew, "Treat me as you would want to be treated if you were in my position." The relative fairness of his system spurred its growth. All drug dealers and gangsters—under the new Mexican Mafia "program"—had to pay La Eme a "tax." Boxer figured he'd get more and more of them willing to pay him, instead of others, by keeping the payments reasonable. "I wanted to be seen as a drug dealer–friendly organization," he said with a wry smile.

Actually, he made only blue-collar money—$40,000 to $60,000 a year, maybe $80,000 in an especially good year. But for a man in prison for the rest of his life, it wasn't just about big bucks. "It's not the money in your wallet," he theorized. "The wealth is in the strength of your crews." Power and influence were what he craved. He explained, "I know I can say any-time that I need $5,000, a car, or gifts for my family. Boom! It will be done. I need that guy killed. And it was done efficiently."

Huck became his overall crew chief who collected the money on the twenty-fifth of every month and forwarded it to Pelican Bay.

Most serious communications were done through the "trusted confidante" who made those three hundred visits to Pelican Bay from December 1993 through April 2002 and relayed orders back to Huck. There were also kites shipped out secretly and regular old U.S. mail. The operation grew and grew.

Brothers from the Eastside Clover gang oversaw a crew in Lincoln Heights, another community that borders East Los Angeles. The brothers came aboard after Huck kidnapped one of them, stuck a gun down his throat, and robbed him of some cocaine, cash, and a truck. Huck went back for a 1965 Chevy show car and stole that too. Henry complained that the collector automobile had sentimental value and he wanted it returned. Enriquez let him buy his own car back for $3,500. The Sanchez boys sold cocaine and marijuana and once on board paid Boxer another $500 a month.

Gennie was a drug dealer in San Bernardino, a rapidly growing bedroom city sixty miles east of Los Angeles. She ran her operation out of a bar called Los Campos, and some thugs falsely claiming to be Eme associates were shaking her down. Boxer found out about her plight from another Mafia member and decided to take advantage. He sent an invading crew to the rival extortionist's house and had him beaten, robbed, and warned—to stop harassing her or anyone else at the bar. After that, Gennie's crew was good for another $300 a month.

"Caballo" of Artesia-Chivas was a prolific methamphetamine cook whose operation produced several pounds of "crank" a week. He sold pounds of marijuana as well. Boxer said Caballo once killed a man who shot and wounded his son. He ran a crew of other meth cooks and paid Enriquez $500 a month for protection.

Caballo and Fat Pete Rincon sliced up a bar owner named Benjamin "Amin" Castro and extorted him for $7,500 and a car. The vehicle went to Enriquez, who signed it over to a crew member who had just been released from prison and had no car. Amin dealt methamphetamine out of the Golden Dragon, a tavern he operated in the Highland Park area northeast of Los Angeles. It was a haven for criminal activity, and Boxer ended up with a partnership in the joint. A drug dealer on Amin's crew was actually a female deputy sheriff, and she owed him money. Enriquez took care of that too. He sent a crew to invade her house. They beat her up, fired a random shot to scare the hell out of her, and collected the unpaid debt. Amin paid regularly.

Old stand-by heroin dealer Flo was still good for $400 a month, and so was Twisting Jenny.

A Mexican national drug dealer named Nacho from Sinaloa paid $500 a month like clockwork, even if he was back in Mexico for a visit.

Three gangsters out of the Huntington Park area—Speedy, Lazy, and Daniel—even kicked back $150 a month to Boxer for using his name to deal drugs on a couple of prison yards.

Shady and Boy, who ran a crew from the Lennox area of South Los Angeles, were both good for another $500 a month. Shady initially paid Boxer a $40,000 "tribute" for Mafia protection of his operation on the streets.

"Snoop," a crew member and "earner" who operated out of 190's territory as well as Cerritos and Norwalk, owned a landscaping company he bought and used to launder his Eme-gained drug profits. Snoop also paid tribute to Boxer.

Again, the money wasn't huge, but it accumulated nicely. It wasn't long before Boxer had tens of thousands moving through the bank. An inmate at Pelican Bay could only spend thirty-five dollars a month at the prison store. There were no expenses at PBSP. The state took care of everything. "So it's a wonderful little scam," said Enriquez. "A wonderful little scam."

Boxer Enriquez eventually had crews working for him in cities all around the greater Los Angeles area, including Artesia, Azusa, Bell Gardens, Cerritos, downtown Los Angeles, East Los Angeles, Hawaiian Gardens, Lennox, Lincoln Heights, Norwalk, Palmdale, Pico Rivera, Riverside, Sante Fe Springs, Victorville, and Whittier.

At the same time these dealers were paying Boxer a "tax" on their profits, they were also encouraged to buy all their dope from Huck. It was the plan Boxer had envisioned for the Mafia from the time he and other carnales first started organizing all the gang meetings a few years earlier. "Our objective is twofold. To become the wellhead, we [La Eme] supply the oil [dope]. Plus, we tax the gas pump [the dealers]. We supply. We tax. So we're making money from the well and the pump."

In reality, Boxer knew that the crew bosses, known as "ballers" or "high-rollers," made the real money—six- to seven-figure incomes. They lived in their own homes, had plenty of cash, and drove luxury cars and SUVs fixed up with all the extras. "I am the low-end earner," noted Enriquez. "It's trickle-up economics, not trickle-down." At the same time, the program was expanding the reach of the Mexican Mafia. "We are creating a righteous organized crime group," explained Boxer, "with multiple crews and multiple net groups overseen by other Mafiosi in different territories. That is the true objective. Look toward the future."

Brutality was always the preferred method used to keep detractors in line. Even crew chiefs such as Toker sometimes needed a reminder. He drove a late-model SUV, his wife bought a new Infinity, and he moved into a new house. "This guy was making big money on my name," insisted Boxer, "and all I was asking for was little tidbits." Yet Toker had a bad habit of periodically not paying his taxes. On one occasion, Huck's crew had to tune him up with a little fists-to-the-face action, and still he would "slow-poke" on his payments. Finally, Huck and company paid him a distinctly memorable visit. It wasn't for the squeamish. Two of Toker's fingers were slowly bent back farther and farther until there was no more give. There was a snapping sound as the bones broke, accompanied by a shriek of unmistakable pain.

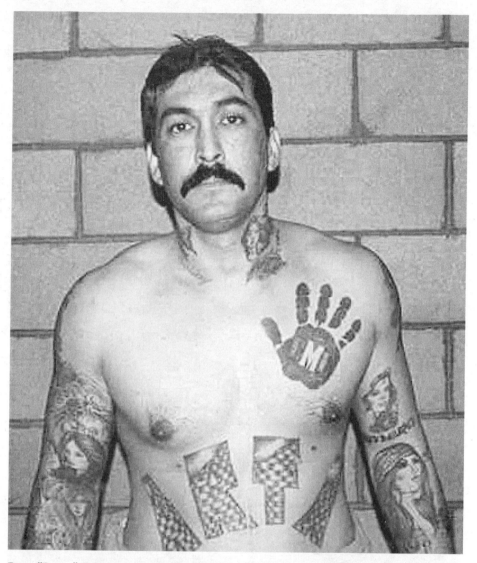

Rene "Boxer" Enriquez at Wasco State Prison in 1997 (in transit from Pelican Bay to the Mafia RICO trial in Los Angeles) with the Black Hand tattoo prominently displayed on his chest as an advertisement to other inmates that he is a member of the Mexican Mafia. The word "ARTA" on his stomach is short for his original street gang, Artesia 13.

Rene at the age of about fourteen had already been jumped into Artesia 13 despite warnings from his father to "stay away from those hoodlums." By this age he was a hard-core user of PCP, had a lucrative business selling the drug to other junior high students, and often woke up in a drug-induced haze.

John (Rene's little brother), Rene at age eight, and Rene's nephew Albert Provencio together at their grandmother's house in Boyle Heights, a neighborhood east of downtown Los Angeles that is heavily influenced by a large street gang called White Fence.

Lupe and John Enriquez, Rene's parents, in 1974, in a warm moment during their fifteenth year of a stormy marriage.

Rene and his mother, Lupe, in 1985 during a visit at California's Folsom Prison shortly after Rene became a member of the Mexican Mafia, also known as La Eme.

Boxer Enriquez *(top right)* at the Folsom Prison Armory in 1985 shortly after he became a member of the Mexican Mafia. One of his mentors was Eme's Raymond "Huero Shy" Shryock *(back row, second from left)*. All six inmates in the picture are homeboys from Boxer's original neighborhood gang, Artesia 13, including Sammy "Negro" Villalba *(lower right)*.

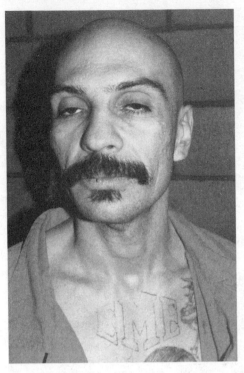

Described by an FBI agent as a "stone killer," Mexican Mafia hit man Jose "Bat" Marquez, EME tattooed on his chest, bragged to other carnales that his exploits on both sides of the U.S./Mexican border were "like James Bond."

Some of the sixty-one firearms found in a Tijuana warehouse when Mexican police finally arrested Bat Marquez on November 22, 2003. The arsenal included automatic assault rifles, shotguns, handguns, and an array of killer knives. There were bulletproof vests, police shirts and caps, and evidence of a torture room with handcuffs.

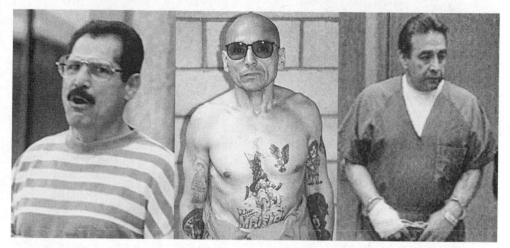

Daniel "Black Dan" Barela, one of Boxer's mentors, read the Bible every day but had a "kill-first-talk-about-it-later attitude," according to one gang detective.

La Eme member Salvador "Mon" Buenrostro, MAFIA tattooed on his stomach, bad-mouthed de facto La Eme boss Joe Morgan and was stabbed twenty-six times in the attorney room at the L.A. County Jail.

Benjamin "Topo" Peters shouted, "Die like a man, you punk!" as he and Boxer Enriquez carried out the jailhouse hit on Mon Buenrostro. Topo is seen here during a court appearance following the attack. His right hand is bandaged because of a knife wound.

Joe Morgan, a murderous jailhouse legend, joined La Eme at the age of forty and within a few years was dubbed the "Godfather." He lost his leg during a robbery and that earned him the nickname "Peg Leg." No one dared call him that to his face.

Jacques "Jacko" Padilla, EME tattooed on his chest, was a cellmate who Boxer describes as "a ruthless businessman and a great thug, but he never was a killer."

Gilbert "Lil Mo" Ruiz was sponsored for membership in La Eme by Boxer, who said Lil Mo "didn't hesitate to kill when you asked him."

Darryl "Night Owl" Baca was a tall, heavily muscled carnal from Artesia 13. Boxer cut him in on his business enterprises and the two ended up trying to kill each other.

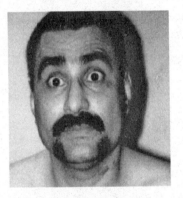

Ruben "Tupi" Hernandez plotted to take over the Godfather spot in the Mexican Mafia, became an unbearable "nutcase," and ended up getting stabbed seventeen times by other carnales in a federal lockup.

Daniel "Cuate" Grajeda, a dangerous, black-hearted, murderous, self-professed Mafia fanatic, prayed to Aztec gods and became Boxer's nemesis.

Examples of drugs smuggled into Pelican Bay State Prison, a maximum security penitentiary in California. Strips of cellophane-wrapped marijuana secreted inside a row of Ritz crackers, tar heroin ironed out and plastered inside the pages of a legal document, and other narcotics pressed inside a pack of Chips Ahoy cookies.

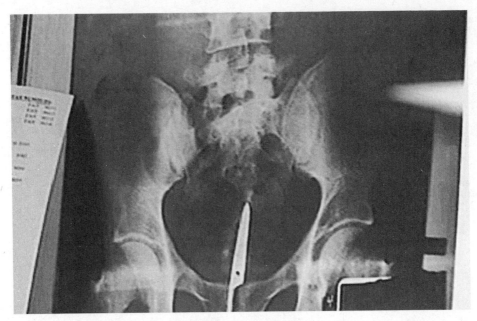

An X-ray photo of a jailhouse knife secreted, or keistered, in an inmate's rectum. Boxer never left his cell without carrying a weapon in this manner. It was a matter of survival.

This inmate at the L.A. County Jail was stabbed more than four dozen times by camaradas and left for dead. His body was wrapped in a sheet and stuck under a cell bunk. His death was ordered by La Eme's Ernest "Chuco" Castro—upset because the victim had pulled a gun on him out on the street.

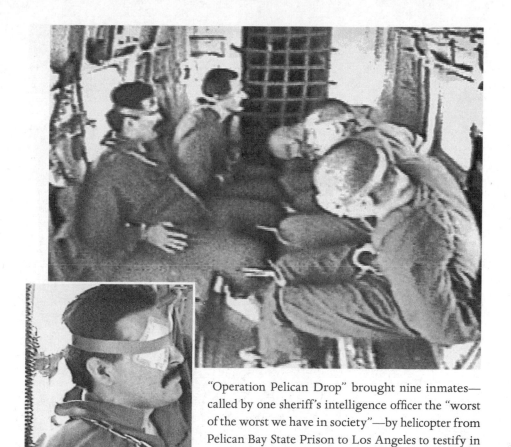

"Operation Pelican Drop" brought nine inmates—called by one sheriff's intelligence officer the "worst of the worst we have in society"—by helicopter from Pelican Bay State Prison to Los Angeles to testify in a murder trial. The "high risk" inmates, including Boxer Enriquez, were waist-chained, leg-chained, handcuffed, bandoleer-chained across the chest, blindfolded, and chained to the floor of the helicopter.

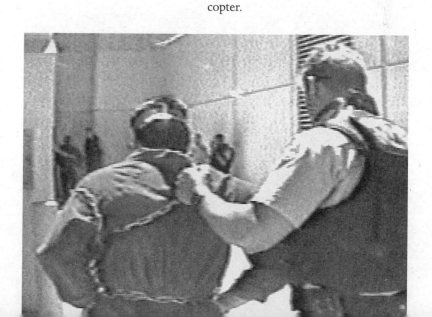

Packs of Sureno inmates are seen stabbing blacks in the biggest riot in the history of Pelican Bay State Prison. It broke out on February 23, 2000, sparked by racial tensions and sanctioned by two La Eme members. Forty inmates were injured, most by stab wounds. Guards after the riot found an unprecedented eighty-nine shanks dropped on the yard.

Fifteen inmates were injured by gunfire from guard towers and thirty-three-year-old Miguel "Sharky" Sanchez died in a pool of his own blood after taking a round in the head while attacking a black inmate with a mob of Sureno gang members. Surenos were ordered to keep stabbing even if guards fired live ammunition. One inmate explained, "It's always you do, or be done."

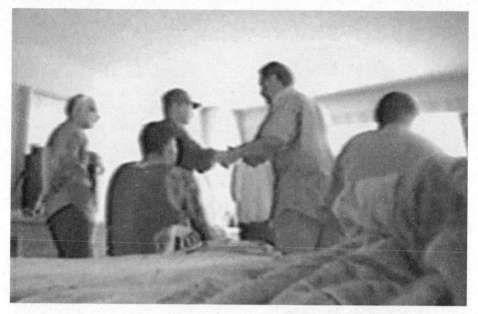

Luis "Pelon" Maciel *(wearing baseball cap)*, the orchestrator of the Maxson Road murders, is inducted into the Mexican Mafia by a dozen other carnales meeting in a southern California motel room.

Huero Shy Shryock *(left)*, who ordered the Maxson Road murders and is by reputation responsible for as many as one hundred hits, walks the streets of El Monte with Pelon Maciel.

Jimmy "Character" Palma seen here in his death row inmate photo at San Quentin, has the name of his gang tattooed across his neck—Sangra. He begged his homeboys to let him do the hit so he could make a name for himself. He shot and killed a mother and two of her small children.

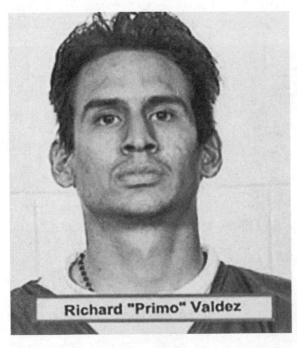

Richard "Primo" Valdez

La Sangra gang member Richard "Primo" Valdez, once a promising Little League baseball player, was the triggerman who killed two Mexican Mafia dropouts during the Maxson Road murders.

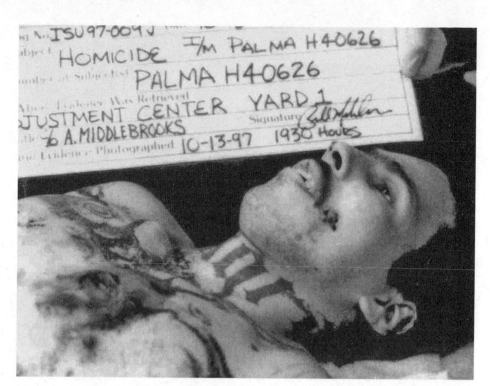

Character Palma, four stab wounds in his chest, lies dead on the death row yard at San Quentin. La Eme ordered his death. "He killed babies and he had to go," explained Boxer Enriquez.

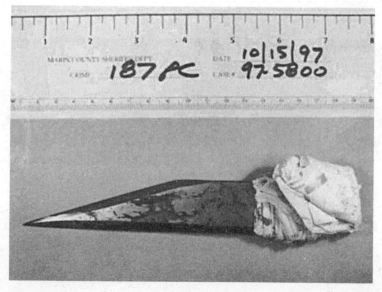

The jailhouse shank used to murder Character Palma, left on the basketball court near his body by a Mafia assailant who was never officially identified or prosecuted.

Maria Moreno *(below)*, shot in the head at close range, lies dead on the floor of the one-room residence where she lived with her brother and four of her children. Her six-month-old son, Ambrose, lying on his back on the blanket and pillow in the foreground, was shot through his right eye. Laura, his five-year-old sister, a bullet through her chest, was found snuggling up close to her mother—her bloody handprint was on the back of her mom's shirt as if she had reached out for comfort.

Mexican Mafia dropout Anthony "Dido" Moreno, EME tattooed across his knuckles, was the first to die in the Maxson Road murders as he drank a beer on the front steps. He took a bullet in his right ear and became an example for the Eme rule that read "blood in, blood out."

Dido Moreno and Gustavo "Tito" Aguirre, both heroin addicts and La Eme dropouts, were also marked for death because they were ripping off drug connections who were paying taxes to Huero Shy Shryock and the Mexican Mafia.

A smiling Rene Enriquez hugging his mother, Lupe, during a visit at the Los Angeles County sheriff's substation in Walnut, California, in 2002, a few months after he dropped out of the Mexican Mafia.

Rene Enriquez surrounded by his two sons, twenty-seven-year-old Bobby *(left)* and twenty-four-year-old Rene *(right),* in 2006 during a visit at the same Walnut substation.

Rene's son Bobby, Rene, older brother Marc, and father John Enriquez during a 2002 visit at the Walnut substation.

Later, Toker actually sent a picture of himself to Boxer with the two broken fingers in a splint. He got the message.

"Topo" was from a gang called Sotel in South Los Angeles. He was approaching middle age when he got out of prison and hooked up with Boxer's twenty-five-year-old niece. She was basically a little tramp—an offshoot of the first marriage of Boxer's mother—and she wrote to her uncle that she was dating a nice guy. Then Topo started writing letters and eventually asked for "some help" to get on his feet. So Boxer made arrangements for one of his crews to give the guy a pound of methamphetamine, free of charge, to cut up and sell on the streets for a potential of thousands of dollars in profit. He expected a payback. Three weeks went by, and he never heard a word from Topo. He wrote. No response. He telephoned. The calls weren't returned.

Meanwhile, Boxer heard from another source that Topo had bought a car. Niece's boyfriend or not, this was not acceptable behavior. Three months went by before Boxer wrote him a final note: "Look, man, I did you a favor. All I want is to keep it real. I will be your best friend. You're my niece's old man. I need to know where you're coming from because this is wrong. I extended my services to you, and I expect you to be real with me."

Topo sent word back that some youngsters had ripped him off. He lost all the dope. That wasn't the right response. "This is my philosophy," explained Boxer. "I don't care what happens to you. Make sure I get my money. I don't care if you flush your dope, or if the rain damages the package, or it's stolen. Make sure I get my money!"

"Canicas," a camarada from a gang called City Terrace, worked on one of Boxer's crews. He was told to pay a visit to Topo. "Give him a little physical therapy" to get him with the program, instructed Boxer. Canicas's view of physical therapy turned out to be more of a surgical procedure. He brought a pair of wire cutters and chopped off Topo's pinky finger. Boxer later got a flood of letters from his relatives asking him if he was insane or what? Canicas had delivered the severed finger to the "trusted confidante" in a plastic bag. On first sight, it looked like one of those toy gag fingers sold at a magic-novelty store—only this was the real thing. It scared the hell out of them.

Boxer congratulated Canicas for "keeping the fear of the Eme on the streets."

No one was exempt from disciplinary action. Lorie was a meth dealer who was once married to Boxer's older brother Marc. She started causing some problems with the crew, showing up at their houses, badmouthing them, sometimes threatening them. Lorie created such a loud scene at Toker's house one night that the police showed up. Toker was arrested on an INS violation and taken to jail. That took a major earner off the streets. Enriquez felt that she was "abusing her relationship with my family." Huck and Fat Pete were sent to make a house call with orders to "tune up" the former sister-in-law. "They beat her up pretty good," recalled Boxer, "and that sent ripples through the whole crew. They even did it to a girl." There were no exceptions.

Back at Pelican Bay, Boxer was celled up with his old crime partner Jacko Padilla, who reputedly had a prolific crew of his own out on the streets with solid Mexican drug cartel connections. They were getting packages every week with a prune-size ball of heroin stashed inside each one. As a result, the two cellmates were high every day.

Heroin came sealed inside cereal boxes and packs of caramel corn. Cocaine was stashed inside Oreo cookies and bars of soap. Marijuana came disguised inside Ritz cracker boxes. Children's drawings and greeting cards were soaked in methamphetamine. Pharmaceutical drugs in the shape of pills were pressed inside Chips Ahoy cookies. Tar heroin was sealed inside two postcards stuck together to look like one.

Boxer and Jacko had so much heroin that they gave it away to other carnales. "Ninety-five percent of the brothers are heroin addicts," according to Boxer. "And the vast majority of inmates suffer from drug addiction. It's part of the gang subculture along with low self-esteem. The bottom line is, that's just who we are. We are not recruited for our sterling reputations, but for being antisocial, maladaptive people." One week four inmates overdosed in their pod. Forty-year-old Eme member Manuel "Musky" Castaneda from Maravilla actually died from an overdose of heroin when he was Boxer's cellmate.

"I remember several times waking up on the floor of my cell with a syringe still in my arm," recalled Boxer. "That's how far gone on dope I was."

Officers periodically searched the cells and often intercepted a package. That didn't stop the flow. "We have so many methods of smuggling dope," said Boxer, "that if one gets cracked, we find another way. We had it coming in on cycles: as one arrived, another one was already on the way." And there was no deterrent. If an inmate serving a life term was caught with drugs, he was given a 115, a disciplinary note in his prison file. It meant nothing.

Shipments of heroin were also protected as legal mail with real or fake attorney names on the envelope or package. It was a system that worked in County Jail, and it worked at Pelican Bay. Again, prison regulations prohibited officers from reading legal correspondence, and tar heroin pressed between sheets of legal documents got by rather easily.

Boxer claims that 80 percent of the heroin and cocaine smuggled into PBSP was arranged by him or Padilla. "We have twenty-four hours a day to sit back and plot ways to get drugs into the prison, and correctional staff have a limited amount of resources at their disposal to detect them." Ten thousand pieces of mail a month go to inmates at Pelican Bay.

There were a half-dozen times during his stay at PBSP when his dope supply temporarily dried up and he had to kick his habit cold turkey. "Jacko and I were in the house just dripping sweat and vomiting profusely—terrible, horrific withdrawals. I thought I was going to die. And we'd look at each other and say, 'Never again. Never again!' There was an uneasy pause and then, 'Yeah, but write your person and make sure they get that next package here.'" That's how it always ended up.

Boxer fashioned syringes out of the metal ink cartridges inside ballpoint pens: "We'd pull the cartridge out of the pen, remove the little ball from the tip, and sharpen the shaft to a point. It would look similar to the needle device used to pump up a basketball. Then we'd fill an eye dropper with liquid heroin as if it were a syringe and fit the sharpened pen cartridge tightly into the open end of it. Now we had a clear eye-dropper tube attached to the needle. We'd then jam it into a vein, squeeze the rubber bulb at the end of the eye dropper, and shoot the heroin into our bloodstream. It was brutal, like injecting yourself with a nail, but it worked. The blood squirted out of your arm after removing the makeshift needle, and I'd have to grab my arm and apply pressure for about ten minutes before the bleeding stopped."

Eventually, Boxer was diagnosed with early-stage hepatitis C, most likely the result of sharing dirty needles with others. A whopping 60 percent of inmates at PBSP are estimated to have hepatitis, caused mostly by needle sharing for drugs or tattooing and in rare cases by sexual exposure. Boxer had interferon therapy, with injections every two days for a year, and it seems to have worked. His viral count is zero, and no serious liver damage has been detected. As unabashed dope fiends, he and others stole the needles used for the interferon injections and used them to shoot up heroin.

Padilla had EME tattooed in large letters on his left breast after Boxer arranged for him to become a made Mafioso. He was always a fun-loving guy but grew serious when he became a carnal. He told Boxer, "We're not lads anymore." Still, they were good friends. Three separate times they were cellmates at Pelican Bay. "He was argumentative. He'd start an argument and then blame me for it. I'd say, 'Fuck this,' and move out. I was probably to blame for some of the disagreements. But Jacko was a good buddy."

At one point, the two buddies started sniffing heroin instead of injecting it.

Boxer knew that his older brother Marc had been diagnosed with rapidly advancing AIDS, hepatitis C, and cirrhosis after years of sharing dirty needles with other hypes. There was an article in *San Francisco Frontiers* magazine in June 1999 about the medical neglect of inmates in California prisons. The article specifically mentioned an ashen-faced Marc Enriquez coughing up blood and defecating with "bright red blood" in his stools while being housed at Corcoran State Prison. That news scared Boxer and Jacko, but not enough to give up dope. Their solution to combat AIDS/HIV was to snort instead of inject heroin. That was their method of using for a couple of years. Boxer said, "We thought it was classier and had this false perception, a focused moral standard that we weren't shooting up. It was ridiculous! We were still heroin addicts. In retrospect, it's almost comical."

CHAPTER 25

Baby Killers

"WHO'S GOT A GUN WITH A SILENCER RIGHT NOW?" BELLOWED HUERO Shy Shryock.

A dozen Mafiosi sat in a San Gabriel Valley motel room talking about guns and murder. There was the crunch of potato chips as Perico Ochoa pulled them from a small bag while he listened. But it was Shy's deep voice that resonated across the room from the chair where he sat in the corner. He wanted someone killed.

"I don't know if you ever heard of this brother named Dido from Monte Hicks," he continued.

He explained that Dido was forty-four-year-old Anthony Moreno, a Mexican Mafia member who had dropped out more than a decade earlier and now lived in a small rental property not far from Huero Shy in El Monte. The Mafia rules said, "Blood in, blood out." As far as Shy was concerned, Dido had earned himself a death sentence for leaving La Eme: "But there are all kinds of people in the pad. There's a whole bunch of youngsters and kids and all kinds of shit, so I gotta figure out how to. I need a silencer is what I need."

Shy leaned forward and told those gathered at this January 4, 1995, Eme meeting that Dido was also hanging out with another Mafia dropout.

"He's hanging out with that Tito from Norwalk."

Tito was thirty-five-year-old Gustavo Aguirre, another heavily tattooed Mafia dropout. Both he and Dido were hard-core heroin addicts. And word on the street was that Dido was still representing himself as Eme and "taxing" people. Tito was ripping off drug connections who had been paying taxes to Huero Shy and the Mexican Mafia.

Huero Shy first and foremost wanted Dido dead. "I just want to kill him. I don't wanna . . . there's kids and everything in that house, man."

Boxer Enriquez was in prison at Pelican Bay, but Huero Shy was one of his mentors, one of the carnales on the streets whom Boxer trusted not to interfere with his interests on the outside. He was tied closely to Huero Shy, and Shy—prolific killer that he was—was about to make a big mistake with this new murder plot. It would backfire in a way that would disgust even other Mafiosi—putting the mob on TV newscasts across the country and in newspapers with a headline theme no one liked: baby killers! "It was so ghastly," said Boxer, "it hurt La Eme's image."

That wasn't all. This time, while Huero Shy talked cold-blooded murder, there were informants in the room and hidden FBI surveillance cameras recording the conversation for future racketeering prosecutions.

And what would unfold in the coming days illustrates, perhaps better than any other story in this book, how the burgeoning Mexican Mafia terrorizes not only other bad guys but the innocent. These events also show how La Eme's glorified mystique infects the minds of young people to the point that they too aspire to be cruel monsters. The community at large is left to pick up the pieces.

During the past year, Huero Shy had been working "real close" with a camarada he felt had "gone way above and beyond the call of duty." He was twenty-five-year-old Luis "Pelon" Maciel from a gang called El Monte Flores.

Pelon was a small man—just five feet seven inches tall and 130 pounds —with a shaved head and a scraggly mustache. He had tattoos all over his back and stomach and had been a gang member for only a few years. Before that, he was into disco music, had long hair, and belonged to a "party crew" called Showtime that made the rounds to all the "flyer" parties they could find. He went to jail for traffic tickets, nothing more, and apparently came out wanting to be a gangster.

He was "jumped in" to the gang around 1993. The same day he went out and had a big EMF, for El Monte Flores, tattooed on his stomach. A homeboy who wants to remain anonymous said, "He changed like overnight. Nobody knew him. He was never around the neighborhood. And now he wanted to make a name for himself." He hooked up with another EMF gangster named Carlos "Diablo" De La Cruz and started doing a lot of robberies and extortions. Eventually, they started working for Eme member Frank "Frankie B" Buelna—using his name, beating people up, and collecting money. Frankie B liked it, but then he got busted and went back to prison.

That's when Huero Shy took over the area. Frankie B had recommended Pelon, and he won Shy's trust as a Mexican Mafia associate willing to do anything: robberies, extortions, beatings, stabbings, murder. "He started doing all this crazy shit," recounted a gang member who does not want to be identified, "taking cars, hitting border brothers, hookers, everything, even taking stuff from his own people. He was running the whole show in the San Gabriel Valley. We were terrorizing everybody."

A year earlier, El Monte Flores gangsters did a drive-by shooting on a rival gang and mistakenly killed a one-year-old infant on the porch. Baby killing was not acceptable, and the Mafia sent Pelon to discipline the gang member who made the errant shot. He stabbed his own homeboy thirty-five times. Amazingly, the target lived, but the statement was made—no baby killings.

"This motherfucker is sharp. He's taking care of a lot of business, and I want to make him a carnal," demanded Huero Shy, his big voice again dominating the room.

It was April 2, 1995, and Mafiosi—a deadly dozen—were meeting again at a local motel to discuss their business. Again, they didn't know it was being videotaped secretly by the FBI and that two among their ranks had turned government informant.

Huero Shy wanted to make Pelon Maciel a member of the Mexican Mafia.

He was quickly asked, "Who's this guy?"

"His name's Pelon from Monte Flores."

No one in the room knew who he was except Huero Shy Shryock, but that didn't stop him from making his pitch: "I know you vatos don't know him, but take my word for it, the motherfucker's down. I'm not talking just about violence either. He takes care of business real good, and he has downed a whole lot of motherfuckers in the last year. And he went against his whole neighborhood for us. He's been fighting with them, he's down. And when . . . his homeboys killed that one-year-old baby a few months ago, he's the one who took care of 'em."

However, promoting membership for Pelon didn't go as easily as Huero Shy thought it would, and there was a reason for that. Boxer Enriquez explained: "There had been some recently bad choices of new carnales, and there was talk among the brothers at Pelican Bay to maybe put a temporary halt on new memberships—a moratorium."

Pelon knocked on the door and walked into the motel room where the gathering carnales had begun discussing his possible selection as a new Mafia brother.

"That's Pelon," said Huero Shy.

Most of those in the room stood and shook his hand—Chuco, Perico, Gibby, Cowboy, Champ, Tonito, Victorio, and China Boy among them. Then Pelon was asked to leave and wait downstairs at the bar.

There was still a burning concern in the room, especially from Perico. Boxer explained later that "Perico had just paroled from Pelican Bay and felt he had a lot of juice. Plus, Perico and Huero Shy had been cellmates in the 1970s and had a falling-out. Since then, there had always been some animosity between them."

"How many brothers here know the guy?" asked Perico.

"Nobody here knows him."

"Well, see, that's the thing. How about giving some of these other brothers a chance to know the dude?"

"In my heart I don't know him," said a voice from the corner. "I never ran with him. I never drank with him. I never partied with him."

"Well, I've raised my hand for the vato," Huero Shy retorted. "Now you vatos make a choice. That's all I can do."

"All right, let a few brothers get to know him," reasoned Perico, "and the next junta it will come to a vote."

"Just give us some time to know him!"

"He's earned everything or I never would have brought it up, Perico!"

Ten minutes into the discussion some in the room started to chime in to support Huero Shy.

"I'll agree to him because of the way I respect Huero," conceded Gibby. "If Huero says he's a hell of a motherfucker, then he's a hell of a motherfucker."

Chuco waved a white rag and made a signal over his head as if he were a football referee indicating a touchdown, as Huero Shy pushed the debate forward: "I think it's time. He deserves it. He's got it coming."

The votes started to roll in for Pelon.

"I'm going to go on Huero's word right here."

"I've just got to go with Huero's say," agreed Gibby.

"Huero ain't going to sit here and lie to us."

"Ya know, Pelon," relented Chuco, "I'll go with him. He sounds good to me."

Yet not everyone was on board.

"It takes only one veto to deny a member," Boxer explained later. "A no vote is an automatic veto—no questions, ifs, ands, or buts. This is a vetting process that has proved reliable in the past."

Back in the El Monte motel room, the voice of another brother again pointed out that there was talk of a possible moratorium on new members. Everyone there had to live with their vote in the future. What if they made a hasty choice now?

"Everybody who said yeah has to go down with him," warned Perico.

Huero Shy—known for his explosive temper—popped. "Ya know, my brother, drop it, man. Just drop it! Fuck it! He's my camarada, he'll be my camarada. Just drop it, all right!?"

His short outburst was met by brief silence in the rest of the room. A few minutes later, there was a consensus. Pelon was voted in. The discussion had taken about twenty minutes.

Huero left the room and returned with Pelon Maciel. He shook his hand. "You're a carnal." The new brother made his way around the room trading quick handshakes and tentative hugs with his new big homeys— sealing his pact with the devil.

Perico looked into Pelon's eyes. "There are certain reglas and guidelines that we go by. When the brother gets a chance, I'm pretty sure he's going to run 'em down to you, explain it to you, man, and we're real serious about it, ya know, real serious about it."

Any doubt about that would be erased in the near future.

Three weeks later, Pelon Maciel softly handed his one-year-old son Joseph to the Catholic priest who had just performed the baptism ceremony at St. Marianne Paredes Church in Pico Rivera. Joseph was his third son—all of them under the age of seven—with common-law wife Monique Pena. They decided to have the christening on the same date as little Joseph's first birthday, Saturday, April 22, 1995.

The Maciels were a working-class family. Pelon's father and mother had their own metal polishing shop and raised nine children—two boys and seven girls.

As the priest cradled the newly baptized child in his arms, Pelon posed next to him with his wife and the two godparents. Little Joseph was dressed all in white with a silky shirt, shorts, socks, and tiny patent leather shoes.

Pelon wore a black sports shirt, gray slacks, and a wide grin on his face as someone snapped the family portrait.

It was like a scene from Francis Ford Coppola's classic film *The God-father*. The Maciels had gathered for a baptism—the Christian sacrament of spiritual rebirth. Pelon reached out and took his child back from the priest, again broke into a big smile, and posed for another fatherly photo, knowing all the time that he was the mastermind of bloody, gang-style, multiple murders planned for later the same day. The midday christening was followed by a reception and birthday party that would last well into the night—intended to be a great alibi.

"Give the baby to Louie," said a woman's voice as the family video camera recorded it all for posterity.

A couple of dozen children, family, and friends now gathered outside in the yard at a relative's house in Montebello. Little Joseph was in the arms of his godmother. "I give you my godson," she said, "who I just brought out from church with the sacraments and holy water he received." She passed the child to his father, who replied, "I receive my precious son who came out of church with the holy sacrament and holy water that you received." Pelon handed the boy to the godfather, and he in turn gave Joseph to his mother. All had recited the same phrase. Pelon hugged the godmother and laughed heartily.

There was more laughter when Pelon reached into his pocket and came out with a handful of change and threw it in the air. Even before it hit the ground, eager children scrambled for a piece of the unexpected booty. "There's a quarter right there!" pointed out Pelon as a five-year-old boy quickly reached for it and stuck it in his pocket.

Grandparents, aunts, and uncles were seated in the shade eating. Pelon was nearby grabbing a piece of chicken off the barbecue, stripped down to a sleeveless T-shirt, any hint of a wholesome family image belied by the gang tattoos marking his arms and peeking up through the top of his shirt, all set against the warm southern California sun.

"Hit it," instructed Pelon as he later helped the birthday boy with a small baseball bat. Together they took a meager swing at a large yellow Tweetie Bird piñata standing on the grass before it was hoisted from a tree branch overhead.

"Get it!" The adults howled as small boys and girls—one after an-other—stepped up and took a shot at the papier-mâché creature dangling from a rope. Eventually, one of the older boys cracked open Tweetie, and the cartoon figure bled candy all over the grass. Pelon delightedly joined in with the kids as they fell to their knees, scooped up the sweets, and jammed them into their pockets.

"Happy birthday to you!" sang the entire gathering as Monique held the birthday boy in her arms, standing over a picnic table and a white-frosted sheet cake. Mom then playfully pushed a handful of the sticky icing into Pelon's mug, and he gleefully did the same to his sister Maria. His laughing wife too ended up with a mustache and beard made of cake topping.

Somewhere around midafternoon amid the family festivities, Pelon—a full-fledged Mexican Mafia member for less than a month—slipped away. He had a murder to set up.

Tito Aguirre saw them pulling up—two carloads full of young gangsters—and he ran into the house and hid in the bathroom. He was convinced that Huero Shy and Pelon were out to get him for ripping off dealers who were paying taxes to the Mafia.

Pelon stepped out of the blue Pontiac Cutlass and walked up the driveway with two other gangsters. Those in the fully loaded second car, a 1992 blue Jeep Wrangler, never got out. This was a reconnaissance run. Huero Shy was nowhere to be seen. This was Pelon's gig now.

Dido Moreno, the Mexican Mafia dropout and target, was standing in front of the single-story house where he lived with his thirty-eight-year-old sister Maria, four of her six children, and sometimes Tito too. The rent was $350 a month. It was a little dump—actually one house split into two, making one residence in front and one in the back. All of them lived in the rear section, which was one room the size of a two-car garage with a fireplace, love seat, full-length sofa, refrigerator, food storage closet, television, four mattresses spread out on the floor, and a bathroom located in one corner. The lot was surrounded by a four-foot-high chain-link fence with a driveway gate that was chained and padlocked at night. It was located at 3843 Maxson Road in El Monte, a two-lane residential street in a lower-income area where older cookie-cutter houses were mixed in with apartments.

Dido was standing next to his slightly younger brother Alex, who lived up the street, as Pelon and his henchmen came sauntering up the drive. They all shook hands. Witnesses would later say that the conversation, which appeared to be about drugs, became loud and argumentative. But in the end, Pelon gave Alex and Dido Moreno forty dollars worth of free heroin. Alex told police a month afterward that Pelon said he gave them the dope "because he liked them," and his crew would be back later to sell them some more. Pelon knew that anyone under the heavy influence of smack would be less able to resist.

Dido, Alex, and their sister Maria were all hard-core junkies.

Pelon returned to the family birthday party assured that his hit men now knew the layout of the Moreno house and exactly who to kill. His orders seemed clear. Take out Dido and don't leave any witnesses. Maciel was from the El Monte Flores clique, but he had recruited a gang of assassins from the ranks of a rival San Gabriel neighborhood called La Sangra. He felt that picking a crew from a different gang would throw suspicion away from him.

Back in Montebello, the birthday party had moved inside—a big banner in the living room read, HAPPY BIRTHDAY JOSEPH. There were baby presents to open, and Monique appreciatively held up the toys and baby clothes that emerged as the boxes were unwrapped. Pelon sat around the table and grinned until his pager went off. He left to meet with the hit team one more time. He had a homeboy drive him and Diablo back to his apartment in El Monte.

Eight miles to the east in Alhambra, twenty-nine-year-old Anthony "Scar" Torres, twenty-two-year-old Richard "Primo" Valdez, and twenty-one-year-old Jimmy "Character" Palma were sitting around laughing and doing lines of speed. All of them were members of the La Sangra gang. Next to them in Scar's bedroom were guns laid out on the floor.

Scar was a portly 200-pound thug packed into a five-foot-eight-inch frame. He lived there with his mother. Sadly, the ugly scar that defaced the entire left side of his head happened when his mother was boiling liquid on the stove and accidentally spilled it on him when he was just a child. Maybe that was what made him so angry inside. According to police records, local detectives thought he was good for as many as ten murders, but they couldn't prove it and he was never charged for them. His mother thought he was acting strangely that night. She confronted him, and he explained that he had to do something: "We don't want to do this, but we have to do it." Scar was the La Sangra shot-caller, and the Mafia had told him it had to be done.

Primo was taller and thin, and his face was dominated by a funny, oversize nose. He did a lot of PCP and a year earlier had been involved in a "payback" drive-by that resulted in the death of a rival El Monte Flores gang member named Juan "Johnny Boy" Dominguez. In another time, he had played Little League baseball.

Character grew up in El Monte and was a kid who seemed to have a deep emotional need to belong. In his early teens, he played basketball in a police recreational league for at-risk youth. One of the cops told his mother that it might be a good thing to get him out of town and away from a bad group of friends. She did it, but he ended up in Youth Authority anyway, met some gang members from La Sangra, and joined up with them. He had the word SANGRA tattooed in big letters that ran across the entire front of his neck. He lived with his younger sister and her husband and was dating Pelon Maciel's sister at the time.

As the house loaded up with four other gang members, Scar's nervous mother went next door to spend the night with her daughter.

Not long after, the gangsters grabbed their guns and headed out the door.

Nineteen-year-old Daniel "Tricky" Logan, who was being raised by his grandmother, had his blue, four-door 1987 Nissan Maxima. Tricky had no serious criminal record and was more of a gang lightweight. He slipped into the driver's seat as Scar piled in next to him and Character and Primo climbed into the backseat.

Twenty-nine-year-old Jose "Pepe" Ortiz, a hard-core gang member always ready to do La Eme's bidding; twenty-five-year-old "Creeper," a loudmouth braggart who was more of a doper than a serious gangster; and twenty-two-year-old "Mateo" all got in a second vehicle—Mateo's maroon 1991 Ford Thunderbird. They were the backup car.

Back at his apartment, Maciel was pacing back and forth—anxious, waiting. Then the blue Nissan Maxima pulled up, and Character climbed out of the backseat and walked up to Pelon, now lingering outside. Pelon gave him some heroin and asked him if he was ready to take care of some business for him and if he had everything he needed to take care of it.

"Yes, we're packing," answered Character. He also said a second backup car was following them to help take care of the business.

Pelon hurriedly turned to the homeboy who had driven him to El Monte and said, "Let's get back to the party"—his alibi.

On their way to the crime scene, an overly excited Character begged Scar to let him do the hit. He wanted to "make his bones" in the gang, be respected as a true killer. Scar finally relented. He would later tell police: "I was going to do it myself, but this guy wanted it so bad. He wanted to make a name for himself." Scar remembered that he had seen children in the house during their afternoon reconnaissance run, and he reminded everyone, "No babies, no babies, I don't want any part of that."

Their headlights were turned off as they drove up Maxson Road in the dark and spotted Tito Aguirre on the sidewalk. He saw them too and took off running, down the sidewalk, straight to Dido's place, where he disappeared up the driveway and into the house. It was about 10:30 P.M.

The Nissan Maxima trailed him and pulled to a stop at the end of the same driveway at 3843 Maxson Road. The gate to the drive was padlocked shut. A short time later, three young men dressed in dark clothing got out and calmly walked up the neighbor's adjacent driveway, toward the Moreno residence in the rear. Tricky Logan, wearing a baseball cap, hunched down in the driver's seat and waited in the car.

The Ford T-Bird backup drove on by and settled into a spot on the street next to Zamora Park, about two hundred yards away. They waited too, ready to kill cops or rival El Monte Flores gangsters who might feel inclined to spoil their mission.

Character and Primo easily vaulted the four-foot chain-link fence as a drunken, drugged-out Dido Moreno sat on the front steps drinking a beer. Six-year-old Paul Moreno was sitting on a bed just inside the door, watching television, when he noticed two men talking to his uncle outside. He remembered some conversation about drugs, and then there was an eruption of violence that no child should ever have to witness.

Primo pulled out a .357 Magnum revolver and put a single slug into uncle Dido's right ear. There was a crash from his beer bottle breaking on the asphalt as the Mafia dropout fell sideways onto the pavement—dead.

Little Paul saw the gunman quickly pull a stocking cap down over his face. It was now a mask with only the killer's eyes glaring through the open door. The boy jumped to the floor and hid along the wall next to the open doorway.

His mother, Maria Moreno, stood and tried desperately to shut the sliding-glass door to keep the intruders out. It didn't do any good. Two gunmen now muscled their way inside. There was the flash of a large chrome-plated .45-caliber handgun in her face, and Character, at close range, ripped a bullet into the left side of her skull. She dropped with her face in the stained carpet and died. An unsuspecting neighbor heard a little boy's voice yell, "Mom!"

Primo turned his revolver on Tito Aguirre, probably figuring that, with the Mafia order that no witnesses be left alive, he was fair game. Tito had been on the couch pretending to watch TV and must have gotten up to run. A .387 slug caught him in the back of his left shoulder, and as he fell between the wall and a bed, a second bullet from close range blew off the top of his head. Later autopsy reports would show it was a contact wound. His brain matter splattered against the wall.

The worst was yet to come. Character was in a killing frenzy. He aimed his .45 at five-year-old Laura Moreno, Maria's daughter, and the bullet entered her back and came out her chest. She fell next to her mom.

The horror wasn't over. Six-month-old Ambrose Moreno, Maria's youngest, was lying back on a blanket and pillow in the middle of the floor. Character apparently stepped over the mother's body and, like a wild man, leveled his .45 one more time and delivered a fatal shot through the baby's right eye.

At some point, for some unknown sick reason, another slug was shot into the buttocks of Maria Moreno as she lay dead on the floor next to two of her children.

During the carnage, Scar kept watch, poised outside with a double-barreled, sawed-off shotgun.

The two killers left more rapidly than they came, jumping the small fence back onto the neighbor's driveway and crawling back into Tricky's getaway car along with Scar. Neighbors celebrating a birthday party across the street saw them all pile into the Nissan Maxima and speed away—headlights still off. Some had heard the shots and ran inside for cover until the police came.

Six-year-old Paul, who had witnessed the massacre of his family, followed the killers out the door, jumped the fence, and ran to his next-door neighbor's house. His hands, feet, shirt, and pants were covered with blood as he furiously beat on the door and told them, "My momma's been shot!" Immediately, they called police.

Meanwhile, the three Sangra gang members in the backup car never heard a shot, but they heard an outburst of sirens. A police car flew past the park. Mateo said, "Let's get out of here!" They did.

A pager and a call to Pelon Maciel notified him it was done. Whether he knew it or not, so was he and all the other callous gangsters who hatched a plot that ended up killing babies.

Boxer Enriquez said: "No one was in accord with killing babies. It was just dishonorable for us [La Eme] to participate in the killing of women and children, particularly innocent victims. If someone is a player and a woman is involved and they have to be whacked, so be it. We do that—but not kids. It was just a horrific crime that goes down as a particularly black chapter in Mexican Mafia history. Someone was going to pay for what happened on Maxson Road."

Officers Ron Nelson, Carlos Zamora, and Gary Gall were the first El Monte police officers on the scene—five minutes after the call came in at

10:30 P.M. As they walked up the drive together, a neighbor was holding survivor Paul, still in his bloody clothes, and several others were pointing next
door, explaining that someone had been shot. The policemen walked over to
the chain-link fence. Meanwhile, Officer A. Phillips arrived and approached
from the other side. He first spotted a body and called to the others, who
climbed over the fence. Paramedics were radioed in immediately.

They found Dido Moreno's lifeless body lying on his side near the steps,
his head surrounded by a large pool of blood, and a beer bottle smashed on
the pavement next to him. A tattoo that read EME ran across his knuckles.

Four feet away, they could see a pattern of more bodies inside the house.
Officer Nelson pushed back the door. Directly to his right was Maria Moreno's hefty body facedown on the floor, motionless, a large bloodstain across
the back of her shirt that emanated from the wound in her head. Officers
Zamora, Gall, and George Mendoza—who had arrived with Phillips—
followed him inside. A police cadet who arrived with one of the officers was
sent out front to flag down the paramedics.

Two small children were right next to the mother. A bloodied little
girl, Laura, with a bullet through her chest, was facedown and snuggled
up close. Her bloody handprint was left on the back of her mom's shirt, as
if she had reached out for comfort. She was breathing, just slightly—deep
short breaths. An officer checked her pulse. There wasn't one.

Two feet away, baby Ambrose—wearing a diaper and a red-and-white
infant's jumpsuit—was lying on his back, arms raised slightly upward
toward the ceiling, as if asking for help, eyes open, a small amount of blood
oozing from the corner of his mouth, and a perfect hole circled by gunpowder burns just below his right eyebrow. He was lying on a tiny white baby
blanket and a blue-and-white pillow that now had a bullet hole in it.

Off to the left, Tito Aguirre's body was on the floor, lying on his right
side, wedged between a bed and a wall near the bathroom, his left leg
propped up on the bed, his eyes open, a pool of blood around his head, as
bloodstains and brain matter dripped down the wall.

Officer Mendoza, who had four children of his own, picked up the
dying Laura, held her in his arms, and talked to her softly so she could hear
someone's voice. Then he quickly lost it. He began yelling and screaming,
"Where are the paramedics?" Mendoza said it was "the worst thing I've ever
seen" in more than twenty years as a cop.

It was awful, but what the four cops saw next was heart-wrenching
and would be forever seared in their memories like a hot poker of ugly
truth. Across the room, their eyes were introduced to a tiny two-year-old

girl named Sarah, hiding next to the white refrigerator, walking in a tight circular motion, glancing around, dazed and confused, and sobbing uncontrollably. As the child moved toward her dead mother and cowered near the body, the sobs were mixed with a terrified screaming sound. She had witnessed the massacre of her family. Officer Nelson—a bachelor with no children of his own—gently scooped up the diminutive child survivor, took her outside, and handed her over to an arriving female paramedic, hoping and praying that motherly instincts would help soothe the little girl's pain.

Investigators would later say that the only reason Sarah and her brother Paul were not murdered too was because Jimmy "Character" Palma ran out of bullets.

Paramedic Chris Cano and his partner had just finished responding to a "nothing call" and were making dinner plans before heading back to the El Monte fire station. He was the senior medic on the night shift. Then they heard a shooting call, which was not that unusual, but a request for a second ambulance was a bit abnormal. He turned on the scanner and could tell from the police radio traffic that this was "something pretty big."

There were reports of multiple bodies down. He stepped on the gas.

He and his partner, Tom Tecata, arrived at the same time as another paramedic unit. The scene was far worse than he could ever have imagined. "This was the most horrible thing, the most horrible thing I've ever seen."

First they encountered Dido Moreno lying outside, and the ugly wound in his head told them he was DOA. He had been drinking and threw up when he was shot. The stench of vomit mixed with blood was horrendous. Yet the smell of blood alone, although familiar to them, this time was overpowering. After stepping on scattered brain matter to get inside the house, they discovered why. Blood was everywhere.

The other paramedic team, Rich Campos and August Duarte, saw five-year-old Laura take her last gasp of breath as they came through the door. They took her limp body from Officer Mendoza and immediately went to work. Both medic teams could tell the child's mother was gone and turned full attention on the two children. Cano and his partner, knowing six-month-old Ambrose had no signs of life, still tried to resuscitate him. For Christ's sake! It was a baby.

Cano then saw Tito Aguirre's battered corpse in the back of the room, went to check, and found the top of his head gone, brains gruesomely decorating the wall. Cano knew he was gone. He returned to help his partner.

Other arriving firefighters joined in furiously. All they could think about was saving the lives of these children. The chances of survival were slim to none, but their humanity kept screaming in their ears: for the love of God, these are babies—save them! Neither child was breathing on their own. An ambulant bag was used to try to get the six-month-old to breathe. Paramedics placed a tube into Laura's lungs, basically trying to breathe for her too. IVs were set up to replace the blood loss. They intently listened for an encouraging sound—not knowing then that the bullet had collapsed her left lung and pierced her heart, literally tearing up her insides.

After handing the lifeless body of five-year-old Laura over to the paramedics, Officer Mendoza walked out onto the lawn and threw up. He wasn't the only one that night to lose his dinner.

"It was so sad," bemoaned Cano, "to see a mom and her two children just lying there side by side, her brains on the floor, and her kids next to her." Firefighters and policemen—most of them with children of their own—were screaming we need this or we need that. The sights, the smells, and the sounds caused a complete sensory overload.

Cops and firemen—breeds of humanity whom many people mistakenly believe are callous, uncaring, and inured to this kind of experience—were emotionally drained as well. "The fact," said Cano, "that there were people out there who were actually capable of killing children. You wonder, these kids didn't do anything. I mean, the six-month-old baby had a chance. The five-year-old girl had a chance. And their chances were taken away from them. That's when it all started hitting me, especially having kids of my own.

"I just think, what if someone was to come into my home and kill me, kill my wife, and then kill my kids. And the worst part is the fact that the few moments that that little girl was alive, you wonder if she knew what was going on. Did she know her mom was being killed? It's just, a kid should never have to have those feelings or see that. And the next thing, she's shot."

After transporting the two children to separate hospitals—neither made it alive—Cano and his partner returned to the scene and walked through it again for documentation purposes. Then they headed back to the station. Cano had to use a water hose to wash the blood, brain matter, and pieces of skull from his boots. Normally, after a call, he and other crew would sit around and discuss it, critique what they'd done, and plan what their responses might be in the future. Often the adrenaline was still rushing and everyone was active and talkative. This time it was solemn. Barely a word was spoken between them. Each man dealt with what he'd seen in his own private way.

Officer Nelson—on the job for three years and himself the son of a small-town police chief—had started the night on the graveyard shift. He worked through the morning hours, went home, and then fell into an uneasy sleep. He woke up in time to catch the six o'clock television news. Sitting on the couch, he watched the story about the grisly Maxson Road murders and broke down in tears. *What a heinous, senseless, cowardly act,* he thought.

Paramedic Cano—who became a police officer in El Monte a few years later—is convinced that he will "never forget it." He explained: "Part of it will be with me forever. Things that are done just horribly to children . . . I think in a way kills part of you, kills your personality or your insides, blackens you a little bit more, and it just really bothers you."

It certainly bothered Joe Moreno, victim Dido's forty-two-year-old brother, who also lived in the area. That same April 22 night as the murders, he showed up at the crime scene and reported to a police officer that he believed a man named Huero Shy either was the killer or had recruited someone to do it. The next day he added the name Luis "Pelon" Maciel.

That same day, eight hundred miles away, Boxer Enriquez, sitting in his cell at Pelican Bay State Prison, was watching television news when he first heard that La Eme executed a family, including a six-month-old child and a five-year-old girl. He looked over at his new cellmate and said, "That can't be right."

Darryl "Night Owl" Baca, a convicted murderer and Eme member, shook his head in disbelief. "Fuck! They're killing babies."

In the days immediately following the Maxson Road murders, there was massive news coverage of the killings, and the reports tied the massacre directly to the Mexican Mafia. Boxer was among those who didn't appreciate the growing negative publicity: "We saw it on *The World News.* It was all over the news. We [La Eme] were all painted with the same brush—baby killers, baby killers. And it's never been us. We don't kill babies."

A relative of Anthony "Scar" Torres, one of the driving forces behind the killings, was also especially unnerved by the murder of babies. So much so that the person confided in someone at her job that Scar and his friends were the Maxson Road murderers. El Monte detective Marty Penney, a gregarious gang cop who always had his ear to the ground, was sitting at his desk at the police community relations office when he got the call three days after the murders. The person on the other end of the line wanted to remain anonymous. They set up a meeting, and cops ended up with a list of solid suspects.

Then, on May 15, during a jailhouse interview with Penney and homicide detective John Laurie, suspect Scar Torres, off the record, identified Jimmy "Character" Palma as the one who shot the kids. Scar had been arrested in an unrelated attempted-murder case. Earlier the same day, Character turned himself in to his parole officer to go into drug rehabilitation. He denied he was part of the Maxson Road murders.

Near the end of July, another informant told investigators that he overheard Scar and Character talking about a week after the murders. He said Scar asked Character, in an angry tone, "What's wrong with you!" And Character shot back, "I don't give a shit. I'm crazy. I'll kill anyone."

Los Angeles County Sheriff's Department homicide detectives had the killers' names and worked at a methodical pace to put the case together.

Rene Enriquez said that "the Mexican Mafia hierarchy was completely appalled" and the Maxson Road massacre continued to be the talk of Pelican Bay State Prison. He remembered that "even the hardest-core La Eme members were shaking their heads in disgust." In his own pod area there was Topo Peters, Jacko Padilla, Lil Mo Ruiz, Bruiser Tolento, Grumpy Padilla, and Musky Castaneda—all Mafiosi. Boxer said, "Everyone agreed they couldn't put up with hits like this." No self-respecting mobster had any outward compunction about killing, but this was different.

On weekly visiting days, small groups of inmates are escorted together to the visiting area. The visiting room itself consists of two long, back-to-back rows of small, secure cells. On the back side of each prisoner's visiting cell is a perforated-steel door. Inmates are able to communicate with each other by calling out to those situated adjacent to them or behind them.

For the next few weekly visiting days, the Maxson Road murders became the primary topic of discussion. Cuate Grajeda reached out to Boxer. "This made the clica look bad. Whoever did this has to go."

The talk about Maxson Road extended into the prison law library, where inmates were kept in separate booths, also equipped with perforated-metal doors, for individual study. A court decision had allowed for inmates in the library to speak to each other. Enriquez sat near David "Spider" Gavaldon the day after he heard the news. Spider said, "Whoever called this has to go, and it was your homeboy who called this shit."

It had surfaced quickly that Huero Shy Shryock was the one who ordered the hit. Shy too became a main topic of conversation. Boxer and his cellmate Night Owl, who was also from Artesia 13, kept hearing from other Mafiosi, "That's your homeboy."

"You don't know for sure it was Shy," argued Boxer. There was some sentiment for executing Huero Shy because he had ordered the killings. He'd also sponsored Pelon Maciel for membership in the organization. Boxer knew that his enemies in the mob could also use that against him, being a close ally of Shy's.

Meanwhile, Huero Shy Shryock didn't waste any time before sending a letter to Enriquez asking him to tell the other carnales he had nothing to do with ordering up dead babies. Boxer remembered the letter saying: "I didn't ask him [Pelon Maciel] to kill the babies. I asked him to kill Dido and this other guy, two dropouts. And then they went and did this on their own. I swear to God I didn't do this. I give you my word, brother. I didn't do this."

Boxer Enriquez believed him and stood by Shy. So did others, and eventually Huero Shy Shryock managed to get a pass.

"But you know what I really knew?" added Boxer. "I knew he inadvertently did it. That's his nature. In his big booming voice, he probably said, 'Kill 'em all. Kill all those motherfuckers.' That's what he would say all the time. And I'd bet that's what he said to this guy [Pelon]. 'Fuck 'em all. Kill all them motherfuckers.' And that's exactly what he did. Maciel did what he was told."

On September 28, 1995, a murder indictment was unsealed naming Anthony "Scar" Torres, Jimmy "Character" Palma, Richard "Primo" Valdez, and Daniel "Tricky" Logan. All were in custody by then except Valdez, who had moved in with his mother in Salt Lake City, Utah, within a week of the murders. Valdez enrolled in junior college there and worked in a supermarket. He turned himself in after his sister read in the newspaper that he was wanted. Primo denied that he had anything to do with the killings.

On December 6, 1995, a grand jury indicted Luis "Pelon" Maciel and Jose "Pepe" Ortiz. Ortiz was already in state prison on another charge. Maciel was arrested a week later coming out of a motel with his girlfriend in the nearby city of Rosemead. His wife had kicked him out of the house three months earlier for having an affair.

"Mateo" and "Creeper"—who were in the backup car the night of the murders—were never charged. Neither was La Eme's Huero Shy Shryock. Federal prosecutors had other trial plans for him. They let the state prosecute all the Maxson Road defendants, and the feds would go after Shy during a massive Mexican Mafia racketeering trial down the road.

* * *

In June 1997, gunmen Jimmy "Character" Palma and Richard "Primo" Valdez, convicted of all five murders the previous December, were sentenced to death by lethal injection at San Quentin State Prison. They were twenty-three and twenty-four years old at that time. Palma sat their silently as the sentences were read. Valdez screamed an obscenity at the judge. During the trial, Valdez—at one time a promising Little League baseball player—threw a Kleenex box at a sleeping juror and hit him in the head from about twenty feet away.

Anthony "Scar" Torres, thirty-one years old, was sentenced the same week to life in prison without the possibility of parole for his role in the murders.

Twenty-year-old Daniel "Tricky" Logan, the driver of the getaway car, received a prison term of 129 years to life.

And thirty-one-year-old Jose "Pepe" Ortiz, a passenger in the backup car who helped give directions to the Moreno home, was also sentenced to 129 years to life behind bars.

Jimmy Palma hadn't even been at San Quentin for three weeks when it happened on October 13, 1997. The first two weeks were spent in processing, and now he was allowed out on one of the small death row exercise yards. There were about a dozen other inmates out there with him—all of them associated with La Eme or the Aryan Brotherhood. It was only his second time out on the yard. He'd just finished a sweaty game of basketball and was arguably a little worn out. Character was standing in the area frequented by Mexican Mafia members and associates when the knife plunged into his flesh. It was over quickly. The baby killer was dead—four stab wounds in his chest, a fatal one to the heart. No inmates came to his aide. The assailant was never charged with the murder. In fact, he was never officially identified.

"There's a raw sense of justice in that," reflected Boxer Enriquez. "He had it coming. There was no remorse for doing this guy. He killed babies, and he had to go. There is justice, and there is the death penalty in California. Sometimes it just happens that the Mexican Mafia carries it out."

In January 1998, twenty-eight-year-old Luis "Pelon" Maciel laughed when the court clerk read the jury's recommendation that he get the death penalty. Two and a half months later, the normally jocular L.A. Superior Court judge Charles Horan didn't think it was funny at all when he sentenced Pelon to die by lethal injection.

During his first week on San Quentin's death row, Pelon Maciel decided the main exercise yard wasn't the best place for him to spend his time. He now goes to a special yard for inmates with safety concerns. Maciel only comes out of his cell accompanied by one or two convicts who have no gang affiliations, as he waits for his official date in the state's execution chamber. That is, unless La Eme can come up with a plan to make it happen sooner.

Deputy District Attorney Anthony Manzella, a tenacious prosecutor who put Maciel away, said: "Most people were already aware of the presence of the Mexican Mafia in the prison system. But few people realize the influence the Mexican Mafia has on street gangs in the community. This case shows just what influence they have."

Manzella grew up in New Jersey and still speaks with a slight Jersey accent developed years ago in a neighborhood that is captured on video in the opening credits of the television show *The Sopranos*. His father, a first-generation Italian-American, was a lawyer who refused to represent mob guys because they didn't meet his standards of right and wrong. His bright son went to the U.S. Air Force Academy and then on to law school at prestigious Georgetown University.

Anthony Manzella considers himself a streetwise attorney who grew up in a place where Italian wiseguys wielded power—more than they deserved. He doesn't hesitate to make a comparison: "The Mexican Mafia is right now where La Cosa Nostra was fifty years ago. We've got a shot at keeping it from growing into what the LCN became."

Boxer had a last word: "The Maxson murders tarnished the Mexican Mafia's image, but really showed it for what it is—a malignancy. In truth, they had more than a little something to do with the killings."

CHAPTER 26

Dead Men Don't Pay

DARRYL "NIGHT OWL" BACA WAS A MEXICAN MAFIA MEMBER WHO had nothing but holes in his tennis shoes and sixty dollars on his books when he became Boxer's cellmate at Pelican Bay in 1995. Enriquez told him, "There is a whole world of money out there."

The two of them had known each other for years. Baca was a year older, a quiet kid who used to get high in Pat Nixon Park and occasionally went to the Enriquez house in Cerritos to score drugs. They were homeboys from Artesia 13—Night Owl lived in nearby Lakewood—who often ran into each other at parties while growing up. Night Owl was a closed-off kind of guy who was incapable of showing emotion, never knew the identity of his own father, and was physically abused by stepfathers and boyfriends of a promiscuous mother who eventually died of AIDS. Darryl lived in apartments, never had a real home, and sometimes had to eat dog biscuits because of the lack of food. "He had no chance from day one," bemoaned Boxer, "and he had serious trust issues."

The two gangsters became better friends when they were locked up in County Jail together in the early 1980s. Once during a disagreement with some *paisas* over a pair of stolen shoes, Enriquez was outnumbered five to one. Darryl came to his aid, gripped his fingers around the neck of one of the adversaries, and lifted him off the ground with one hand. That quickly ended the conflict and cemented a friendship between the two Artesia homeboys.

Boxer was waiting to be sent upstate on his robbery convictions, and Night Owl was facing a murder rap. He had owned and cherished a 1960 Chevrolet Impala low-rider automobile for which he paid a mere $600. A rival gangster made the errant decision to shoot at it. A furious Baca gunned down the offender and killed him. He was arrested, convicted, and sentenced to life in prison at the age of nineteen.

Boxer and Night Owl also did time together at Chino and San Quentin. Baca was a member of the wrecking crew at DVI in Tracy when the two of them were camaradas "making their bones." In fact, it was Night Owl who asked Enriquez to do his first hit for the Mafia at DVI in 1984. Baca was a balding workout machine who stood six feet, two inches tall and had a body frame packed with 190 pounds of muscle. There was also a quiet dignity about him, and in an Eme lineup steeped in dirty politics, he was a squeaky clean carnal. "Darryl was an anal perfect kind of guy, an opinionated naysayer with no business acumen from day one. I made the mistake," said Enriquez, "of cutting him in on my business."

Boxer felt that he always carried Baca—collecting tax money for him and taking care of his beefs out on the street. He cited the Mousie Reyes murder as a perfect example. Michael Reyes, aka "Mousie," of Artesia 13 was a likable little guy who grew up with Baca in Lakewood. They served time together in Juvenile Hall and County Jail. With a boyish face that had the features of a mouse set on top of a tiny body that stood barely five feet tall, Mousie had an especially fitting nickname. He was also a crackhead who dealt nickel-and-dime drug deals as part of Night Owl's crew. He carried a letter from Baca that gave him enough strength to deal on the streets, and he always believed Night Owl had his back. That is, until he ended up dead on September 23, 1998. Mousie and his chola girlfriend drove to a Norwalk house to buy some drugs. There was an argument, and Mousie was stabbed multiple times as he fell to his death on the driveway. Witnesses identified the assailant as Daniel "Poncho" Arredondo of Norwalk 13.

Enriquez claimed that the hit was actually ordered from a federal prison by Mexican Mafia member Ralph "Perico" Rocha, who felt that Mousie was encroaching on his Norwalk drug territory. Baca was indignant that he lost an old friend and a steady earner. More important, his Mafia pride was hurt. Yet he went to Enriquez and asked him "to take care of it." Boxer did. He sent word to his crew boss—through a visit to Pelican Bay by Cynthia Alvarado—that Mousie's death had to be avenged. The green light was on.

On January 4, 1999, hit man Poncho Arredondo—a thirty-eight-year-old tax collector for Mafioso Perico—was standing in front of a heroin dealer's house in Norwalk when a car drove up. A rival gang member popped out of the passenger door, walked up to Poncho, exchanged some harsh words, then pulled out a handgun and stuck it in his face. Poncho turned and ran, but couldn't outdistance a series of 9 mm slugs fired into his lower back and thighs. The getaway car took off without the assassin, who managed to escape on foot and hijack another car to flee the neighborhood. By the time the ambulance pulled into St. Francis Medical Center in Lynwood, Poncho was no longer a Mafia tax collector or hit man. He was just plain dead.

Afterward, La Eme's Perico sent word to Enriquez that the two factions needed to resolve their dispute before this turf war escalated. A deal was made that an Enriquez-Baca crew could absorb part of the Norwalk territory. So Toker was allowed to make more money there in the future without being harassed by Perico's people.

Gonzalo "Sinbad" Navarro, the Norwalk 13 gang member who had successfully followed Mafia orders to kill Poncho Arredondo, was eventually arrested and convicted for the murder. He was fingered by witnesses at the scene and by a number of anonymous callers. Sinbad was thirty years old and would spend the rest of his life in prison for murdering a murderer who offended another murderer—Darryl "Night Owl" Baca.

It was all part of twisted, deadly Mafia business.

Boxer was increasingly annoyed by Baca. He saw him more and more as a "stingy, miserly person and a notorious bean counter." Once, Night Owl wanted to file an inmate grievance because he knew he had seventy-six cents left on his prison canteen books and the clerk wiped it off his account. He was furious over a lousy seventy-six pennies. At the same time, Boxer complained, "I had to collect his tax money from the street. I was carrying him. He never made money on his own and became upset if he was shorted a mere twenty-five bucks." After a couple of years, Boxer told him, "We can't do business together anymore. I'm done."

A correctional officer heard the noise coming from E pod shortly after noon and sent another guard to check it out. He found Night Owl Baca and Boxer Enriquez standing in cell 217, bruised and breathless. The inmates told the guard that everything was okay and they were just playing around. In fact, they weren't. As soon as the officer left, the inmates started throwing punches again. One caught Boxer on the nose, and he was covered with blood. The guards sounded an alarm. A crime incident report filed November 3, 1997, by PBSP correctional officers indicates that the cellmates kept fighting until pepper spray, also known as OC (oleoresin capsicum) spray, was used to break them up. OC is a chemical compound that causes pain and irritation to the eyes, even inducing temporary blindness.

Boxer explained, "It had been building. I took care of him, and he loved it. When I told him the meal ticket was over, he didn't like it." Neither of them took the issue to other carnales. Unauthorized fighting with another carnal was one of the gray rules that could be punishable by death. They patched up their differences and even started doing business again. Then Febe Carranza entered the picture.

Baca's first wife was a gorgeous Mexican brunette with a voluptuous body to match. Her nickname was "Hot Puss," and one day she just took off, knowing Night Owl would never hoot again outside prison walls.

That wasn't a problem for Febe. She was what is known in prison as a "window hopper," someone who visits different inmates looking to hook up with one of them. Baca had met her while she was visiting a camarada from the Avenues known as Demon.

"I knew there was big trouble coming from this chick," recalled Boxer, "a fat, loudmouth cow who had an obscene lust for power." Febe Carranza arranged a quick jailhouse marriage that made her Febe Baca—a Mexican Mafia wife.

After Baca hooked up with her, he tried to micromanage everything. Boxer felt that Febe asked too many questions of other crew members, and he didn't like it. He didn't like her.

Then Cynthia—crew boss Toker's wife whose code name was "Hottie"—visited Enriquez at Pelican Bay and told him they didn't want to pay Baca anymore. He was supposed to receive about $100 a month from Toker and Hottie's end of the business, but they were about $900 behind in payments. Toker and his wife never did like paying both Boxer Enriquez and Baca.

"I'm going to kill her," threatened Baca.

"Leave her alone," argued Enriquez. "Anyone who tries to kill her will get shot."

"Then you're choosing her over me?!" said Baca, following up with a torrent of curses.

First of all, Boxer knew "dead men don't pay." He felt that it made no sense to kill Cynthia: "She was a better business person than her husband. I didn't think she had a killing coming. She was cool people, a good person, loyal to me." Plus, Cynthia was a major conduit between Boxer and his crews. She visited Pelican Bay a dozen times from 1999 to 2002. It was bad business to do away with her.

It was time to sever all ties with Night Owl. Boxer paid him $3,000 and three ounces of methamphetamine for Cynthia's life—making good on her delinquent payments. Baca took the Caballo crew and Flo, along with her ties to the Burgueno family.

It wasn't over. The bad blood between Boxer and Night Owl was boiling.

Enriquez fashioned a deadly metal shank out of a knee brace he was authorized to wear. The weapon was seven inches long and two and a half inches wide. He planned to kill Baca when he got a chance.

Baca planned on killing him.

CHAPTER 27

Chuco Rolls on La Eme

NOVEMBER 5, 1993, WASN'T GOING TO BE A GOOD DAY FOR CHUCO
Castro. About eight o'clock in the morning, he glanced out the picture
window located at the front of his one-story stucco house in Rosemead
and locked eyes with a cop coming his way. Momentarily, his face froze in
a look that said, *Oh shit!* Then he ran to the back of the house and started
flushing bags of heroin. Chuco was on parole, and he didn't want to go back
to prison. "I used to talk to Chuco on the phone almost every day back then
when I was in County Jail," recalled Boxer, "and Chuco would always say,
'I love it out here.' He'd done a lot of years locked up, and he wanted to stay
out on the street."

Now the cops were knocking on his door. During a traffic stop five
days earlier, sheriff's deputies had found two .38-caliber Remington hollow-
point bullets stashed behind the pullout ashtray in Chuco's black early 1980s
Cadillac. That in itself could have been a parole violation, but they'd let him
go. He wondered at the time why they didn't take him in—he felt the heat.
What were the *juras* up to?

In early 1990, the Los Angeles County Sheriff's Department imple-
mented a plan to reduce overtime costs—temporary overtime reduction
assignment (TORA). As a result, the six-man Prison Gang Unit that worked
out of the Special Investigations Bureau of the Los Angeles Sheriff's Department was dismantled. They all went back in uniform on regular patrol duty
or were reassigned to work in the County Jail system.

Only one detective—the one with the most seniority—was left to work
prison gangs all by himself. That was Roy Nunez, a crack detective who
worked black gangs and was actually the prototype for the character played

by Robert Duvall in the movie *Colors*—the older, wiser cop who operates on the streets in a humane fashion. Prison gangs were not exactly his area of expertise. He knew he had to bone up on the subject, and he spent the next few years doing just that. Nunez reached out to institutional gang investigators (IGIs) in the California Department of Corrections and picked their brains about prison gang members and associates. At the same time, he tracked every Eme-affiliated gangster who was in L.A. County Jail from early 1991 to late 1992. Also, he began studying jail mail and even took an eight-week course at East Los Angeles College in Nahuatl so he could understand what Mafiosi were saying to each other in the ancient Aztec language.

Nunez wisely hooked up with Gil Garcia, a parole agent from the California Youth Authority. Garcia was knowledgeable. He worked with the original Prison Gang Task Force in the 1970s when Mundo Mendoza became an informant. Garcia was a great source of information between the older mob and the "Pepsi Generation." Garcia helped Nunez together a link chart that showed the relationship between Mafia members in and outside prison, their associates, and street gang members. They compiled photographs, lists of cellmates, driver's licenses, and the specific cars the bad guys drove. One name that came up in County Jail and later out on the streets was a Mexican Mafia heavyweight and parolee—Ernest "Chuco" Castro. "He was calling the shots," recalled Nunez. "He was the biggest we got." They began surveilling Chuco and stayed on him for weeks.

Boxer Enriquez said that the cops were right about targeting Chuco: "He was an upstanding carnal. No one ever politicked against Chuco or even said a bad word about him. He was the Mafia golden boy who always did the right mob thing, a killer with influence among younger and older brothers, and an idol. We all looked up to him."

Detectives Nunez and Garcia started getting tips off the streets that Chuco was having meetings with large groups of Latino gang members. A confidential informant (CI) told them that Chuco had ordered the gangsters to assault any gang members from Maravilla, an old, established East Los Angeles neighborhood. Boxer explained: "Maravilla was anti-Mafia. It was a gang that openly defied the Eme edict to stop drive-by shootings and refused to pay taxes to the Mexican Mafia." The CI also told detectives that Chuco always kept a handgun nearby for protection, usually stashed in his car, hidden behind the pullout ashtray in the dashboard. Possession of a firearm was a felony for an ex-convict.

Informants also reported that Chuco had recently moved his wife Lorraine and their three small children from an apartment in Alhambra to a home somewhere else. Also, that he stopped every morning at an East Los Angeles drug prevention clinic, received a dose of methadone, and drove his wife to work at the Michelson Laboratory in Bell Gardens. On November 4, 1993, the parole agent set up surveillance outside the laboratory and saw Chuco pick up his wife at the end of the day. He tried to follow them in an attempt to find Castro's new residence, but lost them in heavy traffic.

The next day, undercover sheriff's detectives again found Castro at the methadone clinic and followed him to his wife's workplace, then to Monterey Hills Elementary School, where he dropped off a small child, and finally to his new residence in Rosemead. Investigators now knew where he lived. A later records check found that Chuco had an outstanding traffic warrant—a more than adequate reason to pull him over and look for the hidden handgun.

About four o'clock in the afternoon, the detectives saw Chuco drive away from his house and presumably head off to pick up his wife. He appeared to be alone in the car as he turned at the next street (a dead end), slowly looked into parked cars, made a U-turn, went north on one street, then back south on another as he looked around, as if checking for surveillance. Once on the San Bernardino Freeway westbound, he continually slowed down and sped up, made lane changes without signaling, and then, at a confusing interchange of the 101 and 110 Freeways, made a radical lane change and headed north on the 110. Quickly, he shot down an off-ramp and disappeared. He lost the trailing surveillance team, but at least two other undercover cars were still in the hunt.

Detective Roy Nunez was in one of them, and he followed Castro to his wife's place of work. Because they feared he was armed, two deputies in a black-and-white patrol car were assigned to make the traffic stop when Chuco pulled up. Castro got out of his Cadillac, and Nunez walked up to advise the Mafioso that he believed he was in possession of a firearm.

"I never have a gun in the car when I have my kids in the car," replied Chuco.

The silken-tongued detective calmly asked if he could check for himself.

"Go ahead," answered a confident Castro.

Nunez then discovered two small children sitting in the front seat and an infant strapped into a car seat in the back. The kids were handed over to their mom as she walked up to the scene of the traffic stop, just outside her workplace. Unlike her calm and cool husband, she cursed and threatened the cops.

Inside the car, Detective Nunez found a Kershaw knife in a black nylon case wedged between the driver's seat and the center console. There was no handgun to be found when he pulled out the ashtray and checked behind it—only the two .38-caliber hollow-point bullets.

Nunez strolled back over to where Chuco was standing, opened his fist, and revealed the two live rounds now nestled in the palm of his hand.

"If you're going to ask me about those bullets," said Castro, "I want to talk to my lawyer. Besides, you guys planted them." Nunez put Chuco in the back of a patrol car. The conversation continued for an hour—not like a cop talking to a crook but more like one family guy giving advice to another. The detective and his wife had raised children of their own, and then took in a total of forty-two foster kids over the years. Nunez got the sense that Castro truly loved his wife and cared deeply for his children. He told Chuco the gangster lifestyle was going to take him back to prison, where he would rot away in the isolation of Pelican Bay. There would be no child birthday parties, first communions, or high school graduations to attend. His children would grow up without him. Their dad would be someone they could see during visiting hours a few days a year. Nunez gave the parolee plenty of food for thought.

Finally, Chuco and his family were free to leave. Prior to the Eme member's exit, he lied to Nunez about where he lived, giving his old Alhambra apartment address as his legal residence. He never mentioned the new place in Rosemead, six miles to the east.

By October 1993, two members of the Prison Gang Unit were finally brought back on the squad to help. One was Sergeant Richard Valdemar, a stout, full-bearded, good-hearted man who by now was the unit supervisor and who had a mind that worked like a lie detector when questioning suspects. His knowledge of gangs was unchallenged, and he'd trained so many successful young detectives that they were known as "Valdemar's children."

One of them was detective Rich Lopez, a big guy with a short fuse who played defensive back on a Cal Lutheran College football team that lost in the NCAA Championship game. He was also a star javelin thrower on the track team and a former captain in the U.S. Marines who emulated the Corps values of honor, courage, and commitment. Lopez knew how to think out of the box and had a knack for putting all the little things together to make a successful case—and little patience for those who didn't.

Nunez sat down with Valdemar and Lopez for a brainstorming session. They had the confiscated bullets, two reliable informants who insisted that

Chuco always carried a gun, reports of his participation in a series of large gang meetings, and the fact that he lied about his true address. It wasn't much, but their experience and instincts told them Chuco was a big fish. "A great white shark," said Boxer, "the biggest fish they ever had." How would the detectives get that fish on the hook and bring him in?

The answer was to get a warrant and search his house. There was not an abundance of probable cause, but Lopez wrote it up and a judge agreed to sign it. Some LAPD detectives were invited to go along, and that's when Chuco saw them all coming up the driveway. He knew they weren't stopping by for breakfast.

The dozen cops went through the home like a meticulous housewife looking for specks of dirt. Chuco, his shirtsleeves still wet from flushing dope down the toilet, sat handcuffed on his living room couch. He knew the drill. That didn't mean he had to like it. Before anyone even asked a question, words started flying out of his mouth. "This ain't right! I'll have to go back to prison. They'll want me to kill people. I've killed people I love. It ain't right." His trembling hands were hidden behind his back. The deputies, after initially securing the area, uncuffed his wife and allowed her to tend to their baby and two small children. Maybe these juras wouldn't be smart enough to find what Chuco knew was there. No such luck.

"Look at this!" One of the deputies had discovered something interesting.

In Chuco's bedroom closet, a rug covered the hardwood floor. Deputy Leon Brown peeled the rug back and found a trapdoor underneath. He lifted the door and found a small, concrete-lined crawl space that housed the water heater. That's not all that was there.

Deputy Brown discovered a cache of weapons stored in an athletic bag, including a Mac-10 submachine gun, two .357 Magnum revolvers, two 9 mm Glock semiautomatic pistols, a .45-caliber semiautomatic, and a .44 Magnum with a scary-looking eight-inch barrel. A convicted felon–parolee was not allowed to possess firearms. He had seven. The Mac-10 alone could have him serving ten years in a federal prison. There was another surprise too: $10,000 in cash was stuffed into the same bag. It was part of his cut of tax money collected from L.A. street gangs. He had no receipts or evidence to prove it came from any legitimate source.

Nunez turned to Chuco and said heavily, "You will definitely never see your kids again."

Outside in the trunk of Chuco's Cadillac cops found about a dozen rocks of cocaine in addition to syringes and spoons used to administer doses of heroin. The search also turned up numerous letters about Mafia business.

Boxer believed that "some of those letters had to be from me, telling Chuco I was always behind him one hundred percent." There were also a number of green-light lists that could place Chuco in the middle of a conspiracy-to-commit-murder charge.

Sergeant Valdemar was confident: "We knew he was going to talk."

The team of pleased detectives took him back to the Temple City sheriff's station and booked him. Chuco sat in a small interview room with detectives Lopez and Nunez, and he knew he was done. Besides, he was sick and tired of the whole Mafia mess: the infighting, the politics, and the killing—the killing of people who sometimes were his friends. Not for any good reason, but because some other asshole who happened to be a carnal wanted him dead. If Chuco didn't do it, they'd find someone else to do him. He'd just turned thirty-six years old in August and was strung out on heroin. "He had a really bad heroin habit," said Boxer, "and so did his wife." Yeah, mob life was beginning to look more and more like bullshit.

Roy Nunez had a pleasant, reassuring, fatherly way of talking to a suspect. He explained that Chuco was looking at some serious time, ten years per gun he had in the house.

Rich Lopez noticed that Castro, using his right thumb, kept pushing up against the cuticle on his right index finger. The detective figured it was a nervous tic. "Chuco," he said, "by the time you get out of prison, they'll be serving space burgers."

It was time to go back to prison—perhaps forever—or give it up. He gambled for a life where he could see trees instead of steel bars, eat at an occasional restaurant instead of inside a concrete cell, kiss a child instead of a prison guard's ass, and snuggle up at night against his wife instead of a hard state-issued pillow.

A relative put up the family house as collateral, and Chuco was released on bail. What he had bargained for was going to be extremely difficult. He now had to keep in constant touch with the cops. There was a time in his life when he wanted to kill them, and now he had to depend on them. There was going to be a continual fight with his inner devil. He had agreed to do what in his world was the unthinkable—be a rat.

Valdemar, Nunez, and Lopez knew Chuco Castro was a plum catch. He was one of the most trusted and respected Mexican Mafia members in the Pepsi Generation. He could bring down the whole organization. What did they do with him now?

It was going to take a lot of time, money, and technology to do what they knew needed to be done. The small Prison Gang Unit didn't have the resources to do it. They knew that too.

The feds had money and wiretap expertise. They originally had invited an ATF agent to the Chuco search warrant, but he never showed up. Someone now pointed out that the FBI had been trying to work up an Eme case in the San Fernando Valley but kept coming up dry. Why not call them and set up a meeting?

A few days later, Detective Nunez sat down in a room with an FBI agent and Assistant U.S. Attorney Robert Lewis and broke the case down. The working relationship between the Bureau and local cops is not always a good one. There is a feeling that FBI agents are a bunch of arrogant college boys and girls. "Famous and incompetent" and "fraternity boys with guns" are two of the derogatory phrases sometimes used by local law enforcement officers to describe FBI agents. The locals tend to believe that some of the FBI's finest have no street sense, do have an uncanny ability to screw up a case, and, if the investigation is a success, are quick to take all the credit. On the other hand, the agents often see "the locals" as untrustworthy and not the brightest bulbs in the room.

This partnership was not going to be like that. Jim Myers had dreamed of being an FBI agent since he was a kid and had come to the Bureau after serving as a local cop in Massachusetts. He immediately perceived the importance of the Chuco bust and wanted in. It was a go with the feds.

The task force included Myers, a couple of others from the FBI, and Nunez, Lopez, Valdemar, George Marin, and Carlos Sinaloa from the L.A. County Sheriff's Department. Another detective brought in was Larry Martinez from the LAPD, a tall, lanky homicide cop who looked a lot like a biker with a big old droopy mustache and hair he sometimes combed back into a ponytail. Many of the Mafia murders that Chuco would turn them on to had occurred in the LAPD's Hollenbeck Division in East Los Angeles. Martinez had worked a number of them, and he was good with informants.

Detective Lopez would later say, "Myers was the glue that held the investigation together." Not all the local cops felt that way. Roy Nunez for one, feeling that the feds weren't always up front about what was going on, asked to be reassigned in August 1994.

Chuco was immediately placed in a methadone program to control his heroin habit, and task force cops started meeting with him on a weekly basis. He wore a wire for months and between March 27, 1994, and April 9, 1995, the government actually videotaped fourteen meetings of Mexican Mafia members gathered in hotel rooms to discuss their murderous business ventures. Chuco rented the rooms himself, except on two separate occasions when Huero Shy Shryock and Black Dan Barela booked the room. Barela passed out a box of rubberized non-slip-handle knives to the assembled carnales, as if they were lethal party favors. During one encounter, the Mafiosi were seen and heard talking about the extortion and possible murder of actor-director Edward James Olmos for his indiscretions in making the movie *American Me.* "None of us in the Mafia had any idea that Chuco was an informant," insisted Boxer. "I was shocked when I later found out about it."

During the last weekend of April 1995, sixteen Eme members and two associates were arrested in early-morning raids in the greater L.A. area, including Norwalk, Bell Gardens, and Santa Ana. Among them were two of Boxer's mentors, Huero Shy and Black Dan—who, along with Chuco Castro, several years earlier began organizing the scheme to take over the streets.

None of those arrested offered any resistance. There were no shoot-outs.

Sergeant Valdemar remembers placing handcuffs on forty-three-year-old Huero Shy and saying, "Don't give me any trouble. We're both too old for this."

Huero Shy seemed to agree. "Okay," he replied.

On the following Monday, May 1, the U.S. attorney in the Los Angeles–based Central District of California released an eighty-one-page indictment charging twenty-two Mexican Mafia members and associates with murders, assaults, extortion, drug trafficking, and kidnapping. U.S. Attorney Nora Manella said, "This indictment and the arrests will significantly disable one of California's most violent gangs." It was the first time federal prosecutors in Los Angeles had ever used the Racketeer Influenced and Corrupt Organizations (RICO) Act against a violent criminal enterprise. RICO was enacted by Congress in 1970, basically to destroy the Italian Mafia. The law provides for extended penalties for criminal acts committed as part of an ongoing criminal organization. Charlie Parsons, special agent in charge of the Los Angeles FBI office, said, "[We] prevented forty murders from occurring" by prosecuting La Eme under RICO.

The front page of the *Los Angeles Times* metro section—under the banner headline "U.S. Indicts 22 in Probe of Mexican Mafia"—read, "The 81-page indictment paints a chilling picture of the Los Angeles underworld, signaling an unprecedented degree of organization and ruthlessness in the long and bloody history of Latino street gangs."

Boxer was in the visiting room at Pelican Bay when he overheard Topo Peters and a few other carnales say that Chuco had rolled: "I didn't say a thing as I kept one ear listening to them and the other ear on the visiting booth two-way phone. The news about Chuco was devastating because he was one of my closest allies. He always allowed my crews in the street to flourish and supported me whether I was right or wrong." Mentors Huero Shy and Black Dan were also taken off the streets. "We had a tacit agreement—Chuco, Shy, Dan, and I—that we were together. Most of my support base was moving to federal prison, and I knew I was in serious political trouble. My demise in the organization was coming. It was the beginning of the end."

The twenty-six-count indictment charged that Mafia thugs were responsible for seven murders and seven attempted murders and had plotted to kill at least another eight targets. Among the victims listed were three tied to the making of the film *American Me*, Eme members Manny Luna and Charlie Brown Manriquez, and gang counselor Ana Lizarraga. There was a conspiracy-to-extort charge linked to threats against Edward James Olmos, named in the document only as "Victim Number 1." Ostensibly, those threats came from Boxer. The indictment accused the Mob of "wrongful use of force and fear" to obtain money and property from the Hollywood figure. This racketeering count was later dropped when Olmos refused to cooperate with the prosecution.

Two of those indicted were already doing life prison terms, Benjamin "Topo" Peters—now described by the government as the new Mafia "Godfather" since Joe Morgan's death—and Ruben "Tupi" Hernandez. Both were housed at Pelican Bay State Prison.

Ironically, another indicted Eme co-conspirator, Antonio "Tonito" Rodriguez, had been gunned down in his car on the streets of El Sereno just three days earlier. He was ambushed by members of a street gang called Lowell, a group that was so blatant about defying the Mafia taxing program that they began calling themselves "the Green Light Gang." Many of them would be killed in the ensuing years, including the nineteen-year-old Lowell gang member who shot Tonito.

The indictment recognized that the Mafia had launched meetings to control the estimated sixty thousand gang members in the Los Angeles area: "The main purpose of these meetings has been to organize the Hispanic street gangs into a larger, Mexican Mafia–controlled, criminal organization." Boxer had been part of the foundation of that plan.

The government spelled out how La Eme had arbitrated disputes between and collected taxes from two of L.A.'s largest and most violent street gangs, Eighteenth Street and Mara Salvatrucha, or MS-13.

There was the kidnapping of a local drug dealer who failed to pay $85,000 in taxes, the extortion of another forced to pay $15,000 every six months, and a complaint from a Primera Flats gangster in East L.A. that his gang had already been paying $10,000 a year in taxes and now the Mafia wanted his gang to supply them with guns too.

There were charges that La Eme had "voted on" conspiracies to murder at least two other Eme members: Jesse "Sleepy" Aragon and Frank "Puppet" Martinez. Boxer said, "Sleepy was targeted because he was viewed as worthless, including failure to kill a witness in my murder case. And Puppet was targeted because of his politicking against Chuco and threats to kill three other carnales." Both Sleepy and Puppet were quickly arrested by the wire-listening task force cops to get them off the streets and save their lives.

There were counts accusing the defendants of ordering assaults on jail deputies who were later stabbed by inmates using a broomstick with a sharpened metal point and a shaft with a five-inch metal tip.

In other charges, the Mafia defendants were charged with "hitting" gang members for not paying taxes, for falsely claiming to be an Eme member, for killing a Mafia tax collector, and in one case merely "to make an example."

Before the trial, one Mafia defendant was transferred to another jurisdiction for prosecution and seven others pleaded guilty, including Boxer's old homeboy Sammy "Negro" Villalba. He was sentenced to twenty-four years in federal prison.

"I was left in Pelican Bay with nothing but adversaries around me," said Boxer, "and I began getting feelings of dread. One day on my way to the infirmary for a medical checkup, I suddenly couldn't breathe. As I gasped for air, it made no sense to me. It was a panic attack."

It wouldn't be his last.

CHAPTER 28

A Rat or Just Smart?

ALMOST TO THE DAY, IT HAD BEEN THREE YEARS SINCE CHUCO CASTRO
was arrested and decided to become a government informant when the big
Mafia RICO trial finally got under way in Los Angeles. On November 17,
1996, federal prosecutor Lisa Lench told jurors in her opening statement
that La Eme "controls most of the street gangs in southern California." She
went on to explain how the Eme bosses used the thousands of gang members "as soldiers in the field" to do "a lot of their work for them." "You,"
she stressed, "will have a very unique opportunity to see inside this secret
organization."

A three-tiered rectangular dock was built in the courtroom to hold
the thirteen remaining defendants and their lawyers. Those charged were
also given earphones to listen, if they wanted, to a Spanish translation of
the proceedings. The Mexican Mafia defendants' ankles were shackled and
chained to the floor.

Given rare anonymity, jurors were referred to only by numbers. Their
names were never mentioned during jury selection, trial proceedings, or
afterward. U.S. marshals parked jurors away from the courthouse and escorted them to and from the courtroom in order, Judge Ronald S. Lew
explained, "to keep them [Eme] free of us." Sergeant Richard Valdemar put
it more bluntly: "We were afraid jurors would be identified by the mob, and
that they would kill them."

In addition to the metal detector at the entrance to the Federal Building,
courtroom observers and attorneys had to walk through a second metal detection device set up in the hallway directly outside the doors to the courtroom on the eighth floor. Testy federal marshals were in abundance.

Deputy federal public defender Ellen Barry a month earlier wrote a letter to Boxer Enriquez at Pelican Bay. She said, "We are still trying to negotiate with the marshals about how everyone will be treated in court; at the very least, they're going to shackle everyone's feet. I worry they'll pin down their hands as well, and we will get no help from the judge, who is likely to think someone is going to vault over the bench to get to him."

Boxer says that defense attorney Barry was always Mafia-friendly.

Barry's letter to Boxer was written six days after another explosive incident that happened on October 16, 1996, and delayed the trial for a couple of weeks. It was all caught on video surveillance tape. Sammy Villalba, who had a go-along-to-get-along philosophy that made him a survivor, was joking around in a holding cell at the Federal Building. He'd just gotten out of the hospital, where he'd gone suffering from a bleeding rectum after smuggling in a couple of shanks. Now it was time to use them.

In another holding cell next door, Black Dan Barela was pacing the floor as Tupi Hernandez sat on a bench in the corner with his back to the wall. First Black Dan and then Champ Mendez walked behind a divider into the bathroom and found the hidden shanks inside the toilet plumbing. Jesse Moreno got up to look through a small window in the door to check on the federal marshals waiting outside.

Seconds later, Champ came out of the bathroom, shank hidden behind his back, glanced toward the door, and then came straight at Tupi with a shank to the stomach. Black Dan moved in too. Tupi, taken down to the floor, tried to roll up into a ball to protect himself from the sharp blows and struggled for his life. Barela tried to hold Tupi's arms back so Champ could get a clear kill shot at his throat and heart.

Sammy Villalba and a couple of other Mafia trial defendants stood against the wall next door and listened to the attack.

Federal marshals finally pushed through Moreno at the door, pepper-sprayed the attackers, and saved Tupi's life. He was stabbed seventeen times, but not critically injured.

Tupi had been in a generational battle with Topo Peters to take over the Godfather spot in the mob. So Topo ordered the hit. Boxer said, "Tupi was perceived as 'a nutcase' whose politicking could no longer be tolerated. He became an embarrassment." During a pretrial motions hearing days after the stabbing, he told the judge, "Fuck you, motherfucker!" Tupi had been talking rather loudly in the defendants' dock while the judge was making a ruling from the bench. He responded with the obscenity when the judge told him to be quiet. Moments later, Tupi disturbed the court again with more distracting conversation. The judge admonished him once more, threatening to sick the U.S. marshals on the disrespectful Mafioso. "What the fuck does it matter?" blurted Tupi. "I'm doing three lifes anyway. So fuck you, judge!" Then Tupi spit on the marshal when he walked over to make good on the judge's threat.

During the trial, prosecutors characterized the Mafia as a brutal crime syndicate run from maximum-security cells at Pelican Bay State Prison. The prosecution's first expert witness was Sergeant Richard Valdemar, a twenty-plus-year veteran of gang investigations, who laid out the history and operations of La Eme for the jury in what could be described as Mexican Mafia 101. He estimated the Mafia's membership at 250 to 300 members and numerous associates. He also gave a rundown on each of the thirteen defendants.

The first truly dramatic courtroom appearance came a month into the trial, following testimony from the nearly two dozen law enforcement agents who had laid the groundwork for the government's case. Mexican Mafia dropout Johnny "Kiko" Torres, who wrote from prison volunteering his services to the prosecution, gave a straightforward insider's account of what the Mafia was all about. The thirty-eight-year-old witness said, "I have the perfect résumé for anyone who wants to be a member of the Mexican Mafia." He then laid out how he was serving a fifteen-years-to-life prison sentence for killing a woman—over a drug debt—on orders from Huero Shy Shryock. Besides murders, he talked about ripping off drug dealers, assaults, and robberies, all done in the name of La Eme. Torres had been in and out of youth camps and prisons since the 1970s. The former carnal testified that he'd wanted to be a member of the Mafia since he was a teenager—"for the prestige and fear [Eme members] held over the neighborhoods." The end of his story spelled out the fate of so many others like him. He dropped out in 1983 when other members tried to stab him to death.

The key government witness was Ernest "Chuco" Castro, who spent two months on the stand. He started his testimony with how his Eme life began under the tutelage of Topo Peters while both were housed at the California Institution for Men in Chino. He recounted how Topo told him the way into the mob: "If the Mafia has any enemies, . . . they're also my enemies; so long as I take care of them by stabbing them, then that would deem me eventually a member."

Castro told about the Mafia "code of silence," the reglas (rules), and the expectation that every member would engage in criminal activity to exert the power and control of the Mafia in prison and out in the streets. He explained in great detail what jurors were seeing and hearing in the government's video- and audiotape evidence and gave up-close-and-personal explanations for all the murders and attempted murders laid out in the twenty-six-count indictment. Emerging from the witness protection program to testify, Chuco even told how he'd purchased a 9 mm handgun and an M-1 rifle during his undercover days without the feds knowing about it. He disclosed that he was the one who made and provided the shank for Boxer Enriquez to use in the jailhouse stabbing of Mon Buenrostro. "But Chuco never named me in the indictments," marveled Boxer, "except for a few things for which I was already convicted."

Castro's earnest and believable testimony was devastating for the defense—despite their lawyer's attempts to paint him as a "cockroach" and "a lying rat." In an attempt to destroy Chuco's credibility, defense attorney Ellen Barry, in her closing statement, called him "a one-man crime wave" and "a master manipulator" and told jurors that "Ernie Castro is the heart of this case. And if you don't believe Ernie Castro, you have to acquit."

Attorney Jay Lichtman, who defended Huero Shy, tried to rhyme his way into an acquittal, telling the jury: "A RICO case it is not, Chuco Castro is all they've got."

Obviously, he was wrong.

In actuality, there was much more. Also testifying for the prosecution, and driving a symbolic shank into the black heart of the Mexican Mafia, was James "Apache" Prado, the young Eme associate whom Boxer Enriquez single-handedly had twice vetoed for membership. He, too, having had enough of the violence, gave his testimony and was placed in the prison witness protection system to serve out his life term.

After a six-month-long trial based on 275 audiotapes of conversations between the defendants and their co-conspirators, 14 videotaped Mafia meetings, several conversations recorded at Los Angeles County Jail and Pelican Bay State Prison, 350 photographs and other exhibits, and 125 witnesses, the jury came back with its verdict: twelve guilty of racketeering, murder, attempted murder, and extortion charges.

Only one was found not guilty. That was Victor "Victorio" Murillo. The other defendants broke into cheers when the not-guilty verdict was read. A year later, those cheers would turn into bullets.

Judge Lew sentenced the convicted Mafiosi during a weeklong series of hearings that began September 2, 1997.

Ten Mafiosi were given life in prison without the possibility of parole, including fifty-six-year-old Benjamin "Topo" Peters, fifty-one-year-old

Daniel "Black Dan" Barela, and forty-five-year-old Raymond "Huero Shy" Shryock—all close associates of Boxer Enriquez.

The judge refused to do a wedding ceremony for Topo Peters, who called out in court to his aging fiancé, mother, and another woman, "I love you all." The fiancé's reply was, "I love you too, Daddy."

Huero Shy and Black Dan—during separate sentencing hearings—sat quietly.

One of the goals for prosecutors was to destroy La Eme's power base in state prison by segregating the leaders in federal penitentiaries, in the hope of crippling their organized crime activities. FBI agent Jim Myers felt that the convictions "disrupted" La Eme. He was pleased but not stupid: "They can't work the same way they did before. Their criminal activities have been deterred for a period of time, but it's an ongoing battle with them."

The U.S. Ninth Circuit Court of Appeals, acknowledging that the Mexican Mafia is "an extraordinarily violent organized criminal enterprise," upheld all the convictions and the use of an anonymous jury.

Ernest "Chuco" Castro is still somewhere in the federal witness protection program living a new life as a regular citizen. Boxer Enriquez felt "kinda happy for him, because I knew he got away. I was growing more and more tired of the Mafia life, and I was becoming softer. Chuco helped me understand: if he could walk away—someone that big in the organization—I could too. It gave me encouragement. I didn't think of him as a rat. He just did a smart thing before anyone else [in La Eme] did, and moved on with his life."

In the days after Chuco testified, Sergeant Richard Valdemar and his team took shifts protecting Chuco and his family twenty-four hours a day in an apartment where they lived temporarily in Oxnard. They were all waiting for the federal marshals to come to take custody. Valdemar played with the Castro children and appreciated the fact that Chuco had grown to trust him. Since the beginning, there had been an underlying tension between the two men, cop and crook. After all, more than twenty years earlier Chuco and his homeboys had tried to kill Valdemar and other deputies in the Eastmont Street Massacre. Chuco was critically injured and his homeboy was killed. Some resentment lingered on both sides.

The sergeant finally broke the tension: "Do you remember that day?"

"Yeah," said Chuco. He said it in a way that seemed to acknowledge that Valdemar had shown him a certain kindness those many years ago.

"It felt like a sledgehammer when I got hit," explained Chuco. "The bullet blew the top of my hip bone right out the front of my body. I was paralyzed and thought I was going to die. I couldn't see a thing, but I could still hear. And I heard you walk up and tell the paramedics, 'Hey, work on that other guy [Chuco].'" That suggestion might have saved Chuco's life, and he remembered it clearly.

A few days later, he made another revelation that Valdemar fondly remembered. Chuco told his handlers, "I could never in my life see myself talking to or dealing with police in any way. Now, you guys are like my best friends, trying to keep me alive."

It's a strange world filled with pockets of hope just waiting for someone to open them.

And interestingly, despite Chuco's in-depth dealings with Rene Enriquez, Boxer was not among those indicted, convicted, and sent off to federal prison. Enriquez believed that it had a lot to do with friendship: "He was a good friend who was always there for me. I never doubted his loyalty. He still looked out for me even when he rolled."

Despite the fact that Boxer was not named in the indictment, Mafia-friendly defense attorney Ellen Barry subpoenaed him and thirteen other Eme members down for the trial as witnesses. None of them ever testified. Boxer hesitated to make the trip at first because of his scary out-to-court experience for the Vincent Bruce trial a few years earlier. At the same time, he knew there would be serious Mafia business to take care of on the ride down from Pelican Bay and back. He reluctantly agreed to go along. It would be a death-riddled discussion on the bus.

CHAPTER 29

A Mini—Mob Convention

HEADING SOUTH ON THE BUS TOWARD LOS ANGELES, IT WAS A MINI—
mob convention. They had been called down for the RICO trial, but all
of them knew they were there to take advantage of the system by having
meetings and communicating face to face with one another. Boxer has a
favorite line from the movie *American Me*: the main character, played by
Edward James Olmos, says, "The State was so lame it paid for the game."
That's true not just in the movies.

Locked up at Pelican Bay, carnales could be on the same corridor or cell
block and never see each other at all for months or even years. "The only
inmates who have daily access to each other are those seven or eight who
live in the same pod," said Boxer, "and they might not even be Mafiosi. So
fourteen brothers traveling on the same bus for a couple days was big."

Besides Boxer Enriquez, there were many other members of La Eme on
the bus, all of them leg- and waist-chained.* There were cages in the front
and back of the bus with a heavily armed officer inside each one. Inmates
were allowed to walk around, but the guards gave a warning at the outset
that they had a "green light" to shoot. Talking was allowed, but inmates
were expected to keep the noise level down. There were police chase cars,

* Besides Rene, the inmates on the bus were Richard "Psycho" Aguirre of Avenues;
David "Chino" Delgadillo of Geraghty Lomas; Henry "Indio" Carlos of El Sereno;
Victor "Psycho" Gallegos of Santa Monica; Jorge "Huero Caballo" Gonzalez of Eigh-
teenth Street; Jose "Joker" Gonzalez of Big Hazard; Eulalio "Lalo" Martinez of Lomas;
Jose "Bat" Marquez of San Diego; Jacko Padilla of Asuza 13; Daniel "Danny Boy" Pina
of Big Hazard; Gilbert "Lil Mo" Ruiz of White Fence; Jimmy "Smokey" Sanchez of
VNE; and Albert "Bruiser" Tolento of Avenues.

also equipped with shooters, ahead and behind. The bus traveled from PBSP to Folsom, where there was a layover for the night. It went on to Corcoran State Prison the next day before reaching the ultimate destination of West Valley Detention Center in San Bernardino, where they would be housed during their three-week stay from March 21 to April 10, 1997.

Boxer recalled, "There were some white and black inmates on the bus as well, and a few Nortenos, so every time the bus stopped the Mafia contingent would quickly walk to the back and talk secretly."

Coincidentally, the Maxson Road murder trial of the two La Sangra gangsters who shot and killed two children and their mother, along with Mafia dropouts Tito Aguirre and Dido Moreno, had ended with convictions three months earlier. The two murderers were scheduled for sentencing in June 1997. It had been roughly a year and a half since the killings, and carnales were still talking about the "stigma of baby shooting" left on the Mexican Mafia. There was a quick consensus and a unanimous vote—on the bus ride—that the people responsible for the baby murders had to go. It was this conversation that sealed Jimmy "Character" Palma's execution. Boxer said, "Word was sent to Mafia contacts at San Quentin, and it was done."

The prevailing feeling was that Pelon Maciel should die too. "The debate," said Boxer, "was about who should kill him. The rules said only a carnal should be sent to kill another carnal. Others felt camaradas should be allowed to execute him because he was not a legitimate Eme member." This group argued that Huero Shy jumped the gun and made Pelon during a period when a membership moratorium was in the works.

That debate dovetailed into other serious business. There was a strong sense that too many carnales during the 1990s growth period had been made for the wrong reasons—money being one. The selection process was corrupted from within, and with the rush to infiltrate the street gangs, collect taxes, and extend power on the streets, candidates were not being screened as thoroughly as possible. A small share of Mafia members in one prison, or several brothers on the street, were inducting a new member without properly consulting others. In theory, one no vote kept a candidate out of La Eme, and there was a feeling that not every member was getting that option. "It's a vetting process," explained Boxer. "Traditionally, someone doesn't just come along and hang out with us for a year and then get into the mob. These are, more often than not, camaradas who were raised with us from the neighborhoods, who have been in jail or prison with us, who we have seen under fire engaging in stabbings or murders and other criminal activity over long periods of time. A nominee needs a padrino, or sponsor, who brings his name to a large number of brothers for examination—to see if somewhere along the line he was branded a coward, a homosexual, or a snitch. It's important to have charisma, magnetism, ferocity, and what's known on the streets as 'heart.' There needs to be a willingness to kill for La Eme. You have to be a Mafioso!"

Of course, in practice that was not always the case. For example, Boxer cited China Boy Arias from his own Artesia 13 neighborhood. He said he'd never even heard of him when Smilon Gallardo made the guy because he had a lucrative drug operation going on. "And this new member was also cutting into my share of the neighborhood, cutting off a piece of my pie, and I should have been afforded the opportunity to say yes or no," complained Enriquez.

Boxer pointed out that Pelon Maciel of El Monte Flores, the shot-caller in the Maxson Road murders, had never even been to prison—highly unusual for a Mafia candidate. "I'm sure he did things for Huero Shy," observed Boxer, "but nothing in particular for Eme."

Boxer went on to explain that Phillip "Chano" Chavez of Verdugo was granted Eme membership solely based on his ability to generate money for carnales Tupi Hernandez and Braulio "Babo" Castellanos of Florencia 13. "While Tupi and Babo were in San Bernardino County Jail awaiting their triple- and double-murder trials, Chano was on the mainline working an extortion ring. Chano would grab a weak inmate who had a lot of money, perhaps a lucrative drug dealer, hold him at knifepoint in their module, and force him to sign over cars, boats, and money to his wife on the outside." They jokingly called it "Operation Wildebeest," after the large, not-too-smart African antelope with an oxlike head and horns that is always easy prey for lions and crocodiles. "Chano," insisted Boxer, "never even did a stabbing for the Mafia but would always split the wildebeest take with Tupi and Babo."

Then there was Art Romo, a fake community activist who helped Eme veteran Sana Ojeda organize a shaky gang truce in Orange County. "Ojeda made him a carnal," said Boxer, "and reaped the profits of Romo's real profession—big-time drug dealer." That is, until Romo got caught moving 260 kilos of cocaine (with an estimated street value of at least $2 million) and entered into a plea agreement that made him the first to sign a declaration admitting he was a member of a criminal street gang called the Mexican Mafia. That opened the door for district attorneys throughout California to prosecute Eme members more vigorously under the Street Terrorism Act. Orange County deputy DA Jeff Ferguson, who prosecuted the Romo case, called it "the first chink in the armor. It exposes them [Eme members] to tremendous sentence enhancements that they never had before, probably the most crucial of which is, conviction of being a street gang member is now a strike in California." Romo's admission that there was a Mexican Mafia made it possible for the state—with new gang enhancements—to hand out even stiffer prison sentences than the feds in some instances. It also allowed for greater restrictions on Eme parolees and probationers. Romo settled for twenty years.

In short, it was felt that some Eme members were making new carnales with an eye to feathering their own beds, not taking care of the growth of the Mexican Mafia as a whole. Along with that attitude there seemed to be a philosophy emerging among brothers on the outside—both new and old—that they ran the streets and that those in prisons should only run the prisons. "They were righteously stealing the profits and territories of the Mexican Mafia brothers in Pelican Bay," vented Boxer.

So the mini–mob convention voted to impose a moratorium on new memberships, and it was enforced for the next five years or so. The books were closed in California. During that period, the only new members who were recognized were those made by brothers in the federal prison system.

Another murder plot was also developed during the RICO trial stay at West Valley Detention Center. Defense attorney Ellen Barry gave Boxer legal folders full of wiretap and videotape transcripts to examine. Perhaps she hoped he might find something that would discredit the prosecution or help the defense. Boxer asked for the information because he had his own ideas: "The transcripts were a good way to monitor the pulse of the Mexican Mafia. I wanted to know what was going on, what the brothers were talking about, especially if that included 'talking shit' about me. It was all about preparing myself to meet other carnales in the political arena." In the documents he read that Chino Delgadillo was taped calling Richard "Psycho" Aguirre a rat. That's a serious politicking violation under the Mafia reglas. Unfortunately for Chino, he came down on the bus, and so did Psycho. And both were scheduled for the return trip back to Pelican Bay.

"We like Aguirre," Boxer noted. "We think he is a sociable good guy." So he was told what Chino had said about him. Now it was open season on Delgadillo, who was kind of an unpopular politicker type anyway. "You know we're going to take care of this," Boxer told Aguirre. "He called you a rat!"

It's fair to say that Chino probably felt the negative vibes reverberating around him. Meanwhile, others for now were playing him off, including Boxer: "It's difficult sometimes when you look a guy in the face day to day, tell him, 'Hey, how ya doing?' hang out with him, make him feel at ease, but you're going to kill him at the end of the day."

Boxer carried a knife and a handcuff key, but it was decided that they would also strangle Chino on the bus back to PBSP. The plan was to first remove the cuffs. Then, from the seat behind Chino, one carnal would apply the "hammer lock"—a strangulation maneuver that requires the killer to lock his forearm across the victim's windpipe and cut off his ability to breathe. A second carnal would simultaneously stab him. A third was assigned to head off the cops in the aisle of the bus. They figured that on the first leg of the trip from San Bernardino to Lancaster State Prison, sheriff's deputies on the bus would be armed only with Mace and batons. "Again," explained Boxer, "it's a statement. The Mafia wants people to know we do these blatant hits out in the open. Tell the cops its business is just to sit down, wait till we're done. We do it with impunity, and every act of violence causes terror, which translates into finances because we get our way when people fear us."

There was a hitch. Everyone was split up and transported in smaller vans. The cops changed the type of handcuffs normally used and covered the inmates' heads with hoods. SSU agents picked them up in some other vans at Lancaster and drove them to Corcoran State Prison SHU.

There was still one more chance to get Chino. A bus was dispatched to take all of them to the final destination at Pelican Bay. Sitting in the back, Boxer's hands were already shaking from the building adrenaline rush that preceded a fatal attack. "It's your call," he told Aguirre. "We're ready to take Chino out. We do it now or he gets a pass."

In the meantime, as the bus passed through Mendocito County, Delgadillo denied he ever said or did anything to indicate Aguirre was a rat. He even apologized if there was some kind of misunderstanding.

Psycho Aguirre had full support from all the Mafiosi on the bus. He had been called a rat, and the green light was on Chino, but in the end he decided to give him a pass.

Other carnales, looking at each other sideways, saw it as an act of cowardice. Boxer observed, "Aguirre was a diminished person in their eyes." In the conscientious world, he did the right thing. No decent, intelligent person actually kills someone over a verbal accusation or insult. Normal people maybe exchange some harsh words, work out their differences, or just ignore the insult and move on with their lives. This was not that world.

The mob world is diabolically different. It's a world where people can die over the slightest sign of disrespect.

On this same bus trip, Boxer was approached by another carnal, Jose "Bat" Marquez, who had plans to escape across the border and make their wicked world bigger and more profitable than ever.

CHAPTER 30

Boxer, Bat, and the Tijuana Drug Cartel

HE WAS GREGARIOUS AND OPEN, ALWAYS JOKING, A LITTLE GUY WITH a shaved head, only five feet, seven inches tall, with tattoos covering his stomach and chest and running down his arms from the top of his shoulders to his wrists. Three-inch block letters spelling out EME were tucked neatly below his neckline. His name was Jose "Bat" Marquez, and he was originally from a gang called Del Sol in Chula Vista, south of San Diego. His street name had been Dingbat—"I guess he was just so crazy in the way he used to act," explained Boxer Enriquez, "he used to get high on sherm (PCP) all the time"—but the moniker was shortened to Bat after he became a member of the Mexican Mafia, and he didn't like to be referred to as Dingbat anymore. It was not a nickname worthy of a Mafioso.

Boxer had never met Bat until he showed up on the bus headed to the RICO trial. He observed that Bat was "on the edge of his seat all the time," both figuratively and literally. Thirty-seven-year-old Marquez was seeking out carnales with strong established crews to do some business, and he plopped himself down next to Enriquez to talk. Boxer wasn't necessarily well liked, but he was respected as a good organizer and a dedicated killer. And that's what Bat liked about him.

Bat had a reputation as a killer too. In fact, Mexican authorities believe he was one of a group of San Diego gang members, most from a clique called Logan Heights, who in 1993 machine-gunned to death Cardinal Jesus Posadas Ocampo as he sat in his limousine at the Guadalajara airport. It was a paid hit for the ruthless and rich Arellano-Felix Organization (AFO), also known as the Tijuana Drug Cartel. Some say the Catholic cardinal was assassinated because he spoke out against the violent billionaire cartel bosses.

Others believe his limo was mistaken for that of rival drug lord Chapo Guzman, a fierce Arellano-Felix rival.

In any event, law enforcement on both sides of the border believe that the assassination was spearheaded by David "Popeye" Barron, who was sponsored in 1992 by Bat for membership in La Eme. Barron, also from Logan Heights, became a top hit man for the cartel, moving back and forth across the border enlisting recruits from his old barrio to do cartel dirty work. He was Bat's closest associate. Authorities believe that the two of them shipped tons of dope across the border and left a trail of bodies in their wake. Boxer knew that what Bat and Popeye were doing was extremely important to the future of La Eme: "We had finally broken the Mexican Mafia out of the prison setting and entered into the international aspects of the mob. Bat and Popeye were at the vanguard of this undertaking. They took us international."

Popeye Barron had EME tattooed on his stomach, intertwined with a field of human skulls, some with beady red eyes, representing his many victims. The San Diego gangster was in tight with the notorious Arellano-Felix brothers. They ran a murderous multibillion-dollar drug enterprise, and four of them were at the top of the most-wanted lists of both the FBI and the Drug Enforcement Administration (DEA), with multimillion-dollar rewards offered for their capture. Barron won the trust of the brutal AFO brothers when he helped a few of them escape from a Puerta Vallarta discotheque in 1992 when enemy Guzman cartel assassins shot the place up looking to rub out the competition. After that, the AFO brothers dubbed Barron "Caballero Honorable," or honorable gentleman, for his perceived heroics. It was cutback to "El C-H" for short, and that became his new identity.

Pete Ahearn, special agent in charge of the San Diego FBI office, described Barron as "a ruthless, vindictive, egotistical thug—nothing more, nothing less. The intimidation is what I think the Arellanos respected in him, that people were afraid of him, and rightfully so, because he was a stone-cold killer."

In a June 25, 1994, FBI undercover videotape of a Mexican Mafia meeting at the Days Inn Motel in Monterey Park—the same meeting at which Mafiosi talked about actor Edward James Olmos being "fair game"—Bat bragged about his Mexican exploits with Popeye Barron, claiming they were "like James Bond." Marquez was heard saying, "I'm hotter than a motherfucker" south of the border. He talked about Popeye doing hits for the AFO, including "busting up that vato [the cardinal] at the airport," moving large quantities of drugs, and planning to steal rocket launchers and grenades from a Long Beach armory. Bat boasted, "I got this contract. They want this motherfucker [Chapo Guzman]. They want to give us two million bucks. You're going to get money for any hit." He claimed he wanted to "help other brothers" out by setting them up down south.

Six months later, Bat Marquez was arrested in San Diego for being a felon in possession of a gun and was sent back to prison.

Now, as he sat next to Boxer Enriquez on the bus, he renewed the pitch he had given those carnales at the motel meeting in Monterey Park two years earlier. Bat said he was getting out on parole soon and would return to Mexico and reunite with Popeye Barron.

He wanted to set up a "hit exchange" with Enriquez and his crew.

Boxer said, "You know, that's a good idea. If we want someone hit, we can import the killers from Mexico. The Mexicans want a hit done, we can export our killers over there." Marquez promised that the pay would be generous. He also explained that he had AFO cartel connections to supply massive amounts of drugs for Boxer and his crew.

Enriquez didn't hesitate. "We'll get someone down there to see you, and we'll talk about it some more."

There was no question, in Boxer's mind, that Bat Marquez was heavily involved with the multibillion-dollar AFO Tijuana Drug Cartel and had bold plans to cement his position there and expand his business with Eme contacts in the United States, such as Boxer Enriquez. In addition to the 1994 FBI surveillance videotape, officers with the California Department of Corrections gathered other intelligence through an Eme informant, who explained: "Bat's plan is to take all the brothers up for parole that have two strikes [in California] to Tijuana so they can racketeer over there [Mexico] and not face 'three strikes' here."

The same CDC intelligence document explained that Bat was still in contact with Barron: "And he wants to take over all of TJ and Baja California and restart a new Eme in Mexico where all the drugs are at. Popeye [Peye] has already established himself in Mexico and is greatly feared by the drug families over there. Peye is the main hit man for the Arellano-Felix brothers and is the one who killed Cardinal Ocampo at the Guadalajara airport, and is the one who planted a bomb in front of the hotel at a *quincinera* in Guadalajara."

The confidential memo went on to say that Mexican *federalis* had confiscated homes that belonged to Popeye in Baja and Rosarito Beach and that, as a result of those actions, the attorney general was assassinated. It said that Bat felt that Popeye had been a contractor for the AFO long enough and that it was time to propose a new plan "that the Eme gets half of all drugs or profits that pass the border. But Peye tells us he needs an army of soldiers and brothers to accomplish this. So Bat devised a plan to send brothers and camaradas over to Peye. . . . Bat tells me if they get enough soldiers and brothers across the border, and the Felix brothers [the AFO kingpins] refuse to accept their offer, that they will go to war and assassinate them. All the 18th Street factions and 'wanted' [criminals on the run] in TJ are now under Peye's control. This is why we made Peye a brother. So that these 'Chicanos' would listen to Peye."

Boxer felt that the plan to take on AFO bosses "was overzealous. We would end up in a big unproductive war. And what eventually happened was the relationship between La Eme and the AFO became more symbiotic."

The CDC's informant also insisted that Popeye was a "terrorist" with major supplies of assault weapons, drugs, and money and connections in Europe, Colombia, Japan, Jamaica, and Italy. And he talked about the influence that Popeye and Bat had with politicians, judges, military officials, and law enforcement. Those contacts extended to a bail bonds company, U.S. embassy workers, Department of Motor Vehicle employees, Border Patrol agents, a San Diego County sheriff's deputy, and even social services workers—the informant specifically mentioned Rachel Ortiz's government-funded Barrio Station project in San Diego. Boxer pointed out, again, that "all those contacts were and are important to La Eme."

The same CDC intelligence memorandum laid out Bat's proposal to restructure Eme tax collections in southern California as well: "He wants to just wipe out [rob/kill] all the dealers, unless they're willing to work with the Eme and sell Peye's shipments only. They sell for the Eme or get all their drugs confiscated and either killed or chased out. Bat wants to end taxing, and force dealers to sell for us for a percentage of the profits."

The secret document noted that Bat had already proposed this "to Chuco and the brothers in a meeting," but they chose to stick with their method of strong-arming dealers on a smaller scale and collecting tribute from local gangs. Boxer believed that "some other carnales didn't have the vision. Bat did."

The confidential memo also warned that Bat would flee to Mexico as soon as he was released from prison.

He did. It was about six months after the RICO trial bus trip and his conversation with Boxer. The FBI had been alerted that Bat Marquez was planning to jump parole and head south of the border to rejoin Barron and his bloodthirsty killing machine. In June 1997, the Mafioso was under surveillance—different law enforcement agencies taking shifts—when he drove into traffic and vanished.

On November 25, 1997, two Mexican Army soldiers who were part of a special unit designed to hunt down the ruthless Arellano-Felix brothers were sitting in a blue Chevy Suburban parked outside a government courthouse in Tijuana. The two drug fighters were massacred in broad daylight, making it six men from the same detail executed on the streets within months. There were so many holes in the side of the truck that it looked like a big blue slice of Swiss cheese. More than five dozen casings from AK-47 assault rifles littered the pavement. According to official records, agents believe that Bat was one of the hired guns. "The Arellano-Felix brothers," noted Boxer, "liked Bat's ferocity and willingness to participate in violence, but he was crazy."

The day after the two Mexican Army drug fighters were executed, Jesus Blancornelas, the outraged editor of a local newspaper called *Zeta*, boldly named David Barron, aka El C-H, as the leader of the AFO hit team.

The day after the article appeared, Blancornelas, riding in his red Ford Explorer, was ambushed on his way to work at the newspaper office. Again striking in broad daylight, eight gunmen joined Barron in a well-planned attack, firing from all angles, more than a hundred bullets ripping through metal and shattering glass with frightening precision. The newsman's driver and bodyguard, Luis Lauro-Valero, was killed. Four of the high-powered rounds found their mark on Blancornelas. He nearly bled to death, but none of the wounds was fatal. The sixty-one-year-old editor, who spent months recovering from his wounds, said he felt as if he "was dreaming" when the bullets started flying. "It's incredible," he said, "the number of bullets that went through the car." He thanked God for his survival. "Death, he said hi to me. He gave me a hug, then he let me go."

Death also gave David Barron a hug, and this time the Grim Reaper didn't let go.

Police believe a ricochet bullet from one of Barron's own crew struck him in the eye and penetrated his brain. Dead on the spot, his lifeless body slumped against a short concrete wall on the edge of the sidewalk, as if someone had released all the air from a big blow-up doll. El C-H was dressed in jeans, tennis shoes, and a red sweatshirt that nearly matched the color of a large pool of blood that circled his carcass. The hired assassin still had a grip on the twelve-gauge shotgun he was carrying. Witnesses say the "Caballero Honorable" was on his way up the walk to finish off Blancornelas at close range.

Investigators believe that Ignacio Hernandez Meza, aka "Wolfie"—a gang member from the Pasole neighborhood in Oceanside and one of the hit men who ambushed Blancornelas—was later executed by cartel henchmen for firing the ricochet bullet that killed Barron.

Boxer Enriquez speculated, however, that Bat himself may have wanted Barron out of the way: "I think that Bat did it. . . . And if Bat's not getting his cut," he's not above killing. "The Mexican Mafia destroys everything it touches, and one rule is never get a brother involved in your business because he'll destroy it. I think that's what Bat came to understand. They were business partners. Popeye was stepping all over Bat's toes while he was busted, and I actually think that's probably why Popeye got hit."

Still, just months after Barron was killed, Boxer—lured by the prospect of huge profits—sent his "trusted confidante" to Tijuana to meet with Bat Marquez and talk business. It began with a lengthy series of three-way phone calls with a Bat contact in San Diego, a woman named Angel. Boxer said, "My 'trusted confidante' eventually hooked up with Angel in San Diego, who changed cars twice and went through a routine of countersurveillance driving techniques before ending up at the border. Bat personally walked across, picked up my representative, reentered Mexico, and got into a maroon-colored, armor-plated SUV equipped with a two-way radio communications system and police scanner. There were a couple of chase cars following as they drove in circles around Tijuana for a couple hours—more countersurveillance driving—before landing at Bat's house up in the hills. There were two vicious-looking pit bulls in the front yard, one chained close to the front door and the other roaming freely. Heavily armed pistoleros surrounded the place, and there was constant communication with the AFO contacts scrutinizing Bat's every move."

Bat's place sat on top of a hill, and there was a view of TJ and the border from his balcony. In reality, it was probably a short ten-minute drive to the border.

Later, recalled Boxer, "there was a short trip to a small ranch Bat owned in nearby Rosarito Beach. It was about a ten-minute drive to the ocean and a honky-tonk boardwalk of restaurants and nightclubs. He had horses, and they went riding in the countryside. Bat was consuming doses of methamphetamine along the way."

Back at the Tijuana house, Bat asked Boxer's "trusted confidante" to stay for dinner. Expecting a tasty, authentic Mexican meal, they sat down at the kitchen table and were served good old American Hormel hash out of a can. "Unbelievable." Boxer laughed. "It was ridiculous."

What wasn't ridiculous were the massive amounts of drugs Bat wanted Boxer's crews to sell across the border. He had access to ephedrine (the main ingredient in methamphetamine) in fifty-five-gallon barrels and cocaine, heroin, and marijuana. "Fifty pounds at a pop," recollected Boxer, "hundreds of kilos at a time. He wanted my people to handle it, and I had to assume responsibility for it. I was a thousand miles away and locked up in prison. It was too big. If something went wrong, I could easily get whacked for it. More important, the way they play in Mexico, my family would have been prime targets too. I couldn't take that chance." He passed on the lucrative offer.

That didn't slow Bat down for a second. U.S. DEA agents say he took over Barron's killing machine and hooked up with an Arellano-Felix drug boss named Gustavo-Rivera Martinez, a fugitive who had a $2 million price tag on his head.

A year later, Marquez was indicted in Mexico for murder and attempted murder. Besides being a suspect in the execution of Cardinal Ocampo, the assassination of the two Mexican Army soldiers, and the attack on newspaperman Blancornelas, Bat was responsible, Mexican officials believed, for at least twenty murders, probably more. He allegedly strangled a marijuana dealer with a pair of panty hose for refusing to barter on a price, and he fatally shot an associate and his girlfriend in front of their five-year-old child for reneging on a $2,000 drug debt. He was also a suspect in at least a half-dozen murders on the U.S. side of the border, though he has not been charged or indicted on those counts.

Michael Vigil, special agent in charge of the San Diego Field Division of the Drug Enforcement Administration, called Marquez "a stone killer. This man has absolutely no remorse about taking another human life . . . an executioner, an individual who has kidnapped, not only rival gang members but law enforcement officers and others, and taken them to areas and then tortured, and then killed them."

At the same time, he was a suspect for moving tons of drugs across the border.

In August 2001, a federal grand jury in San Diego indicted Bat Marquez and Gustavo-Rivera Martinez on a list of drug charges for smuggling 1,000- to 2,000-kilogram loads of marijuana and 200-kilogram loads of cocaine into the United States by boat. Bat continued to elude capture.

Boxer Enriquez claimed that Bat even had a daring plan to break La Eme's Raul "Huero Sherm" Leon out of Pelican Bay State Prison: "Leon was set to take methamphetamine to accelerate his heartbeat and then complain about chest pains so prison staff would transport him to Sutter Coast Hospital in Crescent City. It's a small-town hospital with no serious security force. Gunmen were expected to intercept Leon at the emergency room and rush him off to a waiting helicopter for an escape to Mexico, courtesy of Bat and the AFO. An Eme dropout later claimed Huero Sherm even sent him on a couple of dry runs to the hospital. The plot was thwarted by the dropout's admissions. They were actually going to implement this plan."

Then, on November 22, 2003—more than six years after he jumped parole in the United States—a bald, flabby-looking Bat Marquez was arrested by Mexican police in a working-class neighborhood of eastern Tijuana. Federalis found tons of marijuana and an arsenal of sixty-one firearms inside the warehouse where he was caught, along with eight alleged members of his crew, ranging in age from seventeen to fifty-nine. The cache of weapons included automatic assault rifles, shotguns, handguns, and an array of killer knives. There were bulletproof vests, police shirts and caps, and evidence of a torture room with handcuffs. Bat was shipped to a prison outside Mexico City and vowed to fight extradition back to the States. Shortly after his arrest, explosives were smuggled into his prison cell, and he tried to blow his way out. The DEA's Vigil said, "It was a big explosive. However, a lot of the explosive did not detonate. Otherwise, the whole wall of his prison cell would've disintegrated."

Two months later, it became clear what had led to Bat's arrest. The San Diego County District Attorney's Office named two Mexican Mafia members, Marquez and Roberto "Tawa" Marin, and thirty-five gang associates in a sweeping fifty-two-count indictment charging them with methamphetamine dealing, possession of assault weapons, robbery, kidnapping, attempted murder, and conspiracy to murder two civilians.

Cops got a tip that the Old Town street gang in National City, six miles southeast of San Diego, asked for and received Bat's permission to kill a local police detective who was actively pursuing cases against the gang. Government agents claimed that a Bat lieutenant, Arturo "Nite Owl" or "Primo" Torres, had a military background and was supposed to spearhead the detective's murder.

Local, state, and federal law enforcement launched an investigation to make sure the plot to kill an officer never materialized. It didn't. During eight months of wiretaps, detectives found Bat in Tijuana, tweaked out on methamphetamines and up until four o'clock in the morning talking about drug deals and murder. In the end, they were able to pinpoint where Mexican officials could find and arrest him.

Deputy District Attorney Mark Amador, a gang division prosecutor who coordinated the investigation, said, "Everyone knows he [Bat Marquez] controls the streets of San Diego." He described Bat as the "infamous" leader of an Eme-controlled drug distribution network that taxed all local dealers under a reign of terror. "And that's exactly the control La Eme needed," emphasized Boxer. "Bat had street savvy. He knew that if brothers had crews, he could supply them with dope, plenty of dope."

One of the Bat-related gangsters who was arrested, already on probation for a terrorist threat conviction, was caught with three guns and a list of seventy witnesses who had testified before the grand jury. San Diego County district attorney Bonnie Dumanis said, "Some had been threatened, intimidated, attacked, stabbed, or shot by members of this ruthless gang." According to court documents, one woman was held hostage for more than fifteen hours because the gangsters thought she had talked to police about an attempted murder. They threatened to kill her, poured hot sauce in her eyes, and cut her long hair off after ordering her to strip naked.

Investigators say others had their noses broken or were tortured with cigarette burns.

And all the time, federal agents stressed, Bat maintained his ties to the Tijuana Drug Cartel.

During a February 2004 interview in Mexico with a Fox 6 television reporter from San Diego named Pete Fuentes, Bat said he was just a high school dropout who grew up in Chula Vista and worked as a house painter. He told Fuentes he was arrested in Tijuana by machine-gun-toting men, dressed in black, who put a hood over his head, beat him, stuffed him into the trunk of a car, and put him on a plane to Mexico City. "I thought they were going to kill me," he said. Marquez denied being an AFO hit man or a drug dealer and had "no idea" who David "Popeye" Barron was. He claimed he signed a confession in Baja because he was tortured. Marquez managed to tell the reporter with a straight face, "I ain't done nothing at all."

On January 27, 2007, Jose "Bat" Marquez was extradited back to the United States. He was flown into a private airport in San Diego, wearing khaki pants, a white T-shirt underneath a blue bulletproof vest, and handcuffs. Bat was escorted by federal marshals, surrounded by cops with big guns, and taken in a convoy of government-owned SUVs to the Metropolitan Detention Center, where he remains. Trials are pending in both federal and state courts. If convicted, he will most likely never see the outside of a prison again.

Two of the Arellano-Felix brothers—who ran the billion-dollar Tijuana

Drug Cartel—are now in the U.S. prison system. That too could favor La Eme's position with Mexican drug kingpins. Boxer noted, "Who runs the prisons? The Mexican Mafia does. The overall impact for the mob is huge. La Eme can have them [Tijuana Cartel bosses] killed or protected. It gives us great influence with Mexican drug lords."

"And other drug cartels will come along," predicted Boxer. "This relationship with the AFO is no onetime thing."

CHAPTER 31

It Was Just Business

MARIANO "CHUY" MARTINEZ—BOXER'S OLD PINOCHLE PARTNER AT Folsom back in the mid-1980s—was on the outside running so much action that quite a few other brothers wanted him dead. Enriquez didn't feel that way. He liked Chuy, and for good reason. After Black Dan and Huero Shy were convicted at the RICO trial and locked up in the federal system, it was Chuy he counted on as a reliable Eme contact on the street. "He was a Mafioso who allowed my business interests to flourish. He knew Huck, my crew chief, and wouldn't hesitate to lend a helping hand anytime I had a turf dispute. Unlike some other carnales, Chuy never attempted to move in on my territories. He had a thriving operation of his own throughout the Los Angeles basin and understood there was enough business for both of us. That's why we got along so well."

Boxer and Chuy had been made within a month of each other at Folsom in 1985, lived on the same tier, walked the yard together, and bonded. As Mafiosi, said Enriquez, "we were in our honeymoon phase." More than a decade later, both knew their honeymoon with the mob had turned into a bad marriage.

Chuy was a burly, tough cholo with a shaved head and huge bushy mustache that spread across his face and drooped down at the edges in the style of Mexican revolutionaries Emilio Zapata or Pancho Villa. He was a fearless killer who had been shot so many times himself that he had bullet fragments lodged in his head, chest, and spine. On the other hand, he didn't do drugs, spoke fluent French, loved playing chess, and had more than a mild passion for Snickers candy bars. During Christmastime, he had a ritual of passing out presents to poor children in the Varrio Nuevo Estrada neighborhood where he grew up in East Los Angeles. "Prior to his membership in La Eme," added Boxer, "Chuy was a big PCP dealer who often went to Hollywood's famed Brown Derby restaurant, and he hung out with a singing group called Tierra."

Boxer said, "Chuy had strong business acumen and knew how to make money." In his late thirties, Martinez owned a video store and a restaurant, had a share in a nightclub called Luminarius, and drove around in a gray late-model Cadillac DeVille. It was all from drug profits and Eme taxes collected from street gangs in many different parts of Los Angeles. There was little doubt—with a dozen other Mafia heavyweights locked up forever after their 1997 RICO convictions—that Martinez had become a cash machine. "He was raking in huge amounts of money," according to Boxer. And a number of Mafia brothers in Pelican Bay State Prison thought Chuy was keeping too much of it for himself—not sharing the wealth.

Part of the problem, according to Boxer, was "that Mafia heavyweight Topo Peters told Chuy he could direct Eme activities on the streets. Unfortunately, he sent the same message to Victorio Murillo—the only Eme member found not guilty in the RICO trial—who was living in a town called Visalia in California's Central Valley. Topo was just trying to get some money from both of them, but it pitted Chuy against Victorio."

On December 13, 1997, several Mexican Mafia members, including Victorio, met at the Mirage Hotel in Las Vegas—arriving in luxury automobiles and limousines—to discuss the future of Mariano "Chuy" Martinez. During the meeting, Charles "Chacho" Woody—a reputed multiple murderer—volunteered to put the hit on Chuy whenever the mob wanted it done. Unfortunately for him, there was an informant in the room wearing a wire and the FBI was elsewhere in the hotel taking it all down.

That informant was John Turscak, aka "Stranger." He wasn't even a Mexican—his family was from Czechoslovakia—but he grew up in the thick of gangbangers in Highland Park (Northeast L.A.), and at thirteen years of age he had joined the Rockwood gang based in Echo Park. He'd had a relationship with cocaine since those early years and was involved in shootings—an arrest for robbery at sixteen was a planned murder that was foiled by police. During years in prison for robbery and false imprisonment, he did approximately ten stabbings—most at the direction of La Eme—killing inmate Gabriel "Pato" Rodriguez at Folsom in 1990. Boxer "met him once in the law library at Pelican Bay. He looked weird, and I thought he was an idiot, but he was made after he left prison." The twenty-six-year-old Turscak was long-haired and scruffy-looking, more akin to a head-banging heavy metal devotee than the shaved-headed gang members of his age group.

Out on parole in late 1996, the loud and talkative Turscak quickly violated his terms of release by hanging out with other gangsters and testing dirty for cocaine. He was headed back to prison, but the feds offered him an alternative—in April 1997 he became a $2,000 a month paid informant for the FBI. In the months that followed, Turscak continued to have chronic problems with nose-candy and the feds paid $1,500 to send him to drug rehab. Also during his time as a snitch for the government, the Czech Mexican Mafia thug—unknown to his FBI handlers—continued to wrangle up Eme extortion payments on the street. This presented a problem for Boxer: "Turscak got out on the street and tried to tax my crews. He demanded one hundred dollars for every ounce of dope sold by Huck [Boxer's crew chief]. I had Huck call Chuy, who then sent word to Turscak to stay away from my crews. And I wired instructions to Huck—if Turscak or his camaradas tried to collect taxes from any of our crews, tell them, 'If you try to take this, you are stealing directly from Boxer.' And if Turscak insists on payment, kill him."

All the while, Chuy Martinez refused to meet personally with Turscak, who felt snubbed by the prosperous Mafia shot-caller. So, expanding on his duplicitous dealings with the Federal Bureau of Investigation, Turscak participated with others in several plots to kill Chuy.

Six days after the Eme powwow in Las Vegas, Chuy pulled his Caddy into a Montebello taco stand about nine-thirty at night with his fiancé, Jessicka Barreto, and a male companion. Gunshots ripped through his windshield, doorjamb, and radiator as Chuy pushed his girlfriend down on the seat and stepped on the gas to escape. Four bullets tore into the driver's side, and fragments struck Chuy in the left side of his head and right hand. Bloodied but alive, he drove to a nearby hospital and was treated for his wounds. Unbelievably, the other two riding in the car were not hit. Boxer heard the news the next weekend during prison visits: "I thought it was getting serious. These guys were going to move on me too—on my street operations. It boiled down to greed. Guys like Turscak and Woody wanted control. We had solid street crew operations, and they didn't. It was a move by them to weaken our position and political standing in La Eme."

Shortly after he got shot, Chuy Martinez set up a meeting with Turscak in a passenger lounge at Los Angeles International Airport—he knew each of them would have to pass through a metal detector to get in. The talk accomplished nothing. Boxer got a letter from Chuy. "He was outraged that they tried to kill him," Boxer said. "He thought it was a cowardly attack, and he vowed to whack all those guys [who plotted against him]."

Meanwhile, Turscak had audiotaped (for the FBI) the explanation by the murderous Chacho Woody of his conversation in December with forty-year-old Roy "Lil Spider" Gavaldon from Canta Ranas about his willingness to kill Chuy. According to Woody, Lil Spider said, "I'll kill everybody you dudes want me to kill, to let the brothers know I'm in." Gavaldon wanted to be a member of the Mexican Mafia. Ironically, Lil Spider was the husband of Cynthia Gavaldon, the woman Boxer Enriquez had ordered dead seven years earlier. In the Mafia culture, murder never seems to be an antidote to more murder. Boxer felt nothing but disgust for Lil Spider: "He was an outsider who would do anything to get into the organization, and I always opposed him. I knew he would only be an enemy. And if he'd really cared about his wife, he would've killed me. The truth is, he didn't care about her, and he had her hustling on the streets to support his drug habit while he was in prison. It's just business."

In March 1998, Turscak got a letter from an Eme member at Pelican Bay, and he turned it over to his FBI handlers. It read: "[Chuy Martinez] is no longer holding honor as a carnal! He has in the past to present violated the law of our ordinance *carnalismo* [brotherhood]. However, on behalf of all us carnales *verdaderos* [true brothers] here, Chuy . . . must go!!"

Boxer said, "Everyone in the Bay was saying kill Chuy because they were jealous of his success. I did what I could to politic in his favor, but it did little good." The carnales smelled blood.

In April, a frustrated Turscak, unable to get to Chuy, sent orders into L.A. County Jail to assault two of his associates instead. Mafia henchmen beat up Chuy's nephew in his cell, but he survived without serious injury. One of his crew members was stabbed and hurt badly, but managed to survive. On April 8, after the attacks, the FBI monitored another telephone conversation in which a Mafia member advised Turscak to deal with Chuy and forget about the people around him.

Later on that same day, Turscak assured another carnal, "I will set it up," referring to a hit on Chuy.

The next day, still having doubts that Turscak would actually carry out the hit, an FBI agent personally contacted Chuy Martinez at his parole office and warned him that his life was in danger—giving no details. Chuy, forever the gangster, scoffed at the feds' offer of protection. "Chuy wouldn't take protection," explained Boxer, "because he could deal with it on his own. That kept him honorable in the eyes of the mob. He was a stand-up guy."

Shortly afterward, there was a twist of events. A gangster Turscak had tried to enlist to do the hit in turn surreptitiously passed the information along to Chuy. A couple of days later, heavily armed Chuy Martinez crew members tracked Turscak down and opened fire on him, his wife, and their infant son as they walked out of his mother's house in Atwater Village. It was Easter Sunday. Miraculously, no one was hit.

The scare drove Turscak underground for a week—out of contact with his FBI handlers. Meanwhile, the feds had finally had enough of his double-dealing. FBI and parole agents arrested him on April 30, 1998, and put him back behind bars. His days as a paid government informant were done.

On April 4, more than three weeks earlier, fifty-two-year-old Victor Murillo had been shot and killed in a dirt parking lot near a Greyhound Bus station in Goshen, a little farm town in the Central Valley not far from his home, 160 miles northwest of Los Angeles. Murillo ran a lucrative co-caine, methamphetamine, and heroin operation. Agents speculated that he was whacked for his refusal to share drug profits with younger Mafiosi, or possibly because of a false perception that he secretly cooperated with law enforcement to win an acquittal a year earlier in the RICO trial. Boxer Enriquez had a more direct theory: "Victorio was one of the brothers who met in Las Vegas and decided to kill Chuy. Chuy did the right thing and killed Victorio first. Chuy is the epitome of what a Mafioso should be—he was smart and took action."

With Murillo dead and Turscak locked up, Chuy Martinez pushed forward with his drug operations. According to federal records, Chuy had at the very least two dozen gangs paying him taxes—north, south, east, and west of the City of Angels. Also, his faction controlled all Eme activities in L.A. County Jail. He still wanted Turscak dead too. Boxer said that he received a wila from Chuy in coded language that said basically: "Back me up on this murder, and I'll continue to back you up on the streets."

On November 17, 1998, federal agents received information that Max "Mono" Torvisco, Chuy's right-hand man, said Turscak would be killed either in prison or when he got out.

The next day, there was no waiting when it came to wiping out a close associate of Turscak's, a big drug dealer named Richard Serrano, who was spotted hanging out at a Montebello auto body shop. After Chuy got the word, investigators say that he got on the phone and directed crew members

to kill Serrano and all potential witnesses. According to later courtroom testimony, Chuy directed the carnage from a nearby location, communicating
on a two-way radio with the hit men. Serrano was cornered in an office by
two City Terrace gang members armed with .380 handguns and executed
while on his knees. The body of Enrique Delgadillo was found next to his,
and Jose Martin Gutierrez was shot and killed while repairing a wall outside the shop. Two others were shot and left for dead but survived. Boxer
recalled, "Chuy had those guys whacked, and it was the hottest topic of the
week [at Pelican Bay]."

Chuy in the weeks following the massacre made it clear to his Mafia
protégé Mono Torvisco that they should go forward with plans to murder
Stranger Turscak. "This was a collective effort of our Eme faction," insisted
Boxer, "to rid ourselves of opposition in the streets and in the prisons."

Then, on February 2, 1999, hundreds of law enforcement officers from
the FBI, L.A. County Sheriff's Department, Los Angeles Police Department,
and other agencies swept down on certain Los Angeles neighborhoods and
more than a dozen outlying cities, arresting Mexican Mafia members and
their associates. A new federal indictment named twenty-seven people
for violating the RICO Act and spelled out Mafia goals to use murder and
mayhem to control all drug trafficking in southern California while using
a vast network of Latino street gangs. The indictment alleged four murders (including the Montebello massacre), three attempted murders, and
thirteen conspiracies to commit murder, four conspiracies to assault or assaults with a deadly weapon, and multiple conspiracies to distribute drugs.
During the arrests, cops found thirty-seven weapons, including an AK-47
assault rifle and a hand grenade.

"Back in the 1950s, we had organized crime dealing with La Cosa
Nostra in upstate New York," said FBI assistant director in charge Timothy
McNally. "It took better than thirty years of indictments of federal and state
prosecutors across the country to put away really the hierarchy of most of
the families.

"The Mexican Mafia is one of our primary organized crime groups on
the West Coast," McNally continued. "They've been around for a long time,
and we are in this for the long haul."

There would be four separate trials over the next two years as the list
of indicted co-conspirators grew to forty-five defendants involved in Mafia
business. Boxer Enriquez was not named. Sergeant Richard Valdemar believed that "Boxer had a smooth operation and stayed under the radar."
Mariano "Chuy" Martinez, singled out as the top-ranking leader for La Eme

in Los Angeles, became the first death penalty defendant to be tried in L.A. Federal Court since 1950.

The star witness in each trial was an articulate, fast-talking former student at Cal State University–Los Angeles: Max "Mono" Torvisco, Chuy's twenty-four-year-old top lieutenant. Torvisco—who had also sent tax money to Boxer from time to time—made a deal with government prosecutors after spending only a few weeks behind bars. A federal death penalty act had recently been expanded, and he didn't want to tempt fate by going to trial himself and possibly ending up on death row.

During his testimony, Mono admitted that he had ordered as many as forty murders, killed three people on his own, and participated in numerous stabbings and shootings. He identified himself as one of four Mexican Mafia members who ran street operations in the greater Los Angeles area, including his mentor Mariano "Chuy" Martinez. He didn't hesitate to tell the jury, "I was the one with the brains."* Mono testified that Martinez referred to him as "my son" as he brought him up through the ranks of Varrio Estrada Nuevo (VNE) and into the Mafia. Typical of mob duplicity, he also admitted that he had been planning to kill Chuy shortly before their RICO arrests. During cross-examination, he was asked if he had any qualms about murdering his mentor. His answer echoed a line from Francis Ford Coppola's movie *The Godfather:* "No. It was just business, nothing personal."

Chuy Martinez, the only RICO defendant ultimately facing the death penalty, was tried alone. He was found guilty of racketeering, drug dealing, murder for ordering the Montebello body shop massacre, and conspiring to murder nine other people, including Mafioso-turned-informant John "Stranger" Turscak.

In a separate trial, five gangsters charged in connection with the Montebello body shop massacre—including the two actual shooters—were acquitted. The jury foreman later said about key witness Max Torvisco: "We found him to be out and out lying about the murders. As soon as we caught him lying, he was dead meat, and so was the prosecution's case."

Rival Turscak pleaded guilty to various RICO offenses and was sentenced to thirty years in prison.

---

* Rene Enriquez claimed that "Mono was never a made member of the Eme," despite his claims otherwise. According to Enriquez, Topo Peters told Chuy Martinez that Mono was voted in, but that was a "boldfaced lie." Enriquez said that Mono was denied membership in votes at Pelican Bay and at the federal Eme faction. He explained, "Topo lied about it because Chuy and Mono were giving money to Sally Peters, Topo's wife, and Peters didn't want those funds to dry up by offending either of them."

Forty-three-year-old Roy "Lil Spider" Gavaldon, who had offered to whack Chuy to "make his bones" in the Mafia, was convicted of racketeering and drug charges. He was sentenced to twenty-one years in prison.

Charles "Chacho" Woody—also originally in on plans to hit Chuy—pleaded guilty to murdering Victorio Murillo and was sentenced to twenty-three years in prison.

On February 19, 2003, Max "Mono" Torvisco—whose testimony in six trials helped produce fifty convictions—was finally sentenced to ten years in federal prison for racketeering. The public and the news media were barred from the heavily guarded courtroom during the proceeding. Mono fidgeted as he stood in front of U.S. District Judge Dickran Tevrizian awaiting the decision. Brian A. Newman, Mono's defense attorney, had asked for a lesser sentence. He pleaded that his client "is in extreme danger for the rest of his life." No one argued with that assertion.

During Chuy's trial, defense attorney Mark Overland tried to paint him as a peacemaker who tried "to stop the gangbanging and the killing of innocent people." It didn't quite work. Chuy was convicted on multiple counts. However, on March 29, 2001, the jury deadlocked 7–5—during the penalty phase of the trial—on whether to give Mariano "Chuy" Martinez the death penalty. U.S. District Judge David O. Carter was forced to declare a mistrial and sentenced Chuy to life in prison plus 130 years.

Chuy went off to a federal penitentiary forever—joining Black Dan Barela and Huero Shy Shryock. Boxer Enriquez lost his last strong Mafia ally on the street: "It further deteriorated my political base. All my support on the streets was gone now. I found myself in turf battle after turf battle, arguing with one carnal after another, and it was wearing me down. I was left in Pelican Bay, drifting. The wolves were circling."

CHAPTER 32

Race Riot Madness

THE SKIES WERE OMINOUSLY DARK WITH CLOUD COVER, AND THE ground was already dampened by a light rainfall as a collection of inmates started to file out onto B-yard at Pelican Bay State Prison. Each prisoner had to stop for a quick full-body search before being released out into the general population mainline. One hundred yards away, in the maximum-security SHU, Boxer Enriquez was taking an after-breakfast nap on his cell bunk. It was like that every day, but February 23, 2000, wasn't going to be just like every other day. Two Mexican Mafia henchmen—without the knowledge of Boxer and other carnales—had already guaranteed it. "Two boneheads," lamented Boxer, "sent out orders to kill as many black guys as possible."

It was about nine-thirty in the morning by the time the last of about three hundred inmates took a place somewhere on the open field. Some of them were dressed in rain hats and body-length yellow slickers because of a light drizzle in the air. A small group of black inmates stationed themselves at the parallel bars and chin-up bar as a few pulled off a series of reps on the apparatus. A dozen or more sat at a couple of picnic tables on the grass, and several others stood at the yard perimeter trading stories. Groups of four or five walked around the track as a few jogged by themselves. On the concrete basketball court, black inmates played on one end as two teams of Mexican inmates (Surenos) staked out territory for a game at the other end.

Surenos were forming in small groups across the yard, some standing in huddles, others plopped down on the tops of picnic tables by the dozen. Customarily, many of them spent their time on yard 4 playing soccer, but not on this day. There was something else on their agenda. It was a wet and chilly morning, but still, every single Mexican prisoner chose to go out on the yard—not unprecedented but unusual. Word was spread "to act natural" so the blacks wouldn't suspect that danger was lurking.

Jose "Clever" Sanchez was a Mexican Mafia associate from a southern California gang called Toonerville. He was doing ten years for robbery and was the shot-caller on B-yard as the leader of an Eme governing board called the Mesa. Boxer explained: "The Mesa was a selected group of four or five camaradas, maybe one from each cell block, that made collective decisions on how to run the mainline yards for La Eme. The *Meseros* replaced the *llavero* (keyholder) system where just one camarada had total control to make decisions. Several years earlier, we eliminated the llavero concept because it was causing conflict on the mainlines. More than one camarada was claiming the right to be the llavero. The Mesa seemed to cut down on abuses of the single boss notion and kept the drugs and other black market activities running smoothly."

A year earlier, a black inmate named Monster Blevins somehow had insulted or disrespected a Sureno known as Panter, or Panther. It seems the Eme Mesero at the time approached the black shot-caller on the yard and asked him to discipline Blevins for his disrespect. He refused—a snub to Eme/Sureno prison dominance. The stage was set for a massive retaliation.

According to a criminal complaint, Clever Sanchez allegedly directed the manufacture and distribution of thirty new jailhouse shanks and gave orders to Surenos "to kill as many blacks as possible." "If you can kill a nigger," Clever told one associate, "kill a nigger if you can." Boxer noted, "There is a lot of racism in prison." Clever had allegedly laid the venomous groundwork for what would become the largest prison riot in Pelican Bay history.

"It's going to happen right now," Clever is alleged to have said at about 9:35 A.M. as he took a short stroll over to the side of the running track that reached around the perimeter of B-yard. He had already pulled his weapon from the hiding place in his rectum. Marbel Simmons, a black inmate, was taking his morning run as he came around the corner and headed down the stretch. Clever lingered on the inside of the track—as one inmate would later describe it—"like a tiger waiting behind the bushes for their prey to run by."

There was an echo on the yard from the force of Clever's knife slapping into the unsuspecting jogger's back. He grabbed on to the victim's shirt to keep him from running away, but the larger Simmons managed to break free, stumble, and escape. The preplanned riot was on.

The entire yard erupted into what one inmate would later call "madness." The blacks were caught by surprise. They were also heavily outnumbered as roving packs of armed Surenos took them down and stabbed them over and over again. A repeated blast of commands came over the yard public address system: "Get down!" The crazed inmates ignored the warnings. Tear-gas canisters rained down on the action within seconds of the initial outburst of violence, cutting visibility to zero in some spots. There were black men on their backs fending off blows with their bare hands as shafts of steel came at them like three or four driving pistons. The yard was painted with large white and gray clouds of gas and trickles of red blood soaking into the green grass. Puffs of dirt launched from the grass as guards started firing rubber bullets, then a half-dozen warning shots with live ammunition.

Back in the dungeonlike SHU area, Boxer recalled, "I heard pod doors opening and the jingle of keys as guards scurried around ordering, 'Lockdown modified program. Go straight to your cells. Don't stop at any doors!'" The small doggie-walk recreation yards attached to the SHU had open-air ceilings, and Boxer caught a whiff of tear gas as the metal door opened to allow an exercising SHU prisoner back to his cell.

On the mainline, the constant hollering of hordes of Surenos was deafening, punctuated with the crack of Mini-14 rifle fire from three correctional officers in the gun towers. The threat of gunfire seemed to have little effect. Clever had allegedly given orders to keep stabbing even if guards started shooting live ammo into the yard. He said, "If they start firing, keep pushing harder." Mostly they did. A Sureno who does not want to be identified explained: "There's no saying no. It could cost your life, could cost you getting hit, targeted. So no is not an option. It's always you do or be done. That's the way it is."

During the first four minutes of rioting, groups of attackers periodically stood down about three times, but within seconds were again on the attack. At one point, a surge of black power even drove the main force of Surenos back, but it lasted only about a half-minute.

Initially, there were only about a dozen correctional officers on the yard. They used pepper spray and batons to try to break up the skirmishes, but it did little good. Sergeant Hank Akin said, "Your nerves come up. You don't know what's going on. You don't know whether you're going home. You don't know if you're going to get killed or not."

A few inmates who returned from the SHU yard told Boxer that, in addition to the gunfire, they heard verbal commands—"Yard down!"—from the mainline public address system. "I didn't know what or why," recalled Boxer, "but I knew something serious was happening out there."

Outside, fewer than a dozen blacks had their backs against the wall at one end of the basketball court as more than twice that many Surenos cornered them, some swinging toothbrushes with razor blades mounted on the tips. One of the blacks was coldcocked by a Sureno in the pack, and as he fell back he was literally swarmed. It was about five minutes into the fracas. The same gangster who had knocked him down kept on coming. There was the sound of gunfire, and the attacker fell to the pavement. The mob hesitated for a second and then took off running. Thirty-three-year-old Miguel Sanchez, a Sureno known as "Sharky," wasn't with them anymore. He was dead on the spot, a bullet hole in his head, a puddle of blood forming around his still body, which was faceup on the concrete basketball court, partially obscured in a fog of smoky tear gas.

It was a death knell that brought the riot to a halt. Correctional officers pulled Sharky's body to the side and administered first aid, but it was too late.

Unbelievably, Surenos around the yard were on their haunches still ready to leap into action again. Four minutes after the fatal gunshot, there was another surge of Sureno violence, but it didn't last long. More than a hundred guards had filtered out into the yard with armfuls of plastic hand-cuffs. Fortunately, there were forty officers from another shift who just happened to be at PBSP that day for training. Many officers had emptied their canisters of pepper spray. Under a haze of residual smoke, dozens of inmates were cuffed behind their backs and proned out on the ground. Stretcher bearers were taking away the wounded. It truly looked like a damn battlefield.

At the end of a quarter-hour of rioting, one inmate was dead. Forty in-mates were injured, most of them from stab wounds. Fifteen were wounded by gunfire.

In the SHU, correctional officers now slapped "boots" on the cell doors—bars with a padlock and strap that jammed the door to keep it from opening. "Why?" asked Boxer. The guard offered no reply.

Later, officers reported that twenty-four live rounds were fired during the riot, approximately a half-dozen of them warning shots. During the cleanup, guards found an unprecedented eighty-nine prison-made weapons on the yard.

In an article in the March–April issue of *Peacekeeper,* the California Cor-rectional Peace Officers Association magazine, Pelican Bay chapter president Chuck Alexander said: "It's unfortunate that one inmate died from gunfire. But had the officers not used lethal force to end the incident, how many more inmates would have been killed in the attacks? And if we'd have just stood back and let them kill each other, we'd have been criticized for not doing anything."

Boxer Enriquez and other upper-echelon Mafiosi were just as perplexed. Locked up in the nearby SHU section of the prison during the entire riot, they could only wonder, "What was that all about and who called it? After all, doesn't La Eme run the yards?"

It turned out that riot leader Clever Sanchez had been corresponding—via kites—with La Eme's Alfie Sosa. The fifty-seven-year-old Sosa and his cellmate, thirty-nine-year-old Eulalio "Lalo" Martinez, had given their blessing to the riot. The hot-tempered Alfie was "a deadly snake possessed by legions of demons."* Boxer believed that Alfie and Lalo were also " bonafide racists, just hard-core racists. I don't know if they got beat up by blacks when they were kids," he said, "but they are just hell-bent on creating racial tension."

A few weeks later, an unrepentant Alfie and Lalo owned up to their role in giving the go-ahead for the riot. Boxer said, "Alfie—high on meth and doing push-ups in his cell—was laughing about it. It was pure arrogance not to forewarn the other carnales. Most of us disagreed with it because it ultimately prevented us from making money on the mainline. It drew a lot of heat."

In fact, CDC officials tightened prison controls after the riot. Normally, the general population was locked down only between the hours of 9:00 P.M. and 6:00 A.M. A new modified program had them locked down twenty-three hours a day for the next two years.

"This was no small thing," stressed Boxer Enriquez. "A camarada was killed. Multiple Surenos were shot. And Alfie and Lalo left other carnales in the dark about it." It was the biggest riot in Pelican Bay State Prison history.

However, as if the devil was looking out for his followers, the bloody and deadly riot launched an unintended consequence for mob opportunity. Boxer and the carnales closest to him were ready to take full advantage of it.

---

* Mendoza, *Mexican Mafia*, p. 148.

CHAPTER 33

Phony Peace Talks

POLITICIANS IN SACRAMENTO WERE GOING BALLISTIC OVER NEWS OF the bloody prison race riot, and so were bosses at the California Department of Corrections. They didn't want another riot under any circumstances.

Pelican Bay warden Robert Ayers was exasperated. There was fear that if all the general population inmates were released back onto the mainline yard, there would be another full-scale riot—maybe more deadly than the last one.

At the same time, prison reform politicians were pressuring the warden. They wanted to know why the inmates were being locked down nearly all day, every day. The reformers felt that such a policy was inhumane.

It was a great setup for Mafia manipulation. Boxer Enriquez laid out the plot: "Prison officials really didn't want to deal with us, but we could deliver a service that they couldn't. We [La Eme] were going to guarantee peace on the yards—no race riots and no attacks on guards. In return, we would get the hardline carnales released from the restrictive SHUs and put back on the mainline where we could take care of Mafia business."

Days after the riot, Jacko Padilla showed up at Boxer's pod and walked over to his SHU cell. Normally no personal contact was allowed, but now prison officials were searching for a solution to end the violence.

"Hey!" said Padilla.

"What are you doing in here?" queried a surprised Boxer.

Jacko slipped him a bindle of heroin as a gift and said, "They're negotiating with us."

Shortly after the riots, representatives of the Black Guerilla Family prison gang approached the warden with a proposal. They told him that he had lost control of the prison population and they could help him get it back. The BGF plan revolved around one simple premise: release prison gang heavyweights from the SHU facility and put them back onto the general population yard to restore order. The BGF argued that it was the younger gangsters on the yard who were out of control and that only their criminal mentors had the clout to reel them in and settle them down.

It was the desperate warden who took the bait. Members of the rival Aryan Brotherhood were then pulled into this "peace plan" discussion. Jacko caught wind of the talks and, without ever admitting he was an Eme member, volunteered to speak for the Mexican Mafia. The warden wanted no more race riots, no further attacks on correctional officers, and assurances of peace and tranquillity on the yard. He decided to form a negotiation committee composed of twelve inmates—four from the BGF, four from the AB, and four from La Eme. They would be allowed to meet by themselves in a conference room to come up with a viable peace plan.

Jacko's first choice to serve on the Mafia delegation was Boxer Enriquez. "I want you to be there cuz you got my back," explained Padilla. "Everybody knows that you're down."

"That's what I am? I'm the shooter?"

"Yeah."

"Okay," agreed Boxer.

Jacko was the businessman. Official CDC records indicate that he was always connected to the drug cartels and flush with profits—he had plenty of money to grease the tracks. Boxer was a feared leader and a man of action. Together they picked two more carnales to serve on the bogus peace committee.

They needed voices with serious credibility to reach the entire Mariposa at PBSP. Daniel "Danny Boy" Pina fit that bill. He was a forty-one-year-old carnal from Big Hazard in Northeast Los Angeles who helped kill La Eme's Moe Ferrel at Folsom in the mid-1980s. "Danny was a suave carnal, well respected among older and younger members," said Boxer, "and he had a great rap. He could persuade a drowning man to give up his life preserver."

The next pick was forty-four-year-old Jorge "Huero Caballo" Gonzales of Eighteenth Street, a tall, lanky, alabaster-skinned, workout fanatic who had the body of a Greek god, a face that looked like television cowboy Roy Rogers's horse Trigger, and a bald spot large enough to be a parking lot on top of his big head. During a Mafia restructuring in the mid-1980s, he'd served as an Eme commissioner at Folsom before that concept was dropped because of power abuses. He also killed a man on the cell block there. Boxer felt that "he was a political wave rider, and I didn't trust him." At the same time, he knew that "Huero Caballo was a powerful figure who had the ear of members in all generations."

Boxer may have been signed on as "the shooter," but he was determined "to become the speaker for the whole group." First, he helped convince the warden that it was necessary to poll all the other Mexican Mafia members at PBSP. "We didn't even have a plan at first." Boxer laughed. "We were just getting out the door." Then the Eme contingent spent the next few months, two hours a day, a couple of times a week, being escorted around to SHUs to speak with three dozen or more locked-up Eme members. Under the guise of peace talks, Boxer said, "we took care of Mafia business instead—tried to unify the mob, curb factional infighting, quash individual beefs, and establish a new hit list to wipe out Mexican Mafia members seen as detractors."

Jacko had a policy: "give the Indians beads." So every time the guards released them into a pod to speak with a Mafioso, Padilla eased a couple of grams of heroin into his palm. "It immediately eased the conversation," explained Boxer. "We came bearing gifts and made them think they were all a part of this. But we had our own agenda."

Boxer wanted to use this opportunity "to take out his rivals." Angel "Stump" Valencia of La Sangra was one of them. Stump was about five feet tall and was packed solid with about 200 pounds of well-defined, raw muscle. He had EME tattooed on his chest in Old English/German text and another tattoo on his arm that read ANGEL with EME underneath. He was a forty-three-year-old jokester who was always tagging new inmates with nicknames, and despite his short stature, he was a hell of a prison-yard basketball player in his day. "In truth," Boxer said, "Angel was a miserable soul who committed his first murder when he was only in the eighth grade. His father and some of his gangster associates wanted to test Angel, took him to a dope house, and told him to kill a junkie nodded out in a chair as they pinned back his arms. He was only thirteen years old and stabbed the stranger to death. Not long after that, he unsuccessfully tried to strangle his own hard-ass father. His father used to lock him in a closet with a quart of beer when he was a child just to get him out of the way."

Angel was doing life for taking part in the Moe Ferrel murder, and he was a staunch ally of the treacherous Cuate Grajeda. There was always a black cloud hanging over his head.

Lalo Martinez had possession of a kite—supposedly written by Angel Valencia—that spelled out a plan to kill the family members of rival Mexican Mafia members. Boxer was alarmed: "I thought we had some sense of honor, and killing family members was taboo. If that was allowed, not only was a carnal susceptible to Mafia politics, but so was his family. The Angel-Cuate faction believed the threat of killing family would stop Eme members from dropping out. I thought it would create added distress for a carnal and more defections. It would also hurt recruitment of new members." So the so-called peace team took the wila around on their goodwill visits to other mobsters and solidified support to whack the Stump. It later turned out that the note was actually written by Cuate Grajeda himself. Boxer in fact had "recognized Cuate's handwriting immediately" but used the note ruse to take down Angel. Then he had two of his enemies "in the hat." He felt that, with Angel and Cuate on the lista, the enemy Grajeda faction would be neutralized.

Boxer then came up with a plot to invite either Cuate or Angel to the peace talks and kill him. The negotiation meetings were held in a conference room right across from the guard's central control booth in D-facility. There were no guns in there. All the participants were seated around a long table. The representatives from La Eme, BGF, and AB sat across from the hopeful warden, a three-man delegation from the skeptical Special Services Unit, and naive representatives from the offices of state senators Tom Hayden, Richard Polanco, and John Vasconcellos. There were little place cards on the table in front of each seat with the participant's name. The Mafiosi had handcuff keys ready to casually unlatch their chains with their hands under the table. "When everyone's guard was down," proposed Boxer, "stab him [Angel or Cuate] to death." He emphasized: "Stay on him until he dies."

"Yeah," Danny Boy agreed, "let's do it!"

Jacko got nervous. "No!"

He was the voice of reason. Padilla saw the big picture, and he was right. The Mafia had to use this peace talk as a front to get released from the SHU, and an act of violence would only destroy that objective. "We wanted to get back out on the mainline," realized Boxer. "That's what we really wanted out of all this." There was more freedom to run the prison rackets out among the general population. The SHUs had definitely cramped the Mafia's game. The isolation virtually stopped face-to-face communication with most of the other members. "What is the first thing that destroys a marriage?" observed Boxer. "Lack of communication." Furthermore, the only plausible way to kill someone in the SHU was to have an inmate's cellie do it. That caused constant paranoia. Additionally, five to eight inmates always living together in the same pod area would often grow tired of each other and start politicking among themselves. "We had guys coming out to the visiting room talking bad about everybody," observed Boxer. "There was a lot of dissension in the mob ranks because of the constant isolation in the SHU."

Eventually, the peace talk table "hit plot" against Angel or Cuate was scrapped. There was nothing altruistic about that decision. It was done out of pure self-interest. "The prison administration already thinks we're the devil," realized Boxer, "and that hit would have ruined everything for the future." They had given their word there would be no trouble. The warden and his staff would probably have been fired. Most importantly, the Mafia members would never get back on the mainline. Boxer agreed. "We'd never get another opportunity to come back to the negotiating table again. It [the hit] would have created such a bad taste in their mouths [the CDC] that they'd never believe us again." At the same time, he knew the Mexican Mafia cloaked its evil intentions in "a guise of honorability that their word was good. In reality, we would have sacrificed him [Angel or Cuate] in a hot tick if it would have furthered out interests."

Meanwhile, Boxer and Jacko utilized this time to enhance their own images and power as Mafia shot-callers, agree upon a new lista, and neutralize their enemies.

During the escorted visits to other cell blocks, Boxer had some interesting encounters. He walked into a pod with Jacko and Danny and saw David "Big Spider" Gavaldon from Canta Ranas. He and Boxer were made during the same time period at Folsom. Spider was more than six feet tall and light-skinned with few tattoos; in the early days, he was an easygoing, likable "goofball" with big puffy hair and a pompadour. Now he was bald and bitter after years in Pelican Bay, an epileptic whose antiseizure medication made him moody. Boxer said, "Spider had a look of sour anger embedded on his face, as if he'd been sucking on lemons all his life." There were no other carnales on his block, so he pretty much ran it—badly thought Boxer.

He had good reason to harbor animosity toward Boxer, who, a decade earlier, had needlessly ordered the murder of his sister-in-law, Cynthia Gavaldon.

Boxer felt the bad vibes, and he walked right up to Gavaldon's cell door. He'd heard from others that "Spi" had badmouthed him. He wanted to let it go.

"What's wrong? You have a thing with me?"

"No," said Gavaldon. "I don't have a thing with you."

So Boxer moved on to other business. He knew that Mon Buenrostro, the carnal he and Topo Peters had nearly stabbed to death in L.A. County Jail, was living on the same block.

Spider directed him to the upper tier and quickly added, "Fuck that rat!" Famed Los Angeles defense attorney Leslie Abramson, who once represented Mon in court, wrote favorably about him in a book she wrote about her life. Spider thought that made Mon a rat. In fact, to Boxer's knowledge, Buenrostro had never ratted out anyone. In fact, he'd never even officially dropped out of La Eme or debriefed. The Mafia merely ostracized him after trying to kill him for badmouthing the powerful Joe Morgan. And, as Boxer now noted, "Mon never even did that. Cuate Grajeda lied about it. He was truly hit for nothing."

Boxer walked up the metal-toothed steps to see Mon and on his way noticed an Aryan Brotherhood member named Gavin "Irish" Shine, who was on the hit list of the Brand (another term for the AB prison gang). Boxer had known Irish for years and liked him. He was no punk, but a killer—much like Mon—who got caught up in politics and became a prison gang pariah. Irish had a request.

"Rene, these guys are talking bad to us, man," explained Irish. "We're not punks. We're men. Can you do something, man?"

There were eight vocal camaradas on the tier below, none of them more than twenty-seven years old. They were heaping unmerciful verbal abuse on Irish and Mon, calling them cowards and rats. Spider had instructed them to do it. Boxer told Irish he'd take care of it.

Mon didn't hear Boxer coming down the catwalk. When Boxer stopped in front of his cell, Buenrostro had his shirt off, exposing ugly scars all over his torso, evidence of Boxer's own brutality. Mon had a team of four fierce-looking polar bears tattooed just below his solar plexus, with the word MAFIA spelled out underneath in big block letters across his stomach. Now a large ugly scar cut vertically through the middle of the word MAFIA and obscured the face of the lead bear—the tattoo was misaligned, all twisted and sewn together by surgeons who'd saved his life. He suddenly noticed someone's presence and grabbed for his shirt to cover up his shame.

"How you doing, man? It's been a long time," said Boxer softly.

"What's up, Rene?"

The hurt in his voice matched the scars on his body. He told Boxer how Joe Morgan had threatened his son. He reminisced about how Morgan was now dead and Topo Peters was dying of cancer.

"It's just me and you now, Rene."

"No," Boxer replied. "It's way beyond that. You have no support. We stabbed you for Joe, and no one is going to reverse that just because he's dead. You're done, Mon."

The two battle-worn Mafiosi had a good talk. Boxer explained that he knew the stabbing "was really over nothing," and that Cuate Grajeda's "always shifty spin on the truth" exacerbated the conflict. He didn't apologize.

"It was just business," remarked Boxer.

Then he asked his old foe what was happening with the young camaradas in the lower tier. Mon's eyes welled up with maddened moisture as he related the way he was disrespected, called a coward, a rat, and a PC.* He was none of those things.

Boxer made his way back downstairs and called the young camaradas to the edge of their cell doors. He said, "That guy up there is Mon. He's an ex-carnal. And Irish, he's AB. They're both on the lista. Do you have knives?"

The response was bold. "Yeah, we got knives."

"Well, you better carry them, because those guys are killers. And they will kill you if there is ever an open door between you and them."

There was more than a little flash of fear in their eyes.

"You guys shouldn't be talking shit through the bars to these guys. Whatever Spider is saying is not right. That's not our style. I'm the carnal who hit Mon. We whacked him for business. I treat him with respect even though I tried to kill him. He was a carnal for a reason, not because he's a punk or a coward. He's a killer. This guy is a man! As for Irish, he's crazy and will cut your heart out and feed it to a dog. He's not a rat. He's a man!"

The look on the camaradas' faces told Boxer the message was sinking in.

He wasn't finished. "Now, you called them rats and cowards. You started this situation. It won't end. You better be ready. They are on the lista, and you can do them if you want, but I guarantee you they will butcher you first if they get a chance. I'm not kidding."

Boxer walked back up the stairs. "Remember, Mon is a professional. And the same goes for Irish."

As Boxer passed by Irish on his way out, he noticed the AB killer's grateful eyes were saying, *Damn right!* He was touched.

---

* A PC is an inmate who is locked up for his own protection. Someone—who on the general population yard—might be subject to attack.

Mon's face was hurt but proud. "Gracias," he said. "You took my membership from me, but you let me be a man."

Boxer walked away feeling good. "I think at that point," he recollected, "we made our peace with each other. It wasn't personal."

It was another one of those twisted Mafia codes. "A false sense of righteousness in the organization," mused Boxer, "where you could whack a guy and still say he's a man. It's just weird."

As the weeks flew by, the Mafia delegation let prison administrators and politicians believe they were on a peace mission. The Mafiosi never lost sight of the fact that it was a great scam to maybe get back on the mainline and take care of business.

Finally, after weeks of meetings with the warden, politicians, and rival black and white prison gang members, the peace talks were shut down.

On May 5, 2000, Rocky Rushing, an aide to Senator Tom Hayden, wrote to Boxer Enriquez:

> I am deeply concerned that the peace process is in a grave state. Department of Corrections brass from Sacramento is unwilling at this point to support Warden Ayers. That's why negotiations have been shelved for the time. . . . If the peace process is killed, Senator Hayden, Polanco, Vasconcellos and other progressive legislators in Sacramento will be upset. On the other hand, allowing you guys out of the SHU could possibly upset the Governor, maybe CCPOA and others—especially if large-scale violence is not reduced. But there seems something even more fundamental at play here than the Department wanting to pass on a difficult decision. Having you guys let out of SHU to help keep the lid on riots breaking out would be tantamount to a public admission that the Department relies upon inmates to keep order. Never mind that this relationship between line staff and inmates exists and is routinely utilized in many ways—often brutal ways. Still, making that admission has apparently proven too large a pill to swallow for many in the Department. It seems like the ball is now in our [the politicians'] court.

Boxer had to chuckle. Senators Hayden, Polanco, and Vasconcellos went out of their way to champion the Mafia as victims of the system. He knew the truth. La Eme saw them as "foolish, self-righteous, extremely liberal politicians who did the mob's bidding." Whether they did so knowingly or unknowingly didn't matter. They were used.

Near the end of the so-called peace talks, Boxer Enriquez and the others waited in the conference room for a meeting with three representatives of the Special Services Unit, the investigative arm of the California Department of Corrections. There was George Ortiz, special agent in charge; Joe De La Torre, senior special agent; and Brian Parry, assistant director of the Law Enforcement and Investigations Unit (head of the SSU). Parry was the one who did most of the talking and especially caught Boxer's attention.

Brian Parry was a feisty Irishman who grew up in Long Island, graduated from the University of Dayton in 1972 with a degree in police administration, and headed west to take a job as a parole officer. Mafia legend Joe Morgan was actually part of his original caseload. Parry became an SSU agent in 1981, and eight years later he, his partner, and LAPD detective Jack Forsman sat in a chilly surveillance van outside Topper Aleman's house in East Los Angeles looking for Boxer as a suspect in the murders of La Eme's David Gallegos and Cynthia Gavaldon. In other words, Parry helped put Boxer away. And unlike the politicians, Parry had been in hand-to-hand combat with gangsters and other crooks willing to take his life. He was under no illusion that Mafiosi were victims.

As Parry looked into the conference room, he saw the faces of nine of the most dangerous crooks in the CDC system—all waiting to talk with him. There wasn't a single correctional officer in the room. They were all parked outside in the corridor. He thought to himself, *If there is a diabolical plan afoot here, it will be ugly before the cavalry arrives.*

Parry turned to the men he was with and before entering the meeting room said, "I hope you didn't wear your best suit—it could get bloody in there." Then he walked inside and shook Boxer's cuffed hand.

"Hey, Boxer, how you doing?"

"It's Rene, Rene."

"Okay. Rene."

Boxer was five feet, nine inches tall, and he noticed that the top of Parry's balding head only reached him at eye level. Yet the SSU boss carried himself with confidence. He was cocky and pugnacious, gritty but friendly, serious but humorous. Boxer liked him, but his instincts told him this wily lawman wasn't likely to be fooled. He was right.

Parry knew that "gang leaders wanted a free rein on the mainline. They wanted to be released to the mainline in exchange for stopping prison violence. Well, our answer to that was—stop participating in prison violence yourselves. We know that some of these folks were directing others to commit violence, and we were not going to empower them to go out and do our job. They deserved to be in the SHU for valid reasons—their own acts of violence and fomenting others to do the same. Plus, we had intelligence that some of these gangs were planning serious assaults on their rivals once they were out for a while. So we weren't about to turn over the run of the prison to a bunch of gang leaders."

Parry knew the history as well. There was the Inmate Catalyst Program in the early 1970s that had allowed gang members to control the yard. There was still a myriad of stabbings and assaults.

During the 1980s, the CDC went into the segregation business—six major prisons devoted to housing different gang factions. The gang bosses took over the prisons, dominated other inmates, and then turned their violence on staff.

Parry also knew that since the implementation of the SHU program in 1989, violence in the prison system as a whole had plummeted. Now there just wasn't enough bed space for every bad guy who deserved to be in there.

In short, he didn't believe Boxer and the Mafia's pitch for peace. He was all too familiar with the Mexican Mafia's deadly game.

The phony Eme peace brokers lost this little war of the wills. They might have fooled a handful of politicians and special-interest groups that egged them on for prison reform, but not the cops who had spent a lifetime close-up examining the patterns of their criminal behavior.

Boxer Enriquez and his brothers would stay locked up in the SHU.

CHAPTER 34

Growing Mob–Weary

THE INFIGHTING AND MANIPULATION WERE NEVER–ENDING. THE UPPER– echelon Mafia members were all locked down in Pelican Bay SHU, but on weekends they were all out in the visiting area taking care of mob business and politicking against each other. Openly, they ordered hits, sent messages, and gave instructions to underlings or their wives about drug deals and territory disputes eight hundred miles away in Los Angeles. It became clearer and clearer to Boxer Enriquez that none of them "could see beyond that little box of gang life."

His former cellmate Darryl "Night Owl" Baca was no exception. All that was left of their former partnership was bitterness and vengeance. They still lived in the same pod but were in separate cells. Baca was on the second tier, and Boxer was on the lower tier. Immediately after the argument they had about Night Owl's desire to kill associate Cynthia, aka "Hottie," the two enemies had vowed to meet in the upper-tier shower and fight to the death.

Three days a week Baca was a tier tender who helped with some routine maintenance duties. He went to take a shower after completing his tasks, delaying for an hour, waiting and hoping the on-duty guard would forget he was there. Boxer rolled up his massive knife in a towel and shouted to the same guard to pop his door—he too wanted to shower. The correctional officer complied but insisted that Boxer stay on the lower tier. There was one shower upstairs and one downstairs. "You were chicken," chided Baca as he came by his new enemy's cell door the next day.

A week later, the two rivals tried the same gambit to set up their mortal combat. This time Boxer, knife rolled up in his towel, automatically headed for the upper-tier shower to face off against the waiting Baca. As he headed up the stairs, his heart was racing and his sweaty hands were trembling as the fingers of his right hand reached inside the towel and gripped the shank handle.

"Baca, where you at?" asked the guard.

"I'm in my cell drying off."

In fact, he was still locked in the upper-tier shower, hiding. Boxer was about ten feet away when he heard the remote-controlled lock on the shower door disengage. Camaradas in the other cells felt the tension and had their eyes wide open, expecting blood to flow soon. Boxer knew that Baca, always in top physical condition, was bigger and stronger than he was. It wouldn't be difficult for Night Owl to overpower him in a fight. He needed to act swiftly, deliver an overhead death blow, and hope his opponent would bleed out on the floor.

The shower door rolled open a few inches, then suddenly reversed itself and slammed shut. Boxer heard the guard say, "Wait, I think Baca is still in there." The correctional officer's instincts were right. He knew something was up. Returning to his cell, Boxer flushed his knife, expecting a search to follow.

A few days later, while undertaking his tier duties, Baca stopped by Boxer's cell and said, "We need to stop this. We're friends. It doesn't look good to the camaradas." He stuck his pinky through a hole in the metal mesh door, and the two carnales shook fingers. Boxer went along, but he "knew it wasn't over."

In the following days, Baca shot dirty looks at Boxer as he went about his tier tender duties. In the meantime, Boxer had acquired a new Plexiglas knife. Camaradas used string as a saw and cut the shank from a Plexiglas sheet that covered the cell doors of inmates known for gassing officers.* It took two inmates—one in the cell and a tier tender from the outside—about twenty minutes to cut a strip all the way across the bottom of the Plexiglas shield. Boxer secretly grabbed hold of the new knife every time Baca came around his house.

---

* Gassing is a common prison attack method used by inmates on correctional officers. It involves throwing a mixture of urine and feces into an officer's face. It is especially threatening and potentially deadly given the high rate of AIDS/HIV and hepatitis C among inmates.

Not more than a few weeks had passed before Baca couldn't resist shooting off his mouth. Walking by Boxer's cell, he again complained that Enriquez had cut him loose in business.

"You picked a chick over me!" he sneered.

"You're talking like a nigger," chided Boxer, knowing that black inmates were seen as loud and disruptive. It was no small insult in a prison environment steeped in racial animosities. The taunt was meant to sting and it did.

"I'm going to make you scream," threatened Baca as he moved on in a snit.

"We'll see who screams," countered Boxer.

Minutes later, Boxer heard other cell doors pop open down the row. Against prison policy, the guard was letting Night Owl Baca make deliveries of canteen items. Correctional officers are supposed to make these deliveries themselves. It was part of Baca's latest plot to get at his archrival.

Eventually, Night Owl stood in front of Boxer's cell. He had on Converse tennis shoes that were laced up tight and an "evil look" in his eyes. Both were a signal to Boxer that something was up.

"Crack this door so I can give him his canteen," shouted Baca to a guard in the control booth.

Boxer jumped up from his bunk and reached for his knife, fumbled to remove the cellophane wrapper he used to keister it, and cocked back his arm ready to attack. The cell door slid open a mere six inches as he heard Baca call out, "Open it some more."

Baca had a bag of Dixie cups in his left hand and a washcloth in his right. Hidden underneath was a small razor blade poised to strike. He reached to hand the bag over. Boxer knocked it to the floor as Baca, razor in his right hand, slashed out at his wrist. All it caught was air as Baca jumped back to avoid the overhead swing of Plexiglas aimed at his heart.

The electronic door slammed shut between them. The guard was alerted by the commotion.

"Why didn't you come out?" taunted Baca.

"Why didn't you come in?" scoffed Boxer as an adrenaline rush of fear shot through his system like a streak of lightning. At the same time, it felt good to see Baca jump back to avoid the plunge of his blade. So, with a nervous chuckle, he delivered a final verbal blow: "You almost got your punk ass stabbed."

Boxer still planned on killing Baca if he ever got a chance—maybe during escort to the law library or the prison medical facility. Neither of them ever left his cell without a knife and handcuff key hidden away. Boxer felt that Baca "was a lousy, greedy businessman who turned his back on me over a buck."

It wasn't the first time that he'd felt betrayed by another Mafioso he thought was a good friend. He'd also become distrustful of his old pal and partner in crime Jacko Padilla. Several years earlier, the two of them had been cellmates. Both were lingering in a visiting room corridor after completing their visits. They stood chained together with Carlos Diaz of San Diego—Boxer in the middle position—all waiting to go back to their cells. La Eme's Mark "Turtle" Quiroz of Colton was locked up in a holding cell ten feet away, also waiting to be processed in or out for a visit.

Boxer was passing the time talking to Carlos when he noticed that Jacko was having a conversation with Turtle. Then he noticed Turtle suddenly pointing a finger in his direction. "Your cellie," he heard Turtle say to Jacko. Then out of the corner of his eye he saw Turtle make a thumbs-down motion with his right hand, followed by a gesture that imitated a stabbing motion. He was telling Jacko to kill Boxer—his cellmate and friend. Jacko nodded his head, as if to say okay. Boxer pretended he didn't see it, but it already felt like a stab to his heart. He wondered, *Is there any pure loyalty at all in the mob?*

Back in their cell, Jacko was acting a little distraught as the two cellies made small talk. Boxer had his knife out, ready, waiting for his friend to make a move. He didn't. Instead, he left to take a shower. Boxer figured he'd gone for a shank. Later, he imagined his friend would try to stab or garrote him as he slept. Instead, Jacko announced that he was going to cell up with Steve "Smiley" Castillo—an Eme associate and jailhouse lawyer—to get some legal work done. He moved out a week later. "I knew then," said Boxer, "something was wrong. Some Mafioso had put me in the hat, on the lista, for reasons unknown to me."

Now Night Owl Baca and Jacko Padilla—former friends and allies—were plotting against him.

It made Boxer sick: "I knew I had killed for La Eme when others had been scared to kill. I'd been involved in kamikaze hits beyond the normal devotion to the Mafia, and dedicated my entire life to being the best Mafioso ever." Now it didn't make any sense at all. The Mafia merry-go-round of murder would never stop. "It would only get worse," he realized. The pointless realities of a life in La Eme were "growing more and more tiresome." There were stinging reminders all around him that he was "wasting his life in the mob."

In 1993 Joe Morgan, the reputed Godfather and ultimate Eme icon, died alone in prison of cancer at the relatively young age of sixty-four. His loss didn't seem to make much difference to anyone. Boxer remembered an institutional gang investigator asking him after Morgan's death what would happen. "The mob was here before Joe died," he reflected, "and it will be here after."

In February 2001, the same fate befell Morgan's reputed successor, Topo Peters, who also died alone in prison of cancer at the age of sixty. He was the product of an abusive alcoholic father who left when Topo was eight and an overly protective mother and grandmother who always made excuses for him. Sadly, Topo told a prison psychologist in 1987 that he "saw himself as a dummy." A prison evaluation report done months before he died noted that Topo "has warned CDC staff that he is a target for assault by Mexican Mafia members due to his illness and the inability to function as an active gang member." The same document quoted him saying, "I'm never going to get out of prison, and I don't want to die here." He did anyway. There were only a half-dozen cars in his funeral procession driving into Forest Lawn Memorial Park in Covina Hills. Fewer than two dozen mourners fit under one small awning at the gravesite. Boxer said coldly, "He was a dope fiend and a liar with no more credibility in the organization. We were going to kill him. He did us a favor by dying. No one cared."

A month later, feared executioner Mike "Hatchet" Ison, another Mafia strongman and potential successor to Morgan, got into a pushing match at a sleazy bar on San Francisco's skid row. He stabbed a guy in the back with a three-inch buck knife, ran, and was chased by a half-dozen black men who beat him to death with pool cues and an aluminum lawn chair. The fifty-four-year-old Eme stalwart had spent his last days as a crackhead living in a flophouse hotel. "An addict on his way out," remarked a detective on the case. "He didn't die a very glorious death." Cops felt that Ison's murder wasn't even worthy of prosecution.

Boxer had idolized these murderous Mafia legends but was realizing that they ended up as nothing and with nothing. "They were men with limited outlooks who settled for a life behind bars—men who chose to destroy rather than build. Their choices were faulty and often driven by serious drug addictions that clouded their judgment and crippled their potential. All your ethics are destroyed by drugs."

Inside the SHU at Pelican Bay, an environment built to isolate and contain prison gang predators, there was no mainline prey. So Mafiosi more and more turned on each other. Boxer learned that "friendship in the mob is bullshit, and I grew tired of it." It was becoming increasingly clear to him that "we [Eme] are the dregs of society. We have every personality disorder known to man and kill people for ridiculous reasons."

Tupi Hernandez, who had challenged Topo's authority and was stabbed into humiliation at the Federal Building, had lost his mind. The organization ostracized him after he was hit. Boxer saw him in the PBSP visiting room—disheveled-looking, all bug-eyed and paranoid—and Tupi whispered that there was a surveillance camera hidden in the heating vent of his cell. Hernandez actually believed that Topo had planted the secret device (which didn't exist) to spy on him. Boxer heard later that Tupi "was standing around in his cell naked, talking to himself. He's a nutcase!" That was a fate worse than death.

Boxer had seen most of his support base disappear when Black Dan Barela, Huero Shy Shryock, and Chuy Martinez were all shipped off to federal prison. "I always had affection for those guys," recollected Boxer. "In their eyes I could do no wrong. They were my political support." They were gone.

Lil Mo Ruiz was just as good as gone. In 1997 he was stabbed by his cellmate, Eme member Lalo Martinez. Mo was hit because of a dispute with the Cuate Grajeda camp over a plan to murder Topo Peters's stool pigeon brother-in-law. Mo asked that the hit be delayed as a courtesy to Topo, who was in Los Angeles for the federal RICO trial at the time. The Cuate faction didn't want to wait and felt that Mo was backing up a rat. Mo's troubles didn't end there. He screamed when Lalo stabbed him, and then yelled, "I have AIDS!" It was a ruse to make Lalo back off by making him think he might get an HIV infection from Mo's blood. That was seen by other mobsters as an act of cowardice. Boxer believed, "Mo is through. He doesn't realize it. He and his homeys at White Fence think he's okay, but he's not." Boxer tried to get Mo a pass but couldn't get it done.

Darryl "Night Owl" Baca still wanted Enriquez dead. And Boxer could no longer trust his longtime pal Jacko Padilla. His other loyal friend, Chuco Castro, was buried somewhere in the federal witness protection program. Boxer envied Chuco's new life—a second chance—living with his wife and children under an assumed name, free of the suffocating Mafia politics.

CHAPTER 35

Man Is Made or Unmade by Himself

RENE "BOXER" ENRIQUEZ WAS NEARLY FORTY YEARS OLD. HE WAS tired of the whole Mexican Mafia mess and secretly wanted out. Yet none of the alternative choices—snitch, debrief, or die—seemed any more appealing.

Meanwhile, there was something else that for years had been slowly changing Boxer's outlook on life—books. He was a high school dropout with no interest in education, but years earlier he had begun to read: "I had difficulty reading when I was a kid because I really didn't apply myself in school, but when I got to prison I became a reader." It stemmed from an episode in L.A. County Jail back in the early 1980s. A young Boxer spent all his time gambling and horsing around. Charlie Rose was a big, fat, greasy-looking outlaw biker who one day asked him to grab a bunch of books off a library cart that came around the tier.

"What are you doing?" asked Boxer.

"I'm reading," he said. "I love to read. Rene, you'll understand when you get to prison. Books will be your best friend."

The next year at Soledad State Prison, Boxer was thrown into solitary confinement after instigating a prison skirmish. He started reading Stephen King novels and then *The Count of Monte Cristo*. Later, during the ensuing years at Pelican Bay, he became a voracious reader. "Once I learned one thing, I realized how little I really knew, and wanted to broaden my understanding of something else." He graduated to some of the classics. *The Red Badge of Courage* taught him that "fear was normal. It's how you deal with it that counts." There was Machiavelli, the Italian statesman whose doctrine denied the relevance of morality in political affairs. It hit close to Boxer's amoral world. Author John Steinbeck's earthy novels about the nobility of the common man more than held his interest. He perused Shakespeare's *King Lear, Romeo and Juliet,* and *Taming of the Shrew* and began quoting the English playwright to other inmates.

Ernie "Neto" Nunez was a short, olive-skinned gangster from Azusa 13 who combed his hair straight back and wore a catfish mustache with long, wispy hairs spreading across his upper lip. He was also known as "lying Neto" because he had a little problem with the truth. Boxer listened to him tell a fresh whopper about killing a cougar with his own bare hands. "Neto," he said, quoting *Hamlet,* "to thine own self be true."

"What does that mean?" answered a confused Neto.

"Be true to yourself—don't lie," admonished Boxer.

Another time he leveled a prison-hardened gangster who madly denied he had stolen something with "Methinks thou dost protest too much."

Books were increasing his vocabulary and opening up a whole new world to him. Much of what he read would have been introduced in good high school English classes, but he never went. Now Boxer began to educate himself. He would pass a high school equivalency General Educational Development (GED) exam with above-average marks—upper ninetieth percentile—in writing, reading, and social studies.

Boxer read biographies about people as diverse as Italian Mafioso John Gotti and artists Frida Kahlo, Diego Rivera, and Georgia O'Keeffe. He added, with a huge knowing laugh, that his "favorites are still horror novels," for their pure entertainment value.

He taught himself algebra and studied sociology and psychology, taking an independent study course in abnormal psychology from Cal State Northridge. The term paper he wrote was entitled "Psychological Degradation and Isolation," and he queried other inmates about the effects of their incarceration in Pelican Bay SHUs. He completed a ten-lesson course in fundamental economics from the Henry George Institute in New York; a course entitled "Discovering Psychology" from LaSalle University in Mandeville, Louisiana; a course in the Ten Commandments from the Catholic Home Study Institute at Loyola Marymount University in Los Angeles; and a series of courses about sight from the Hadley School for the Blind in Winnetka, Illinois, including "An Introduction to Personal Computers." "I wanted to know what people were talking about when they mentioned a mouse or a cursor," he explained. "Just because I'm a prisoner doesn't mean I have to live in a cave."

During the late 1990s, his brother Marc sent him a copy of James Allen's

As a Man Thinketh. It was the same self-help book his father had forced him to read when he was a teenager. The premise was: "As a man thinketh in his heart, so is he." This time the message was striking. Allen wrote: "A noble and God-like character is not a thing of favor or chance but is the natural result of continued effort in right thinking, the effect of long-cherished association with God-like thoughts. An ignoble and bestial character, by the same process, is the result of a continued harboring of groveling thoughts. Man is made or unmade by himself."

It was an epiphany for a developing Boxer. "I didn't even realize it before that my dad was trying to give me a lesson in life." He was getting ready for a change.

CHAPTER 36

Missing Life

THE DAYS AT PELICAN BAY BEGAN AT SIX O'CLOCK IN THE MORNING with a "bird bath"—plugging up the sink with plastic, filling it with lukewarm water, dumping it over your head with a used milk carton, then soaping up and rinsing as needed. There was always a morning cup of hot brewed coffee. Inmates made it with a makeshift "immersion heater" created out of headphone wires and staples plugged into the TV cord. Boxer did a few exercises before the breakfast food tray arrived. All meals in the SHU were brought to your cell and shoved through a small slot in the door, just like feeding animals at the zoo. Boxer usually "wore away the morning hours writing letters, reading, studying for a correspondence course, and waiting for the lunch tray to arrive."

He could always tell what the other inmates in his pod were doing by the sounds he heard: "The rustling of paper told me someone was reading. The squeak of a tennis shoe signaled exercise. Muffled dialogue meant someone was watching television." Inmates were required to use special headphones—little ear buds inserted into the inner ear—to listen to television quietly. However, ears got sore with the buds stuck inside during a long day of TV watching. So inmates took an eight-by-eleven piece of paper, rolled it up into the shape of a megaphone, and placed the ear bud inside the small end. The result was a small cone-shaped speaker that amplified the sound. It was placed above the television or on a bunk, and an inmate wouldn't have to wear the ear bud.

Televisions are prized possessions. All have a clear plastic outer shell so guards can see that no parts are missing or nothing is hidden inside. An inmate loses his set forever if a shank is made from TV parts. "As a consequence," explained Boxer, "not many weapons are made from television sets."

Some of the inmates sit in their cell with the light off and watch television all day long, wasting away. "Those are the people who go nuts in the SHU," according to Boxer. "Stagnation in prison is intellectual death. There are inmates who do nothing but watch the soap operas and Spanish novellas. They are called 'soap opera connoisseurs,' and some of them are nearly brain-dead." Arguably, the TV for them is much like a life support system, because if someone pulled the plug on the set, they'd die. Even Boxer admitted, "I watched *Days of Our Lives* every afternoon for eleven straight years."

Boxer observed, "A number of the Mexican Mafia members, including Darryl 'Night Owl' Baca, studied Nahuatl most of the day." The ancient Aztec language is used to communicate back and forth between cells without correctional officers understanding the conversation. It's used in correspondence too.

Chess is a popular game in prison, and some of the great players believe they could kill Boris Spasky's king without ever using a shank. Boxer noted, "They have twenty-four hours a day to study the game. Inmate chess masters each have a numbered board in their cell, and they shout out their moves to their opponent down the row. The opponent is never seated across from you, unless the match is with a cellmate." Super prison chess aficionados even play occasional matches through the mail. It helps keep them sane.

Each inmate gets ninety minutes a day at the walled-in, doggy-walk recreation yard. Bodies that don't take advantage of the exercise time atrophy as quickly as the minds that watch TV all day. Plus, a visit to the rec area is the only chance a SHU inmate gets to look up at an open sky, usually a cloudy one in a frequently rain-soaked Crescent City. Those minutes of looking toward the heavens through a wire-mesh screen are the only connection to the great outdoors.

The afternoons are like the mornings, and the nights are like the afternoons until an inmate turns off his cell lights. It's a lonely life too. "The loneliness eats away at you," said Boxer. "I've always felt alone. You are alone, and you are lonely." The lack of physical contact is excruciating. "How can you value the loss of something as simple as the smell of a girl's skin in your nose?" asked Rene.

All things considered, Boxer felt that "the SHU didn't bother me all that much." He spent ten years locked up in Pelican Bay SHU, and much of his ten years in prison and jail before that were spent in quasi-solitary confinement—high-power and administrative segregation. The personality of an extrovert forced him "to maintain interaction with people even when I didn't feel good." Mechanically he seemed fine, but "I knew the isolation was taking a toll on me." By the late 1990s, he'd experienced a few more anxiety attacks. On one occasion, Topo Peters arranged for him to be called out to the visiting room so they could talk. On the way there, he "felt that same dread"—a fearful anticipation that cramped his lungs and stole his breath.

Boxer began to quantify the depth of despair and depression: "On the general population yard, there was noise from soccer games, basketball, the verbal jostling between inmates, and the hum of conversation. In the SHU, there was an almost morose quiet, punctuated by the sound of metal gates opening and closing, and the clang of food trays being delivered and collected."

He was haunted by all the things he'd missed. "I think about going to walk barefoot on the grass. I dream about being able to do anything I want anytime I want to do it, have any type of food, or look up at the stars at night—simple things. Once I was being pushed on a gurney into the local Crescent City hospital for a knee operation and I heard a baby cry. I said, 'Wait a minute!' The guard said, 'It's just a baby.' I hadn't heard one in a decade. It struck me, 'Wow! That's life.' You know, I even miss my old mangy mutt Goliath too. I miss my dog."

Then there was the dread of a phone call. There were only two types of phone calls an inmate could receive at Pelican Bay—a serious illness in the family or a death. On August 23, 1996, the feared phone call came. The death of any loved one can tear at the heart, but the loss of a young loved one hurts even more. Rene's nephew Mark, his older brother's son, died unexpectedly from an aneurysm. He was only fifteen years old. Boxer remembered that "he'd recently visited me at Pelican Bay, along with my son Bobby. They were friends. Mark had the letters MERE embroidered above the bill of his baseball cap. It stood for Marc Enriquez and Rene Enriquez, in honor of his father and me. I was touched." Tragically, it was a symbol of young Mark's love for two men who had in truth forsaken him. The sadness was magnified by the reality that Boxer, locked up in prison for most of the dead boy's life, "could do nothing to help." He wanted to cry, but instead he had to choke back his emotions: "Tears were a luxury a Mafioso couldn't afford to show—it was considered weakness." Prison staff were standing there listening as he received the news. He didn't even know them, and how could a Mexican Mafia killer expect any comfort? It all seemed so cold, and it was. "One of the most difficult things for me to do," according to Boxer, "is to wait for those calls.

"The most profound fear I have," continued Boxer, "is getting that call about the death of my parents." His father, who has suffered a stroke and has trouble articulating words, is in his late seventies, and his mother is four years younger. Rene knows that "I've caused them a lot of emotional pain, and I wish I could take it all back." Now, in their last years, he can't be there to help them. "I wait for my parents to leave me, and I can't be by their sides," he said regretfully. "I have to be hundreds of miles away and wait for that phone call, and some stranger to advise me in a cold, standoffish way that they are dead. You want more than a phone call when your parents die. It's a reality I find difficult to face."

Meanwhile, his older brother Marc was dying from AIDS, hepatitis C, and cirrhosis after years of intravenous drug use in and out of prison and having sexual intercourse with a wife who died from AIDS. "Everyone is starting to die around you," noted Rene, "and it also brings you to the realization that you are missing life."

The irony of Boxer Enriquez feeling sorrow over impending death is not lost on him: "I mean, we [Eme] are the brokers of death. We kill people and joke about it with a black, wicked humor without any regard for human life. Then it happens to our family or us, and it takes us aback. We're mortal?! Our families are mortal?! How dare God do this to us." The cessation of life humbles everybody. It's a piercing truth everyone has to accept in the end. Rene had that figured out: "That's one thing that's humbled me—is death."

Prison visits in the later years became more and more difficult for his parents. During his ten years at Pelican Bay, his dad managed only three trips to see him, and his mom made fifteen trips. His mother Lupe said, "It becomes so sad, like you buried your son but he's not buried. In everything you do—dinnertime, celebrations—something is missing. I cry a lot for my son. No one can see inside a mother's heart, the pain, suffering, hopes that I have over and over to see him free before I die. That's the only thing I wish to make my life complete, but that's not in my hands. Eventually, I'll die waiting."

Besides the imminent death of his parents, other things were gnawing at Rene's psyche. The two grown children he had were in reality almost strangers. Only Bobby ever came to visit him at Pelican Bay—six trips. How much of a father can someone be during prison visits? Boxer was proud that "Bobby became the first member of our family to graduate from college. Unfortunately, I couldn't be there to celebrate the achievement." His other boy, Rene Jr., gave him a baby grandson and granddaughter, neither of whom their imprisoned grandpa has ever seen. He wants "to hold them, see their little smiles, and hear their laughter." His parents and son Bobby were the only immediate family members who ever came to visit him during ten years at Pelican Bay.

Boxer's stark realization was that he had "gravitated toward gang violence and then blew my whole life on it. In retrospect, it was a terrible waste. I often think of the phrase, 'This is a wasted life.' And that's how I feel. I wasted my whole damn life. There are so many regrets. If I could change it all by the snap of my fingers, I would."

More and more Boxer yearned for release, but he truly didn't know how to break the grip of the Black Hand. He began to discuss his frustrations with his "trusted confidante" during visiting days at Pelican Bay. The no-contact visits required SHU inmates to communicate through a glass window via closed-circuit telephones, and Boxer knew correctional officers sometimes monitored the conversations. So he usually tried to disguise his thoughts using prison "carnival talk." In May 2002, during a Saturday and Sunday visit, he verbalized considerations he had about leaving La Eme in a more direct manner: "This is so much bullshit! I'm tired of all this politics. Every time I come out here [visiting booths] it's politics, politics—every damn visit. If it's not me battling for turf or fighting with business partners that I don't want to do business with anymore, it's guys [carnales] going to kill this person or that person, or do this or that. It's ridiculous."

Lieutenant Ernie Madrid was the new institutional gang investigator at Pelican Bay. He was a serious, short, stocky, tobacco-chewing ex-Marine who spoke with a western drawl and wore cowboy boots and shirts, tan jeans, a bolo tie, and a big silver belt buckle he'd won riding bulls during a rodeo competition at the Camp Pendleton Marine base. Madrid grew up in a small rural northern California town called Happy Camp. He lived with his five sisters, mother, and a father who worked in a sawmill for thirty-five years. During high school summers and for a time before he went into the Marine Corps, he worked on a cattle ranch. Madrid served on a ship offshore during President Ronald Reagan's war on the island of Grenada and spent vacation time hunting big game with a bow and arrow. The former Marine didn't need to watch an old TV episode of Superman to know that he believed in truth, justice, and the American way.

Madrid spent four months reading confiscated Mafia letters and ran profiles on the Eme members housed at PBSP. During his research, he came to the opinion that Boxer Enriquez seemed to be the most influential Mexican Mafia figure, and one of the most intelligent. La Eme was looking at Enriquez as their leader, thought the lieutenant. He also noticed a certain thoughtfulness that he felt was out of character for a mob hit man. In one of the Boxer letters he read, Madrid noted, "He was talking about sunrises and sunsets and the fact that he wanted to hold his kids." While serving as a correctional officer years earlier, he'd had a few random conversations with Boxer and came away thinking that "he had a mean Mafia attitude with a killer look in his eyes." The man unfolding before him now seemed different.

Also, the lieutenant monitored visits and heard Boxer talk about the continuing frustrations of his existence in La Eme. He thought the time might be right to make a move. So he secretly set up a meeting without the Mafioso's knowledge.

Boxer was dressed in his white boxer shorts, T-shirt, and tennis shoes. There was a handcuff key hidden inside his mouth and, as always, a knife secreted in his rectum, prison-style. He knew Darryl "Night Owl" Baca still wanted him dead, and he was ready to strike first if a fresh opportunity arose. As prison policy dictated, he was handcuffed and leg-chained as two guards escorted him to the infirmary.

A sudden call to the doctor's office alone didn't alarm him. Boxer was part of an experimental interferon treatment program for hepatitis C. Every six months medical attendants took his vital signs and gave him a physical examination to make sure he was a sustained responder. In the back of his mind, another curiosity alert was going off. "The escorts were acting strangely," he remembered. Earlier, the floor officer who delivered breakfast "had a big round-eyed look that telegraphed something different was going on." Boxer guessed that the guards' instincts signaled more trouble between him and Baca and the fact that they both had knives. Or "maybe another inmate dropped a kite to administrators" about the Baca-Enriquez feud?

Near the end of his medical visit, Boxer's floor officer slid up and said, "The secret squirrels want to see you."

"What do you mean, 'secret squirrels'?"

"Lieutenant Madrid, the IGI, he wants to talk to you. Do you want to talk to him?"

"Sure."

Boxer never refused to talk to the IGIs. He'd heard there was a new one.

Why not talk to him? They always wanted something—maybe a cop had been threatened and they wanted him to smooth out the friction. As far as he was concerned, "a good rapport with prison staff wasn't a bad thing. I had to live with them every day. Periodic accommodations were made to make life easier for both sides." Some correctional officers—against policy—had at times let Boxer and a few other Mafiosi out on the tier together to talk. Others turned their backs to drug use as long as it wasn't too blatant. A few female guards on occasion even offered sexual favors, or just mild flirting. In exchange, Mafiosi would make sure guards weren't shanked, speared, or gassed. There was always an undercurrent of tit-for-tat behavior. Contrary to popular belief, there is even an unwritten understanding among inmates that allows for correctional officers to give a beat-down to a convict who truly deserves it. In any event, Boxer knew that "when the shit hits the fan, they [prison staff] have to know you are a stable personality they can go to."

In addition to his escort, additional correctional officers came out and cleared the corridors. It was done in a way that dripped of secrecy.

"What's going on?" asked Boxer.

"We want to make sure no one sees you."

"I don't care," scoffed the bold Mafioso.

Yet inside, he began to feel "something big was happening." This was not a routine visit.

He asked again, "What the hell is going on?"

Boxer was led to a small hideaway holding cell located near the prison library. Correctional officers removed his restraints through a slot in the metal-mesh door, and he took a seat on the toilet and waited. A distinct fear that was unfamiliar to him crept into his brain. "They're going to approach you," he thought. "I knew I was susceptible." The pace of his heart quickened. His mind raced with thoughts that threatened his loyalty to the Mafia code of silence. "Don't do it, Rene," said the voice in his head. "Don't let them talk you into it. Just hear what he has to say, and ask to go."

CHAPTER 37

Dropping Out of the Mob

RENE "BOXER" ENRIQUEZ HEARD THE *CLOP—CLOP—CLOP* OF COWBOY boots coming down the corridor toward the holding cell where he sat waiting. The clopping stopped in front of the cell door, and there stood the sturdy cowboy turned prison guard. He was about Boxer's age and had a slightly receding hairline, brown hair slicked back on the sides, and a full, rusty-colored mustache. There was no slouch in his posture, and he exuded an air of powerful confidence, a recognizable quality of leadership. Boxer thought he "looked sharp." Also, he could see the big, silver rodeo belt buckle highlighted through the slot in the door. There was a cowpuncher sloped over in the saddle and an engraving that read, END OF THE TRAIL.

Boxer stood and walked to the door. Against policy, an open palm reached through the slot, and he felt the officer's firm grip as they shook hands. Their eyes met squarely.

"Boxer, I'm Lieutenant Madrid," he announced.

"Rene, please," came the response. "I don't go by Boxer. I never liked that name. What's on your mind, Lieutenant Madrid?"

"Well," said the lieutenant, "I'm going to tip my hand here, but I think it's worthwhile." He sat down in a straight-back chair next to a small table in the corridor and told Rene to take a seat. Madrid pulled out a small can of Copenhagen chewing tobacco, grabbed a pinch with his fingers, and dropped it into his mouth.

Boxer settled back onto the toilet, using it as a stool.

Madrid tapped his tobacco can against his other hand, as if he were trying to figure out what to say next. Then he threw out a verbal lariat: "Rene, I think you're in trouble."

"I'm not in trouble," Enriquez said defensively. "I want you to understand right now I'm not in trouble. I don't need anybody's help." Mexican Mafia machismo went into overdrive as he coolly denied even being a carnal. His steely eyes didn't betray the lie, but his hands were trembling. He was in trouble all right, and he knew it.

Madrid explained that he had been monitoring visits and had detected that Boxer was ready to leave the Mafia.

"I don't have a damn thing on you," the lieutenant assured him, "but I remember you ten years ago, and I'm looking at a different man today."

"What do you mean by that?"

"I profiled you. Not another Mafia guy alive—who has money—helps put their kid through college and sends gifts to family members on the right days." Madrid had no doubt that the man who sat across from him through the metal door was still a warrior, but he felt that his heart had changed. He felt that this Mafioso had seen enough blood and had come to realize he was fighting on the wrong side. The lieutenant was careful not to use the name Boxer.

"Rene, I think you're ready."

Madrid's instincts told him this bull ride was about over as he reached into his pocket and pulled out a small tape recorder. He pushed PLAY without saying a word, and Rene "Boxer" Enriquez heard his own voice played back to him: "I'm so fucking bone-weary tired of this shit."

Unmistakably, it was part of the conversation he'd had a few days earlier with his "trusted confidante" in the Pelican Bay visiting area.

He heard the click as Madrid turned off the recorder. It served as punctuation before the western drawl continued in a direct and reassuring manner. "Call me stupid or crazy," said the lieutenant, "but you want to drop out [of the Mafia]. Rene, let me take you out of this. Let me help you. You don't want to be this anymore, do you?"

No one had ever approached him like that. It was disarming. He looked down at his sweaty hands, and they were shaking uncontrollably. Enriquez was truly frightened by what he was about to do. He'd been involved with La Eme for more than twenty years. It was the heart of his entire adult life. The devil owned his soul, but the Mafia had a lease on it.

"The shit out there [in the prison] doesn't scare me," he told Madrid. "You scare me. I don't know what the other world is anymore."

"Let me take you there. I'll show you."

"What do I have to do?"

Instantly, he noticed a gleam in Madrid's eyes. "He knew he had me. He'd caught me at the right moment."

Enriquez wanted some assurances. They moved to Madrid's nearby office, and Boxer noticed the lieutenant's secretary, sitting at her desk, "had a look of fear in her eyes" as the Mafia kingpin entered her safe haven. A call was made to the Special Services Unit offices in Sacramento, and Enriquez spoke with the SSU director and special agent Devan Hawkes. Rene had known Hawkes for years. He remembered him as a young gang investigations officer when Pelican Bay first opened in 1989, then as a sergeant, correctional counselor, special agent with SSU, and gang specialist. Hawkes was a sincere, soft-spoken, trustworthy man who had planned on being a geologist before he was sidetracked into the Department of Corrections. His own upbringing in a dysfunctional family—a series of stepfathers and a sister lost to drug addiction—perhaps had prepared him well for a career devoted to making things right. He was also smart—a nemesis for La Eme.

"Rene, I don't believe it," said Hawkes. The news that a manipulative, murderous Boxer Enriquez was ready to drop out of the Mexican Mafia was not that easy to digest quickly.

"I don't believe it either," offered Rene.

"How do we know this is real?" wondered the skeptical SSU agent.

The Boxer part of him was "a little pissed off" by the response, but he understood. He also liked Hawkes and wanted him to personally do his debrief. Madrid would join the more experienced SSU agent throughout the process, mostly acting as Rene's handler. Enriquez wanted immunity from future prosecutions, but Hawkes's smooth, nonthreatening style of interrogation had him already giving up certain information on the telephone. Suddenly, Boxer snapped back into a defensive position and tried to broker some kind of a deal, making demands. As he would readily admit years later, "I saw too many movies."

Hawkes softly explained the debriefing process to him. CDC policy mandated that Miranda warnings were not given to inmates who debrief so that information handed over to prison staff is only used administratively, not for criminal prosecutions. According to the department operations manual, the purpose of a debrief "is to obtain sufficient verifiable information from the subject which adversely impacts the gang so the gang will no longer accept the subject as either a member or associate. . . . A debriefing is not for the purpose of acquiring incriminating evidence against the subject." Also, the debrief is designed to convince prison staff that an inmate has truly dropped out of the gang. That done, staff is obligated to place the inmate in protective custody and keep him safe from possible retaliation.

After the phone call to Sacramento, Rene asked what to do about the belongings he still had in his cell. Madrid told him that correctional officers were already moving it to his new quarters.

"It was comforting," remembered Enriquez. "He took control of it. It was almost as if he were saying, 'I've got you, Rene.' He was protecting me. I was befuddled and felt like crying—the emotion was lumped up in my throat," he said, like a big chunk of indigestible meat. The lieutenant walked him back to the holding cell in the prison administrative building, personally unlocked the door with a key, and shook hands. Then, in total violation of prison policy, the legendary crook and the ex-Marine cop embraced. They'd known each other for an hour, and already it felt like they were longtime friends.

Boxer Enriquez had dropped out of the Mexican Mafia.

Rene Enriquez had realized there had to be more to life than wasting it.

It was 11:20 A.M. on March 22, 2002. The news of his defection shot through the prison as quickly as a round from a guard's Mini-14 rifle. Lieutenants and captains had been buzzing in and out of the office when Rene was talking to SSU agents on the telephone. Later, as the escort came to take him to his new cell in protective custody, there was a stale sense of dread. Madrid was there to shake his hand again. "You're making the right decision. It will change your life." Other cops came by and told him the same thing, assuring him that what he'd done "was going to save lives." Already, Rene wasn't so sure.

He was internally shaken as he headed down the corridor to the protective custody block 150 feet away. "I didn't want to go there—didn't want to be a PC. But I wanted to get it over with quickly." Conflicting emotions were tearing him up inside. Rene had asked that the corridors be cleared so inmates couldn't by chance see him. That didn't stop prison staff from looking—every doorway was filled by a curious cop or two. He felt "dirty and ashamed." The distance he had to travel was only fifty yards—the width of a football field. He felt it was the "longest, most shameful walk" he ever took.

That night he couldn't sleep. The next day he tried writing out some of his Mafia history for the coming debrief, but he snapped. *I'm not writing this shit,* he told himself. Madrid came to see him at noon, and Enriquez noticed him first stop to talk to a young correctional officer named Rivers Drown, who was a devout Christian. The youthful guard was the gunner on the tier and had a military bearing that soldiers would describe as "squared-away." He was also a member of the Special Emergency Response Team (SERT) at the prison, a SWAT-like unit that was headed up by Lieutenant Madrid. Officer Drown glanced over at Rene as he spoke to his commanding officer.

Rene, minutes later, felt the water well up in his eyes as he met with Madrid and angrily told him he had made a mistake by dropping out of La Eme. He felt terrible. "I don't know why I did this," he told the lieutenant. "I think I made a mistake." The Boxer ego began to think he was tricked into making the decision. Madrid assured him that all dropouts felt that way at first, that he had no worries and should try to get some sleep.

Later that day, Rene heard the opening pop of the heavy metal door that kept him in his cell. Officer Drown, the young gunner, called him over to the gun booth that overlooked the pods. Rene looked up, and the gunner's hand reached down with a personal note. It read: "My wife and I are praying for you. You took a bold step in your life. I know your family is in danger, but you did the right thing. People care for you. P.S.—I'm on Madrid's crew." He added that he didn't know if Rene wanted to talk or not, but he would be available to chat. The hardened convict's throat constricted with emotion, and he couldn't say a word. He turned and walked back to his cell, barely making the short distance before he broke down crying. "No cop had ever talked to me this way," recalled Rene. "He reached down into my soul. He said he prayed for me, and I didn't even know him. I was touched deeply by the kindness of his gesture." However, it wasn't enough to sustain any belief that he had actually done the right thing.

The old Boxer personality fell into a deep depression. He was a proud Mafioso schooled to be hard-hearted, an addict conditioned to blind his emotions with drugs, a carnal trained to beat any bout with sensitivity, and a soldado required to fight back tears. Now the walls of his protective custody cell couldn't shield him from his own tortured feelings. In the darkness of night, tears dampened his pillow as he cried like a man who had lost everything. Words of regret ripped through his sleepless mind: *You just destroyed yourself. You are nothing now. You gave up everything. Why did you do it? You didn't have to do it. You didn't have to do it!*

His knife had always been a security blanket. It was almost an appendage of his prison being. He never left his cell without it, and it was always close by when he was locked down. A couple of days after dropping out, he had flushed it down the toilet along with his handcuff key—believing he wouldn't need them anymore. Now he felt stripped. There were anxiety attacks when he left the cell to talk with Madrid, to take a shower, to work out in the mini-yard attached to his pod. "I would almost panic," remembered Rene. "Everywhere, always, I had a knife." Not anymore.

In the days that followed, gang investigators showed him he'd moved to the top of the Mexican Mafia hit list. He knew that the rule was "blood in, blood out" in his deadly universe. "Nobody wants to die," he said. "I'll do everything to protect my life. But it's the total rejection that bothered me more. My entire Eme career I'd worried about being placed on the lista—that I would be ostracized. Being placed on the lista means the organization is rejecting you. It's a terrible feeling to be ostracized from a community that is already ostracized from society itself." Also, the Boxer alter ego knew he would lose his crew, the money it generated, and all the respect and power he'd gained as an upper-echelon de-facto leader in the Mafia. He feared that "there would be nowhere to go for acceptance" and that he would end up "as nutty as Tupi Hernandez."

A voice from a cell located to the left of him came through the ventilation system. "Hey, Rene, you're going to be all right." It was an inmate named Richard Rich, aka "Richie Rich," a dropout from another prison gang called the Nazi Low Riders (NLR). He had long hair down to his shoulders, boyish good looks, and no tattoos. Richie Rich came from Fontana, a town an hour's drive west of Los Angeles that had seen organized Ku Klux Klan activity as recently as the 1980s.

"You're going to go through this depression for a while," uttered another voice from a cell to the right. That one belonged to "Buckethead"—a fat, heavily tattooed, more than mildly obnoxious NLR dropout who came from Orange County, a comparatively conservative Republican part of southern California that spawned pockets of an active racist Skinhead movement.*

Richie Rich and Buckethead began what Rene would later describe as "NLR therapy." The two had dropped out of the NLR about six months earlier and were familiar with the mood swings Rene would encounter in the days ahead.

Their therapeutic advice echoed through the vents with regularity.

---

* Similar to the relationship between Surenos and La Eme, the Skinheads are fodder for recruitment by white supremacist prison gangs. Because most of the Aryan Brotherhood members were locked down in Pelican Bay SHU, the NLR developed on mainline yards throughout the California penal system. In 1995 the CDC validated Nazi Low Riders as a bona-fide prison gang threat along with the Mexican Mafia, Nuestra Familia, and the Aryan Brotherhood.

"We know you were an Eme big shot."

"The worst stuff will happen in the first few days."

"We're all of the same status here."

"No one will judge you."

They shared their own psychological journeys and walked him through each stage of emotional healing. "It was actually very cathartic to talk to those guys," maintained Rene. "They were effective, knew exactly what they were talking about, and I found it very comforting."

Then, on a Sunday morning two weeks after he dropped out, he awoke from a much-needed deep sleep with a sharp realization: "You don't have any more worries. It's over. That's it. No more Mafia politics. No more anxiety about whacking people. No more jostling for position. The world is going to be okay."

Suddenly he felt great. The Mafia was truly a pack of predators who inevitably found prey within their own perimeters. Clearly, he was free of that twisted bizarro existence that confused right and wrong. Some would forever see the Black Hand on his chest as a kind of scarlet letter, but that was their problem, not his anymore.

Rene was full of regrets, but the remorse tank was running on empty: "I have a sense of guilt for participating in some things, especially the murder of Cynthia Gavaldon. But for the most part, these are heinous, horrible, brutal criminals who are getting killed by other criminals. I don't feel any sympathy for those guys. Maybe it's a rationalization on my part, trying to minimize or compartmentalize my crimes, but I don't have any remorse for those guys. It's a brutal world. There's not much room for compassion."

On June 5, more than two months after he dropped out, special agent Devan Hawkes arrived to handle the official debriefing. "I knew Devan had integrity," said Rene, "and he had an uncanny ability to tap into informants. He already knew secret information about me, things I did for the mob, and he knew his stuff." The debrief took several days and eventually filled more than fifty pages of information related to Mexican Mafia activities—murders, assaults, extortions, robberies, burglaries, and drug deals. It listed almost five hundred names of Eme members and their associates. There was no going back now.

During the first few months, Enriquez met daily with Madrid, giving him an in-depth education about La Eme. He described the different codes that Mafiosi used to communicate secretly, how visits were set up to conduct Eme business, and how that business was conducted with crews in the streets. He translated taped Mafia conversations recorded in the visiting rooms and gave advice on which carnales to target as potential Eme drop-outs and how to reel them in.

There were meetings with the warden, an FBI agent, a U.S. attorney, a Los Angeles County sheriff's deputy who worked gang intelligence, and a collection of other California Department of Corrections investigators.

Lieutenant Robert Marquez, a gang intelligence expert at Pelican Bay, said, "It was the first time we had an Eme defendant who could lay it all out for us. We never had anyone before of Rene's stature. He explained how Eme infiltrates different organizations, uses inmate rights to advance their own agenda, and manipulates our rules in the prison system for their own benefit. We began to understand how it works for the first time. He went beyond what is required of a normal dropout."

Rene had more than a few suggestions on how to interfere with Eme operations:

1. *View the Mexican Mafia as organized crime and a domestic terrorist group.* "It's not just a prison gang," warned Enriquez, "or just a bunch of guys shooting heroin. It's an organization." An organization that foments violence, spreads the cancer of drugs, has influence with tens of thousands of Surenos, calls the shots on who lives and dies, and plans to expand its reach. "It corrupts everything it touches," added Rene.

2. *Shut off Mafia communications.* He suggested that the CDC seek injunctions to prevent Eme members from communicating with other Mafiosi, associates, or facilitators. This would include no telephones, no correspondence, and no visits. "You have to shut down all communications," said Rene. "Without communication, the Mafia members in prison dry up."

3. *Totally isolate Eme members in prison.* Rene suggested housing them in an area separate from all other inmates. "Place them in such isolation" he said, "that they can't talk to anyone but prison staff. Take them away from the camaradas and Surenos who do their dirty work for them."

4. *Prevent Eme members from receiving money.* "Every bit of money they have," stressed Rene. "Because they value their money, and it's all generated by illegal activity."

5. *Seize the funds Eme members have in prison trust accounts.* "This is all illegal money," said Rene. Mafia members get money orders and personal checks from $50 to $500 a pop on a monthly and sometimes

weekly basis. It's cumulative and goes right into a prison trust account. They fill out a form called the trust withdrawal computation and then are entitled to release money to anyone of their choice. "It's the perfect method to cleanse money," he explained. "There is so much money leaving and entering the prison—tens of thousands of dollars moving on and off the books on a regular basis, dirty money that is laundered with the help of the CDC system." Rene invested his drug "tax" dollars in U.S. Treasury bonds, CDs, and double-e series U.S. savings bonds. Then he redeemed them later as clean money, all through the prison trust account. He and other inmates legally set up interest-earning bank accounts at Bank of America in Crescent City. Some Mafiosi even play the stock market. "Every cent of that money is criminal money," asserted Rene, "small fortunes of laundered money used to purchase homes, commercial real estate, and small businesses. It doesn't take a rocket scientist to figure out a Mafia member is receiving money from illicit sources. And no inmate keeps $20,000 on his books for bubble gum and candy bars."

6. *Prosecute Eme wives, family members, girlfriends, and other facilitators who aid and abet Mafia crimes.* "These people are knowingly participating in Eme activities, delivering drugs and messages, and the mob could not conduct business without them. They are co-conspirators. Not indicting them is like partially treating an illness, taking half your antibiotics and not killing off the infection. Prosecuting their wives and loved ones is a deterrent. The one thing we do fear is our families being hurt, people we value going to prison. That's what we fear."

7. *Prosecute all in custody for criminal conduct, including murders, even the cold cases.* Rene noted, "There are numerous incidents of murders, assaults, and narcotics trafficking each year that go unprosecuted. An Eme member understands he can sell or imbibe drugs or kill his cellmate and get no punishment except for a disciplinary report in his file. He already has an indeterminate SHU term because of his Mafia affiliation, so what else can the system do to him? We [Eme] have the sense that no one is going to prosecute, so let's do it. There's an air of impunity in the mob that we're the ultimate authority figure in the gang subculture and nobody can stop us."

8. *Seek capital punishment for murders.* "What's really needed is the ultimate sanction because a lot of carnales are simply incorrigible and irredeemable. Another life sentence does nothing. One life sentence

in California is as good as ten life sentences. So what's the difference if I pick up ten more along the way? The Mafia only understands and respects a violent power greater than them. It's the biggest-bully-on-the-block mentality. We'll kill you, but if there's a bigger force that can kill us, maybe we'll hold back.

"However, I don't believe the death penalty is a deterrent for future Mexican Mafia members. It might be more of a deterrent in Texas, but not in California, where a man can sit on death row for twenty years or more. He could die of old age, hepatitis, or get stabbed on the yard before the state kills him. There's no immediate threat of dying here. It's politicized. Furthermore, the publicity from further indictments and trials for heinous crimes can even enhance a Mafia career. In fact, dying from a lethal injection at San Quentin might place the recipient into legendary Eme status, a carnal dying for the cause.

"But here's the bottom line on the death penalty for prolific Mexican Mafia murderers. The only way to stop them is to kill them. They are wholeheartedly involved in the furtherance of Eme and its criminal objectives. That means murdering people. So these are carnales that have such low value on life, even their own lives, that they are willing to sacrifice themselves for other brothers who are ultimately going to betray them. And here's the point—what good is there in keeping people like that alive?

"After all, that's how we do business. The Mafia rectifies everything with violence. I mean, Mafiosi try to negotiate and intimidate, but if Eme has a problem with a guy and all else fails, we ultimately kill him."

Rene made an hourlong videotape presentation—at the request of his CDC handlers—to play for state legislators in Sacramento, spelling out the threat of the Mexican Mafia and how it all works. State and local gang investigators had expressed their concerns many times before, but Rene "Boxer" Enriquez, an articulate upper-echelon Mexican Mafia killer, started to command the attention of CDC bureaucrats in Sacramento.

He also made a video clip for La Eme's Angel Valencia. Rene's instincts told him that Angel too had had enough of Mafia politics. Basically, he told his old adversary that it was over. Mafia politics destroyed everyone. Mafiosi knew Angel was part of a plot to kill family members, and there had been plans to execute him during the phony PBSP peace talks in 2000. Gang investigators pulled Valencia into a conference room and showed him the tape. "What!?" he joked. "I'm supposed to drop out because of a videotape?" Then he did—after twenty-five years in the mob. It was as if all he needed was an invitation.

During this same time period, David "Chino" Delgadillo of Gheraty Lomas, an ex-Marine who had used his military training to teach others how to kill on the streets and in prison, dropped out of the Mafia after twenty years. He'd had a final run-in with Eme fanatic Cuate Grajeda.

Three high-ranking Mexican Mafia members had dropped out within a month—and all were now advising CDC gang intelligence officers on how to break La Eme. One PBSP gang investigator said, "We wanted to deliver a death blow to La Eme, at least knock them back ten to fifteen years. We knew we could do it by seizing their trust accounts, cutting off communications, visiting privileges, and mail. At the same time, we'd house them separately from Surenos and the rest of the prison population. They would become a wilted flower and die."

CHAPTER 38

A Wonderful Break

PELICAN BAY GANG INTELLIGENCE OFFICER LIEUTENANT ROBERT MAR-
quez said, "Rene Enriquez was above and beyond the majority of Eme
members at Pelican Bay. He had a level of sophistication that made it almost
impossible to nail down everything he was doing. As I became more aware
of Eme, it was apparent he was among the top five. I never thought he would
leave the gang."

And when he did, the news traveled quickly to the ranks of law enforcement in southern California, sometimes referred to as "the Gang Capital
of America." Sergeant Richard Valdemar was still working with the FBI's
Mexican Mafia task force in Los Angeles, and he immediately saw value in
Rene "Boxer" Enriquez. He filed the paperwork that authorized a long-term
trip to L.A. and a fresh Eme debrief for the FBI.

Two deputies from the L.A. County Sheriff's Prison Gang Unit stood
outside Rene's cell about ten o'clock in the morning on July 24, 2002. The
members of Valdemar's unit didn't really look all that much like cops. They
could pass on the street as just regular Joes, and that's how they wanted
it. Mike Duran, a mustached deputy with a Cuban ancestry, was one of
them—an astute, efficient, good-natured, smart-aleck cop.

Duran asked Rene, "Are you afraid of flying?"

"I'm a mobster," answered Enriquez. "Why would I be afraid of
flying?"

The deputy cracked up laughing as he slipped waist chains around his
prisoner for a plane ride to Los Angeles. *He's real nice,* thought Rene.

His partner was Deputy George Marin, a jolly, rotund Mexican-American with a heart of gold and a talent for writing warrants and other paperwork to prosecute Mafia cases. "I loved George immediately," said Rene.

Deputies Duran and Marin would essentially be his caretakers for the next year. What he liked about them most was that they both treated him, not like some murderous monster, but like a human being. The two of them had no shortage of good humor. There was a lot of laughter in their presence, and it was refreshing for a convict who had been locked down 24/7 for more than a decade—with people who wanted him dead.

A young FBI agent named Glen Hotema was also along for the ride. He was assigned to evaluate Rene's worth to the Bureau. Enriquez found him "a bit standoffish."

A turbo-prop, twelve-seater Beechcraft King Air airplane sat on the tarmac. It belonged to the L.A. County Sheriff's Department. Lieutenant Ernie Madrid and his SERT team sharpshooters from PBSP, armed with automatic rifles, kept watch for any unwelcome intruders. As Rene boarded the aircraft—bound in leg chains, waist chains, and handcuffs—the pilot was wearing a flight suit and shoulder holster with a 9 mm Baretta.

The lawman pilot warned, "If you do anything stupid, I will shoot you."

"Okay," said Rene. "I'm not going to be any problem."

Three and a half hours later, he could feel the airplane descending. He looked out the tiny airplane window and saw "little reservoir lakes below and a landscape dotted with little swimming pools in backyards. I spotted the *Queen Mary* ocean liner permanently docked in Long Beach Harbor as a tourist attraction. The water in the port looked filthy.

"I stepped out of the plane at Long Beach Airport, and the whole world changed. It was sunny and warm compared to the normally chilly, rainy, drizzly days at Pelican Bay." In sharp contrast to the echoed dullness of a prison cell, "there was the sound of noises from the city." Rene noticed that he "could smell exhaust fumes. Even that odor seemed pleasant and real. I was overloading with environmental stimulation"—with sounds and colors that had become only memories for him.

His handlers walked him ten feet to a waiting van. It was pitch-black with curtains and dark windows, a surveillance vehicle, driven by a tall, serious, deep-voiced SSU agent named Dan Evanilla, a prison gang expert with a couple of master's degrees and a work ethic that had no patience with laziness.

They joined a fairly long caravan of law enforcement vehicles. No one would tell Rene where they were headed. *It's like a scene out of the movies,* thought Rene. He peeked through the window curtain and checked out all the cars on the freeway, spotting an expensive Ferrari. "That's a come-fuck-me car," he told the nonplussed FBI agent. Looking up front through the driver's window, he saw a sign for the 605 freeway and then the Cerritos Mall: "This is Cerritos," he noted out loud. "I used to live just down the street." It was midafternoon when the caravan pulled up to the rear entrance of a satellite sheriff's station, miles east of downtown Los Angeles. Agent Evanilla walked the prized Mafia dropout to a holding cell, and Rene noticed the jailer "looking at me like I'm an animal." She had a hard jailer's edge. No punk. Her name was Kelly Ford, and she knew from his reputation that Rene was considered dangerous. Yet, Rene said, "she was fair and turned out to be really nice." She stepped out of the room while her new prisoner was strip-searched.

Rene had a small cell block all by himself. Except for one ten-day trip back to PBSP, it would be his new home for more than a year. On occasion, the jailers brought him home-cooked food, and in return he made them origami mobiles. It was one of the skills he had taught himself while passing time in prison.

On that first day, the FBI's Hotema brought him cheeseburgers, fries, and a strawberry milkshake from a stellar southern California fast-food chain called In-and-Out. "It had been thirteen years since I'd eaten something like that," said Rene appreciatively, "and it tasted so delicious." This time around, that was about all he was going to get from the FBI. Sergeant Valdemar brought Rene down mainly to see if the feds could do some cases with him. There were nearly a dozen meetings with assistant U.S. attorneys and FBI agents discussing the murder of Jimmy "Character" Palma on death row, Rene's Artesia crew, the LAPD Rampart dirty cops scandal, the Aryan Brotherhood prison gang, and Darryl Baca's crew. In the end, Rene didn't get involved in any of these cases. Sergeant Valdemar later explained that "the FBI just couldn't see the benefit in using Enriquez, didn't see his value."

Warden Joseph McGrath did see his value. On October 26, 2002, he sent a Lear jet and a SERT team to pick up Rene and bring him back to Pelican Bay to be a witness for the state attorney general in a civil case filed by an inmate named Anthony Escalera, *Escalera vs. Pelican Bay State Prison*. Sureno prisoners had been on constant lockdown—not allowed out on the yard—ever since the prison race riot in 2000. Escalera challenged the fact that only Surenos were on lockdown and filed the lawsuit to force the state to allow them all back out to the mainline yard.

Before boarding the plane in Long Beach, Rene stood on the tarmac with more than a dozen cops and smoked a cigar. "It was an amazing thing for me," he exclaimed. "It was, like, wow!" Two days later, there were snipers stationed on the roof of the Del Norte Courthouse in Crescent City when he went to testify for the state. He recognized one of them—outfitted in full SWAT gear—as Rivers Drown, the young Christian correctional officer who had been so kind to him when he initially dropped out. Inside, Rene sat behind a screen in the packed courtroom, identified only as "Inmate #25" and a recent Mafia dropout. He testified about the relationship between Surenos, La Eme, and the riot. In the end, the trial judge, finding the lockdowns were unconstitutional, eventually ruled in favor of the Sureno inmates.

In the meantime, the California Department of Corrections and Pelican Bay State Prison were involved in another bitter lawsuit that threatened to cost the state millions of dollars. It was called *Castillo vs. Alameida* (CDC director Edward Alameida).

Steve "Smiley" Castillo was a gregarious jailhouse lawyer with a big snaggle-toothed grin who had become part of PBSP folklore filing lawsuits on behalf of the inmates. In 2002 *Castillo vs. Terhune* (warden Cal Terhune) won fourteen points of reform and redress regarding the SHU program. Castillo's prowess in prison law had endeared him to the Mexican Mafia. Jacko Padilla, a friend of Castillos's, wanted to "make" him. He argued that the Mafia needed intelligent members. Angel Valencia also sponsored Castillo for membership. Boxer and others vetoed the idea. Even though Castillo was doing time for a murder, Enriquez felt that he was a "Poindexter type"—not a worthy killer.

Castillo's latest lawsuit had the potential impact of a bone-crusher shank plunging into the bowels of the CDC. He was challenging the entire SHU system, claiming that it was capricious and cruel and that the department had failed to follow up on reforms issued as the result of his previous legal action (*Castillo vs. Terhune*). If he won, prison gang members could be released back to the main yard—no more 23/7 in a solitary confinement cell. La Eme shot-callers knew what that meant—more freedom to personally control prison rackets on a day-to-day basis, to communicate face to face, to deal drugs, and to kill whoever they wanted when they wanted with their usual impunity. Castillo was on to something big.

Moreover, Castillo had the support of some powerful former and current state legislators, including Senator Gloria Romero, chair of the Senate Select Committee on the California Correctional System; Senator John Vasconcellos, former chair of the Public Safety Committee, who, according to his website, "stopped cold the decade-long rush to more penalties and more prisons"; former two-term senator Richard Polanco, once chair of the Senate Prison Committee, who championed *Castillo vs. Terhune;* and former senator Tom Hayden, 1960s radical and ex-husband of controversial movie actress Jane Fonda, who saw himself as something of a gang expert, having written a book published in 2004 titled *Street Wars: Gangs and the Future of Violence.*

Tony Rafael, who in July 2007 published an insightful book called *The Mexican Mafia,* described Senator Hayden's work as a "profoundly muddled and often dishonest examination of Southern California and national gang culture."*

During his debrief, Rene Enriquez had described the Mafia's interest in using politicians Romero, Polanco, Hayden, and Vasconcellos to further La Eme's goals. It worked quite simply. "One of our objectives is to infiltrate legitimate politicians," explained Rene, "if not by overtly corrupting them, through subtle corruption by having our voices in place. Romero, Polanco, Hayden, and Vasconcellos listen to Steve Castillo, and Steve Castillo listens to La Eme." That said, one Mafia goal was to shut down the SHU system.

Rene expounded on Romero's reputed ties to Steve Castillo and Castillo's strong relationship with La Eme's Jacko Padilla. During the 2000 peace talks that followed the Pelican Bay riot and a couple of subsequent inmate hunger strikes organized by Castillo, the mob didn't miss the significance of politicians who came to see them, sent their aides to follow up, and joined their causes. "They could be used to the benefit of La Eme," explained Rene.

During this trip to PBSP, Lieutenant Madrid set up a meeting for him and Rene to meet with Jacko Padilla. Enriquez felt that his old friend was also "tired of the Eme politics," and he talked to him about dropping out. If Jacko turned and testified in the lawsuit, it would "neutralize Steve Castillo and his bogus arguments to shut down the SHU program." Padilla was mildly receptive, but nervous.

The next day, Rene met with the warden and three top CDC administrators who were eager to shop for a prosecution team and launch a massive Eme investigation.

On November 5, 2002, Madrid and some of his SERT officers drove Rene back to his new jail quarters at the Los Angeles area sheriff's substa-

---

* Rafael, Tony. *The Mexican Mafia.* New York: Encounter Books, 2007, p. 38.

tion. He was "excited" about his expanding role as a quasi-gang consultant for law enforcement.

A week later, at the request of the director of the Department of Corrections, he did another hourlong videotape, again spelling out the operations and insidious intents of the Mexican Mafia. The in-depth interview was done by Lieutenant Madrid as agent Evanilla listened in. This presentation was headed to the state's number-one executive—Governor Gray Davis.

On Thanksgiving Day, detective George Marin arrived with his daughter, son, and niece carrying a platter overflowing with home-cooked holiday turkey and other trimmings. "It showed me cops were humans," said Rene. On another occasion, Marin's wife cooked him breakfast, and his teenage daughter sent audiotapes with religious messages. She wrote, "I'm praying for you. Jesus loves you." "I was so touched," said Rene.

In a January 3, 2003, meeting with assistant CDC director Brian Parry and agent Dan Evanilla, Rene Enriquez agreed to help the Special Services Unit in its prosecution of La Eme.

On February 3, Sergeant Valdemar, frustrated by the feds' lack of interest, decided to explore the possibility of bringing state indictments with the help of Rene. To interview him Valdemar brought in his favorite deputy district attorney, Anthony Manzella, who, as a young prosecutor thirty years earlier, helped put serial killer Charles Manson away forever. Manzella put crooks in jail for ten years and then became an L.A.-based litigation partner in a New York law firm for seventeen years. Having made enough money to live comfortably for the rest of his life, he decided to rejoin the district attorney's staff to end his career putting bad guys away—real bad guys. He'd done a number of dangerous Mexican Mafia cases—one of them put Luis "Pelon" Maciel, the mastermind of the Maxson Road murders, on death row.

Manzella felt that Rene was "smart," but there was a problem. "I wanted to keep working with him [Rene Enriquez]," said Manzella, but under California law, it "was years too late to make any kind of deal" to reduce or vacate Enriquez's twenty-to-life prison sentence. Then an understaffed Sheriff's Homicide Bureau decided that they didn't want any part of it. District attorney investigators felt the same way. A frustrated Sergeant Valdemar was also eventually pulled off the case. Manzella couldn't do it all alone.

During the first quarter of 2003, Rene did a training videotape about the Mafia for an LAPD task force and another for the U.S. Bureau of Prisons. Different local detectives trickled in to talk to him about a handful of Eme-related murders, and he offered information that helped them build their cases. That was it.

Fourteen months in L.A. was "a wonderful break" from the drudgery of SHU living at PBSP, but no big cases came out of it for Rene—and no deals from the feds or the local cops. He headed back to prison.

CHAPTER 39

You Can't Play by the Rules

CDC ADMINISTRATORS HAD AGREED TO TRANSFER RENE ENRIQUEZ closer to home at Lancaster State Prison, about seventy-five miles north of Los Angeles. First, he had to spend three months in a Transitional Housing Unit (THU) on the mainline at Pelican Bay. It was a trial period made to test his ability to live peacefully in an open unit with other inmates. Another Mafia dropout walked up and told him the routine when he arrived, and then left him alone on the yard. Rene kicked off his shoes and socks and started walking barefoot in the grass. He'd only had concrete to stand on for more than a decade. It was a hot June day, and he "smelled manure baking on the lawn, and felt the soft green blades poking up through my toes and massaging the bottom of my feet." He started "chicken scratching the turf," as if he were a little kid. There was "a lump in my throat as I experienced a simple freedom."

In the coming weeks, he trained pigeons on the yard. "I started by feeding them bread, sunflower seeds, and Top Raman noodles off the toe of my shoe. Eventually they ate right out of my hand. It got so they would fly in by the dozens when I made a *prrrrr* sound, and they followed me around on the ground like a trail of ducks." He'd throw rocks at enemy seagulls that tried to attack them and called the pigeons "my little dogs." "It was something I could care for," explained Rene, "and I loved them." Soon Mafia dropouts Angel Valencia and Chino Delgadillo were helping him tend to his flock.

He worked as a clerk in the IGI's office deciphering Mafia mail and audiotapes. Rene also had listened to loads of surveillance tapes—shipped down from PBSP—while incarcerated at the Los Angeles County sheriff's substation. A familiar theme developed during his translations. Senator

Gloria Romero, a former psychology professor, was, according to an inmate's relative, communicating with Eme associate Steve Castillo, and in the mind of Rene and several gang investigators, she was being used by the Mafia. The same was true, they felt, for her aide Rocky Rushing, who had earlier worked for Senator Tom Hayden during the PBSP peace talks. Sham talks were being used by the Mafia to secretly tend to their prison business.

Romero had become a vocal critic of the California Department of Corrections—suggesting that correctional officers and administrators were responsible for even more than brutality and corruption—and held the purse strings to its nearly $6 billion budget. After Eme associate Castillo filed his lawsuit designed to shut down the SHU, his cause was championed by Senator Romero. The Los Angeles–area politician—whose Senate biography described her as a "dedicated social activist and aggressive prison reformer"—planned Senate hearings to explore inmate Castillo's contention that "hundreds of prisoners" were misidentified as gang affiliates with "flimsy and trivial" information and held in the SHU unjustly for indeterminate amounts of time.

Castillo and his lawsuit were also backed by an inmate rights group called California Prison Focus (CPF). One of the people working with CPF is "Bato," a reputed Mexican Mafia member. Rene tells it this way: "He's a made guy who has a veiled front as an activist." Bato was also a two-strike felon acquitted for his alleged part in a 1971 San Quentin prison uprising that left three prison guards and two inmates dead.

CPF's president, Ed Mead, was a convicted domestic terrorist who served eighteen years in prison for blowing up a Safeway supermarket in the 1970s to show support for Cesar Chavez and the United Farm Workers. He had been officially banned from Pelican Bay. The United Farm Workers helped Romero get elected, and she was an active partner with CPF in so-called prison reforms.

Charles Carbone was CPF's attorney. Although he could point to a number of prison reform measures he had championed over the years, he was widely viewed by law enforcement as merely "a mob attorney." Rene Enriquez and his former Eme brothers wouldn't argue with that characterization.

Jesse Enriquez was another man who claims to have had Senator Romero's ear. He was Eme member Jacko Padilla's former father-in-law. Rene Enriquez (no relation) knew that Jesse and Jacko were very close, despite the fact that Jacko was no longer married to his daughter. And according to what Jesse claimed on the PBSP surveillance tapes, Jesse was also a confidant of Senator Romero and Steve Castillo. Jesse regularly alternated his visits with inmates Jacko and Castillo, and he talked about what he characterized as his cozy relationship with the senator.

Rene had warned his debriefers that La Eme was "trying to get influence in the Senate to force the CDC to the negotiating table, implement more prison rights, and get released from the SHU." Devan Hawkes and Lieutenant Ernie Madrid, during a gang task force meeting in Los Angeles shortly afterward, tried to get the FBI to tap the phones of Senator Romero, her aide Rocky Rushing, and Jesse Enriquez. No taps were ever authorized.

During a trip to Pelican Bay in June 2003, Romero met with five prison gang members: three from La Eme, one from Black Guerilla Family, and one from the Aryan Brotherhood. One gang investigator called the meeting "peculiar" and described Romero's attitude toward the staff as "snooty and condescending." At one point, she challenged an officer's qualifications to investigate the Mafia.

According to prison surveillance tapes of meetings between Jesse Enriquez and prison inmates, Enriquez claimed that he kept meeting with Romero and other politicians, convincing them that conditions at the Pelican Bay SHU were inhumane. Jacko Padilla was caught on tape appreciatively describing his ex-father-in-law as "a slick old fogy." Romero moved ahead with her plans for a Senate hearing to examine the effectiveness of the SHUs, focusing on the validation process that identified inmates as Eme members. The hearing date was coordinated with the timeline of Steve Castillo's lawsuit designed to shut down the SHUs altogether.

In the meantime, Deputy Attorney General Gregory Walston was litigating the Castillo case for the state: "There was a lot of political cowardice to undermine the will of the Department of Corrections to have their day in court. Correctional officers sincerely felt that [SHU] policies were not just constitutional but necessary to protect the lives of officers from some of the most dangerous criminals there are. This was not a decision that should have been decided politically." Meanwhile, Walston said, the state "was more and more focused on settling to save money," and he didn't want to settle the case at all. He felt that money won by Castillo and CPF would end up in the hands of gangster-crooks—to buy drugs and orchestrate hits. So Walston sought Rene Enriquez's advice on how to battle Castillo's legal action. "How can we break Castillo?" asked the government lawyer. It was simple, counseled Rene: "Jacko Padilla is close to Castillo. Get Jacko to drop out of the Mafia, and Castillo's lawsuit will disappear."

Rene, Angel Valencia, and Chino Delgadillo—all recent dropouts offering their counsel to government investigators—concurred. Rene says that all three of them advised, "You can't play by the rules. Toss ethics out the window. You are dealing with murderers here."

So the deputy attorney general set up a humbug visit with Rene's former cellmate and friend, Jacko Padilla. He threatened to make Padilla a hostile witness for the state and divulge the fact that he met secretly with Lieutenant Madrid several times to talk about Mafia business. "Jacko may have thought he was working Madrid in those meetings," said Rene, "but it was the other way around." Padilla was visibly shaken.

Several days later, Lieutenant Madrid pulled Jacko out of his cell. The IGI, under strict orders from the warden, reluctantly threatened to leak information that Padilla was cooperating with authorities. Previously, he had assured Jacko that everything they discussed was strictly confidential. Padilla, knowing he was being extorted to influence Castillo, felt double-crossed and left angry. The strong-arm tactic had backfired.

After that encounter, a diabolical male voice left a message on Lieutenant Madrid's telephone: "I'll blow your fucking head off!" Also, a wila was found in a prison transportation van spelling out that a hit had been placed on the cowboy lieutenant.

On August 3, 2003, Jesse Enriquez was recorded telling his son-in-law Jacko Padilla that he would be getting the names of "three canaries" (Eme informants) scheduled to testify at Romero's Senate hearing. He claimed that a Senate aide was going to supply the names. Those were Rene "Boxer" Enriquez, Angel Valencia, and David "Chino" Delgadillo. This was a serious security breach. Rene believed that Senator Gloria Romero or her aides must have been leaking sensitive information to Jesse Enriquez, and he was passing it to the Mafia. In his opinion, the organization was using her office to further their objectives.

A correctional officer filed a report saying that he heard Castillo on the yard telling another inmate that Senator Romero "works with us."

Around that time, the *Los Angeles Times* printed an article about an inmate hunger strike at Pelican Bay designed to help close down the SHU. Jesse Enriquez was interviewed for the piece, and gang intelligence officers complained that it erred in making the California Prison Focus lawyer Carbone and Steve Castillo look credible.

In July, Steve Castillo had been stabbed by his cellmate and seriously injured. The hit man was Ray "Termite" Vara, allegedly sent by Eme's Daniel "Cuate" Grajeda. Boxer, along with more than a dozen hard-core Mexican

Mafia members, always "thought hunger strikes were a boneheaded idea." Their thinking was that the Mafia wasn't a political group. Boxer Enriquez had been among those who believed that, "if the mob wanted to make a statement, let's just kill a couple of cops during visiting." "That was the Eme way," argued Boxer, "not some nonviolent demonstration or hunger strike." Eventually, Castillo was hit—a genuine Mafia protest by the rival Grajeda faction.

Senator Romero called the prison shortly after the attack on Castillo. According to CDC investigators, she seemed to believe that the hit had been a CDC setup.

In truth, Castillo was the man trying to get Mexican Mafia members out of their SHU accommodations and was given thanks with a shank. Immediately, he began talking to prison staff about "rolling over." He'd had enough of La Eme. Soon after the stabbing, CPF attorney Charles Carbone called the warden and demanded to have an immediate telephone conversation with his prized client.

Then Jesse Enriquez quickly arranged to visit Castillo and delivered a message to hold firm, go back to the SHU, and not get locked up in protective custody. Jesse Enriquez again claimed to Castillo that he was working closely with Senator Romero, her aide Rocky Rushing, and CPF lawyer Carbone. Jesse Enriquez met with his former son-in-law Jacko Padilla on August 2, the day before he met Castillo. According to Enriquez, the crooks and the politicians feared that the Senate SHU hearing and the lawsuit were dead if Castillo dropped out of the picture. Devan Hawkes said, "That caused us concern that Romero was getting involved in Eme. That she would discourage his [Castillo's] dropping out. If he did, he would tell the truth about La Eme, and that would ruin their whole case" against the SHU. There is no evidence that she urged Castillo to stay in the Mafia.

Castillo also tried to get a warning out to Romero to check under her car for a bomb. He knew La Eme still wanted her support, and the senator could be killed if she backed off her anti-SHU stance. After that, Castillo returned to a cell in the SHU and cut off all communications with Romero. The California Highway Patrol (CHP) came to the prison twice to investigate the bomb threat. Padilla was interviewed. Ultimately, the CHP determined that the Senator was in no danger because she planned to go forward with her plans to have a hearing.

Jim Moreno, a former college linebacker who was the senior special agent at the Special Services Unit, was also under pressure to make the hearing and the Castillo lawsuit go away. He was further incensed by the death threats made against Lieutenant Madrid and a subsequent Eme "green light" put on gang intelligence officer Lieutenant Robert Marquez. Moreno made a special visit from Sacramento and vowed "to break" Jacko Padilla. Rene Enriquez, serving as an adviser, stood with a lieutenant just a few feet away in a corridor behind the IGI office and secretly listened to the conversation. He heard Moreno "menacingly threaten to destroy Padilla's Mafia career, his father-in-law, and entire family. He wanted Jacko to roll so badly he shipped him out to Corcoran State Prison on a midnight express" and made other Mafiosi "think Padilla was cooperating." "Jacko was stressed," remembered Rene, but he held on.

On September 15, 2003, Senator Romero convened a hearing of the Senate Select Committee on the California Correctional System. She opened the proceedings by saying, "It is much more expensive to house an inmate in a SHU." Then Romero explained that she wanted "to focus on the validation process," about which she had "very serious concerns," including "due process rights . . . being utilized by CDC . . . a lack of oversight of the process by which it is determined whether a SHU inmate continues to be an active gang member or associate." She complained that "a validated gang member could conceivably spend the rest of his life in a SHU." The senator posed the question: "Are we, as community members, safer because of SHUs?"

Rene Enriquez, speaking from an insider's view, thought the senator was "naive." "She doesn't understand," explained Rene. "There are Eme members like Cuate Grajeda and Huero Sherm Leon who are just bitter, vicious, evil men who have no place in society. All they seek to do is destroy because they are miserable and want others to be miserable."

Next to testify at the hearing was former state senator Richard Polanco, who was introduced by Romero as "instrumental in addressing this issue [SHUs]." Polanco noted that he grew up on the gang-infested Eastside of Los Angeles. He then criticized the "debriefing" process for depending on "snitching." He questioned the CDC's method of defining gang membership as "too subjective a methodology" and complained that the gang validation process depended on "rather old information" supplied by inmates.

"Polanco is an idiot," said Rene. "He's advocating the complete shutdown of the SHU. He was dumb because he blindly went forward and jumped on the liberalization of prisoner rights and so-called Draconian SHU conditions because it was the politically correct thing to do."

Another speaker at the hearing was CPF attorney Charles Carbone, introduced by Romero as an "integral player in the discussions with the California Department of Corrections in reforming the Security Housing Units." Carbone disapproved of the SHU policy as "punishment through segregation on a prisoner according to their potential to commit violence, rather than any actual act of violence." He complained that gang officers were poorly trained, and he described debriefing as "the McCarthyism model"—one in which inmates "are simply naming names" without evidence of wrongdoing. The CPF attorney recommended "increased visiting" and "phone calls with family members" to help rehabilitate SHU inmates.

"Ridiculous!" said Rene. "There are worse places than Pelican Bay SHU. Besides, it should be worse. Hard-core Mafiosi should be stripped down in cells until they are ready to leave the organization. That appears to be torturous treatment, but it keeps them from communicating with the outside world. Prison gangs—Eme in particular—will not stop. They are a constant threat to society. Some of them need a dirt nap, dead and buried—that is the only solution for them."

The gist of the Senate committee hearing was that many of the 1,500 SHU inmates were unfairly validated as gang members and held for indeterminate terms at Pelican Bay, Corcoran, and Tehachapi.

Jailhouse lawyer and Eme associate Steve Castillo debriefed sometime after the Senate hearings and told gang investigators that in truth he knew of only one inmate who was ever placed in the SHU after being validated incorrectly—a Mafia associate who was mistakenly identified as a full-blown carnal.

One longtime gang investigator said, "It was all a lie perpetrated by Prison Focus and Castillo. We knew it was a lie. All their arguments were bogus. What was most disturbing was they had a senator who was backing them [on their arguments]."

In fact, Castillo later sent a letter of apology to Senator Romero, explaining that he had lied to and manipulated her.

Steve Moore, assistant director of the CDC Law Enforcement Investigations Unit, ordered Devan Hawkes not to look into Senator Romero or her aide Rocky Rushing and their possible relationship with La Eme. Moore felt that there wasn't evidence warranting an investigation and in any event, that it was not the CDC's place to investigate the person who oversaw the agency. He felt that should be up to the FBI or California Highway Patrol. They didn't do it either.

Rene was disillusioned. He'd listened to hours of surveillance tape about Senator Romero, Rocky Rushing, Steve Castillo, Charles Carbone, Jesse Enriquez, Jacko Padilla, and others with an interest in changing the SHU policy that so impacted La Eme.

Sergeant Richard Valdemar was "disappointed with CDC." He, like others, wondered why a state senator would take such an interest in the prison conditions of the Mexican Mafia.

There was growing pressure from CDC headquarters in Sacramento to settle the Castillo lawsuit. Deputy Attorney General Gregory Walston quit his job in frustration. Walston went into private practice: "There was conflict between the politically minded people in the AG's office, and it was annoying. It was preventing my client [the correctional officers] from having their day in court."

The Castillo case was still set to go to trial in December 2003. Warden McGrath pressured Rene to testify for the state, threatening to call him as a hostile witness. Enriquez cockily asked for some relocation money and other considerations, and his demands weren't met. "These people [top CDC executives] were duplicitous," observed Rene. "They didn't want to go after the mob. They only wanted to kill the lawsuit."

There were also other video surveillance videotapes shot in the PBSP visiting room implicating Eme members and their associates in murder and other crimes. The tapes disappeared, and so did any attempt to prosecute the offenders. They had a high-ranking Eme member operating as an informant within the Mafia's ranks, and Rene said, "The CDC still wouldn't do anything." He finally decided that the CDC had a "deliberate indifference" to the entire Mafia mess. Rene stopped cooperating. He had found that politics are everywhere—not just in La Eme.

CDC director Edward Alameida resigned in December 2003. He was caught in a storm of allegations that he impeded investigations into charges that Pelican Bay correctional officers committed perjury in inmate abuse trials. Alameida denied the allegations. Senator Gloria Romero, a vocal opponent of the director, wanted his head on a stick.

It was not until May 2004 that the CDC finally entered into a settlement agreement with Prison Focus on Castillo's lawsuit. The CDC ended up making certain concessions in its administration of the SHU program: giving inmates the right to challenge evidence that they were in a prison gang and requiring investigators to detail how a piece of evidence indicated gang affiliation. Gang investigators felt that the agreement seriously compromised their ability to properly do their jobs, especially since it watered down the importance of facts obtained from informants.

None of that mattered much to Rene Enriquez anymore. In August 2003, he was transferred to a facility closer to home—Lancaster State Prison, seventy-five miles north of Los Angeles. Living on the mainline, he was hoping for a less complicated, Mafia-free, drug-free existence.

Lieutenant Ernie Madrid lamented that "we had this tool [Rene Enriquez] who was willing to work with us—dynamic and intelligent. Why were we going to let all this work go? The answer I got was budget and politics." Madrid also worried that "Rene is not the kind of guy who will sit in prison and rot away unnoticed."

CHAPTER 40

La Eme Spreading Like a Cancer

CALIFORNIA STATE PRISON AT LANCASTER (CSP) WASN'T A DAY CARE center. It was still a level-four institution filled with murderers, attempted murderers, kidnappers, carjackers, rapists, robbers, burglars, and pumped-up, shaved-headed, tattooed gangsters who would make a suburban house-wife's heart stop if she saw one walking toward her on the street. At the same time, it was no Pelican Bay SHU. Rene could spend his days "stand-ing on grass smoking cigarettes in one of the three big prison yards and look up at blue, cloud-free skies and feel the southern California sun bathe my skin with warmth." In a large open space where an inmate could walk freely inside the cell block, prisoners played backgammon, chess, check-ers, or cards at little tables. There were roll calls two times a day so that guards could account for all inmates, but to a man who had spent more than a decade in relative solitary confinement, Lancaster was "freedom." Plus, there was no Mafia politics swiveling his brain. He had a job working on the grounds crew, and at first he enjoyed the change from his more dungeon-like existence at Pelican Bay.

However, there were immediate drawbacks. The cell block where he lived and the yard he walked was a protective custody (PC) facility filled with inmates he'd always distained—gang dropouts, snitches, and sex of-fenders. "It was horrible," said Rene.

There were other adjustments to make as well. The years of solitary confinement had made him "jumpy around crowds. I didn't like to be sur-prised. So I stayed away from the bustling chow hall, preferring to eat in my cell." Some inmates still thought he was a "sleeper" for the mob—there only to kill Mafia enemies on the sensitive-needs yard. They were wary of his presence. There were guards too who had nothing but skepticism and scorn for this former Eme hit man turned PC inmate. Who could blame them? Ironically, he found the correctional officers at Pelican Bay to be "the best" in their treatment of inmates.

One old family friend recalled her first visit to see Rene at his new Lancaster digs: "He was nervous, and his hands were sweating. He'd never been among families and visitors on visiting day. If he heard a fast movement, he jumped up."

There were stark reminders of why he left the mob life. A couple of Mexican Mafia associates on the yard walked up to Rene and said, "Hey, I killed a guy for you." Rene recalled, "I had no idea who they were, what I'd asked them to do, or why. It showed how empty the whole Eme process is and how everyone is used."

Yet the Boxer part of Rene still had an ego that could fill Dodger Stadium. People still feared him, and he wasn't totally ashamed of his former reputation. In fact, he still relished the attention it accorded him—even on a PC yard. Freddie "Veneno" Gonzalez, another Mafia dropout at Lancaster, told him, "You're just a regular Joe now—get used to it." He couldn't.

Within weeks of his arrival at Lancaster, Rene "felt abandoned. People who were supposed to change my life didn't change my life. They just extracted information and dumped me." He became depressed.

Rene had been clean and sober for more than four years. His sobriety came during a realization at Pelican Bay that he was nothing more than a jailhouse junkie. He wanted "to show my sons and my parents that, even in prison, I could be more than a washed-out heroin addict." That was no small accomplishment considering that about only 3 percent of heroin addicts ever give it up for good. Suddenly at Lancaster, however, the allure of drugs was as strong as a naked woman lying in his bunk.

A number of inmates kept asking Rene if he got high. Then a prisoner named Aaron Jeffro of Gardena said, "I'll give you a gram of heroin to get on your feet." Rene and his new cellie, a Norteno from Sacramento named Louie, slammed. He felt home again as the opiate flowed through his blood, caressed his brain, and massaged his ego. Heroin seemed like an old friend, but much like La Eme, it always stabbed him in the back.

"I wanted to start getting money and dope again," said Rene. He looked around the yard and saw old tatted gangsters who acted tough but weren't real mobsters. Rene felt that they were "mentally weak." "I'm going to have some position somewhere," he rationalized. "I just can't stand being a no-account." He started hustling dope on the yard, smuggling methamphetamine into the prison every week through a girlfriend visitor, and stayed high as much as he could. He was gagged on dope as he headed across the yard and ran into Johnny Duran, a former Eme associate from San Diego who had found Christianity behind bars. Johnny introduced himself to Rene.

"Jesus loves you," assured Duran. "When you're ready, we'll be here."

Rene shook his hand and didn't give the encounter a second thought. He was forcing himself to get out of bed each day, thought about whacking someone to grab another case and a transfer, and drowned himself in any intoxicating substance he could get his hands on. "I drank until I blacked out and was shooting dope until I couldn't see—I didn't care anymore." His son Bobby, who had just graduated from UCLA, came to visit his father and could see he was on a downward spiral.

"What's the matter, Dad?"

Rene could see the disappointment on his son's face.

"Look what you're doing to yourself. Please stop using," Bobby pleaded. "I don't want to see you like this."

Locked up in prison for nearly all of Bobby's life, Boxer hadn't been much of a father. In truth, the young man was saved by his grandfather, who tried to make up for the mistakes he made with his own sons. Bobby was the first college graduate in the family. Rene was bursting with pride and hope for him. His drug-weary eyes filled with tears, and he cried.

Desperate to get ahold of himself, Rene later wrote a letter to a former high-level SSU contact who had moved on to another job. Agent Dan Evanilla was sent to see him instead. He was an earnest, clean-cut, no-nonsense guy with grown kids—all championship swimmers who went to college with the help of scholarships. Discipline seemed to be an Evanilla family virtue.

The old Boxer alter ego had just finished slamming some oxycontin and meth when a guard popped his door and said there was someone waiting to talk to him. Rene looked down and saw that his shirt was dripping wet from the rush of drugs. "I put on sunglasses, grabbed a baseball cap, and pulled it down low on my head"—as if to hide his deteriorating physical condition.

Evanilla, wearing a green jacket, was sitting next to gang investigator Steve Preciado and his lieutenant when Rene was escorted into the room.

"How you doing?"

"What's happening, homes?" Evanilla said in greeting as he reached out his long arm to shake hands. It amused Rene how Evanilla always talked to him in street language. The man couldn't look or act more like a cop, but Rene "respected him" as one of the good guys.

"Take off your glasses," ordered the tall lawman.

Rene slowly peeled the lenses from his face.

"You're on drugs!" said Evanilla. It wasn't a question.

"No," lied the beaten Mafia dropout.

"You're fucking up, Rene."

"I ain't using."

The lie came just as easy the second time, but he knew no one was buying it. Preciado and his lieutenant were chuckling in their disgust. They'd been recording his phone calls and knew all about the small drug-smuggling operation he'd been running for weeks. Rene was busted, visits were cut off for three years, and he was taken to administrative segregation to serve out more punishment. He knew he was done with SSU. Evanilla could only deliver a negative report.

During nine months in "the hole," Rene never abandoned his drug habit. It was a cycle of doom. "I hustled and sold everything I had to buy heroin or meth." If he couldn't get his drugs of choice, he "used codeine or wine to take off the edge." It was more of the same when he returned to the PC yard. One day he looked around his "house" (his cell), and there was nothing. "I'd hocked everything I owned for drugs."

Rene made an appointment to speak with David Foote, the lieutenant on his yard.

"Get me off the dope block and put me on the Christian block," he pleaded.

Shortly afterward, Rene walked into the block that housed many of the protective custody inmates who were born-again Christians.

"You remember me?" someone asked. "I'm the guy who told you Jesus loved you."

It was Johnny Duran from San Diego, a year and a half after Enriquez had run into him on the yard. "Yes," said Rene. He needed a safe haven.

He was clean for two weeks, slipped once using some heroin, and then stayed clean for a month. In December 2005, some new visitors came to see him, and they offered him another chance to change his life.

Three L.A. County sheriff's deputies, working on a task force, were waiting to see him. They had a flow chart outlining the drug operation of Mexican Mafia member Darryl Baca.

One of them was a soft-spoken young deputy with a friendly manner named Jeff Bosket, the son of a homicide detective. He asked, "Can you help us with this?"

Rene didn't waste any time waiting to answer.

"Yes," he offered. He didn't want to jack these cops around. Maybe they were his salvation.

FBI agent Glen Hotema, who'd talked with Rene two years earlier, hadn't completely overlooked his value. He had been the one to recommend that these task force deputies make a trip to Lancaster.

Bosket told Rene, "Okay, we'll be back."

"No," he pleaded. "Get a court order and take me now."

Bosket for the next few years would become Rene's trusted custodian, chief cop, counselor, and caregiver, all rolled into one.

On December 22, 2005, Detective Jeff Bosket, carrying a stun gun and a 9 mm Baretta, and Detective Joe Villanueva, armed with a 9 mm Baretta of his own, escorted Rene to an undercover car and drove the Mexican Mafia dropout to the L.A. County sheriff's substation in Lancaster. There the ex-Mafioso and the two deputies boarded a Drug Enforcement Administration (DEA) helicopter for a short flight to another jail facility east of downtown Los Angeles. He moved for months from one satellite lockup to another, partly for his own safety.

In February 2006, Rene received one of those phone calls he feared in his dreams. His father had had a stroke. "I lost my composure and was sobbing on the phone. 'My pop is dying. I don't want my pop to die.' " His father didn't die but was left with impaired speech. It was difficult to understand his words. "After the stroke, the first time I talked to him, it wasn't my dad. He wasn't the same man. It was sad." It had taken years to quell the anger and open up communications with his father, and now it was nearly impossible to have a conversation with him. It was not only sad, but a bitter irony as well.

Then, on August 8, 2006, while Rene was housed temporarily in the San Bernardino County Jail—Bosket got a tip about an execution plot. According to the detective, another Eme member, who was housed in the same facility on a different tier, used a jail trusty to deliver a message to a Sureno inmate celled next to Rene Enriquez. That message ordered the prisoner to kill Boxer. There was no doubt the Mafia still wanted him dead.

Meanwhile, Rene continued to work with local and federal law enforcement on a myriad of Mexican Mafia cases.* They involved multiple murders in and outside prison walls, drug trafficking, and extortion. He acted as an invaluable resource, providing detailed knowledge of the inner workings of La Eme and its cast of players. Rene Enriquez in effect became something

---

* Some are still active and cannot be discussed in this book.

of a Mafia consultant working on task force projects with names such as "Operation Anaconda," "Operation Knockout," and "Operation in the Hat." He has made a series of training videos for local, state, and federal law enforcement groups.

Still, his reputation as a hardened Mafia hit man followed him and put him in the middle of a murder-for-hire plot. While housed at another suburban Los Angeles–area jail in 2004, Rene was celled up with a convicted Cuban-born drug dealer named George Martinez who headed up a narcotics-trafficking operation that smuggled multi-kilo loads of cocaine from Mexico into the United States and Canada. The thirty-seven-year-old Martinez had lived in a $2.5 million house in Downey and owned restaurants, apartment buildings, and a fleet of expensive automobiles that included an armored Mercedes-Benz and a Ferrari Spider. Wiretaps by a federal drug task force caught Martinez saying that he had made at least $8 million in drug profits before he was arrested in 2004. Rene said, "Martinez believed his wife was stealing all his hidden money, was beating their children, and was having sex with his attorney while he was wasting away in jail." The extravagant woman had $250,000 of Louis Vuitton luggage. Martinez hired Rene to kill her for $100,000: "He wrote out instructions telling me how it should be done. He wanted her shot—not in front of their children—and requested that the body be dumped in Mexico with a note pinned to her chest reading, 'Sigue hablando soplon' (Keep on talking, rat)." Rene snatched the note for proof and on several occasions wore a wire taped to his skin under a loose Calvin Klein sweater or hidden inside a pair of Billabong shorts. It was all under the tutelage of Bosket and other task force officers. Rene found it "nerve-racking, but the officers convinced me I was saving the woman's life." George Martinez, already looking at decades behind bars, is facing a new trial and a lot more time in prison.

CHAPTER 41

Trying to Be More

SITTING IN THE BACK OF AN UNMARKED POLICE CAR, RENE HEADED down the I-10 freeway toward the federal courthouse in Los Angeles to meet with some FBI agents and assistant U.S. attorneys. He was in leg irons, waist chains, and handcuffs, but his eyes were free to roam. It was one of those rare opportunities he had to see the outside world. The roadway was congested, but he liked it. The slow-moving cars gave him a chance to study the distraught faces of motorists cursing the traffic or barking into their cell phones. He saw one woman behind the wheel good-naturedly singing away, but for the most part the expressions were bitter and hurried. Yet for a man whose day would end back in a concrete enclosure, it was real life. "Those people don't realize they are blessed just to be in traffic, even to drive an old beat-up car," said Rene. "I don't think they realize that, take the moment in, and say this is a beautiful day. Each day is another chance to accomplish something positive, just to embrace life."

The cop car cruised down an off-ramp and turned onto a busy down-town street. There was a young mother walking with her child and a man strolling with his dog. Hungry customers waited at a little greasy spoon taco cart parked at the edge of the curb. Rene took it all in: "These things strike me as life. People pass it by every day, taking it for granted." The detectives pulled up to a stoplight. A black homeless man and his girlfriend stood on the corner with a shopping cart full of junk and a sign that read WILL WORK FOR FOOD. Their eyes met Rene's as he looked out the window at them, and the homeless guy gave him a little wave. He felt sorry for them. Then he started to wonder if they were really poor people or just crack addicts hustling change for their next rock of cocaine. *How can you determine that?* he thought. Caring people become jaded when they realize that their donated dollar really buys a chunk of dope instead of food. It's just a hustle. Rene also knew there were people in and out of law enforcement who "were thinking the same thing" about his defection from the mob.

The unmarked car pulled into the underground garage at the Federal Building. The trip had taken about an hour across the freeway and traversing downtown streets. "I had a blast," said Rene, who wondered, as he witnessed people's hurried lives, "if they really understood how blessed they were to be alive."

Rene Enriquez knew that it's highly likely he will die behind bars after spending most of his life in prison. He had served more than eighteen years on a fifteen-to-life sentence, and there's been almost no chance of parole for him, considering his notorious Mafia background. Now, through his cooperation with law enforcement, he was hopeful that someday he might be released from custody.

He did not want to end up the same way as his mentor, Daniel "Black Dan" Barela, who died alone in his cell on January 17, 2007. Guards at the U.S. Penitentiary in Victorville, California, watched on surveillance cameras as the sixty-one-year-old Mafioso was released from his solitary confinement to take a shower. A half-hour after Barela returned to his cell, officers found him down on the floor with no pulse, not breathing, and "vomit coming from his mouth and nose." He was taken by ambulance to the Victor Valley Community Hospital emergency room. Four armed federal agents guarded the doorway to his room when he was officially pronounced dead of a heart attack at 11:25 A.M. The coroner's report indicated that Barela had a "history of chronic heroin abuse," and toxicology tests found traces of opiates in his system. It also noted an upper arm tattoo of a skeleton wearing a sombrero that "appears to be 'Death.'"

On March 12, 2007, Rene's older brother Marc died from complications due to AIDS after years of intravenous heroin abuse. He was serving a parole violation at the California Institute for Men in Chino when he fell to the floor of his cell in a convulsive state and never regained consciousness. Sadly, Marc died while still a slave to the needle. "He refused to go to rehab. It was like he wasn't my brother anymore. Marc wasn't Marc," lamented Rene. "He was a handsome man who wasted away. He never worked and was in and out of prison his whole adult life, mostly for drug-related thefts. The brother I want to remember is the happy-go-lucky guy who loved to go fishing with me, always got the girl, and never wanted to hurt anyone.

He was my charismatic big brother—my hero." Marc died in prison as an AIDS-riddled junkie.

In the end, Marc was in a coma on life support for several days before family members gave doctors permission to pull the plug. His father, mother, sister, and younger brother John—who overcame a drug problem of his own, turned his life around, and was working as a surgical technologist—all came to visit Rene after Marc's death. Tears fell like raindrops. "I never cried like that before with my family," said Rene. "I hadn't seen my sister Perla in eighteen years, and as soon as I saw her I broke down crying." Like so many families wracked by the evils of drug addiction, many of the tears fell as symbols of what could have been.

Rene has been clean and sober since November 2003 and is determined at the very least not to die just another jailhouse junkie. About two and a half years after he dropped out of the Mexican Mafia, Rene for the first time in his prison career willingly participated in a mental health evaluation with a state forensic psychologist. Dr. Elaine L. Mura asked him, "What would you change if you could alter only one thing in your life?" His answer was: "Drug abuse . . . without drug use, the possibilities would have been endless. . . . I think drug abuse is a portal to the Mexican Mafia." He no longer wants to be a drug addict.

"I have to be more," said Rene, "than the worst thing I've done in my life. I don't want to kill anyone ever again. My greatest desire is to be a better man. I want my sons to someday be able to say that their father was a good person who made a lot of terrible mistakes but finally learned—that I ultimately had some positive impact, made a difference."

In the fall of 2004, gang investigators at Pelican Bay State Prison froze the inmate trust accounts of fourteen Mexican Mafia members in an effort to stop mobsters from using the state to launder drug profits. The documents have been sealed by a Superior Court judge pending investigation, but Eme member Raul "Huero Sherm" Leon led the list with $23,000 in his account, one of two carnales with more than $20,000 in trust accounts. Two others had more than $10,000, and seven other members had accounts ranging from $1,700 to $5,200. The trust accounts were designed for inmates to keep a few hundred dollars on hand to buy toiletries and canteen food items. Gang specialist Devan Hawkes believed that Eme members had been laundering "millions of dollars" of illegally gained profits through their prison trust accounts; investigators wanted the courts to seize the ill-gotten profits.

In 2006 about two hundred top prison gang members were moved into one "short corridor" at Pelican Bay to disrupt gang communications. There the isolated Mafiosi were separated from the camaradas who normally did their dirty work. All mail was monitored and stamped so it could be traced from prison to prison, allowing for gangsters and their accomplices to be prosecuted for ordering hits or setting up drug deals through the mail.

A few Mexican Mafia members had prison visits cut off altogether, and several Eme wives were marked for prosecution for aiding and abetting in mob business. Devan Hawkes said that Rene Enriquez "was an instigator in it [the measures to disrupt Mafia business] moving forward."

Rene also worked with representatives of the Greater Los Angeles Catholic Archdiocese to educate human rights and prison reform groups about La Eme. He said that "well-meaning" leaders of civic organizations often "do not understand who they are dealing with when it comes to the Mexican Mafia." These groups may believe they are promoting good works when they support inmate peace talks or hunger strikes by sending letters, faxes, or e-mails to prison officials, but the truth often lies elsewhere. Rene said that the Mafia "utilizes the legitimacy and power of churches and prison reform groups only to further the interests of the mob. Prison administrators often succumb to the pressure generated by these valid organizations that are in fact doing the bidding of evil without even knowing it. Anything we [La Eme] touch, we corrupt. Human rights advocates complain about cruel and unusual punishment without realizing these guys in here [SHU] are really killers. Put five of them together and somebody is going to fall dead on the yard. These are really cynical, cold, calculating, brutal murderers—Eme people who are beyond redemption. Do-gooders should run from them like their hair is on fire."

Rene Enriquez knew that the Mexican Mafia is glorified in the minds of tens of thousands of young people—just in southern California—and he wanted to change that perception. "Maybe I can't help older people because they have already chosen their path in life," said Rene, "but I can help kids." He was hopeful that his telling of the ugly truth would discourage others from making the mistakes that he made. While in California State Prison in Lancaster, he helped start a program called Prisoners Reaching Out to Educate Children and Teens (PROTECT). It's a prison-based project run by ex-prison gang members who use videotaped messages and in-person lectures at the prison site to keep young people away from drugs and gangs.

In October 2007, Rene, qualified by the court as a Mexican Mafia expert, testified for federal prosecutors against a La Eme member and six associates in what was the first-ever RICO prosecution against gang members in

San Diego. He was nervous for days prior to his testimony: "It was so difficult—a personal struggle. I was raised not to cooperate with authorities, and even though I had been doing that, my subconscious was nagging at me." He had never before personally testified in a criminal trial against a member of the mob, or anyone else for that matter.

Sitting on the witness stand, "I started swallowing with a lump in my throat. My voice was shaky. I said to my mind, *Don't let me break down here.* It was the most difficult undertaking I've ever experienced." Rene was on the verge of tears when Assistant U.S. Attorney Todd Robinson asked, "Is this difficult for you?"

Rene started stuttering and was afraid to blink, thinking that would unleash the tears that were building up in his eyes. He looked over at the jury and saw a middle-aged black woman: "She saw the water in my eyes, and she felt what I was feeling. I'm testifying against my former brothers." He turned his entire torso toward the jurors and said, "I'm sorry. I'm so nervous." The courtroom—packed with other prosecutors, FBI agents, U.S. marshals, and other cops—was silent. Federal prosecutor Robinson's mother—also in the gallery—would later tell her U.S. attorney son that Rene came across as "very sincere."

The one Mexican Mafia member on trial was Ricardo "Gato" Martinez. He was the boyfriend of the controversial Varrio Logan social worker Rachel Ortiz. She and Gato had once come to visit Rene in L.A. County Jail years earlier. Rene—looking the defendant straight in the eye—testified that Gato was "a well-known high-ranking member of Eme" with "thirty years in the organization." During Rene's five days of testimony, he remembered, Gato "would look at me grandfatherly. I felt compassion for him. He was overweight and gray and looked old. I felt sorry for him. And I felt I was somehow killing him."

Federal prosecutors at the conclusion of the two-month trial ended up with seven convictions—Gato and six Mafia associates. They were found guilty of numerous racketeering offenses, including murder, conspiracy to commit murder, drug dealing, and money laundering. Weeks before the trial, two others had pleaded guilty to similar charges, including La Eme's murderous Raul "Huero Sherm" Leon. "I had looked forward to testifying against Huero Sherm," said Rene. "He killed people for petty reasons, ordered executions for the slightest of reasons."

After the racketeering trial, an FBI supervisor told Rene, "You should be proud of yourself." Another told Rene that he testified "better than an agent." And yet another said that he "sounded like a college professor" on the witness stand. Shortly afterward, Rene agreed to speak at a training session for more than two dozen federal agents and prosecutors in San Diego. He felt good about it.

Rene Enriquez now has a new life in WITSEC, a witness protection program for cooperating inmates who are still locked up. "Every day for seventeen years as a carnal I worried about Mafia politics, hidden motives, visiting room posturing, enemies, indictments, and being placed on the lista. I know I am a priority hit, but it doesn't bother me anymore. Now I'm at peace. I'm not looking over my shoulder. If I do go somewhere and get killed, then I lived by the sword and I died by the sword. That's the way it is. But to my knowledge, no one has been murdered inside the WITSEC program. Now I really don't have to worry about the opinions or whims of Eme members who want to kill just to make themselves look good. I feel liberated from that. So in a sense, I am free. I feel good about myself. It's okay to be weak. My weakness is my strength."

"Gang life," learned Rene, "is like falling into an abyss." It's no life. Or rather, it's a life with no future. A life spent staring at concrete walls. A life peering through steel bars and hoping to get a glimpse of something new. It's never there. What is there is the always lurking possibility—when an inmate does step outside his cell—that his last breath will be stolen quickly in a burst of brutality. Being locked up in a prison cell and dying a violent death are not exactly great options, but those are the overriding choices for an active gang member. Life can be so much more.

Meanwhile, Rene Enriquez sits on the edge of his thinly mattressed bunk in a small cell, and his mind races with regrets. There is a new woman in his life—an old friend he married several years after dropping out of the Mexican Mafia—but he gets to see her only during visiting hours a couple of days a week. Other relatives, busy with their own lives, rarely come to see him. He eats when others tell him he can eat. The lights go out not when he wants to sleep but when the state decides it's time. His movements are restricted by a heavy metal door that spans the entrance to the modern-day cave in which he lives. He accepts that, "if I have to die here [prison], then I die here, but I don't want to die in prison. I want to die at home with my wife and family nearby, next to my dog. I want to be a regular guy, even just for one day."

The Black Hand is still tattooed boldly on his chest, but it now reminds him of what he was—not what he is trying to be.

Afterword

SINCE RENE ENRIQUEZ DEFECTED FROM LA EME, THERE HAVE BEEN A number of new Mafia prosecutions in southern California:

- On April 24, 2006, La Eme's Darryl Castrejon was one of four gangsters charged in connection with a Mexican Mafia contract murder. The forty-eight-year-old Mafioso was caught as a result of undercover surveillance by the Los Angeles Interagency Metropolitan Police Apprehension Crime Task Force (LA IMPACT). The case is one of nearly a dozen filed by IMPACT after a sixteen-year-old wannabe gang member gunned down a California Highway Patrol officer as he emerged from the Pomona courthouse. Castrejon was charged with being the shot-caller in the area, which was ruled by a Mafia-related street gang called the Twelfth Street Sharkies.
- On June 16, 2006, the Mafia's Raul "Huero Sherm" Leon was named as the prison-based ringleader in a San Diego federal racketeering and drug conspiracy case involving thirty-six street gang defendants with ties to La Eme. The indictment spelled out a massive drug conspiracy and three murders, including the execution of an extortionist who claimed to be a Mexican Mafia member and an inmate at a state prison. Also, prosecutors charged three gangsters in connection with the shooting of a twelve-year-old boy who survived. It was the first time in San Diego that federal prosecutors had used RICO to go after gang members. FBI agent in charge Dan Dzwilewski said, "Simply put, they are urban street terrorists who rule by violence. They are the closest thing to traditional organized crime in San Diego."

- On September 12, 2006, Eme member Ruben "Nite Owl" Castro and ten Eighteenth Street gang members were indicted in another federal racketeering case in which they were charged with controlling the narcotics trade on the entire Westside of Los Angeles. The feds said that thirty-six-year-old Castro oversaw the operation from a cell in the highest-level maximum-security federal prison, in Florence, Colorado—often referred to as "Supermax"—where he was serving a life sentence. Prosecutors say orders were relayed through Castro's girlfriend who also collected the feria.

- On December 12, 2006, the Drug Enforcement Administration spearheaded the arrest of two Mexican Mafia members and nineteen associates in San Bernardino County in what was described as a nationwide methamphetamine trafficking operation. Agents seized $1 million worth of meth, $1 million in cash, and fifty-six guns. La Eme's forty-two-year-old Salvador "Toro" Hernandez and his thirty-eight-year-old brother Alfred face criminal conspiracy charges. Agents said that San Bernardino has become the hub for meth produced in Mexico and distributed across the United States.

- On December 18, 2006, La Eme's Peter "Sana" Ojeda—the mobster who first began to organize street gang "taxing" in Orange County, California—was sentenced to fourteen years in federal prison. The sixty-four-year-old mobster was one of twenty-eight gangsters sentenced to prison for terms ranging from two to twenty-four years as the result of federal racketeering convictions. The indictment alleged dozens of criminal acts as the Ojeda organization taxed gang members and drug dealers on the streets of Orange County and in the Orange County Jail and prisons. Those who resisted were assaulted by Ojeda enforcers.

- On April 27, 2007, another multi-agency gang task force arrested thirteen gangsters who were funneling "tax" money to La Eme's Richard "Psycho" Aguirre, who was serving a life prison sentence at Pelican Bay State Prison. Investigators said that two camaradas loyal to Aguirre enforced control of the entire Coachella Valley, 130 miles northeast of San Diego, with killings, assaults, and home invasion robberies. Seventy-five-year-old Jovita Aguirre, Psycho's five-foot-one-inch mother, was charged with collecting payments and passing orders for her Mafioso son. Cops confiscated fifty guns and a live pipe bomb during an investigation dubbed "Operation Clean House." The trial is pending.

More investigations are in the works, and there is plenty of evidence to suggest that La Eme is spreading its power and influence across the United States.

Let's start in the nation's federal prison system. During RICO cases in the late 1990s, the feds thought that these indictments would diminish the organization's power to scatter convicted Mexican Mafia members among federal prisons across the country—split away from La Eme's base in the California system. Daniel Vasquez, a former San Quentin warden turned consultant, said, "All it seems to do is spread the seed—the seed of a bad plant."

Already there is a separate, four-man federal Eme Commission. The commissioners are Rudolfo "Champ" Reynoso, Ruben "Rube" Soto, Phillip "Negro" Segura, and William "Willie" Gouvieia. According to Rene, "they have ultimate authority, or *palabra*, over all Mexican Mafia dealings in the federal prison system, including the making of new members." Law enforcement intelligence believes that Soto had already established a relationship with celebrated Italian godfather John Gotti at the U.S. Penitentiary in Marion, Illinois, before the "Teflon Don" died of cancer.

On April 21, 2005, the federal Eme faction demonstrated their bold and violent presence in the U.S. penitentiary system. Sixty-four-year-old Manuel "Tati" Torrez, a longtime Mexican Mafia member, was beaten and stomped to death by at least three other Mafiosi at the Supermax prison in Florence, Colorado. The facility, sometimes called "the Alcatraz of the Rockies," was built to house the most notorious inmates in the nation. It was the first time in the decade-old prison's history that an inmate was executed by other prisoners. The Fremont County coroner called it a "vicious" beating with severe injuries to the face, neck, and chest. Why Torrez was eliminated is not clear. What is clear is that La Eme didn't hesitate to do it in broad daylight on a mini-yard at the nation's most secure penitentiary.

Rene Enriquez warns that La Eme is "spreading like an incurable cancer." While incarcerated at the U.S. Penitentiary in Marion, La Eme's Ralph "Perico" Rocha in 2001 wrote to Rene Enriquez at Pelican Bay—using code words—that he was "trying to get involved in the NAFTA [code for Mexican drug cartels] to expand *negocios* [business] overseas *y* [and] borders . . . the family [Eme] is looking to open a few more restaurants [legitimate businesses] in Colorado, Texas, Chicago, etc." After beating another in-prison attempted murder case in federal court, Perico was paroled in March 2007.

In February 2008, Perico was shot and wounded on the streets of

Norwalk. Rocha's injuries were minor, but investigators say he was hit under orders from La Eme's Jacko Padilla—Rene's former cellmate and friend. Two months earlier, Jacko's wife and five others were arrested and charged with trying to murder Rocha and another Mafioso for encroaching on Padilla's drug turf in the San Gabriel Valley. Their trial is still pending. According to cops, Rocha and Rafael "Cisco" Gonzalez-Munoz pilfered tens of thousands of dollars from drug dealers in Padilla's territory. Sheriff's detectives say that the orders to hit Rocha came from Padilla at Corcoran State Prison, and that Rocha is still on the lista. No charges have been filed.

In December 2005, the FBI opened a National Gang Intelligence Center in Washington, D.C., to help coordinate a new "National Gang Strategy" with local and state law enforcement. As happened with the Italian Mafia in previous decades, the Federal Bureau of Investigation has been late to the party. Its interest in the growing national gang threat was piqued when members of a group called Mara Salvatrucha, or MS-13, began to proliferate in the northern Virginia/Washington, D.C., area. MS-13 started in Los Angeles during the 1980s with a bunch of Salvadoran war refugees and moved east, where gangsters killed three federal agents and demonstrated their penchant for hacking up victims with machetes. The National Gang Intelligence Center estimates that there are eight thousand MS-13 members in the United States spread across thirty-one different states, with an additional twenty thousand members in foreign countries. The FBI in 2005 formed an MS-13 National Gang Task Force.

The irony here, according to retired L.A. County sheriff's sergeant Richard Valdemar—arguably one of the nation's foremost experts on La Eme and other street gangs—is that "MS-13 is the junior varsity. MS-13 pays tribute to La Eme. That number '13' marks MS loyalty to the Mexican Mafia." He insists that "La Eme is the big-time, not MS." The prominent "13" that is part of the MS logo, in fact, stands for the letter "M." And that "M" stands for Mafia—the Mexican Mafia. That "13" marks loyalty to La Eme, just as it does for the vast majority of other Latino gangs in central and southern California.

Albuquerque, New Mexico, in 1995 was hit with a plague of violence that confounded local law enforcement. The homicide rate doubled as gang members from Los Angeles took over the crack trade in a high-crime area of southeast Albuquerque already known as "the War Zone." One L.A. gangster said, "When we went out there, we went out there like a big missile. And they didn't have no guard up. They didn't have no bullets to fly when we came with the missile." Detective Rich Lewis, an Albuquerque city cop, for four years partnered up with Bureau of Alcohol, Tobacco, and Firearms (ATF) agent Gary Ainsworth to uncover the biggest racketeering case in history for the U.S. attorney in that city. More than one hundred weapons were seized, including AK-47, SSK, Mac-11, and Tech-9 submachine guns. Fifty defendants went to prison for murder, attempted murder, and drug dealing. They were a mix of cholos from southern California gangs in East Los Angeles, West Los Angeles, South Los Angeles, Norwalk, Duarte, Lennox, and the Inland Empire. A rock of cocaine that sold in L.A. for three dollars could be sold on the streets of Albuquerque for twenty bucks. The trigger-happy gang members, many of them rivals at home, worked together to take over the drug trade on Albuquerque's streets. They commonly identified themselves as Sureno 13—"13" a symbol of loyalty to the Mexican Mafia—and some of their drugs were traced to La Eme connections. A shot-caller from Lennox with Mexican Mafia ties tried to keep the peace among the Sureno factions and ensure a continual flow of drugs.

A murderous clique from a Compton-based gang called Tortilla Flats swept into Oklahoma City in 2001 and quickly used murder, threats, and violence to take over the local drug trade. The heavily armed crew was led by a Mexican Mafia associate who proudly posed for pictures holding an assault rifle. Along with large quantities of methamphetamines and cocaine—conservatively estimated at more than $4 million in street value—cops confiscated enough military-issue C-4 explosive to blow up a small building. A federal task force put sixteen defendants in prison for terms ranging from four to thirty years. One of the convicted gang members, who does not want to be identified, said, "We were sent by the Mafia."

Eighteenth Street, a gang with an estimated membership of twenty thousand in the Los Angeles area, has also been identified by the FBI as a National Gang Strategy "priority group" with ties to thousands of other Eighteenth Streeters in El Salvador, Honduras, Guatemala, and Mexico. Eighteenth Street has a rogues' gallery of Eme shot-callers who influence its operations, including Ruben "Nite Owl" Castro, Jorge "Huero Caballo" Gonzales, Felipe "Chispas" Vivar, and Frank "Puppet" Martinez.

Federal prosecutors say Puppet Martinez was receiving $40,000 a month in "tax" payments throughout most of the 1990s, including three years he spent in Pelican Bay State Prison. Bruce Riordan, a former assistant U.S. attorney in Los Angeles who prosecuted Puppet, said Eighteenth Streeters were running their drug operation "like a McDonald's franchise. It was busy all day." The Columbia Lil Cycos, one small clique of Eighteenth Street that operated out of a tiny neighborhood in the MacArthur Park area just west of downtown Los Angeles, netted about $250,000 a month for eight years. Eighteenth Street dealers were put on shifts so that drugs could be sold on the street twenty-four hours a day. The feds, during a RICO case, found that rent collectors were making eight to ten grand a week. Young up-and-coming gang members were raking in $1,000 a week for themselves. Anthony "Coco" Zaragoza, a workhorse hit man with "18" boldly tattooed on his face, was receiving nearly $300,000 a year while locked up in prison.

Luis Li, a former federal co-prosecutor in the case against the Lil Cycos, said, "They patterned themselves after East Coast organized crime. And they relished the trappings." One gang shot-caller, living in a ritzy Burbank compound, had a framed picture of actor Al Pacino as *The Godfather* hanging on a wall in his office. There were expensive low-rider show cars, SUVs, Mercedes-Benzes, fancy jewelry, jet skis, and costly helicopter rides. Prosecutors believe the Lil Cycos were collecting about $4.5 million a year and washing the money through a couple of restaurants, a used-car lot, and a juice bar. Gang accounting required that all the cash be marked so that the Mexican Mafia knew who was paying taxes. "They ran it essentially like a corporation," explained former assistant U.S. attorney Li.

Puppet Martinez, EME tatted on his chest, was at the top of the money chain. Prosecutor Li explained that "every decision went through him." Investigators said that while Puppet was in prison in 1994 he ordered the execution of a rival Mafia associate who tried to move in on his territory. Carlos "Truco" Lopez and his aunt, Donatilla Contreras, were ambushed with AK-47 submachine guns and left for dead.

FBI agents discovered that Puppet's wife, Janie Garcia—known as "the Lady Boss" or the "Black Widow"—had nearly a half-million dollars in cash stashed away at three houses. The feds found $10,000 hidden in a vacuum cleaner and another $40,000 stuffed into a duffle bag. Lefty Cazales, another tax collector, was executed in a pool hall after he disrespected the Black Widow by making a $10,000 payment in $1 bills. The hit team finished Lefty off with a close-up round in his mouth.

Bruce Riordan left the Los Angeles U.S. Attorney's Office in January 2007 as deputy chief of the Organized Crime and Terrorism Section and accepted the new position of gang czar in the L.A. City Attorney's Office. He joins other law enforcement gang experts in saying that operations such as the Lil Cycos are being replicated by the dozens for sure, and that most likely hundreds of Sureno street gangs are under the auspices of the Mexican Mafia. Riordan said, "La Eme is the single most organized criminal enterprise in America today, and they represent the single greatest threat to the internal security of the nation because their power is derived from a 'choke-hold' on the prison system at the federal, state, and local levels. That power is growing rather than receding in the years since 9/11, when law enforcement took its eye off the ball. Eme was battered and bruised in the late 1990s and into 2000–2001—on the verge of extinction—but law enforcement at every level left the field, and Eme has undergone resurgence. Today they are at the pinnacle of the crime pyramid in the USA."

Since 2005, U.S. attorney prosecutions in Los Angeles have sent forty-one members of the Vineland Boyz gang to prison as part of a federal racketeering investigation called "Operation Silent Night." The average sentence ranged from ten to twenty years in prison, with fifteen defendants put away for more than twenty years and five for mandatory life. The Vineland Boyz case specifically linked the gang to four gangland murders, including the execution of a Burbank police officer, and laid out a drug-trafficking operation that spread from Hawaii to Indiana, Kentucky, North Carolina, and New Jersey under the watchful eye of La Eme's Michael "Mosca" Torres. The Vineland Boyz for years would buy a pound of meth for $7,000 and sell it in Hawaii for $25,000.

Meanwhile, according to Rene Enriquez, La Eme's Anthony "Tony" Palacios has set up a drug operation in Hawaii, Gilberto "Shotgun" Sanchez has moved to Florida, Jaimie "Payaso" Tinoco is now in Connecticut, and a new carnal known to Enriquez only as Mike was made in New York and is expected to establish a foothold there.

Mexican Mafia groups have also formed in Arizona and Texas.

Around 1974, Hispanic inmates at Arizona State Prison formed a prison gang and named themselves La Familia. Shortly after, a few Eme members from California got busted and ended up in the Arizona prison—where they schooled La Familia on how to get business done Mafia-style. La Familia was eventually endorsed by California Eme and became the Arizona Mexican Mafia. About a decade later, some homegrown Arizona crooks wanted to be Eme but didn't care for any affiliation with California. They started the New Mexican Mafia without the original Eme's endorsement. The two groups are bitter enemies.

The New Mexican Mafia staged a failed plot to kill the director of the Arizona Department of Corrections in 1998. In 2000 two New Eme members were charged with killing a police officer during a botched robbery. By 2003 more than a dozen members of the New Mexican Mafia had been prosecuted by U.S. attorneys for dozens of crimes, including racketeering, drug dealing, money laundering, the execution of eight prospective witnesses, and a plot to kill the Phoenix detective who worked the investigation. They were sentenced to the Federal Bureau of Prisons. Frank Marcell, chief of intelligence for the Maricopa County Sheriff's Office, said: "It was anticipated that these members would be placed on a 'hit list' once they set foot in the federal prison system because of the long-standing feud with the California-allied Arizona Eme. To the surprise of us in law enforcement/corrections who monitor these groups, it appears that has not happened. All indications suggest a truce has been established between all Arizona Mexican Mafia factions, and they in turn have reached out to Eme members in California and the federal prison system. This phenomenon is ominous. Imagine the consequences of all Southwest states falling under the umbrella and direction of the California Mexican Mafia. As a criminal syndicate, they are unmatched, and it appears their power-hungry tentacles are reaching farther and farther."

The Texas branch of the Mexican Mafia, called Mexikanemi, or La EMI, was formed in the mid-1980s. It also started in prison and has a constitution that describes the group as a "criminal organization" that works "in any criminal aspect or interest for the benefit and advancement of Mexikanemi. We shall deal in drugs, contract killings, prostitution, large-scale robbery, gambling, weapons, and everything imaginable." Federal indictments in 1993 and 1998 named more than two dozen Mexikani ranking members and associates in conspiracies that involved heroin, dirty money, guns, and fourteen murders. Mexikanemi is not officially linked to California's Mexican Mafia.

In the meantime, La Eme has been growing for years, mostly under the radar of national law enforcement, and it is a mob in search of a new criminal empire. Rene Enriquez confirmed law enforcement fears: "Mafia commissioners in the federal system and leaders at Pelican Bay State Prison want to establish a treaty with Hispanic criminal organizations, i.e., Latin Kings back east, Texas Syndicate [in the] Midwest and Southwest, Nuestra Familia in northern California, as well as already established factions of La Eme in Arizona, New Mexico, and Texas.

"The objective of the treaty would be to control distribution for all major cartels as well as to expand each organization's influence to a national level rather than a regional level. In five to ten years, you will see all of this come to fruition. This is the new domestic terrorism. The Mafia is like a malignancy—slowly and quietly metastasizing and metamorphosizing."

The Department of Justice estimates that there are 30,000 gangs in the United States with 800,000 members having an impact on as many as 2,500 communities. Just about half of those gang members are of Hispanic descent. Rene Enriquez said that La Eme wants a piece of all their action.

Chris Swecker, assistant director of the FBI's Criminal Investigative Division, told a congressional committee in April 2005: "Gangs from California, particularly in the Los Angeles area, have a major influence on Mexican-American and Central American gangs in this country and in Latin America." That comes as no news to members of La Eme.

At the same time, law enforcement estimates put the number of Latino gang members in southern California alone as high as 100,000 members. Arguably, the Mexican Mafia's Black Hand reaches out to all of those who call themselves Surenos. It's a sizable army committed to wrongdoing, and there is irrefutable evidence that they are in fact moving throughout the country, infecting our population with drugs, death, and a diabolical sense of duty.

Gang expert Richard Valdemar offered this insight: "What we see [in the Mexican Mafia] is what the Italian Mafia was in the 1920s or 1930s. They're on their way to another place. Thank God most of them are heroin addicts. It keeps them from doing what they have the potential of doing."

Rene Enriquez picked up on that same theme: "I don't think the public understands the ramifications of what the Mexican Mafia has grown into—and right now it's in its nascency. There is a big shift toward making guys who aren't lifers and do not use drugs. The organization is only fifty years old. Compare that to the Italian mob that has been around for hundreds of years."

Brian Parry, a former special assistant to the assistant secretary of CDC and now a consultant, said, "Eme is the new La Cosa Nostra."

The potential is frightening. There are no more than 150 to 300 made guys in La Eme, but in southern California their army of loyal Latino gang members numbers in the tens of thousands. La Cosa Nostra in the United States never had anything close to those numbers to build on.

Los Angeles city gang czar Bruce Riordan had more to say: "Individual 'brothers' of the Mexican Mafia wield power in the nation's prisons and on the street that would make Tony Soprano 'blush.' *The Sopranos* is merely an exercise in nostalgia. Today the real power is in the Sureno Nation, and the Sureno Nation is ruled by La Eme. La Cosa Nostra has no influence in the nation's prisons, no influence in the Southwest, and no influence over street gangs. La Eme has influence over all three, and is using that power to take control of the nation's drug trade. La Eme calls the tune for the drug dealers in the Southwest, and the drug dealers dance to that tune. La Cosa Nostra left the drug trade to La Eme, and La Eme made the most of that decision."

Glossary

AB: the Aryan Brotherhood prison gang
Abeja: an Aryan Brotherhood member
Bay, the: Pelican Bay State Prison
BGF: the Black Guerilla Family prison gang
big homey: a Mexican Mafia member
bone-crusher: an extremely large jailhouse knife; shank
Brand, the: the Aryan Brotherhood prison gang
brother: a full-fledged Mexican Mafia member
call it a day: to drop out of the Mexican Mafia
camarada: a trusted associate of the Mexican Mafia
carnal: a full-fledged Mexican Mafia member
carnal de la palabra: a brother of his word, a man of his word; an influential Eme member
check in: to enter protective custody
chuchulucu: knife or shank; Spanish for "candy bar"
clavo: drugs
crew chief: the person who handles all illegal business for an incarcerated Mexican Mafia member
cucui: a boogeyman, monster, or devil; a shadowy figure to be feared; someone who lurks in the darkness waiting to harm or kill
dope: drugs
dropout: a "made" Mexican Mafia member or gang member who defects from the organization
Emero: a Mafioso
facilitator: a woman who aids or abets in criminal activity for an incarcerated Mexican Mafia member, usually a wife or girlfriend
farmero, or farmer: derogatory term for a Nuestra Familia prison gang member
favor: a hit for the Mexican Mafia

feds: Mexican Mafia members serving time in federal prison; also U.S. government agents

feria: money

fiero: knife or shank

flip: to cooperate with law enforcement

handle: to arrange a hit

hit: to kill or try to kill someone, usually by stabbing, shooting, or strangulation

homeboy: a gang member from your own neighborhood

homegirl: a female gang member from your own neighborhood

hoop: to keister, or secrete contraband in the rectum

in the car: aligned with a certain group or faction

in the hat: marked for a hit; on the hit list

ixtac: Nahuatl for "white"

jugo, or juice: influence or power, as within the organization

jump in: to give the ritual beating that initiates a gang recruit

junta: a meeting

kanpoleros: Nahuatl for "southern gang member"

keep point: to act as a lookout

keister: to secrete contraband in the rectum, usually drugs or a shank

kite: a small note containing Mafia information

La Causa: Mexican Mafia objectives or ideology

La Eme: the Mexican Mafia

lista: the hit list

llavero: a Mexican Mafia associate who functions as a leader on a prison yard or in jail

Los Famosos: Spanish for "the famous ones," denoting Mexican Mafia members

Los Hemelos: Spanish for "Twin Towers," the newest and most recent addition to L.A. County Jail

Los Senoras: a subgroup of women who act as facilitators to Mexican Mafia members, usually wives or girlfriends

mad-dog: to stare at someone with a sinister, challenging look

made guy: a full-fledged member of the Mexican Mafia

to make or be made: to be inducted into the Mexican Mafia

make your bones: to do a hit for the gang

Mariposa: code word for the Mexican Mafia

married, get: to be inducted into the Mexican Mafia

mayates: a derogatory term for blacks

mesa: an ad-hoc commission on a general population prison yard made up of Mexican Mafia associates

mesero: a member of the mesa or commission that runs a prison yard

miqui: Nahuatl for "to kill"

MM: the Mexican Mafia

Norteno: a gang member of Spanish descent from northern California and an enemy of the Mexican Mafia and southern California gangsters of Spanish descent

notches: the number of hits in which one has participated

Nuestra Familia: a northern California prison gang and enemy of La Eme

osomatli: Nahuatl for "monkey"; used as a derogatory term for blacks

padrino: a Mexican Mafia member who sponsors a prospect for membership in La Eme

palabra: Mafioso's powerful influence, or "word"

Palmas: California Institution for Men in Chino, California

pedaso: knife, or shank

pilli: a Mexican Mafia member (Nahuatl for "honored one")

placa: nickname

pop: to kill, whack, murder

program, the: the concerted effort by the Mexican Mafia to extort all street gangs and drug dealers in California

putting in work: doing work for the gang—drive-bys, hits, drug selling, and so on

rat, or rata: a person who snitches to authorities or testifies in court against gang members

reglas: the rules used to regulate Mexican Mafia members

roll: to cooperate with law enforcement

send home: to kill, as in sending home in a box

Senor: a Mexican Mafia member

Senora: a wife or girlfriend of a Mexican Mafia member

shank: a jailhouse knife usually fashioned out of a metal or plastic object

shiv: a jailhouse knife, or shank

shot-caller: a Mexican Mafia associate or other gang member who functions as a leader

sleeper: a non-associate of the Mexican Mafia who carries out a high-priority hit on a target of the mob

snitch: a rat; someone who gives up information to authorities

Sureno: a southern California gang member of Spanish descent

tax: to extort money or drugs from someone

tusa: Nahuatl for "informant" or "rat"

whack: to kill or attempt to kill

xipe: Nahuatl for "to flay" or "to skin"

Bibliography

"Actor Olmos Seeks Permit to Carry Concealed Weapon." *Los Angeles Times,* April 24, 1993.

Allen, James. *As a Man Thinketh* (1910). Available at: www.AsAManThinketh.net.

Anti-Defamation League. "Bigotry Behind Bars: Racist Groups in U.S. Prisons." *Anti-Defamation League Special Report,* October 1998.

Arizona Department of Corrections. "History of the Arizona New Mexican Mafia." Available at: www.azcorrections.gov/adc/divisions/support/stg/nmm.asp.

Artesia California Profile and Resource Guide. "Artesia, Los Angeles County, California." Available at: www.usacitiesonline.com/cacountyartesia.htm.

"Artesia's History." Available at: www.cityofartesia.us/history.html.

Ayres, B. Drummond, Jr. "Battle Against Mexican Mafia Opens New Front in Court." *New York Times,* November 25, 1996.

Azusa, California, City of. "The City of Azusa." Available at: www.ci.azusa.ca.us/general/history.asp.

Baltazar-Martinez, Sandra. "Coachella Valley's Mexican Mafia Chief Arrested." *The Press Enterprise,* April 27, 2007.

Berthelson, Christian. "Mexican Mafia." City News Service (CNS), December 6, 10, and 11, 1996, and May 30, 1997.

Blankenstein, Andrew, and Richard Winton. "Sweep Targets Vineland Boyz." *Los Angeles Times,* June 22, 2005.

California Department of Corrections. "CDC Facts." October 1, 1992.

———. "Security Housing Unit." Available at: www.cdc.state.ca.us

California Manufacturers and Technology Association. "Gloria Romero." Available at CMTA legislative database: http://cmta.net/legsample.php?leg=romero_gloria.

Cerritos, California, City of. "The Story of Cerritos." June 2, 2005. Available at: www.ci.cerritos.ca.us/library/history/chapter7.html.

Chavez, Stephanie. "Mother's Mission Ends with Sentencing of Five Killers." *Los Angeles Times,* February 1, 1992.

————. "Pair Ambush, Kill Gangs Counselor Violence." *Los Angeles Times*, May 15, 1992.

Colvin, Richard Lee. "A Tense Truce." *Los Angeles Times*, December 26, 1993.

"Convicted: Mexican Mafia." Associated Press, May 30, 1997.

Coulter, Cameron. "For the Defense, Gang Members." *Daily Bulletin* (n.d.).

Decker, Twila, and David Rosenzweig. "Nine Members of Mexican Mafia Are Convicted." *Los Angeles Times*, October 25, 2000.

Dibble, Sandra. "American Linked to Cartel Slayings Arrested in Tijuana." *San Diego Union-Tribune*, November 25, 2003.

Doan, Lynn, and J. Michael Kennedy. "Cerritos Thrives on Cash Cows from Old Pastures." *Los Angeles Times*, September 13, 2006.

Dolan, Maura. "Judge Orders End to Brutality at High-Tech Prison." *Los Angeles Times*, January 12, 1995.

Dominguez, Jeff. "Riot at Pelican Bay—What Really Happened and Why." *Peacekeeper*, March–April 2000.

Egelke, Bob. "Prison Officials Say Pelican Bay Is Tough, but It Works." *Long Beach Press Telegram*, November 25, 1993.

Egley, Arlen, Jr. "National Youth Gang Survey Trends from 1996 to 2000." U.S. Department of Justice, Office of Juvenile Justice and Delinquency Prevention, February 2002.

Egley, Arlen, Jr., and Aline K. Major. "Highlights of the 2001 National Youth Gang Survey." U.S. Department of Justice, Office of Juvenile Justice and Delinquency Prevention, April 2003.

Enders, John. "California's Toughest Prison." Associated Press (n.d.).

Fears, Darryl. "Sixteen Held in Countywide Sweep Targeting Mexican Mafia." *Los Angeles Times*, February 3, 2000.

Feldman, Paul. "Six Arraigned in Mistake Slayings of Two." *Los Angeles Times*, May 13, 1988.

"Folsom State Prison." Available at: www.answers.com/topic/folsom-state-prison.

Ford, Andrea. "Inmate Stabs Prisoner Awaiting Verdict in Shootings." *Los Angeles Times*, February 11, 1993.

————. "Half Brothers Found Guilty in Church Murders." *Los Angeles Times*, February 12, 1993.

————. "Two Sentenced to Death for Murders in Church." *Los Angeles Times*, May 22, 1993.

Furillo, Andy. "Conditions at High Desert SP in California." *Sacramento Bee*, May 1, 1998.

————. "Prison Gang's Pockets Deep." *Sacramento Bee*, October 17, 2004.

Furlow, William A. "Beating Terrorizes Attorney Here." *San Diego Union*, March 22, 1980.

Glazer, Andrew. "Ten-Month Probe of Mexican Mafia Yields Thirteen Arrests." Associated Press, April 28, 2007.

"The Gods of the Ancient Mexican." Appendix to *The Fire Within* by Graham Watkins. New York: Penguin Group, 1991.

Goldsmith, Susan. "Federal Bureau of Violence." *New Times L.A.*, August 9, 2001.

Gonzales, Ruby. "Mass Murder Stunned Police." *San Gabriel Valley Tribune*, April 21, 2005.

Gribben, Mark. "Massacre on French Place." *The Malefactor's Register*, April 12, 2005. Available at: markgribben.com.

Guillen, Marcos. "The Mexican Mafia Exposed." *Los Angeles East Side Sun*, August 31, 1995.

Guthrie, Julian. "Former Prison Gang Leader Killed on Street Pool Cue Assault After Bar Fight." *San Francisco Chronicle*, March 25, 2001.

Guttman, Monika, and Chitra Ragavan. "Terror on the Streets." USNews.com, December 13, 2004.

Harris, Scott. "Jailhouse Lawyers' Get Day in Court." *Los Angeles Times*, July 16, 1987.

Heller, Matthew. "Fourteen Plead Not Guilty in Mexican Mafia Case." *Los Angeles Daily Journal*, May 9, 1995.

Hentoff, Nat. "Pelican Bay Is Our Own Devil's Island." *Los Angeles Times*, December 5, 1993.

Hetherman, Bill. "Mexican Mafia Member Guilty of Murder." *San Gabriel Valley Tribune*, January 31, 1998.

———. "Killer of El Monte Family Laughs at Death Verdict." *San Gabriel Valley Tribune*, February 12, 1998.

———. "Mastermind Could Get Death." *San Gabriel Valley Tribune*, March 1, 1998.

"Holding Cell Fight Leaves Man in Critical Condition." *Los Angeles Times*, February 9, 1994.

"Honor Rancho Scene of Racial Brawling." *Daily News*, December 20, 1993.

Houston, David. "Mexican Mafia: Second Defendant Has Been Sentenced." City News Service (CNS), September 2, 1997.

———. "Mexican Mafia." City News Service (CNS), September 3, 1997.

Insideprison.com. "Mexican Mafia: Prison Gang Profile." Insideprison.com, May 2006. Available at: http://www.insideprison.com/mexican-mafia-prison-gang.asp.

"Inside San Quentin." *California Magazine*, 1993.

Jones, Harry J., and Onell R. Soto. ' "Severe Blow' to Mexican Mafia." *San Diego Union-Tribune*, January 24, 2004.

Karlak, Pat. "Eighty Hurt in Saugus Jail Brawl." *Daily News*, January 10, 1994.

Katz, Jesse. "Column One: Film Leaves a Legacy of Fear." *Los Angeles Times*, June 13, 1993.

———. "Edict to Gangs Follows an Old Pattern." *Los Angeles Times*, October 3, 1993.

———. "Reputed Mexican Mafia Leader Dies in Prison at Age 64 ." *Los Angeles Times*, November 10, 1993.

———. "Clashes Between Latino, Black Gangs Increase." *Los Angeles Times*, December 26, 1993.

Katz, Jesse, and Robert J. Lopez. "Mexican Mafia Tells Gangs to Halt Drive-bys." *Los Angeles Times*, September 26, 1993.

———. "Mexican Mafia's Impact on Gangs Questioned." *Los Angeles Times*, September 28, 1993.

Kingston, Tim. "Medical Neglect in the California Department of Corrections." *San Francisco Frontiers,* June 3, 1999.

Kouri, Jim. "Mexican Mafia's Top Lieutenant Pleads Guilty U.S. Court." *Renew America,* October 4, 2006. Available at: www.renewamerica.us/columns/kouri/061004.

Larocca, Paul. "Police Hit Hierarchy of Mexican Mafia." *The Press Enterprise,* December 12, 2006.

Leeds, Jeff, and Robert J. Lopez. "Gang Kills Member for Shooting Girl, Police Say." *Los Angeles Times,* November 7, 1995.

Littlefield, Dana. "Eme Members Sentenced in San Diego." *San Diego Union-Tribune,* August 2, 2006.

Lopez, Robert J. "U.S. Indicts Twenty-two in Probe of Mexican Mafia." *Los Angeles Times,* May 2, 1995.

Love, Marianne. "La Eme Has Ties Throughout the Valley." *San Gabriel Valley Tribune,* March 6, 2004.

Lozano, Carlos V. "Blacks, Latinos Brawl Again in Court Cell." *Los Angeles Times,* January 5, 1994.

"Man Convicted in Five Slayings Linked to Gang." *Los Angeles Times,* January 31, 1998.

Martinez, Marilyn. "Gang Vendetta Turns Neighborhood into a War Zone." *Daily Breeze,* December 23, 1993.

Mathison, Dirk. "Gunning for God." *Dispatch,* November 1997.

Mendoza, Ramon. *Mexican Mafia: From Altar Boy to Hitman.* Corona, Calif.: Ken Whitley & Associates, 2005.

Merritt, Jeralyn. "Inmate Beaten to Death at Supermax." *Talk Left: The Politics of Crime,* April 22, 2005. Available at: www.talkleft.com.

MEXonline.com. "History of Benito Juarez." Available at: http://www.mexonline.com/benitojuarez.htm.

"Mexican Mafia." City News Service (CNS), June 5, 1995; October 4 and December 3, 1996; September 2, 3, and 4, 1997; May 16 and October 10, 2001.

"Mexican Mafia Hit by Raids." Associated Press, May 2, 1995.

"Mexican Mafia/Open Statements." City News Service (CNS), May 27, 2001.

Meyer, Josh. "Prisoners Are Segregated After Brawl." *Los Angeles Times,* January 11, 1994.

———. "Peace Plan Elusive as County Jails Race War Continues." *Los Angeles Times,* January 17, 1994.

Minaya, Zeke. "Ex-Mexican Mafia Leader Gets Ten Years." *Los Angeles Times,* February 19, 2003.

Moran, Greg. "Members of Mexican Mafia Convicted on Racketeering Counts." *San Diego Union-Tribune,* January 4, 2008.

Morrill, Robert. *The Mexican Mafia: The Story.* Denver, Colo.: Security Threat Intelligence Network Group (STING), 2005.

Moses, Eric. "Mexican Mafia." City News Service (CNS), May 18, 1995.

Mrozek, Thom. "Convict Pleads Not Guilty in Slaying of Four Prostitutes." *Los Angeles Times,* June 26, 1992.

"NAACP, MALDEF Meeting." *Compton Bulletin,* January 25, 1994.

National First Ladies' Library. "First Lady Biography: Pat Nixon." Available at: http://www.firstladies.org/biographies/firstladies.aspx?biography=38.

"Nine from Mexican Mafia Convicted of Racketeering." Associated Press. October 25, 2000.

Okerblom, Jim. "Activist Acknowledges Boyfriend's Arrest." *San Diego Union-Tribune,* February 20, 1992.

"Olmos." City News Service (CNS), October 24, 1996.

"Olmos Rejected in Bid to Carry Concealed Weapon." *Los Angeles Times,* April 28, 1993.

Online Archive of California (OAC). "Biography of John Vasconcellos." April 25, 2003. www.oac.cdlib.org.

"Pair Charged with Murder in Shotgun Slayings at L.A. Church." *Daily News of Los Angeles,* July 28, 1989.

Pelisek, Christine. "Bad Night for the Vineland Boyz." *L.A. Weekly,* June 23, 2005.

"Pete Wilson Political Biography." Available at: http://www.answers.com/topic/pete-wilson.

"Police See Marital Dispute as Main Factor in Church Shooting." Associated Press, July 26, 1989.

"Prison Gang 'Godfather' Breaks Ranks." *BBC News World Edition,* September 27, 2005.

"Prison Inmate Beaten to Death." *Rocky Mountain News,* April 22, 2005.

Rafael, Tony. *The Mexican Mafia.* New York: Encounter Books, 2007.

Ramos, George. "Witness Provides Details of Joining Mexican Mafia." *Los Angeles Times,* December 23, 1996.

———. "Mexican Mafia Case Ready to Go to Jurors." *Los Angeles Times,* May 16, 1997.

———. "Two Sentenced to Death for Killing Five People." *Los Angeles Times,* June 12, 1997.

Rasmussen, Cecilia. "What's in a Name? Clues to a City's Past." *Los Angeles Times,* June 3, 2007.

"Riverside Gang Accord Shatters; Crime Booms." Associated Press, December 11, 1993.

Rohrlich, Ted. "DA Admits Murder Trial Was Unfair." *Los Angeles Times,* August 1, 1990.

———. "Man Fingered by Informant to Be Freed." *Los Angeles Times,* April 5, 1991.

Romero, Gloria. "Majority Leader Gloria Romero." Available at home page of Senator Gloria Romero: http://dist24.casen.govoffice.com.

Rosenzweig, David. "Witness Denounced in Trial of Reputed Mexican Mafia Chief." *Los Angeles Times,* January 5, 2001.

———. "Mexican Mafia Figure Convicted of Three Murders." *Los Angeles Times,* February 15, 2001.

———. "Jury Convicts Three, Clears Two in Mexican Mafia Case." *Los Angeles Times,* November 10, 2001.

———. "Mexican Mafia Member Describes Gang's Activities." *Los Angeles Times,* May 31, 2000, B3.

Rotten dot com. "San Quentin." Available at: www.rotten.com/library/crime/ prison/san-quentin.

Sandburg, Brenda. "Thousands of George Jacksons Are in Prison Today." *Workers World,* September 13, 2001.

"San Quentin: Links in the Chain." *Revolutionary Worker,* August 16, 1998.

Schooley, Wilson A. "A Hunger for Justice: The Passion of Rachel Ortiz." *Human Rights Magazine,* Fall 2000.

"Shocking Court Papers Claim . . . Olmos Paid Extortion Money to Mexican Mafia." *Star,* November 12, 1996.

Soto, Onell R. "Thirty-six Indicted in Mexican Mafia Crackdown." *San Diego Union-Tribune,* June 17, 2006.

Sturkey, Marion F. "Corps Values." From *Warrior Culture of the U.S. Marines* (Heritage Press International, 2001).

Thompson, Don. "Prison Hearings." Associated Press. January 20, 2004.

Townsend, Debbie. "Mexican Mafia 'Taxes' Dealers." *Inland Valley Daily Bulletin,* December 17, 1993.

"Two Arrested in Church Slayings." *Daily News of Los Angeles,* July 26, 1989.

U.S. Department of Justice. "Drugs and Crime Gang Profile: Mara Salvatrucha." November 2002.

"U.S. Targets 'Mexican Mafia.' " Associated Press, May 2, 1995.

Wagner, Dennis. "Murder Trial Shifting to Phoenix." *Arizona Republic,* September 29, 2003.

———. "Prison Gang Members to Plead Guilty in Murders." *Arizona Republic,* December 15, 2005.

———. "Arizona New Mexican Mafia Update." *Arizona Republic,* January 13, 2006.

Wagner, Rob L. "Convicted Murderer Sentenced to Three Consecutive Life Terms." *Ontario Daily Report,* July 12, 1989.

Ward, Jon. "Gang Follows Illegal Aliens." *Washington Times,* May 5, 2005.

Webber, Dawn. "Eleven Inmates Hurt in Second Day of Race Riots." *Daily News,* January 5, 1994.

Welborn, Larry. "A Long Past to Live Down." *Orange County Register,* July 24, 2005.

"Will 'Snitch, Parole, or Die' Policy Become Law?" *San Francisco Bay View,* April 7, 1999.

Acknowledgments

I WOULD LIKE TO THANK THE ENRIQUEZ FAMILY, AND RENE IN PAR-ticular, for baring their lives to make this book brutally honest.

And certainly *The Black Hand* would never have been made into a book at all without the consideration of Mauro DiPreta, editor at William Morrow. I thank him and his editorial assistant, Jennifer Schulkind, for all their assistance.

Clearly, no project such as this can be done without the help of other people sharing their experiences, their advice, and their time. The following is a list of those who helped in some way to make this book possible: Gary Ainsworth, Hank Akin, Mark Amador, Pete Amancio, Antonio Bestard, Pam Booth, Jeff Bosket, Chris Brandon, Bob Buell, Chris Cano, Scott Carbaugh, Dave Contreras, Steve Davis, Joe De La Torre, Leo Duarte, Robert Dugdale, Steve Duncan, Mike Duran, Rich Duran, Bill Eagleson, Bobby Enriquez, John Enriquez, Lupe Enriquez, Dan Evanilla, Jeff Ferguson, Tim Flaherty, Jack Forsman, Sandi Gibbons, Devan Hawkes, Glen Hotema, Chuck Horan, Frank Johnson, Rich Kincaid, John Laurie, Rick Lewis, Luis Li, Mark Lillienfield, Rich Lopez, Mike Lowe, Ernie Madrid, Anthony Manzella, Frank "Paco" Marcel, George Marin, Robert Marquez, Larry Martinez, George Mendoza, Ramon Mendoza, Eric Messick, Dan Moldea, John Monaghan, Steve Moore, Gabe Morales, Thom Mrozek, Jim Myers, Ron Nelson, Roy Nunez, George Ortiz, James Owens, Brian Parry, Marty Penney, Bruce Riordan, Todd Robinson, Roger Ross, Rudy Segura, Dennis Story, Brian Sullivan, Pat Thrasher, Richard Valdemar, Al Valdez, Dan Vasquez, Joe Villanueva, Al Vitkosky, Greg Walston, Steve Weireter,

Gary Whirl, Ken Whitley, Pete Wilson, Daron Wyatt, Mark Young, and Jerry Zamora. I thank them all profusely.

Rene would like to add his own special thanks to: Chris Blatchford, for his integrity and friendship; Jo Jo Beeson, Jeff Bosket, Father Gregory Boyle, Chris Brandon, Nelson Delgado, Dan Evanilla, Andy Flood, Mike Gutierrez, Katie Harding, Devan Hawkes, Sister Susan Jabro, Richard W. Kincaid, Mike Lowe, Ernie Madrid, George Marin, Robert Marquez, Michael Montgomery, Maureen O'Connell, Sister Elizabeth O'Keefe, Brian Parry, Todd Robinson, James Spertus, Richard Valdemar, Al Vitkosky, Michele Barfield, Kirk Gulesserian, Karapet Keoperelyan, Carlos Tomala, and Bishop Gabino Zavala; and his family for remaining by his side through it all.

And lastly to Goldilocks—saying thank you could never encompass the breadth of what you've done for me or the depth of my gratitude to you. But thank you just the same.

Index